Anti-Semitism and Schooling
under the Third Reich

D1595850

Studies in the History of Education
Edward R. Beauchamp, Series Editor

EDUCATIONAL PHILOSOPHY
*A History from the Ancient World
to Modern America*
by Edward J. Power

SCHOOL AND SOCIETY IN VICTORIAN
BRITAIN
*Joseph Payne and the New World
of Education*
by Richard Aldrich

DISCIPLINE, MORAL REGULATION,
AND SCHOOLING
A Social History
edited by Kate Rousmaniere, Kari Dehli,
and Ning de Coninck-Smith

JAPANESE AMERICANS AND CULTURAL
CONTINUITY
Maintaining Language and Heritage
by Toyotomi Morimoto

RADICAL HEROES
*Gramsci, Freire, and the Politics of Adult
Education*
by Diana Coben

WOMEN'S EDUCATION IN EARLY MODERN
EUROPE
A History, 1500–1800
edited by Barbara J. Whitehead

ESSAYS IN TWENTIETH-CENTURY SOUTHERN
EDUCATION
Exceptionalism and Its Limits
edited by Wayne J. Urban

GIRLS' SCHOOLING DURING THE
PROGRESSIVE ERA
*From Female Scholar to Domesticated
Citizen*
by Karen Graves

COMMON, DELINQUENT, AND SPECIAL
*The Institutional Shape of Special
Education*
by John Richardson

GENDER, RACE, AND THE NATIONAL
EDUCATION ASSOCIATION
Professionalism and Its Permutations
by Wayne J. Urban

TRANSITIONS IN AMERICAN EDUCATION
A Social History of Teaching
by Donald H. Parkerson and Jo Ann
Parkerson

WHEREVER I GO I WILL ALWAYS BE
A LOYAL AMERICAN
*Schooling Seattle's Japanese Americans
during World War II*
by Yoon K. Pak

CHARTERED SCHOOLS
*Two Hundred Years of Independent
Academies in the United States,
1727–1925*
edited by Nancy Beadie and Kim Tolley

ANTI-SEMITISM AND SCHOOLING UNDER
THE THIRD REICH
by Gregory Paul Wegner

Anti-Semitism and Schooling under the Third Reich

Gregory Paul Wegner

RoutledgeFalmer

NEW YORK AND LONDON

Published in 2002 by
RoutledgeFalmer
29 West 35th Street
New York, NY 10001
www.routledge-ny.com

Published in Great Britain by
RoutledgeFalmer
11 New Fetter Lane
London EC4P 4EE
www.routledge.co.uk

RoutledgeFalmer is an imprint of the Taylor & Francis Group.
Printed in the United States of America on acid-free paper.
Design and typography: Jack Donner

10 9 8 7 6 5 4 3 2 1

Library of Congress Cataloging-in-Publication Data

Wegner, Gregory Paul.
    Anti-semitism and schooling under the Third Reich / by Gregory Paul Wegner.
        p.   cm.
    Includes bibliographical references and index.
    ISBN 0-8153-3942-9 — ISBN 0-8153-3943-7 (pbk.)
    1. Antisemitism—Germany—History—20th century. 2. Jews—Germany—Public opinion.
    3. Public opinion—Germany. 4. Germany—Ethnic relations. I. Title.

DS146.G4 W385 2002
305.892'4043—dc21
                                                                        2002021350

For
Paula
Mary Clare
James
Tim

Contents

Series Editor's Preface

The RoutledgeFalmer Studies in the History of Education series includes not only volumes on the history of American and Western education, but also on the history of the development of education in non-Western societies. A major goal of this series is to provide new interpretations of educational history that are based on the best recent scholarship; each volume will provide an original analysis and interpretation of the topic under consideration. A wide variety of methodological approaches from the traditional to the innovative are used. In addition, this series especially welcomes studies that focus not only on schools but also on education as defined by Harvard historian Bernard Bailyn: "the transmission of culture across generations."

The major criteria for inclusion are (a) a manuscript of the highest quality, and (b) a topic of importance to understanding the field. The editor is open to readers' suggestions and looks forward to a long-term dialogue with them on the future direction of the series.

Edward R. Beauchamp
University of Hawaii

Acknowledgments

A book of this nature rests heavily on the kindness and generosity of many people. The author wishes to thank the Faculty Senate Committees on Research and Grants and Faculty Development from the University of Wisconsin–La Crosse for funding that made this work possible. Lavonia McCarty from the Interlibrary Loan Office at La Crosse deserves special praise for her determination in securing valuable sources on short notice. Larry Sleznikow from Educational Technologies masterfully transferred images from Nazi curriculum materials onto CDs for the illustrations in this book. Dedicated archivists and librarians in three countries opened collections and offered valuable suggestions in support of the research. Special thanks to Gila Michlovski, Ida Isaac, and Ariella Segev from the Wiener Library in Tel Aviv for providing a wonderful opportunity to access one of the largest collections of Nazi curriculum materials in the world. Zippi Rosenne from the Museum of the Jewish Diaspora in Tel Aviv was instrumental in connecting me to collections of artwork from anti-Semitic Nazi literature for children. Rosemary Nief, senior librarian from the Wiener Library in London, not only opened up the library's vast collection of anti-Semitic images but also shared important background data on Johann von Leers. As always, Germany continues to beckon historians to its large and well-organized archival network. Christian Ritzi, the director of the German Institute for Pedagogical Research in Berlin, heads one of the premier research institutions in the world on the history of education. This institute's vast collections of professional journals and curriculum resources from the Nazi period remained indispensable for this study. Not to be overlooked in this regard is the Institute for Contemporary History in Munich which possesses a huge archival treasure on modern German history. Karin Popp has the author's deepest gratitude for so thoughtfully organizing an excellent time frame for his studies at the institute. Frau Kandler and staff at the Brandenburg Landeshauptarchiv in Potsdam were most diligent in securing access to rare documents on the Jewish question and schools on a provincial level. Not enough can be said about the depth and scope of the documentary collections at the Bundesarchiv Berlin in relation to the NSLB, Kanzlei Rosenberg, and the Education Ministry. The patience of Frau Grüner and Frau Langner in responding to numerous research requests and their suggestions about examining certain documents made this a very rewarding research experience. A most beneficial surprise came at the hands of Manfred Heinemann from the University of Hanover, a man who earlier acted as the author's sponsor as a research fellow under the Friedrich Ebert Foundation from 1983 to 1984. He generously provided access to what the locals call the "poison box," a big collection of curriculum materials and texts from the former Nazi teacher training college for women. Access to the collection, placed under lock and key by the British occupation authorities in 1945, was made possible only very recently. As always, Herr Heinemann contributed his sharp scholarly understanding of Nazi education and a warm hospitality in ways too numerous to recount here. His generosity in opening up the extensive resources of the Institute for the History of Education profoundly shaped the character of the author's research. Professor Emeritus Joachim Knoll from Hannover offered invaluable insights from his own research experience on Nazi conceptions of science education. Stepping into the well-preserved Hannover collection was a rare and unique research trip into a chapter of Nazi curriculum history. Herr Schwill and library director Frau Makowsky also have the author's sincerest gratitude for opening so many doors into this collection.

Growing as a scholar though this research process can also be traced to many contributions from manuscript reviewers. Dewey Bjorkman, a very dear friend and intellectual companion on this journey, offered encouragement as well as much-needed challenges about the substance of the book. Close friend and accomplished scholar Karl-Heinz Füssl from Humboldt University in Berlin, through his deep insights into the history of German education, provided the author with critical challenges about key assumptions concerning National Socialism, educational policy, and the Jews. The manuscript would not have been possible without Edward Beauchamp from the University of Hawaii. He was present from the very beginning and the prospectus to the completion of the published volume. Strong encouragement from this noted historian made the entire project worthwhile. Special thanks are also extended to the University of Wisconsin–LaCrosse Foundation and Noel Richards for grant funding in support of the color reproductions. Above all, any thought of completing such a challenging undertaking would have remained out of reach without the loving support and infinite patience of the author's wife, Paula, and their children, Tim, James, and Mary Clare. The old adage is true. We stand on the shoulders of others.

Tables and Ilustrations

TABLES

ILLUSTRATIONS

INSERT

Introduction

In September of 1919, Adolf Hitler penned a letter to a certain Herr Gemlich that held great portent for the future. In this communication, Hitler expounded on the great danger represented by the Jews for the people of Germany. Anti-Semitism, he wrote, was a logical outcome of this threat, for the Jews "knew only the majesty of money" and, moreover, "destroyed national pride, the strength of the people, through ridicule and the shameless teaching of vice." To satisfy their hunger for power and money, Jews took special pains to control public opinion through the press and to charge exorbitant interest rates in their economic affairs. Drawing from medical terminology, Hitler concluded that a new kind of anti-Semitism was in order to fight this "racial tuberculosis of the people." As a political movement, anti-Semitism could not, Hitler insisted, be determined by "the moments of emotion, but rather through a knowledge of facts." These facts, as Hitler called them, included the assumption that Jews were first and foremost members of a race and not a religion. This implied that Jews were both non-German and foreign in Hitler's perspective on the body politic. In looking ahead, Hitler insisted on the development of a "rational anti-Semitism" supported by a "well-planned legal battle" to "eliminate Jewish privileges." The final goal, the future dictator noted, must be the overall removal of the Jews.[1] Fourteen years later, in the wake of Hitler's rise to power, the sentiments expressed in this letter would find an even more powerful voice in the form of a racial state.

The Nazis were not the first to advance anti-Semitic thinking. Hatred for Jews, sometimes included under the broad rubric of "anti-Judaism," is an ancient phenomenon with roots as far back as the Roman destruction of the Second Temple in 70 A.D. or even as old as the slavery suffered by the Hebrews under Ramses II in Egypt. The term "Semite" originally referred to the family of Semitic languages that included Arab and Hebrew cultures. "Anti-Semitism," in exclusive application to Jews, appeared in the 1840s in a *Staatslexikon* written by Karl Rotteck and Karl Welckerschen.[2] Years later, in 1879, the German journalist Wilhelm Marr coined the expression in founding the Anti-Semite League. What remains of particular importance in understanding the place of anti-Semitism in Nazi ideology and institutional life is that Hitler drew from a long tradition of animosity toward Jews already well established in European society long before he came to power. The ground, as Hitler's letter explained some six years before *Mein Kampf*, was already well prepared. That this development eventually ended in the mass destruction of Jews made the case of German fascism unique in all of Europe.[3]

A crucial development in the history of anti-Semitism, and one which remains of great importance in this investigation, was the emergence of scientific racism in the late nineteenth century that cast new rationalizations for prejudicial attitudes toward Jews. However, scientific racism alone does not explain the successful Nazi exploitation of anti-Semitism for political gain. There was a mystical element in Nazi anti-Semitic thinking tied to a process of mythmaking about the Jew as cultural outsider with powerful historical antecedents originating in the Middle Ages. Part of the Nazi strategy was to link the development of newer, "scientific" justifications for anti-Semitism with older forms of prejudice including blaming Jews for the misfortunes of the German community and keeping alive the ancient claim of Jewish conspiracy. Scapegoating proved to be one of the most insidious and effective Nazi strategies in tapping already long-held German prejudices about Jews. The distinguished historian George Mosse observed that an essential part of Hitler's political genius rested with his uncanny sense of timing and his skillful exploitation of anti-Semitic prejudices for political gain. Jews became Hitler's great foil in his efforts to gain and consolidate power.[4] The consequences for the Jewish community in Europe, and subsequently in other parts of the world, would be most profound.

Aristotle once wrote that any attempt to understand the political values of a culture must take into account the manner by which that culture educates its young.[5] The Nazi process of legitimizing what schoolchildren should or should not know about Jews involved what Raymond Williams called "selective tradition," or "an intentionally selective version of a shaping past and a pre-shaped present, which is then powerfully operative in the process of social and cultural definition and identification."[6] All cultures engaged with the socialization of the young are intimately involved with the process of selective tradition. Examining how Nazi elementary schools articulated a selective tradition of racial anti-Semitism through curriculum policy and teaching materials can contribute to a greater understanding of Nazi ideology. A central dynamic in this process concerned the manner by which the Nazis used the language of science and myth to propagate anti-Semitic prejudices through education. Science, as will be shown in this study, remained inseparable from myth in the racial anti-Semitism legitimized under the broad rubric of school knowledge for Nazi schools.

Still needed in studies on the history of Nazi education is an investigation of anti-Semitism across the curriculum, the major purpose of this book. Anti-Semitic thinking in Nazi elementary education was not confined to one particular school subject or program. More specifically, the proposed study explores how the Hitler regime articulated anti-Semitism as a central element in its understanding of the educated person. Nazi elementary school curriculum remained among the most integrated of the twentieth century. Integrated curriculum, long since a call word for educational reformers of various political stripes, invokes the desirability of drawing connections between and among ideas represented in the various school disciplines, thus softening and even removing the traditional lines of demarcation between them. For the Nazis, race provided a formative conceptual framework for the entire curriculum and, on another cultural level, represented a consistent line of political thinking in support of waging "the war against the Jews."[7]

The power of language in defining the citizen under the Third Reich remains central to any serious study of Nazi curriculum and the anti-Semitic content therein. One of the most insightful studies on Nazi language appeared with the publication of Victor Klemperer's *LTI: Notizbuch einer Philologen*, which came to light in 1957 and is now in its eighteenth edition. As a Jewish philologist, and professor of French literature from the University of Dresden before his dismissal under the Third Reich's racial laws, Klemperer offered profound observations about the various meanings communicated by Nazi language and its presence in the everyday lives of people. LTI, the "Lingua Tertii Imperii," was for Klemperer the language of the Third Reich, a language of mindless fanaticism. The Nazi assumption of power in 1933 marked a shift away from *Gruppensprache*, or the language of groups that concerned itself only with those matters directly affecting the specific interests of the groups involved. In sharp contrast, there emerged the *Volkssprache*, which tried to encompass the "the entirety of life" for all citizens as members of a racial community. The *Volkssprache* "seized all public and private areas of life: politics, the administration of justice, language, the economy, the arts, the sciences, schools, sport, the family, kindergartens and nurseries."[8]

For Klemperer, Nazi language was destitute in nature, employing the same clichés and the same tone while bringing everyone under the same lockstep conformity subsumed under *Gleichschaltung*, the Nazi process of "meshing the gears" of all institutions in German society in order to bring them under the complete control of the regime. In the verb form of *gleichschalten*, Klemperer finds an expression that is "appallingly representative of the basic way of thinking under Nazism."[9] Of course, this kind of conformity demanded that all people defined as citizens of the Third Reich had to think the same way about Jews.

The Nazi conception of racial anti-Semitism did not escape Klemperer's discerning eye and indeed remained a focal point in much of his thoughtful work. "Against innate hatred, there existed no other certainty than the elimination of the hated," he wrote. To Klemperer, this hatred served as a vital stabilizing force supporting both racial anti-Semitism and the subsequent *Judenausrottung*, or the destruction of the Jews. The Jew was "the most important man in Hitler's state" through fulfilling the traditions of scapegoat and opponent. After all, as Klemperer's acid pen recorded, how could Hitler and the Nazi state have come to pass without the Jewish devil? Without the dark Jew there would never have been the radiant figure of the Nordic Teuton. Thinking of this nature required what Klemperer called the highest commandment of Nazi propaganda: to disallow any possibility of critical thought among listeners and to deal with everything in as simplistic a way as possible.[10]

Klemperer's thinking provides part of the context for understanding the language used by Nazi curriculum writers on what became widely known in German circles as "the Jewish question."[11] As Klemperer observed, schools were part of a much larger propaganda effort in the Third Reich. Educating the citizens of the Third Reich on the momentous task of preserving a certain racial heritage for the survival of the Nazi state went far beyond the doors of schools.[12] The racial anti-Semitism expressed in a broad variety of curriculum resources including textbooks, curriculum policy statements, and curriculum guides for teachers under investigation in this study were created by educated Germans. The authorship typically drew from circles of university professors, teacher educators, school administrators, and teachers. What is represented in these curriculums, along with the permeation of overt nationalistic and militaristic tones, is an ideological justification for the oppression and annihilation of the Jews. Supporting this process were the considerable resources of the Nazi propaganda establishment of which schools were an integral part.

Race biology, history, geography, and German literature were counted among those school subjects deemed as special bearers of Nazi race ideology and anti-Semitic thinking under the Third Reich. Beyond these traditional subject matter disciplines, the Nazis would add another curricular thrust under the banner of racial hygiene, more commonly known as eugenics, which remained truly integrative in nature drawing heavily from science, history, and literary myth. The cultural ideals and the ideological core of the Nazi dictatorship are written across the pages of these elements of knowledge deemed important for the young citizen of the Third Reich. In the schools and in Nazi society as a whole, Jews would figure prominently in the definition of the German citizen.

The vast educational enterprise that integrated anti-Semitic teachings into the Nazi curriculum and the large network of people who contributed their intellectual labors to this endeavor cannot be adequately treated in the pages of a single volume. The Hitler Youth and the SS, for example, developed their own curriculums on racial anti-Semitism, partly out of mistrust for teachers in public and private schools. As important as these two groups are to understanding the history of the Third Reich and the teaching of anti-Semitism, their educational programs are considered beyond the scope of this study. At the same time, historical evidence from these two institutions will be integrated periodically for the purpose of clarifying the nature of racial anti-Semitism in the curriculum for elementary schools. Another limitation demands clarification. This is not a history of Jewish schools under the Third Reich.[13] Aspects of this rich history invariably became part of the context for this study and remain an important part of the educational experience under the Third Reich.

The voices of perpetrators are preserved in this study through their articulation of racial anti-Semitism in Nazi education. They number among those steeped in the language of the Third Reich so brilliantly elucidated by Victor Klemperer. Their ambitious project to transform curriculum along racial anti-Semitic lines through the union of myth with science remains unprecedented in history. An equally important development in the long-range scheme of things is that racial anti-Semitism fed upon older, more traditional forms of religious anti-Semitism along with the history of economic stereotypes going back to the days of emergent market capitalism. Older and newer forms of anti-Semitism became intertwined in the Nazi educational experiment. Volkish thinking provided part of the cultural glue for this chapter in the history of prejudice.

Historical context remains important in framing a discussion of racial anti-Semitism under the schools of the Third Reich, in part because the Nazi education edifice did not stand as a clear cut representative of either a continuity or a break with the past.[14] This complex historical relationship extends more specifically to the question of racial anti-Semitism in the Nazi curriculum. The Nazis were the first political culture to legitimize racial anti-Semitism in school curriculum with the full legal support of the state. On the other hand, the ideas presented in this anti-Semitic dimension of school knowledge in Nazi Germany were not new at all. Broad outlines from the history of ideas initiated in the first chapter reveal the union of traditional and more contemporary racial strains of anti-Semitism before the Third Reich.

From this basis, the chapter embarks on an examination of Nazi educational perspectives and curriculum theories as related to racial anti-Semitism. The context established here provides a kind of doorway into the second chapter, which investigates evidence of anti-Semitism in curriculum guides written by a university professor, school administrator, and teacher. Subsequent chapters study the dynamics of anti-Semitic thinking in a more specific sense through curriculums formed for race hygiene, history, geography, and children's literature. Physical education, which garnered among the highest number of instructional hours of any subject in Nazi schools, is not overlooked. While not as overtly anti-Semitic as other traditional school disciplines, physical education bore the marks of the Nazi intent to extend racial thinking to as much of the curriculum as possible.

Chapter 1

The Emergence of Racial Anti-Semitism and Nazi Educational Philosophy

> The mightiest counterpart to the Aryan is the Jew.
> —Adolf Hitler, *Mein Kampf*, 1924.

The political agenda of Nazi Germany drew from centuries of anti-Semitic prejudice and racism in Europe. Although it is not our purpose to examine this long and tortured history, clarification of some of the broad outlines of Volkish thought will be useful in pondering the meaning of racial anti-Semitism in the schools of the Third Reich. One of the most profound legacies associated with the Third Reich is the legitimation of race and racial anti-Semitism in a modern industrial state that had one of the highest literacy rates on the European continent. Another aspect of this legacy is the Nazis' success in translating racial theory into practice. Hitler represents a critical juncture in the history of European racism in that he was the first ruler of a modern state to legitimize anti-Semitism through racial terms. At the same time, the Nazi dictator's political success is at least partially explained by his clever propaganda strategy of integrating more contemporary elements of race with older religious and economic forms of anti-Semitic prejudice.

Essentially, we are drawn into a history of ideas when speaking of German racism and its consequences for education. Central to the investigation is the complex German concept of *Volk* which had its roots in the struggle for German national identity in the Romanticism of the late eighteenth century, the subsequent reaction against modernity, and the rapid industrialization of Germany. Volk represented much more than the broad translation of "people," integrating concepts of race, soul, soil, and nationalism. George Mosse offered a lucid explanation of Volkish ideology and its implications for anti-Semitic thinking:

> The essential element here is the linking of the human soul with its natural surroundings, with the essence of nature. The really important truths are to be found beneath the surface of appearances. . . . According to many *Volkish* theorists, the nature of the soul of a *Volk* is determined by the native landscape.

Thus, the Jews, being a desert people, are viewed as shallow, arid, dry people, devoid of profundity and totally lacking in creativity. Because of the barrenness of the desert landscape, the Jews are a spiritually barren people. They thus contrast markedly with the Germans, who, living in the dark, mist-shrouded forests, are deep, mysterious, profound. Because they are so constantly shrouded in darkness, they strive toward the sun and are truly *Lichtmenschen* (people of light).[1]

One of the great elements of Hitler's success was to link Volkish ideology to a mass political organization under the rule of an exceedingly well organized dictatorship. Racism, then, "increasingly became unadulterated anti-Semitism," with subsequent programs cast for other racial undesirables including Gypsies, the mentally ill and the physically handicapped.[2] With anti-Semitism as the ideological focal point for Nazi racial theory, Hitler drew from a rich literature of Volkish thinkers whose writings had increased in popularity among followers of the political right during the late nineteenth and early twentieth centuries. These writers are of particular importance for our discussion in that many of their ideas would be affirmed by circles of Nazi curriculum writers in years to come.[3]

Among the most strident voices was that of Houston Stewart Chamberlain (1855–1927), the nineteenth-century philosopher and British-born author of *Foundations of the Nineteenth Century* (1900), a book that wielded great influence among Volkish thinkers including Hitler. For Chamberlain, the Germans were authentic carriers of Western culture, the saviors of world history, and in diametric opposition to the Jews, with whom they were involved in a protracted racial struggle. A certain mysticism of race combined with mythology and science emerged from Chamberlain's writings, a relationship that marked the ruminations of other Volkish thinkers as well. In a pattern repeated ad nauseum over the next four decades, Chamberlain drew upon phrenology and skull measurements to emphasize cultural differences between Jews and Germans. The more elongated skull of Germans, so he thought, symbolized a moral superiority over the Jews and all other races.[4] Chamberlain was not by any means the originator of this approach to science, but he certainly was one of the popularizers. He offered a synthesis of thinking on the notion of race at a time when social Darwinism enjoyed growing support among the newly emerging social sciences, especially anthropology.

Chamberlain combined mysticism with a certain kind of realism, something that few of the earlier Volkish writers had done. Like Paul de Lagarde (1827–1891), Chamberlain called for the eradication of Jewish elements from German language and culture as part of the necessary spiritual transformation of the "racial soul."[5] At the same time, he saw the potential of science and technology as means to preserving Aryan culture. Science, when linked to the myth of the Aryan race, provided another means by which racial anti-Semitism could be further legitimized. Integrated within Chamberlain's worldview was the Aryan myth that had already gained a widening literary audience from the earlier pronouncements of Richard Wagner, one of the more influential and fanatical anti-Semites of his time, and the French diplomat Comte Arthur de Gobineau (1816–1882).

Gobineau's *Essay on the Inequality of the Human Races* (1853–1855) interpreted race as the key to world history. There was a profound pessimism in Gobineau's writing that stood as a warning to those who would dare mix the blood of the races. The Aryans, according to the popular myth he helped develop, originated in the Indus Valley and later migrated to central Europe. Members of the white race, which by Gobineau's definition encompassed the Aryans, inevitably mixed their blood with those of inferior races. The resulting degeneration spelled the death of the most intelligent and noble of all the races.[6] Although not anti-Semitic in nature, Gobineau's ideas and the Aryan myth he articulated would eventually find new life in the pages of Hitler's *Mein Kampf* and in the curriculum of Nazi schools under miscegenation, a key element in the Nazi biological conception of citizenship and in Jewish policy. This historical process marked the decontextualization of "Aryan" by both the Nazis and their Volkish predecessors. The term actually referred to the descendants of an early language group in the Indus Valley with no distinctive racial characteristics. Hitler changed the term to mean non-Jewish, on the basis of the fact that Hebrew was a language unrelated to Aryan tongues.[7]

There was a strong strain of Romantic idealism in Volkish thinking, best articulated by two men who were deeply frustrated with German academic life and the education system in the wake of German unification. Paul de Lagarde and Jules Langbehn were among the intellectual vanguard of Volkish thinkers and played a significant role in spreading Volkish ideas to ever-widening circles of citizens from the political right. Their activities symbolized the growing importance of the teaching profession and educational institutions in the late nineteenth century in coalescing Volkish ideals for national renewal. Lagarde, a former gymnasium teacher and professor at Göttingen, spoke fervently about the necessity for creating a German religion to replace the staid and outworn traditions of the Christian church that had failed to carry forth the spiritual dynamism of Jesus Christ. Lagarde yearned for the return of the spiritual harmony that characterized the Middle Ages. A genuine unity among Germans, he wrote in his *Deutsche Schriften* (1878), could only come to pass with spiritual regeneration and a transformation of character. Race was not a pressing issue with this pedagogue. The organic nature of the Volk was connected to German attitudes and character, both of which were severely threatened by the forces of modernity. Germany had to regain its soul. Casting off contemporary Christianity and the stifling legalism represented by St. Paul, Lagarde sought a purer gospel for the Volk.[8]

One of the best teachers in the formation of a new and vibrant German faith rooted in the Volk was history. From Lagarde's historical perspective, such hopes for spiritual renewal would remain unrealized until Germans opened their eyes to the strongest force threatening their existence. That enemy was the Jew. Lagarde's strident anti-Semitism was not racially based nor was it new. His polemic, which drew primarily from religious forms of anti-Semitic prejudice, condemned the Jewish faith as sterile and wholly incompatible with the German spirit. That Jews could ever be considered Germans remained firmly out of the question. His writings warned about the evil nature of Jews conspiring to foment revolution in league with political liberals. As agents of modernity and materialism, Jews were the perpetual cultural outsiders.[9] Although Lagarde's anti-Semitism was not concerned with race, later Volkish thinkers associated with the Third Reich would cast his ideas in racial terms. Not lost on this prophetic figure was the importance of education in transforming national character. The Göttingen professor decried a decline in the learning of German language and literature among youth who often "died of boredom at the end of their school days."[10] Lagarde's idealism, like that of his younger ideologue, Jules Langbehn (1851–1907), gave to Volkish thinking an intellectual substance that resonated among educators under the Second Reich.

The appearance of Julies Langbehn's book *Rembrandt als Erzieher* (Rembrandt as educator) in 1890 infused an even stronger mystical element into Volkish tradition and, moreover, linked mystical Germanic religion to aesthetics. The life spirit of the Volk was linked directly to artistic creativity in Langbehn's view. Nature and landscape were part of the mystical relationship Germans had with the fatherland. Like Lagarde, Langbehn was a Romantic idealist who also railed against institutions that prevented a true unity among the Volk. It was the creative talents of the artist rooted in the soil and landscape that represented Germany's salvation. In sharp contrast with the more senior Volkish writer, Langbehn's work drew strong connections to racial bloodlines in defining German citizenship. While Lagarde condemned Jews primarily for religious reasons, Langbehn attacked Jews because of their racial identification.[11]

Maintaining blood purity was a powerful gospel in Langbehn's conception of the new Germanic religion. Langbehn's writings appeared at a time when racial science was coming into its own and social Darwinism gained a broader audience among social scientists, educators, and politicians. He remains important for the history of ideas in that he was one of the first Volkish writers to articulate ideas about "racial soul." Langbehn helped to popularize the assumption that the physical and spiritual characteristics of human beings were part of a racial dynamic transmitted through bloodlines. The anthropological implications were enormous. Under the banner of science, one could now conceive of a Volk defined by relationships between physical characteristics, cultural attributes, and the inner qualities of racial soul. Jews, as implicitly assumed by Langbehn, did not possess the racial constitution or character to be deemed members of the artistic Volk. Only Aryans were capable of being artists. As a foreign people on German soil, Jews represented an omnipresent threat to German blood purity and an insult to the German conception of art.[12] The contributions of Langbehn and Lagarde led one prominent historian to draw this conclusion: "A thousand teachers in republican Germany who in their youth had worshipped Lagarde and Langbehn were just as important in the triumph of National Socialism as all the putative millions of marks that Hitler collected from the German tycoons."[13]

THE EMERGENCE OF RACIAL ANTI-SEMITISM

The early development of Volkish thought drew from a variety of anti-Semitic traditions both racial and nonracial in nature. A more focused anti-Semitism based primarily on race would emerge in the late nineteenth and early twentieth centuries legitimized with the language of science. What Langbehn had intimated in 1900 symbolized the dual nature of anti-Semitism blending mystical and racial elements. Although justifying hatred for Jews on religious and economic grounds always remained part of the anti-Semitic tradition, and does so in some quarters to this day, social scientists and eugenicists began breaking new paths in what became known as racial science. This new science created rationalizations for treating Jews as perennial cultural outsiders based on biological determinism. Understanding Nazi race education, more specifically the racial anti-Semitic dimensions of school curriculum under study later in this book, demands a recognition of pre-Nazi developments in eugenics and race hygiene.

An important qualification is in order. Race biology and hygiene, as they became known, did not immediately foreshadow the Nazi policy against Jews.[14] This situation changed once the perception of Jews as a racial body became part of contemporary thinking. Eugenics became part of the lexicon of science with the work of Francis Galton (1822–1911), a prominent British scientist and cousin of Charles Darwin, who coined the word in 1883. The term originated in the Greek meaning "well-born" and took on the mantle of a science dealing with the improvement of hereditary qualities of a race or breed. Influenced by the concept of social Darwinism originating with Herbert Spencer (1820–1903) and his perspective on "survival of the fittest," Galton introduced this new science at a time of rapid industrialization, expanding colonialism, shifting populations, and growing concern about public health policies relating to the poor, weak, and mentally unstable. Galton thought that eugenics could become a centerpiece of public policy designed to ensure that "the more suitable races or strains of blood" had "the better chance of prevailing speedily over the less suitable."[15]

From its inception, eugenics took on an international character.[16] In contrast to the English meaning associated with eugenics, the German *Rassenhygiene* (race hygiene) assumed a broader context to include not only efforts to improve the general genetic quality of the population but also measures to increase the birthrate among racially acceptable elements in the population. Race hygiene and eugenics eventually became interchangeable expressions in the writings of social anthropology and race biology.[17] The transformation in this language did not suggest that all eugenicists were anti-Semites. Wilhelm Schallmayer, a noted eugenicist, won first prize in an essay contest sponsored by the industrialist Alfred Krupp that sought the best application of Darwin's principles in the area of law and public policy. Schallmayer's *Vererbung und Auslese im Lebenslauf der Völker* (Heredity and selection in the life history of nations) from 1903 and subsequent writings provided a theoretical framework for eugenics in Germany. Central to Schallmayer's thinking was the formation of a technocratic and rational approach to managing the German population for the purpose of increasing national efficiency. Not an avowed anti-Semitic or Volkish in attitude, he did oppose mixing so-called weaker with stronger racial strains.[18]

Schallmayer's legacy presents a curious historical problem. Along with many other eugenicists of his day, he set down value judgments about those people deemed fit or unfit as citizens of the state. The language of science, technology, and bureaucracy that conveyed Schallmayer's thinking about racial hygiene later resonated in the Third Reich through a brutal managerial efficiency instituted through the Final Solution.[19] Yet, a closer reading of his works reveals another issue that subsequently connected with the Nazi state. Speaking before a gathering of doctors in Munich in 1917, Schallmayer emphasized the importance of education in the preparation of public opinion for ever-widening eugenics measures in the population.[20]

Scientific knowledge, like all forms of knowledge, was and is culturally bound. The racial science that grew in popularity in German academic circles rested on preconceived notions and value judgments about human cultures. One may well ask whose science was practiced and for which political and social ends. Some of the most deeply held racial assumptions about Jews, even when rejected by prominent scientific studies, still found a stubborn defense and remained an intricate part of the German social fabric. Rudolf Virchow (1821–1902), a founding member of the German Anthropological Society, initiated a special study of race in 1871 to test an assumption already posed by French anthropologists that questioned the existence of pure races. In the largest racial study ever conducted in Europe until that time, Virchow surveyed 6,760,000 schoolchildren on the bases of eye, hair, and skin color as well as skull measurements. Was there a German race, and, if so, how much of it remained? Were there any unique physical or cultural qualities that marked one as a Jew or a German? Virchow conducted the survey with Jews and Germans on a separate basis. The results contradicted the belief systems of those who held dear the promise of Aryan racial supremacy and the purity of Aryan bloodlines.

Not surprisingly, Virchow's research findings revealed that racial uniformity did not exist anywhere in the Reich. The myth of the acclaimed blue-eyed, blond-haired Germans as a strong numerical presence in the country took a severe hit. The professor's data revealed that blonds constituted 31.8 percent of the population compared with 14.05 percent for brunettes with mixed types garnering 54.15 percent. The results from the 75,377 Jewish schoolchildren in the survey showed that 11 percent were pure blonds compared with 42 percent with black hair and 47 percent with mixed types.[21] Virchow's study raised serious doubts about racial conceptions of citizenship, especially in regard to the Jews. The myth of race was strong enough among members of the German academic and political elite to largely ignore Virchow's findings.[22]

More in tune with mainline perspectives on race hygiene was the appearance of an influential textbook, *Menschliche Erblichkeitslehre und Rassenhygiene* (The principles of human heredity and racial hygiene), first published in 1921 by Erwin Bauer (1875–1933), Eugen Fischer (1874–1967), and Fritz Lenz (1887–1976). The work, widely used in Germany as a standard on genetics for over twenty years, was authored by leading figures in the German scientific community. Lenz, from the University of Munich, became the first professor to assume a chair of racial hygiene in Germany in 1923. Fischer directed the Kaiser Wilhelm Institute for Anthropology, Human Heredity, and Eugenics in Berlin-Dahlem from 1927 to 1942, and Bauer headed the Institute for Breeding Research, also at the Kaiser Wilhelm Institute. One of the most striking examples of stereotypical language leveled against Jews in an avowed scientific publication is found in the last section of the text. In "The Psychological Differences between the Great Races," Lenz shared the following presumptions with students, other scientists, and politicians:

It is therefore understandable that the Jews distinguish themselves not only through cleverness and activity, hard work and persistence, but also above all through a surprising capability to transfer themselves into the souls of other people and, from this, influence them according to their will. That is why their tendencies and capabilities lead them again and again to enter activities based on the inclinations of the public at any one point in time with connections that bring them success. Professions which tend toward their special predilections and success are, above all, those of the salesman, trader and distributor of gold, journalists, authors, publishers, politicians, actors, musicians, attorneys and doctors . . . The tendency to use too many words stands in sharp contrast to the Germanic taciturnity, the "Jewish haste" in contrast to the Germanic peace and ponderousness. The inner space between people and things, which is characteristic of Germans, the Jew knows nothing about; he is dependent on other people for his way of life. (*Er ist seiner Wesensart nach eben auf andere Menschen angewiesen*.)[23]

As prestigious members of the Kaiser Wilhelm Institute, Lenz and Fischer would go on to play important roles in the articulation of Nazi racial policy. They actively engaged themselves in the professional formation of aspiring doctors and scientists on race hygiene, hereditary doctrines, and genetics. Their contributions toward the administration of the Law for Genetically Diseased Offspring, passed on 14 July 1933, constituted the first step toward the elimination of genetic defectives and those deemed racially inferior, including the Jews, Gypsies, and the mentally ill.[24] In another respect, Lenz and Fischer are connective figures linking Weimar with the Third Reich in that their works were among those frequently cited by Nazi curriculum writers in race education. In an essay initially published in 1925 under the title *Über die biologischen Grundlagen der Erziehung* (Over the biological bases of education), Lenz advocated the formation of a strong racial consciousness among the young as a critical purpose of schooling. The Munich professor reminded his contemporaries that they bore a serious responsibility to future generations of youth in advancing race education. The consequence of not attending to this noble racial purpose was the grave possibility that the Germanic race would die out.[25]

Mentioning Jews only once in his treatise, Lenz expressed additional preconceptions about Jewish intellectual tendencies. A meaningful issue for education, he wrote, was that Jewish children on the average already clearly showed a different nature (*Veranlagung*) from non-Jewish children. There was no doubt that many Jews were intellectually talented, especially in thinking with numbers and abstract concepts as well as psychological empathy, but they revealed less talent for thinking in terms of graphic images and technical construction. Lenz advised educators that compared with non-Jewish children, Jewish children were more likely to exhibit physical and intellectual precociousness.[26] The scientist's seemingly benign tone regarding the Jewish community stood in sharp contradiction with his assumptions recorded several years later in the genetics textbook with Bauer and Fischer. In this volume, Lenz insisted that Jews possessed very little capability for abstract thought and were predisposed toward fomenting revolutions. The predilection of Jews for the healing arts could be explained by the bald assumption that Jews held a greater fear of pain, illness, and death than the Germans.[27]

In a pattern already familiar to a host of Nazi curriculum projects, Lenz added a section to the 1936 edition of the genetics textbook that presented percentages of Jews in Prussia actively engaged in the professions of medicine, law, publishing, and acting without documenting the source. Presumably, statistics advanced the illusion of a more convincing and objective argument that Jews really were not only outsiders but also held a threatening non-Aryan influence in these professions. To add more weight to his argument, Lenz cited the eleventh German edition of Henry Ford's *Der Internationale Jude* (Leipzig, 1923) to illustrate that the American theater had also fallen under the control of Jews.[28] Spreading the word about race hygiene and biological determinism, as well as Volkish nationalist assumptions that undergirded this perspective, found a particularly enthusiastic disciple in the person of Hans F. K. Günther (1891–1968). The philologist from Freiburg and professor from the University of Jena, with the strong support of the medical publisher Julius Lehmann from Munich, became one of the most successful and prolific writers to reach broad sections of the German public on racial hygiene. Günther's name eventually became a household word for a subsequent generation of teachers under the Third Reich. His key contribution was to fuse race hygiene with nationalistic fervor and a virulent anti-Semitism.[29] Günther's best-known work, *Rassenkunde des deutschen Volkes* (Racial science of the German Volk), first appeared in 1922 and enjoyed such popularity that it reached its eleventh edition within five years.[30] The collapse of the Weimar Republic provided a significant opportunity for Günther to advance the teaching of racial hygiene into the German school system with the blessings of the Third Reich.

Günther offered nothing new to the study of race hygiene. But he succeeded in couching the language of racial science, and more specifically racial anti-Semitism, in terms that the lay person could understand. His works were profusely illustrated with facial shots of people representing various races. Like many of his other colleagues, Günther advanced an anthropology of race linking external, physical characteristics of human beings with the inner qualities of racial soul. There was a certain aesthetic focus in much of his writing. Pitted against the beautiful Aryan was the profound ugliness of the Jew as expressed in a series of stereotypes with long traditions.

In no other volume were these stereotypes more graphically depicted than in Günther's *Rassenkunde des jüdischen Volkes*, published during the swan song of the Weimar Republic. Three years before Hitler's assumption of power, Günther's most focused work on the Jews integrated over 300 illustrations of Jews from various countries. The text argued that Jews possessed unique physical qualities that marked them as an inferior race. Appearing once again was evidence of skull measurements used to support certain assumptions about racial classification. Pictures and accompanying measurements suggested that Jews did not possess the coveted *Langschädel*, or the more elongated skull of the creative and cultured Nordic race.[31] Among the multitude of facial images was that of Albert Einstein. Günther completely omitted discussion of his intellectual achievements and simply stated year of birth (1879) with a brief notation about Einstein's appearance, "predominantly oriental with a slight Near Eastern element."[32] In a style that reverberated with the language of the Third Reich, the uniqueness of the individual disappeared under Günther's catalogue of racial observations and stereotypes. The Jewish nose alone earned no less than three pages in Günther's tome. Little was left untouched. Hair, lips, height, eye color, and even mustaches came under Günther's scrutiny in a section on "Jews of the Present."[33]

Behind these detailed and labored descriptions was the power of suggestion. Biological determinism necessitated careful scientific study to demonstrate through enlightened legal practice and anthropology that Jews really were different from the Aryan population. So different were Jews in body and soul from Germans that as an undesirable and racial outgroup, they threatened the bloodlines of the nation. Racial anti-Semitism, as shown thus far, claimed its own history beginning long before the Third Reich. The boundaries between science and intuition were almost nonexistent, often equated, among those engaged in racial science.[34] Even when science contradicted prevailing racial stereotypes, as in the case of Virchow's study of Jewish and German schoolchildren, the mystique of race and intuition proved more powerful than reason.

Volkish thought, considered thus far in broad outlines, symbolized a foundation stone for what eventually became legitimized knowledge implicit in curriculums created for children under the Third Reich. Hitler and National Socialist educators had a rich Volkish tradition from which to draw. They also found a body of like-minded individuals to carry forth the banner of racial anti-Semitism.[35]

NATIONAL SOCIALISM, JEWS, AND THE EDUCATED PERSON

Any serious examination of Nazi views on the nature of race and education, especially in relationship to anti-Semitism, must take into account Hitler's autobiography, *Mein Kampf*, written with the aid of his adjutant, Rudolf Hess, at Landsberg Prison in 1924. *Mein Kampf* is significant for educational historians of the period in that the educational theories advocated by Hitler in its pages closely approximated the official educational policies of the Nazi regime after the assumption of power in early 1933. (See Figure 1.1.) In the case of curriculum formation, the book became a critically important ideological reference work legitimizing educational reform ranging from the preeminence of physical education to the integration of race consciousness.[36]

As revealed in Hitler's letter to Gemlich in 1919, the future dictator had already given serious thought to the prospect of rationalizing racial anti-Semitism five years before penning *Mein Kempf*. In one of his most direct statements on the purpose of schooling, Hitler wrote that the crowning work of the entire educational enterprise

> must be to burn the racial sense and racial feeling into the instinct and the intellect, the heart and brain of youth entrusted to it. No boy or girl must leave school without having been led to an ultimate realization of the necessity and essence of blood purity.[37]

The anti-Semitic dimensions of Nazi school curriculum which represents the centerpiece of this study claimed strong ideological connections to the earlier genesis of Volkish thinking. In no other publication conceived in the German language of the twentieth century, with the possible exception of Julius Streicher's writings, does one find the decidedly virulent kind of anti-Semitism

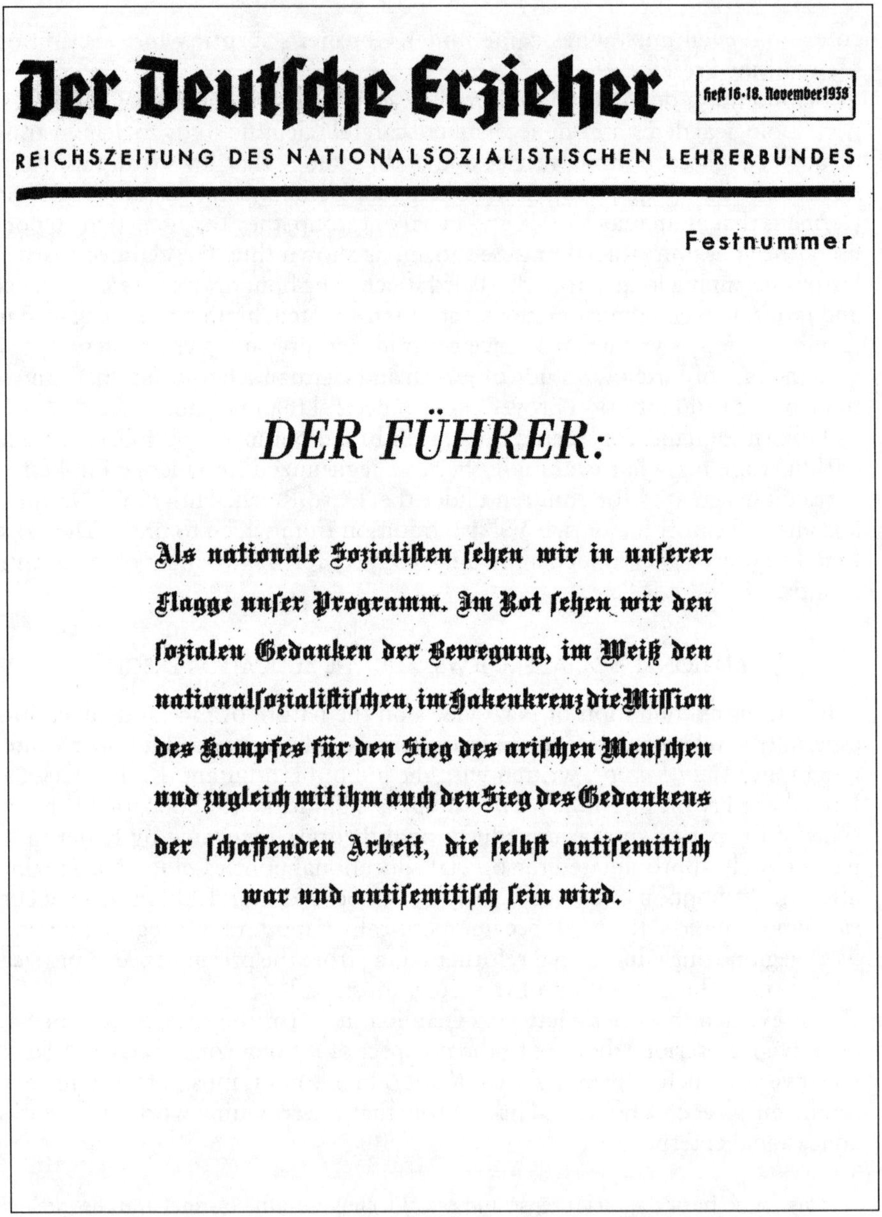

Der Deutsche Erzieher
Heft 16-18. November 1938

REICHSZEITUNG DES NATIONALSOZIALISTISCHEN LEHRERBUNDES

Festnummer

DER FÜHRER:

Als nationale Sozialisten sehen wir in unserer Flagge unser Programm. Im Rot sehen wir den sozialen Gedanken der Bewegung, im Weiß den nationalsozialistischen, im Hakenkreuz die Mission des Kampfes für den Sieg des arischen Menschen und zugleich mit ihm auch den Sieg des Gedankens der schaffenden Arbeit, die selbst antisemitisch war und antisemitisch sein wird.

Figure 1.1 Adolf Hitler on the symbolic meaning of the Nazi colors and anti-Semitism from *Mein Kampf*, cited on the cover of the journal *Der Deutscher Erzieher* (*The German Educator*), 1938. Translation: "As National Socialists, we see our program in our flag. In red we see the nationalistic idea, in the swastika the mission of the struggle for the victory of the Aryan man and, by the same token, the victory of the idea of creative work, which as such always has been and always will be anti-Semitic." From *Mein Kampf*. Trans. by Ralph Mannheim, 1971, pp. 496–497.

expressed in the pages of *Mein Kampf*. There is nothing original about this expressed hatred. In Hitler's diatribes against Jewish blood, one finds images of the shifty merchant, cultural parasite, intolerable usurer, dishonest profiteer, manipulative press agent, evil Marxist, plotting revolutionary, and carrier of all manner of disease destructive to the Volkish body politic. The long and embittered list kept alive the myth propounded in the *Protocols of the Elders of Zion* regarding Jewish world conspiracy.[38] Hitler readily rejected the religious identification of the Jewish community with the enjoinder that the Jew "has always been a people with definite racial characteristics." He contented that the Talmud did not represent Jewish spiritual traditions, but symbolized instead a practical guide on securing worldly profit.[39]

There was a strong strain of anti-intellectualism in Hitler's writings on education. The dictator harbored a strong enmity toward the Gymnasium tradition, which he strongly criticized for making a mockery of the Greek balance between mental instruction and physical training. In his view, the Gymnasium was plagued by a propensity for mental discipline and filled youthful minds with useless bits of knowledge soon to be forgotten. Similar to the educational views of Paul de Lagarde, Hitler insisted that the elite secondary schools contributed to the deadness of the educational system, a system in dire need of a new spirit that would grow out of the Volkish state. The Nazis were not the first to apply Volkish philosophy to the classroom. Two obscure, right-wing pedagogues from the Weimar Republic, G. A. O. Collischonn and Max Maurenbrecher, were among the first to discuss the didactical problems associated with the Volkish teaching of history.[40] The Third Reich was the first to apply the full weight of the state to legitimize this kind of instruction.

Hitler's view of history as a school subject united nationalism with the biological dimensions of racial superiority and blood. The task of the Volkish state, he wrote, was to ensure that "a world history was finally written in which the racial question was to be raised to a dominant position." The German chancellor retained the study of antiquity from the Gymnasium tradition but steeped the subject in combative and racial overtones:

> Roman history correctly conceived in extremely broad outlines is and remains the best mentor, not only for today, but for all time. The Hellenic ideal of culture also remains preserved for us in its exemplary beauty. We must not allow the greater racial community to be torn asunder by differences of the individual peoples. The struggle that rages today is for very great aims. A culture combining Hellenism and Germanism is fighting for its very existence.[41]

The words of *Mein Kampf* were not part of a dead prophecy or, as it turned out, failed visions conceived by an idle dreamer. Albert Speer, Hitler's former architect and armaments minister, would later recall the dynamic role played by racial anti-Semitism in the dictator's worldview. "Hatred of the Jews," he observed, "was the motor and central point for Hitler, perhaps even the only element that actually moved him. The German people, German greatness, the Reich, all of that meant nothing to him in the end." For that reason, Hitler preserved a special animosity for the Jews in the last sentence of his will and testament through linking them to Germany's catastrophic defeat. Speer was among those present to hear Hitler's famous speech in the Reichstag on 30 January 1939 when he warned that if war was to come, the conflagration would destroy the Jews, not the Germans.[42]

The consequences of institutionalizing this racial interpretation of Jewish cultural identity would be great not only for how German schools legitimized knowledge about Jews for young charges but even more so for Jews suffering persecution under the legal process of defining racial citizenship in the Third Reich. The Nazi assumption of power in 1933 set into motion a brutality that would forever change the Jewish community and its relationship to Germany and the Germans. A multiplicity of government racial policies, far too numerous to examine in any detail here, are part of the historical context of schooling in Nazi society. On 1 April of that year, Jewish businesses were boycotted across Germany. Legislation from 25 April limited the percentage' of non-Aryan students, now called foreigners, attending secondary schools leading to university studies. Jewish school enrollments could not exceed 1.5 percent of the student population. The aim was to cut back on the number of Jewish students eventually entering the academic professions.[43]

Of even greater effect that same month was the promulgation of the Law for the Restoration of the Professional Civil Service. The *Arierparagraph*, or Aryan Paragraph, of this measure meant that Jews, as non-Aryans, were barred from civil service and denied admission to the bar. Almost overnight, Jewish judges, lawyers and teachers along with other officials were dismissed from their posts. Jewish ancestry or political reliability became the grounds for dismissing thousands of teachers and school administrators. Berlin witnessed a purge of 130 of the 3,200 secondary school teachers, 230 of the 8,500 primary teachers, and 83 of the 622 head teachers.[44] Jewish doctors, now forbidden to deal with any health insurance plans, found themselves faced with Nazi activists who discouraged patients from visiting hospitals directed by Jews.

Beyond the civil service restrictions, Jews were to experience even more difficult persecution under the name of the law. The Reich Law for the Protection of German Blood and German Honor, part of the Nuremberg Laws from 15 September 1935, prohibited marriage and sexual relations between Jews and Germans. Jews were also stripped of citizenship. Connecting to an old stereotype of Jewish sexual perversion, the Nuremberg Laws made it illegal for Jews to employ German women under forty-five years of age in their households.[45] The seriousness of these mounting restrictions for Jews reached a crossover point on 9–10 November 1938 with the public initiation of the "Night of the Broken Glass." Thousands of Jewish businesses and synagogues suffered destruction across the Reich with the imprisonment of over 26,000 Jews and the murder of at least 90.[46] Especially ominous for the Jews was the absence of any sustained moral indignation against the Nazi regime from the international community for these acts.

According to Victor Klemperer, the difference between Aryan and non-Aryan was all important for citizens living under the heavy arm of dictatorship. The worst experience for him as a Jew under the Third Reich was the requirement to wear the Yellow Star beginning September of 1941. The symbol resurrected old medieval associations with plague and quarantine. Everything changed radically for him from this point onward. Like many other Jews, including schoolchildren, Klemperer was now open to a greater frequency of public humiliations of various kinds. The Yellow Star accentuated the racial classification of Jews and provided Nazi authorities with even more efficient ways of controlling the Jewish population.[47]

Within this larger persecution directed against Jews were institutional measures leveled at the schools.[48] The Bavarian Ministry of Teaching and Culture announced in August of 1933 that Jewish students in the teaching seminar at Würzburg could continue their professional preparations only in Jewish schools and not public schools. The Aryan Paragraph applied to all headmasters in the public schools of Baden beginning in early 1934.[49] Authorities in Land Brandenburg successfully pressed Minister Bernhard Rust to declare an end to Jewish religious instruction in all public schools in March of 1936.[50] Shortly before the close of 1937, the Reich Ministry for Education abolished the teaching of Hebrew in all public secondary schools. At about the same time, the Bavarian authorities barred Aryan teachers from instructing in Jewish schools.[51] Even more ominous was an announcement handed down by Education Minister Rust shortly after the assassination of Ernst von Rath in Paris and the Night of Broken Glass. In a directive dated 15 November 1938, Rust informed administrators that Jewish children could not attend public schools. "It is unbearable," proclaimed Rust, "for German schoolchildren to sit next to Jews."[52]

Public school attendance figures revealed a drastic transformation in the Jewish population. In May of 1934, Jewish schoolchildren in Berlin's public schools numbered 2,777, which constituted 4.9 percent of the public school population. Two years later, the number dropped to 1,172, representing only 1.9 percent of the total.[53] For private schools, which traditionally enrolled the majority of students in the Jewish community, the situation grew worse. By the end of 1938, all state subsidies for the support of these private schools were officially prohibited.[54] Even though often much of the cost for supporting the teaching of Jewish religion in public schools was paid by local Jewish congregations, the Nazis remained adamant in striking down an old school tradition critical to Jewish cultural identity. Protests from Jewish school leaders fell on deaf ears.[55]

Surviving this period is a rare curriculum document that revealed much about the transitory nature of Nazi policy toward Jewish schooling and the Jewish community at large. In 1937, the school department of the Reich Agency for Jews in Germany, an office in the RMWEVB (Reich Ministerium für Wissenschaft, Erziehung, and Volksbildung), released "Guidelines for Establishing Teaching Plans for Jewish Elementary Schools." One of the most prominently stated goals for curriculum development was to prepare Jewish children for eventual migration to Palestine and the "difficult life struggle" pupils could expect after their arrival. Along with general guidelines for classes in Hebrew, religion, Jewish and biblical history, German, music, and drawing was the introduction of "Palestine Studies" in geography.[56]

The general government policy encouraging Jewish migration, as reflected in this curriculum, was short-lived. Escalating anti-Semitic practices, reaching an especially brutal level in November of 1938 with the Night of Broken Glass, essentially nullified these curriculum guidelines for Jewish elementary schools.

The following month, a meeting of representatives from the SS, the foreign ministry, interior, education, state secretary, finance, and Hitler's staff studied statistics for Jewish school attendance. Racially separating Jews from all phases of school life remained at the center of discussion.[57] (See figure 1.2.) A secret directive from the Education Ministry ordered all Jewish names removed from memorial tablets in universities and schools.[58] The situation changed very quickly for Jewish pupils and their teachers. By 15 October 1941, the deportation of Reich Jews to the East was under way. Three days later, Himmler closed the gates of emigration.[59]

ANTI-SEMITIC VOICES AND NAZI EDUCATION

The Jewish experience considered thus far, and the Volkish thinking which supported racial anti-Semitism, collectively represent an important backdrop for the consideration of Nazi writings on the educated person. Hitler's *Mein Kampf* and Nazi racial laws provided an ideological framework for the integration of racial anti-Semitism into Nazi school curriculum. Recent research suggests that ideological conviction alone does not explain why professors, teachers, and school administrators engaged themselves in writing and pub-

Figure 1.2 Two Jewish students derided in front of a class. The blackboard reads: "The Jew is our greatest enemy! Protect yourselves from the Jews!"

lishing curriculums of an anti-Semitic nature. While not to downplay the dynamic role played by ideology under the regime, career advancement was undoubtedly facilitated through opportunities offered by a multitude of publishers interested in printing new curriculums following the party line.[60]

The public face offered by the Nazis to the international community left little doubt about the place of biological determinism and what became commonly known as "the Jewish question" in the life of the school. Walter Scharrer, in an essay translated into English by a London publisher under the title "Jewish Opposition and Secondary Schools," angrily condemned Jews for trying to take over secondary education. In a pattern of propagandistic language that became the hallmark of the Third Reich, Scharrer appealed for the ruthless administration of a cleansing campaign to rid schools of "saucy Jewish brats" and "foreign parasitic invaders."[61] Even the imposition of the 1.5 percent rule for limiting Jewish enrollments was not enough to satisfy Scharrer's agenda:

> But even more rigorous legislative measures would not strike at the root of our difficulties. Let us assume that even one Jewish pupil remained in a class, this same specimen is the stumbling block to proper National Socialist instruction. How can a class, which includes a possibly in itself quite harmless Jewish child, be brought to a proper pitch of racial pride and racial consciousness? How can such a class be rendered immune once and for all against pro-Jewish sympathies, and how can it be enlightened about the unbroken series of crimes committed by World Jewry and Jewish Freemasonry? Both on tactical and educational grounds it is not always advisable to place Jewish pupils under disadvantages in class, to treat them roughly, to bully them, to keep on ridiculing them, or to give them bad reports. Meticulous correctness and painstaking justice have often proved more effective.[62]

In a slightly more diplomatic tone, Minister of Education and Science Bernhard Rust, a former secondary school teacher from Hanover, informed international audiences that Hitler's *Mein Kampf* provided the major direction for schooling in the new Reich. The misguided education traditions of the past often placed an undue emphasis on intellectual development. A new kind of schooling honoring a more vigorous training of the body, the inculcation of values supporting racial purity, and a curriculum inspired by the laws of biology and racial science was the order of the day. The Jews did not escape the Reichminister's commentary on the nature of the educated person. Whose false and harmful education traditions, rooted in individualism and Marxist internationalist perspectives, destroyed the natural bonds of racial community? The consequences of the Nuremburg Laws, he wrote, corrected this misfortune by removing Jewish children from public schools, thus preserving the race instincts of German boys and girls.[63]

In academic circles, there was one voice who, through the pages of the respected *International Education Review*[64] and numerous other publications like *National Political Education* (1932) became widely recognized as a leading philosopher of Nazi education. Ernst Krieck (1882–1947), a faculty member with a strong international reputation from Frankfurt-am-Main and later the University of Heidelberg, reflected a racial anti-Semitism of a multifarious nature. His perspective is also worthy of note in that he wielded influence in translating Volkish thinking into a Nazi philosophy of education. The publication of his essay "The Education of a Nation from Blood and Soil" in 1934 further opened an international venue for his ideas. In language that harkened back to the Volkish ideas of political culture of Chamberlain, Lagarde, and Langbehn, Krieck observed that national growth, rooted in blood and soil, was the key to German history. The Nazi revolution introduced a new purpose of schooling in which biology would go hand in hand with the training of character. Implied but not directly stated in Krieck's argument was the assumption by the state that certain groups of people fell outside the racial bounds of those deemed worthy of education. Jews are not mentioned once in this essay, but the spirit of exclusion is clear.[65]

From his university posts and also as an active member of the Institute for the History of the New Germany with Alfred Baeumler, Krieck assumed a different tack when writing for a specifically German audience. His earlier essay "The Jewish Question" appeared in 1933 in Bauemler's journal, *Volk und Werden*. The professor resurrected a string of Jewish stereotypes associated with finance capital. "Our anti-Semitism," he claimed, "is based on a simple formula: We in Germany do not want the rule of Jews. We want to be the lord of our own house." Krieck certainly was not above citing the historian Theodore Mommsen who allegedly remarked that Jews, beyond any doubt, represented "an element of national decomposition" just as they had when they lived under the Romans.[66] Some three years later, Krieck would be at the center of renewed efforts to cloak anti-Semitism in the language of anthropology. Of greatest significance were his efforts to convince fellow educators that knowledge should be conceived in organic and unified terms. Krieck railed against what he felt was the mechanistic nature of Darwinism and the creation of a false dichotomy between the organic and mechanistic dimensions of reality. Race and blood purity became for Krieck, and many other Volkish thinkers in the Third Reich, powerful symbols of an organic cultural unity. Knowledge legitimized for schools as an integrated organic whole clearly held implications for those engaged in the teaching of the young. In an expression which certainly qualified for Klemperer's LTI, Krieck looked to the formation of a "racial-Volkish-political world view" (*rassisch-völkisch-politisch Weltanschauung*) as a necessity of life for educators.[67]

Among these mandarins was one figure who stood above all in terms of the sheer volume of writings on racial anti-Semitism. Johann von Leers, professor at the University of Berlin and adviser on Jewish affairs in the Propaganda Ministry of Joseph Goebbels, published more books and journal articles on the subject than perhaps anyone else in the Nazi pantheon. While Krieck tried to pass off his anti-Semitic rationalizations as anthropology and science, Leers delighted in steeping his rhetoric in a linguistic violence designed to enlist readers in this unholy cause. In what became possibly a classic in the history of racial anti-Semitism, Leers masterfully employed propaganda techniques of the Big Lie popularized by Goebbels. His book *Wie kam der Jude zum Geld?* (How did the Jews come to money?) from 1939 depicted on its cover a Jew with claws wrapping his arms around a globe. (See plate 1). The Jewish banking conspiracy, personified most radically by the manipulations of the Rothschild family, was to Leers one of the greatest threats to civilization. As master propagandist, Leers realized the power of image in advancing anti-Semitic attitudes and often sought emotional responses of fear and loathing from his audience. In one drawing, he portrayed the banking mogul Solomon Rothschild from Vienna driving two threatening vultures in search of bankruptcies. Another caricature depicted the Jewish community as threatening swarms of bees.[68]

The enthusiastic anti-Semitism expressed in the writings of von Leers was multifaceted in nature and explained, in part, why he remained an important figure in the formation of Nazi racial policy. An earlier piece called *Juden sehen dich an* (Jews look at you) blended sun worship with romantic idealism. The true Aryans of the north, he argued, were people of the light and occupied the center of the cosmos. He reasoned that Aryans, being inhabitants of land often shrouded in mist and fog, possessed a natural propensity for sunlight. All of this implied that Jews were antithetical to the culture of light and dwelled in eternal darkness.[69] The kind of Volkish thinking advanced by Leers took on yet another dimension that reflected a more direct connection to racial science and Nazi legal conceptions of the Jew. To further separate the Jews from the German body politic and strengthen rationalizations for their maltreatment, Leers drew upon one of the most violent forms of anti-Semitic prejudice. Writing in the spirit of the Nuremberg Laws of 1935 that he championed, Leers categorized all Jews as dangerous criminals. Like many of his colleagues, Leers resorted to the language of mathematics by integrating false and unverifiable statistics to demonstrate the criminal nature of Jews and their underworld activities.[70]

The foreword to one of Leers's later works further expanded the Nazi lexicon for racial anti-Semitism. Is the Jew, Leers asked, "an hereditary criminal"? In few other works does Leers exploit old economic anti-Semitic stereotypes of Jews with an undeniable biological twist laced with numerous falsifications. The hereditary background of Jews explained their criminality. After all, so he claimed, wasn't this evident in the traditional Jewish propensity for murder, child pornography, sexual crimes, theft, gangsterism, and fraud in the marketplace?[71] With the blessings of Joseph Goebbels, Leers carefully cultivated connections with the Nazi education establishment, which provided an important venue for his propaganda. The prolific faculty member from the University of Berlin was one of the most frequent contributors to *Die Deutsche Erzieher*, a widely circulated journal of the National Socialist Teachers Union.[72] He was a significant figure, along with other Volkish notables, upon whom the regime relied to propagandize their ideology and the Nazi revolution.

The process of legitimizing racial anti-Semitism through the curriculum also brought into sharp focus the problem of censorship and clearing curriculum materials for publication. Several ministries were involved in the ideological proofing of books and monographs written for school audiences. Education and Science Minister Rust and his staff often exchanged drafts of curriculum writings with the National Socialist Teachers Union and other ministries to ensure ideological purity. Contributing mightily to this circle of censorship was Alfred Rosenberg (1893–1946), whose anti-Semitic and anti-Christian tract, *Myth of the Twentieth Century* (1930), earned him a reputation as one of the leading Nazi intellectuals. The *Myth*, in addition to condemning the machinations of the Jesuits, pitted the virtues and honor of the Nordic race against the subverted values of Biblical Judaism most powerfully represented in the person of the Jewish cattle merchant. If this wasn't threatening enough, Jewish control over the forces of liberalism prevented the rise of the Nordic race. Germany now had the moral responsibility to cut down the inferior races that created this cultural morass.[73]

The self-appointed philosopher, in addition to his many offices, was the "Representative of the Führer for the Supervision of the Entire Intellectual and Ideological Schooling and Education of the NSDAP [Nationalsozialistische Deutsche Arbeiterpartei]." Chancellery Rosenberg actively engaged itself in not only scrutinizing proposed materials for ideological instruction but also in advocating certain points of emphasis in the curriculum. Few other Nazis, for example, spoke with such conviction as Rosenberg in regard to the teaching of German prehistory. The issue was so important for the cause of Aryan supremacy that he personally appointed the new Reich Association for German Pre-History under the direction of a certain Professor Reinerth. Like Heinrich Himmler, Rosenberg sensed a potential in archaeology as a way of scientifically explaining, and thus legitimizing, Aryan racial origins. His dissatisfaction with the quality of writings on prehistory coming off the press early in the Third Reich was a prime reason for Rosenberg's organizing the new Reich Association. Much of what passed for prehistory among many publications, he wryly observed, was both uncritical and based on fantasy. A more scientific approach was in order.[74]

The Third Reich provided Rosenberg with a highly visible podium to extend his anti-Semitic thinking far beyond his earlier work in the *Myth*. As chief of the Foreign Office of the NSDAP, Rosenberg expounded on the Jewish question by raising fears about the *Ostjuden*, or Jews from the East. As did Hitler's ravings in *Mein Kampf*, Rosenberg warned about the devastating consequences for German culture posed by the migration of thousands of Jews from the East to the Reich. Condemning Zionism in the harshest of terms, he repeatedly associated Jews with the threat of international communism. Returning to his discourse was the "abuse of women" through Jewish men lying in wait to take sexual advantage of the defenseless females. The imagery extended to a litany about "power and lack of culture" among Jews seen many times before in other Volkish writings. With deadening repetition, Rosenberg brought readers back to the disturbing concentration of Jewish influence in the legal and medical professions. In like mind with Leers, Rosenberg attacked Jewish politicians as nothing more than veiled criminals who earlier enjoyed protection under the wing of the failed Weimar democracy.[75] Posing as an expert on Jewish religion, the Reichsminister struck at the Talmud with language that both dehumanized Jews and insulted Jewish spiritual traditions. Written in 1937, these words preceded by about a year the Night of Broken Glass when Torah scrolls would be removed from synagogues across Germany and unceremoniously thrown to the ground and burned.[76]

Placed within a larger perspective, Rosenberg's activities in relation to public schools and the issue of anti-Semitism represented but one of many facets of Nazi education policy. Layers of educational bureaucracy revealed other figures who wielded much more influence than Rosenberg in the formation of curriculum. Phillip Bouhler (1899–1945), the Reich representative for literature on school and teaching, was of singular importance not only for the question of school knowledge but also for his other political responsibilities that impacted the practice of medicine. Bouhler, the master bureaucrat, was the business manager of the NSDAP from 1925 to 1934 after which he succeeded Himmler as police president of Munich. In 1934, he became chief of Hitler's Chancellery. Added to these obligations was the chairmanship of the censorship committee, which published lists of approved and condemned books. Eventually, a fateful turn of events would forever associate Bouhler with the Nazi policy of mass murder. Moving up quickly in the ranks of the Nazi hierarchy, Bouhler received an appointment from Hitler in September of 1939 with a charge to organize the euthanasia program with Karl Brandt. This order eventually led to what became known as the T4 killings of the mentally and physically disabled.[77] The high-ranking Reichsleiter, as Rosenberg, Rust and many others would discover, was a force to be reckoned with. Bouhler's answer to the problem of involving so many publishers in the printing of school books was to propose a unified history textbook for elementary pupils in the entire Reich.[78] As noted in chapter 5, the Reichsleiter eventually seized the opportunity to promote his own reader for schools based on a series of stories.[79]

Officials like Bouhler and Rosenberg, with varying degrees of influence, set their own stamp on the process of legitimizing school knowledge. Other institutions contributed even more significantly to this field. Documents from both the Ministry of Education and Science as well as the NSLB (Nationalsozialistische Lehrerbund) revealed a great deal of activity in the proofing and exchange of manuscripts and curriculums from 1934 to 1939 in particular. At times, curriculum proposals showed a kind of radicalism for which Berlin was ill prepared. Herr Haanz, the minister of culture and teaching from Karlsruhe submitted to Rust in early 1939 a curriculum proposal to wipe out all classes in religious instruction and replace them with one unified religious education curriculum for the Third Reich. Such a move supported the Nazi process of centralizing educational policy in Berlin while moving away from the old German tradition of preserving educational policymaking prerogatives in the provinces. Even the Nazis, however, were bound by certain traditions. Religious instruction along Catholic and Protestant lines remained intact in many public schools.

Although Haanz's ideas never reached fruition under the Third Reich, the anti-Semitic implications of his curriculum proposal are worthy of note. Somewhat reminiscent of earlier ideas from Lagarde and Langbehn supporting the emergence of a new Germanic religion, Haanz advocated "a substitute for religious instruction" through lessons centered on "German traditions and German ways." Such a curriculum engendered in pupils a sense of moral reverence for nature, German blood, and the underlying values of National Socialism. In a section on the Germanic worldview, Haanz maintained a nationalistic focus on German heroes, artists, scientists, and key leaders of the people. Nordic fairy tales and myths also remained an important part of the course plans. Religion, now recast as undogmatic and conditioned by race, portrayed Jesus Christ as an Aryan revolutionary and fighter against the Jewish spirit. Among the notable "faith heroes" remembered by the Nazis for their strident anti-Semitism were Martin Luther, Paul de Lagarde, and Ernst Moritz Arndt. This new pantheon of heroes would contribute to national renewal and the foundation of a new faith.[80]

NAZI CURRICULUM REFORM AND RACE

A major assumption advanced thus far is that an understanding of Nazi racial anti-Semitism in curriculum necessitated the articulation of a historical context. That context, as we have seen, is rooted in the history of ideas, more specifically the development of Volkish thinking which, by the late nineteenth century, embraced the science of race. The critical integration of science into an anti-Semitic worldview never wholly displaced the old economic stereotypes or the tradition of religious anti-Semitism. The exploitation of science to serve the ends of the racial state simply made anti-Semitism more virulent and dangerous. For the Nazis, this implied a sense of mission to create an organic and integrated curriculum based on race and biological determinism. Artificial boundaries between body, soul, and spirit would be swept away in order to reach a unity of thinking about the nature of citizenship in the New Germany.[81] The educated, racially conscious person spurned the tradition of humanistic learning espoused earlier by Wilhelm von Humboldt whose reform ideas defined the purpose of the elite Gymnasium from the early nineteenth century onward.[82] Such a transformation of school life under the Third Reich, so claimed Walter Gross from the NSDAP's Office of Racial Political Affairs, demanded nothing less than a revolution of the spirit.[83]

The biological focus for schooling under the Third Reich, with origins already found in *Mein Kampf*, became official for teachers and school administrators through a curriculum policy directive circulated by the Ministry of Education and Science in September of 1933. The directive directly quoted Hitler's autobiography on the importance of children leaving school with an understanding of blood purity and its significance for themselves and the nation. Racial science now assumed a position of preeminence in the curriculum in association with teaching about heredity. In this sense, racial science did not exist as a single standing subject in the elementary or secondary schools; instead, it provided a conceptual orientation for the entire course of study.[84] One of the most articulate curricular voices from the Nazi ranks on this relationship was Rudolf Benze, ministerial adviser to the RMWEVB and later head of the German Central Institute for Education and Teaching while holding the rank of SS sturmbahnführer. "National political education," he wrote, "established on the basis of teaching about heredity and racial science is much more an educational principle which, as applied to all subjects, knows its goal, and joins them with each other inside and out."[85]

Rust's curriculum directive indicated the degree of importance attached by the regime to the Jewish question in the life of the school. Two years before the Nuremberg Laws, the ministry told educators that the preservation of Nordic bloodlines meant the survival of the German racial community. Pupils must understand that mixing their blood with foreign races, especially with Jews, was an act of national betrayal. A wise and informed choice of marriage partner became obligatory. The struggle against degeneration and hereditary disease meant that teachers were obligated to teach about the rationale behind sterilization. In the only international connection in the entire directive, educators learned that legal measures in other countries served as models for the legitimation of German sterilization and racial laws. The United States figured prominently in this context with direct reference made in the curriculum directive to sterilization laws in various states, immigration laws, and what Rust called the "*Negerfrage*," or "Negro question." Family policy in France supported by strict hereditary laws for people from the Far East was also highlighted as yet another example from which teachers could draw.[86]

The curriculum directive from 1933, the first of its kind from the Third Reich, offered a brief glimpse into certain Nazi ideals for school knowledge. Just how extensively this directive applied across the curriculum could be seen in the perception of subjects like mathematics, natural sciences, and foreign languages. In Rust's typically vague rhetoric, teachers were strongly encouraged to develop instructional examples in these classes advancing an "organic attitude toward life" and the "development of informed opinion." Physical education, one of the kingpins of the curriculum, not only was a subject concerned with the health of the body but also modeled "Nordic racial beauty."[87]

The interrelationships between race, state, and culture evidenced in this document, and the racial anti-Semitism implied therein, provided an ideological framework for curriculum writers and publishers of school materials. What remained unresolved at this early stage were the formation of the curriculum itself and pedagogical questions about the delivery of instruction. These concerns would engross a multitude of educators until the end of the Third Reich. The Nazis did not transform German schools overnight. Starting up Hitler Youth formations was infinitely less complicated than instituting a new curriculum supported by appropriate teacher education programs for novice educators and advanced programs for veteran instructors. During the early years of the Third Reich, feverish activity directed toward extending the spirit of *Mein Kampf* into the schools required not only widespread creation of new school texts and curriculum but also the formation of a corps of racially conscious teachers. Candidates for elementary school teaching, according to the plan of study finalized by 1938 for the two-year teacher training colleges, studied four hours of ethnology and racial science a week over the course of the program. (See appendices 3 and 4.) Educating experienced teachers in the ways of racial science was another matter.

The NSLB initiated programs in advanced instruction and teacher seminars in various parts of the country. Most significant about the course offerings in the early years of the Third Reich was the fact that, unlike most other school literature, the schedule for teacher seminars treated race as a relatively minor subtheme. For the summer program from 1934 for the Berlin area, a concentration of thirty teacher seminars on the natural sciences, mathematics, and astronomy included only one on the racial dimensions of biology. Twelve seminars focusing on philosophy, pedagogics, psychology, and instructional teaching included two offerings on race, a class on "The Biological Bases of National Socialist Education: Race Hygiene" and a seminar in Reinickendorf on the philosophy of Hitler in *Mein Kampf* and Rosenberg's *Myth of the Twentieth Century*. Ernst Krieck taught a two-week seminar for teachers at Tempelhoff on national political education.[88] This schedule of teacher seminars suggested that the ideological retooling of the teaching staff was multidimensional in nature with racial anti-Semitism being one among several concerns.

The process of editing new textbooks reflecting the political values of the regime meant that a good share of the schoolbooks did not reach classrooms in significant numbers until after 1935. In one way, this did not present a serious problem since most history textbooks from the Weimar era, used by pupils on a temporary basis until more Nazified books arrived, contained strong nationalistic and militaristic interpretations of Germany's past.[89] Such qualities remained cherished by a regime bent on exploiting racial anti-Semitism for the purpose of cementing national unity and consolidating Nazi power.

The curriculum for the elementary school reflected both continuity and change. The Nazis remained largely committed to maintaining the same school subjects that had defined studies in the *Volksschule* for years. The transformation of these subjects through race ideology was what set the Nazi school agenda apart from previous generations. The weekly class hours for boys and girls under the Third Reich designated music, art, German language and literature, history, and geography as *deutschkundliche Fächer*, or subjects representing the essence of German culture. Beginning in grade five and continuing through the eighth year, physical education for both genders assumed the highest number of weekly class hours with the exception of German. Symbolizing the Nazi support of traditional gender roles, the curriculum required four hours weekly for girls in home economics during the eighth grade with an absence of math or geometry during the same year. (See appendices 1 and 2.)

As the previous discussion suggested, Nazi curriculum emerged out of a context of Volkish thinking that was both nationalistic and anti-Semitic in nature. Racial myths and stereotypes with a long past remained durable even after scientific racism integrated a language of rationality about why Jews were not Germans. The prospect of transforming the character of pupils through the inculcation of Nazi racial anti-Semitism demanded a major propaganda effort. Public schools were not fully trusted with this mission as seen by the growing importance of the Hitler Youth organization as it undertook greater responsibilities in teaching race education.[90]

This development does not suggest a lack of importance concerning the role of public schools in the formation of racial consciousness among the young. The nature of Nazism was such that racial anti-Semitism became part of a larger propaganda strategy influencing all major institutions in German society, from the cinemas to the law courts. To understand racial anti-Semitism in the Nazi school curriculum and its place in the definition of the educated person is to understand something of Nazi ideals for the young. Teachers were not the only professionals participating in the inculcation of Nazi ideals among the young, but they still remained important figures in legitimizing school knowledge on behalf of the regime. They would be joined by others, among the most educated elements of German society, to engage in one of the most unique curricular experiments in the history of education.

Racial anti-Semitism was a critically important dynamic in this process. With years of Volkish tradition and scientific racism behind them, Nazi educators articulated an organic, biologically oriented curriculum in which the Jew became the great foil for all that was wrong with the world. How the Nazis articulated this kind of knowledge through the curriculum is a matter to which we now turn.

Chapter 2

The Jewish Question
Curriculum Perspectives from the Third Reich

> Whoever avoids the Jewish question is my enemy.
>> —Dietrich Eckart, early Nazi ideologue, cited in Werner Dittrich, *Erziehung zum Judengegner*, 1937

> Without a solution to the Jewish question, there will be no solution to human kind.
>> —Fritz Fink, *Die Judenfrage im Unterricht*, cover, 1937

Any serious discussion about racial anti-Semitism in the curriculum of the Third Reich must take into account the thinking of professors of education, teachers, and school administrators actively engaged in forming curriculum on the Jewish question. Again, the purview of this study is limited to the public schools with the full realization that race biology certainly was not restricted to the halls of these institutions. While school restructuring remained in flux during the early years of the Third Reich, the problem of preparing teachers to think more consistently along racial and anti-Semitic lines loomed large for professors from teacher training colleges. Educating a new generation of teachers along with retooling the older and more experienced instructors demanded an articulation of Nazi curriculum in a language that connected to the classroom. The works published on the Jewish question for teachers reflected something of the ideological expectations of the regime, and as Victor Klemperer's treatise on Nazi language revealed, the lexicon of the Third Reich provided another way for the system to rationalize racial anti-Semitism.

Curriculum guides were significant in this process since they filled part of the gap made by the delay in the publication of textbooks with a decidedly Nazi racial bent. School restructuring did not take hold until after 1937 with many new textbooks for the regime not coming out until about that time as well. They also provided teachers and school administrators with a highly concentrated and easily accessible collection of anti-Semitic evidence on which to build lessons. Furthermore, in the eyes of many Nazi education authorities, many of those engaged in classroom instruction needed an ideological retooling. Working with the NSLB, many teachers found themselves engaged in coursework to expand their own knowledge base on racial science and anti-Semitic thinking.

In the vanguard of this pedagogical effort was Ernst Dobers, an especially prolific author of race biology curriculum materials. His professional activity

as a professor of science education in teacher training colleges provided a plat-
form for the advancement of his ideas to a broader audience of public school
teachers and administrators. Part of the legacy of Nazi race educators can be
found in the curriculum guides produced during the 1930s. In the view of Dobers,
the author of the most detailed curriculum guide on the Jewish question, the
challenge of teaching about the Jews in a racial biological sense remained
especially acute for those educators who engaged the minds of the young in
the classrooms of the New Germany. A new curriculum was in order, one which
sought to place the racial view of history and natural science at the center of the
curriculum.

ERNST DOBERS AND THE JEWISH QUESTION

As a professor of genetics and racial science at the Teacher Training College at
Elbing, Dobers quickly established a reputation as a leading educator on content and method regarding Jewish affairs. His book *The Jewish Question: Subject
Matter and Treatment in the School* first appeared in 1936 and subsequently
entered a third edition in 1939. In these pages are found familiar patterns of
anti-Semitic thinking combining old economic stereotypes with scapegoating.
Absent from the book are any arguments about race hygiene or eugenics that
appeared in other textbooks or teacher guides, a topic coming under special
scrutiny in a later chapter. Dobers's work merits our close attention since, as a
biology educator, he articulated the Jewish question in largely historical and economic terms. Once again, in the reflection of Nazi curriculum philosophy, the
content lines between the disciplines remained purposefully blurred. The
racial anti-Semitic historical interpretations in Dobers's volume are more detailed
than one would find in any history or science textbook under the Third Reich.
Teachers, as the major audience for Dobers, learned that economic history
and geography were not treated lightly, especially in relation to the Jews. Neither was the question of teaching methods to be overlooked, as the table of
contents demonstrated. (See table 2.1.)

The foreword written for Dobers's first edition in October of 1936 set a
tone of attack that characterized much of his writing on the Jewish question.
The people of the world, Dobers wrote, were not impressed with the insults and
tricks of the Jews. Citizens could be aroused to think more deeply about this
question through the marshaling of an "overpowering body of evidence" designed
to quell the poison of the Jewish-Bolshevik threat. In Dobers's words, "the
passionate commitment for truth and righteousness," supported by enlightened
propaganda and the "certainty of knowledge," would provide the best kind of
race education for youth about the nature of the Jews and their threat to the
nation. He called on teachers to protect themselves from "empty expressions"
built on a weak conception of knowledge about the Jewish question, which
"around the world stood at such a dramatic point in the racial struggle."[1]

The knowledge legitimized by the Nazi state in Dobers's text conceived of
the Jews as perpetual outsiders incapable of reaching the cultural achievements of the Nordic race. The strong sense of struggle in this work begins
with the Germanic claim to *Lebensraum*, or living space. The study of the living
laws of race in history would show young people that the Germans held rightful

Table 2.1

Table of Contents
The Jewish Question:
Subject Matter and Treatment in the School (1939)

ERNST DOBERS

Foreword
The Subject Matter
  I. Characteristics
 II. Settlers and Nomads
III. Nordic and Jewish
 IV. Examples and Practical Applications
  V. From the History of Jews before Their Emancipation
     1. Until Erzra and Nehemiah
     2. The Jewish Diaspora—a Calculated Lie
     3. Racial Chaos
     4. The Ghetto—Still Another Lie
     5. The Third Lie
     6. Until the French Revolution
        a. The Proliferation of the Jews
        b. Court Jews
 VI. The Emancipation of the Jews
VII. The Great Struggle
     1. The Preparation for Attack
        a. Statistics
        b. Jewified Professions
        c. From Money Lending Jews and Court Jews to Landholding
        d. "Public Opinion"
        e. Political Preparations
               Representative Bodies
               Government
               Monarchy
     2. The Great Jewish Attack against Germany in the World War and in the
        November Revolution
        a. Secret Manipulations
        b. Destruction of the Will to Victory (Defeatism)
        c. The Prevention of Economic Mobilization
        d. The Takeover by the Jews
               Political
               Economic
               Culturally
        e. The Rise of Criminality
VIII. Changing Times
 IX. Outlook
        a. Domestic Policy
        b. Foreign Policy
The Methods
Literature

Table of Contents from Ernst Dobers, *Die Judenfrage: Stoff und Behandlung in der Schule*. (*The Jewish Question: Subject Matter and Treatment in the School*) 3rd edition. Leipzig: Klinkhardt, 1939.

claims to expand their territory. The Jews stood in the way of these aspirations through their misguided and false cultural traditions. In few other places was the contrast greater than between what Dobers termed settlers or farmers and nomads. The perpetually stateless Jews grew out of a nomadic culture without any real ties to the soil. While the farmer offered the "working hand, the planning spirit of a settled people, created values, cleared and cultivated the land, laid the foundations for human culture and customs in the sense of a higher and purer humanity," the nomadic Jew "devastated, plundered, destroyed." Behind all of these contrasts was the implication that the settled farmer was more capable of completing an honest day's labor than the shiftless Jew of nomadic stock.[2]

The racial disparity between Nordics and Jews offered an even greater opportunity to emphasize what were, according to Nazi ideological perspectives, even more profound reasons why Jews must be treated as outcasts. In a relatively brief two-page section of the book, Dobers articulated the most biological aspect of the entire work. The major task of the Nordic peoples, in ensuring their continued existence, was to closely relate the decline in the strength of a people with the struggle for maintaining blood purity and the health of the race. The Jews, who practiced race mixing with the Canaanites from the Near East during ancient times, created the racial foundation for contemporary Jewry. From their origins as "parasitic, predatory Nomads," Dobers concluded, the Jews gained the dubious reputation of crafty traders. Jews remained, in the view of Dobers, the racial composite of Near Eastern and Oriental bloodlines. Combined with the traditional anti-Semitic portrayal as cunning traders, the Jew symbolized for many other curriculum writers "the great antagonist of the Nordic farmer." The economic stereotypes associated with this portrayal of the Jewish trader, whether it be linked to usery or the exchange of goods and services, claimed their own pre-Nazi history. Dobers, and other educators as will be seen later, were well prepared to exploit this kind of anti-Semitic tradition. On another level, what the professor from Elbing glorified in the Nordic farmer was ideologically consistent with the Nazi idealization of the German peasant as the vessel of racial purity for the Reich.[3]

From "examples and practical applications," Dobers cast a narrow historical vision that continued almost to the end of his work in various forms. Again, the strategy of posing cultural opposites played an important role in explaining the author's interpretation of Nordic and Jewish peoples. Dobers's history, as well as his anthropology, are nationalistic and marked by unfounded generalizations to fit his Volkish assumptions about German culture. Germans possessed a long history of struggle for freedom, from Luther's battle with the church for the soul of the German people to Hitler's conflict with the shameful Treaty of Versailles and restoration of German territory and honor. The Jews, on the other hand, made up almost 100 percent of the leadership for communism and bolshevism, which, in Dobers's estimation, was explained by the influence of earlier "desert-Nomadic thinking." Just how this intellectual legacy eventually connected to communism remained unclear in Dobers's treatise.[4]

The science educator integrated brief and undocumented quotations from a variety of sources to support his arguments. Dobers insisted that all of Jewish culture remained ruled by one simple but powerful principle that doubtlessly fed the fantasies of conspiracy theorists worldwide: "All of Israel vouches for one another." One of the ominous indications of this condition for Dobers was the frightening Jewish efficiency in establishing control over the press. Even Bismarck entered the picture, allegedly asking readers to comprehend only one Jew who struts in all corners. In the third edition, that appeared shortly after the Night of the Broken Glass, Dobers added a paragraph that tried to globalize the nature of the Jewish threat. The results of the year 1938 showed very clearly, he insisted, that Jews the world over were concentrating their influence and authority in order to shape public policy in the United States and England. This Jewish "world central," as he called it, with all of its intrigues remained the bane not only for Arabs in Palestine but also for Germans. If this wasn't enough, Jews followed their deepest instincts for political manipulations by hiding behind anonymous parliamentary majorities.[5]

To add an aura of authority to his anti-Semitic reflections, Dobers peppered his work with a host of quotations from notable individuals and statistics to suit his case and, presumably, to benefit those teachers searching for evidence to use in their classrooms. In a discussion about the Jew as "parasite and destroyer," Dobers once again engaged in a gross distortion of history by claiming that Jews were a major cause of the fall of ancient Rome. He liberally quoted Luther's incendiary essay "On the Jews and Their Lies" (1543) in the 1936 first edition with the reformer's angry enjoinder that Jews had gained too much influence among princes and other powers while mistreating others though their propensity for usury. The third edition, in 1939, accentuated even more the role of Martin Luther in the history of German anti-Semitism. The following words by Luther, presented as a solution to the Jewish question, are also noteworthy since they appeared in other curriculum materials as part of a larger justification for the oppression of the Jews:

> First, that their synagogues or schools be set aflame.... Secondly, that their villages likewise be shattered and destroyed.... Sixth, that they be forbidden to practice usury and take from them all money and jewels. And this is the cause: Everything that they have ... they have stolen and robbed from us through their usury, because they did not otherwise have any other competition.[6]

While Dobers was more than willing to use Luther's anti-Semitic invective to justify Nazi policies against the Jews, one important clarification about context must be made. The recent writing of Steven Katz on the nature of Luther's intentions is most instructive in this regard. Luther, Katz observed, "was a great hater, an ecumenical hater, and Jews held a prominent place on his hate list."[7] What remains crucial was Luther's orthodox intent to annihilate the Jewish religion, but not to murder the Jews. In contrast to Hitler, Luther did not articulate anti-Semitism in racial terms. Despite the punitive tone of his writings, Luther remained deadly serious about converting Jews to Christianity. A Jewish rejection of Christianity meant banishment of the Jews, according to Luther, not murder. Katz writes:

> Luther's thinking remained radically different from the absolute assault against Jews represented by racial anti-Semitism. The latter demands the complete bio-

logical extirpation of every Jew. The adversary is not Judaism, but Jewish genes. Nazism inverts the crucial diagnosis: the carrier of pollution is not ideology, religious dogmatics, discrete beliefs in and about God, it is, instead, the carnal being of the Jew, his or her very physical presence, that incorporates the ontological and normative antithesis of history and metahistory.[8]

There was another level of meaning that Dobers brought to readers. Luther's anti-Semitism could be exploited for another purpose. Dobers framed the words of Luther with a sardonic twist. Luther's expanded role in Dobers's third edition was justified with the observation that the writings of the Protestant leader should be recommended reading for all so that people could "get themselves worked up" (*ereifern sich*) over the "barbaric methods" of the "evil Germans" against the "poor Jews"[9] (Dobers's quotation marks). This commentary, coming so soon after the mass arrests and the widespread destruction of synagogues and businesses in the Jewish community in early November of 1938, remained one of the most chilling in all of the curriculum materials published by the Third Reich. The powerful association between Luther's call for the use of fire to destroy Jewish synagogues and schools and the Nazi orgy of destruction that became the Night of the Broken Glass was not lost on the discerning reader.

Dobers was far from finished. The multiple layers of anti-Semitic language coming from this teacher-educator suggested that the Jew would never shake off the perpetual designation as enemy of the state. Dobers used the word *zugelösigkeit,* as part of the language of the Third Reich, to employ a double meaning. In a general sense, the word meant "lack of restraint." When applied to Jews from Dobers's perspective, the expression also implied the lack of restraint associated with anarchy or sexual promiscuity.[10] Both behaviors were associated with Jews by anti-Semites down through the ages. Dobers was especially diligent about attacking what he felt was the immoral nature of Jewish culture. In the second edition, he added the words of Benjamin Franklin who allegedly stated that every country that had allowed Jews to increase their numbers usually experienced a decline in morals. Richard Wagner's vituperative anti-Semitism followed with the characterization of Jews as demons responsible for the moral fall of humanity.[11]

Additional teaching examples prepared for classroom discussions included a more internationalized focus on the activities of Jews. To demonstrate the worldwide influence of Jewry, Dobers raised the example of the United States suffering under Jewish influence through the press and banking system. The connection with Jews in the United States apparently became more of a pressing issue for Dobers since he devoted more detailed attention to this issue in his third edition. Bernard Baruch's role as adviser to President Woodrow Wilson and his work in the armaments industry during World War I was especially disturbing to Dobers. Baruch, one of the most highly placed Jews in the government, became a target for Dobers's acid pen when he insisted that the arms official made a fortune off the backs of non-Jewish casualties in the war. Here, again, was another example of the contrast between peace-loving Germans and war-mongering Jewish profiteers. To further the stereotypical assertion that Jews had a propensity for murder and assassination, Dobers set out to rewrite United States presidential history. The disgruntled office seeker Charles J. Guiteau who assassinated James Garfield in 1881, so Dobers insisted, was a Jew who hid behind a Huguenot name.[12]

Beyond all of these anti-Semitic assertions formed for the presumed benefit of teachers and their charges in classrooms across the Reich was the problem of Jewish lies designed to mislead the public. This is where Dobers, in perhaps one of the most insidious aspects of his work, tried to correct certain historical "misconceptions" about the Jews and their place in the world. In what he called "three lies," Dobers tried to rewrite Jewish history along Nazi lines. It was not true, he wrote, that the "poor Jews" (Dobers's quotation marks) lost their homeland after the Roman destruction of Jerusalem in 70 A.D. and were forced to flee from land to land as a disinherited people. Incredible as it might seem to readers today, the Nazi curriculum writer tried to articulate the Diaspora as a myth with no foundation in historical reality. The truth of the matter, so Dobers asserted, was that a population increase in Palestine before the destruction of the temple forced Jewish families to flow out to the west and east. The great cities of Syria, Egypt, Asia Minor, and Greece and the remaining countries around the Mediterranean offered major vantage points for the "trade and parasitic instincts of the Jewish mixed race."[13] The so-called Jewish instinct, often associated with the biological term "parasite," remained among Dobers's most frequently used expressions. In trying to subvert Jewish spiritual traditions, Dobers looked to the Talmud, which, in his estimation, taught that commerce set the standard for all cultural values.[14]

The second lie argued that various peoples, through a series of laws and cultural practices at the beginning of the Middle Ages, were responsible for forcing Jews to live in ghettos. Dobers categorically denied this contention saying that the Jews themselves were the very cause of this movement. Dobers's reductionist thinking colors almost all of his beliefs concerning the relationship of Jews to the larger culture. The strange customs of Jews, especially in relation to moneylending and commerce, so deeply outraged all peoples of Europe that legal authorities had to erect ghettos to protect the Jews from the hatred of the masses. There were those, the professor from Elbing contended, who insisted on spreading the illusion of "the poor and eternally persecuted, oppressed Jew without rights, defenseless and packed into the ghetto." On the contrary, the Jew, as a foreigner to the Christian faith and German ways, tried to carve out living space for himself at everyone else's expense. The German community must keep the Jews as far away as possible (*hielt Man den Juden so fern wie möglich*).[15] Dobers's challenge to the persecution of Jews was an illusion in itself one of the biggest deceptions in *The Jewish Question*. The Nuremberg Laws had already been in force for almost a year when Dobers's first edition appeared in 1936. Subsequently, the Nazi concentration of Jews into ghettos symbolized an ominous stage in the process of annihilation on the way to Auschwitz.

There was another lie Dobers felt dutybound to expose. This time, he reached back to the Middle Ages. With a tone of indignation, Dobers attacked those misguided souls who believed that Jews were forced into the business of moneylending by various landowners under whom they lived and, moreover, were shut out from all other professions. Again, Dobers sowed an illusion of his own when he insisted that Jews never were farmers or cattle breeders. Jews were first and foremost people of the city with little direct experience in working with the soil. Such a judgment possessed a Volkish edge made even sharper by the accusation that Jews traditionally knew only one law, that of making money. "Impoverishment of the farmer, land speculation, enslavement of the worker in the city, and the formation of a highly complicated credit banking system," all of which held roots in the Jewish community of the Middle Ages, continued to plague contemporary Germans. The Rothschild banking house was to Dobers the penultimate Jewish symbol of these unfortunate economic developments.[16]

Up to this point, much of Dobers's writing focused on economic history as the major context for articulating his ideas about Jews. He continued this emphasis in discussing the formation of the *Wucherjude* or Jews who practiced usury. Race biology always remained in the foreground providing a larger context for Dobers's pronouncements. The migration of *Ostjuden,* or Jews from eastern and southern Europe, constituted a particularly grave threat to the German body politic since they mixed mongoloid and east Baltic bloodlines. The specter of blood mixing between *Ostjuden* and Aryans provided Dobers with another opening to advance his dualistic "us and them" mentality. On one side stood the creative people who earned their living through honest work and exacted just prices, who remained true toward and respectful of their father's customs. On the other side, there existed the expanding world of the Jews as parasitic nomads, a world of high profits marked by the dishonest, thoughtless and unlimited hunt for riches without any forethought about good or evil: "Here, in the darkness of the ghetto alleys and courtyards, were born profit capitalism and modern criminality."[17]

The treatment of Jews as a criminal element, common to the Nazi lexicon, found a most willing spokesperson in education through the pen of Ernst Dobers. To accentuate the stereotype of the Jew as criminal, Dobers added a new set of statistics in his third edition. The professor proved the wisdom once again of Mark Twain's old adage, attributed to Benjamin Disraeli, about the three ways of lying ("lies, damn lies and statistics"). For a change, Dobers actually mentioned the author of these statistics, E. H. Schulz, but his reference remained woefully incomplete. Nowhere does one find either the year, title of the source, or publisher. The gross distortions and falsifications inherent in Dobers's approach, as we shall see in subsequent pages, were not restricted by any means to the professor from Elbing.

The statistics on Jewish criminality via Dobers provided teachers with a convenient way of presenting students with a propagandistic vision of Jewry both simplistic and false in nature. The allegedly close relationship between Jewry and criminality was revealed in statistics about those who received sentences for fraud per 100,000 persons between 1882 and 1901. Forty-three Lutherans, forty-seven Catholics, and ninety-one Jews per 100,000 persons in the general population represented the rate of sentencing for fraud from 1882 to 1891. The rate increased for all three categories, respectively, to 58, 68, and 113 per 100,000 for the years 1892–1901. To further strengthen his anti-Semitic claims, Dobers brought in relative statistics from 1915–16. From these, Dobers concluded that Jews were seven times as likely as Germans to commit offenses relating to the spread of animal epidemics and diseases, nine times more likely to break bankruptcy laws, and twenty-eight times more likely to engage in usury.[18]

Not only were Jews inclined toward criminal behavior from Dobers's standpoint. They were also dangerous because of their historic capability of working themselves into positions of influence. One specific example to come under Dobers's scrutiny were the *Hofjuden*, or court Jews, who, because of their well-known ability to handle financial matters or provide financial resources, became indispensable advisers to princes. Calling them the "bloodsuckers of the German people," Dobers took special pains to described two court Jews, the sixteenth-century financier Lippold from Berlin and Finance Minister Süß from Württemberg, who were hanged for alleged financial abuses.[19] Lippold was especially bothersome to Dobers since he supposedly had the nerve to charge an interest rate of 50–54 percent on his loans. The citizens of Berlin were so angry about this development in 1571, he added, that they stormed the Jewish synagogue in the city and, with great indignation, plundered a group of Jews. Dobers made sure to place this historical memory immediately after a volatile quotation of Martin Luther from "On the Jews and Their Lies" regarding the Jewish lust for money and power.[20]

The vision of Germans destroying synagogues, as noted earlier, remained a potent theme in Dobers's writing and, because of the timing of his commentary, took an even more meaningful tone because of the events in Nazi Germany in November of 1938. Dobers kept pounding away at still other historical developments that explained the unfortunate expansion of the Jewish presence in German culture. The call for equality growing in the wake of the French Revolution eventually led to the legal emancipation of the Jews. In 1812, the king of Prussia issued an edict granting full citizenship to the Jewish community that gave Jews a greater freedom of movement as well as social recognition. Such a change, according to Dobers, "further advanced Jews toward the penetration and rule of the western world." Further complicating matters was the practice of baptizing Jews into the Catholic faith. Dobers was quick to remind teachers that the misguided practice did not change the essential truth that a baptized Jew was still a Jew. The gulf between Jews and Germans could not be crossed through religious conversion.[21]

The immutable law of Aryan blood superiority invariably manifested itself again in the way Dobers framed his arguments. In the third edition from 1939, Dobers added a paragraph to the section on Jewish emancipation that recognized the great difficulties for Jews in reaching high positions in the civil service or membership in the officer corps. This, he insisted in a sharp tone, was not the fault of the legal authorities in the Reich, but rather rested on the unwritten laws of blood from the local population. Something particularly ominous followed in Dobers's writing. The Volk, to their credit, continued to fight against "a total capitulation before the parasitism of foreign bloodlines."[22] The fight against Jewish blood eventually took on even more murderous forms not long after this book came off the press.

Mixed marriages were particularly troublesome to the Nazi worship of blood and kin. Again, the exploitation of undocumented statistics, Dobers's forte, supported his alarmist claims. With about 150,000 mixed marriages in Germany between Jews and Christians from 1875 to 1933, Dobers estimated that with two children per marriage, Germany now had to contend with 300,000 citizens with bastardized blood. The race biological implications spread to Austria where mixed marriages between Jews and Austrians between 1914 and 1930 rose more than 100 percent. To add more punch to his rhetoric, Dobers cited the year 1930 when 420 mixed marriages took place in the Ostmark.[23] This addition to the 1939 printing was understandable in regard to propaganda value and timing since the consummation of the *Anschluß* between Germany and Austria transpired in March of 1938.

The numerous anti-Semitic assertions by Ernst Dobers brought forth thus far all led up to what he called "the great struggle" for the preservation of German blood in which schools would play an important role. In the most substantive part of the guide for teachers, Dobers outlined yet more multiple layers of evidence about the perceived Jewish threat to German civilization. To the discerning race educator, Dobers's writing on the racial struggle represented a veritable treasure of statistics and quotations that could be used in a variety of ways to rationalize the Nazi policy of oppression against the Jews. Berlin, which claimed the highest concentration of Jews in the Reich, became a favorite point of departure for Dobers's argumentation. Berlin came to be known first and foremost by Nazi anti-Semites as the seat of power for the "city Jew." The accuracy of Dobers's data remained highly suspect and his misuse of statistics readily apparent.[24] Students of the history of anti-Semitism would do well to take a closer look at how this Nazi loyalist abused history, economics, and biology in stating his spurious claims. Berlin remained critical for Dobers since the city represented both the hopes of the New Germany under Hitler and a critically important location for Jewish culture and commerce.

In what he called "the preparation for the attack" against the Jews, Dobers adopted combative language laced with the aura of respectability with his legion of statistics. Population levels for Prussia between 1816 and 1910 revealed an increase of almost 300,000 Jews. Additional numbers from thirteen German districts showed that between the founding of the Second Reich in 1871 and 1910, the Jewish population of Berlin alone increased from 36,020 to 90,013, rising to a record 4.35 percent of the population in the city. While almost a sixth of all Germans lived in Berlin in 1905, the city claimed, at the same time, a fifth of all Prussian Jews. Never far below the surface was the implication that something had to be done about "the racial instincts of this city race" that possessed the "blood of the nomad and trader."[25]

The statistics regarding the "Jewified Professions" made the situation appear even more serious. Jews made up 80 percent of Berlin lawyers along with half of the doctors in the city. Enrollments of Jewish pupils in selected elite Berlin *Gymnasien* amount to almost half of the classroom population. The *Anschluß* once again exerted a certain influence in the formation of Dobers's third edition which, for the first time in the author's writing, pointed to Austria's population of professionals as reflecting an inordinate Jewish influence. No less than 75 percent of all bankers in Austria were Jewish, compared with 40 percent of jewelers, 32 percent of druggists, 85 percent of furniture dealers and factory owners, 82 percent of credit inquiry agencies, 85 percent of lawyers, and 52 percent of doctors. In a wry observation, Dobers concluded that the only purely Aryan business in Austria was that of roofing, suggesting that this might be the case because the work was not always safe.[26] The *Anschluß* was not the only significant connection for this parade of numbers. From Austria would come some of the most dedicated officers in the SS, including Adolf Eichmann and Ernst Kaltenbrunner, and a host of other Austrians who administered the concentration or death camps.[27]

Dobers changed the language of attack to paint the Jews themselves as aggressors bent on destroying the fatherland through their "secret manipulations" during the First World War, all to ensure profit margins at the expense of Germans and the war dead. Drawing from Wilhelm Meister's *Judas Schuldbuch* (Munich: Deutsche Volksverlag, 1919), Dobers quoted a pamphlet published by a circle of rabbis in Austria from 1901 that once again reflected the conspiratorial intentions of Jews. "Every war, every revolution, every political and religious change," so it was written, "brings us every moment closer to reaching the highest goal toward which we strive." Not surprisingly, Dobers singled out Rosa Luxemburg and Karl Liebknecht, leading Jewish voices in the Spartacus Movement and the German Communist Party, for special condemnation. His partisan interpretation extended to the November Revolution of 1918, an event that radicalized the German scene thanks to financial support by Russian Jewry.[28]

The professor unleashed yet another set of statistics to show that Berlin Jews like publishing giant Rudolf Mosse had taken control of Berlin newspapers. Max Reinhardt and a host of other Jews directed the vast majority of Berlin's well-known theatres. Writers like Lion Feuchtwanger, Alfred Döblin, and Arnold Zweig published "literary filth and trash." Stars in the Jewish firmament like Walter Rathenau, foreign minister under the Weimar Republic, earlier founded AEG, the biggest electrochemical company in the industry and led by the Jews Felix Deutsch and Paul Mamroth after the war. Adler and Oppenheimer controlled the leather and shoe industries. Orenstein and Koppel was a dominant concern in the construction trades. The Jew Seligmann was general director of the Continental Tire Company in Hanover. German culture and commerce were no longer German. There was scarcely a corner where Jewish influence could not be found.[29]

The massive amount of data brought together by Dobers on the Jewish question for instruction in the public schools, all presented in a tone of urgency, implied the need for some kind of action. Toward the end of his book, in a section under "Changing Times," Dobers presented to teachers the racial implications of the Nuremberg Laws from the fall of 1935 and the necessity of these measures for maintaining blood purity in the Reich. Major revisions in this part of the book for the 1939 edition are evident. In forceful language not seen in the earlier edition from 1936, Dobers challenged his readers to think about "the banishment of the Ostjuden and the agitating, emigrant Jewish blood from the German national community."[30] A long and detailed discussion of various Nazi racial laws applied to the Jews soon followed in the third edition with the clear intention of providing a basic rationalization for the events of November 1938. Dobers avoided any discussion of the physical destruction, arrests, and murders resulting from the Night of the Broken Glass and, as was the general custom for curriculum writers from the Third Reich, any mention of concentration camps for the enemies of the state.[31]

To even the most casual reader, Dobers's contribution on the Jewish question suggested his desire to enflame teachers, and their students as well, with a strong hatred of everything Jewish. Although most of his data applied to German Jewry, the major emphasis in his writing, Dobers wanted young people to know that as "world enemy number one," the Jews posed a deadly threat across the globe. In his foreign policy outlook on the Jewish question, Dobers returned to his tendency of showering readers with a plethora of statistics demonstrating Jewish influence in the political and economic systems from a host of countries. Coming under his gaze were nations that either eventually suffered under the boot of Nazi occupation or acted as belligerents in the subsequent global conflict. Jews, Dobers warned, were a powerful threat in Hungary, Czechoslovakia, Poland, Romania, Italy, Palestine, Latvia, England, the United States, and Australia. There is a prophetic sense of doom in this pronouncement since Jews from a majority of these countries eventually met their end in the death camps.[32]

The form and nature of the evidence presented by Dobers reflected his belief that race biology remained at the center of any discussion about the nature of German-Jewish relations. Dobers's dualistic "us-them" thinking permeated his entire pedagogy. "The racial struggle," he wrote, symbolized "one last ring around human existence." Life itself among civilized peoples never was neutral. In the sphere of the organic, there existed only the rule of "either-or."[33] After treating his readers to an extensive set of statistics and selected anti-Semitic quotations, Dobers tried to impress upon educators the seriousness of the racial struggle and the important place assumed by the schools in joining a single-minded Nazi destruction of Jewish influence in the world:

> The goal is clear . . . The German people, which as the first to dare stand up to the Jew and his pretensions to rule and the first to set the eternal values of the pure race against racial chaos and the subhumans, shall once again be brought to its knees if the Jews nevertheless triumph in Central Europe. If this [German] bastion is conquered, all other peoples will fall anyway to Jewish rule, and therefore this people must stand and maintain itself against the Jew. This example must and will be made in the school and the dream of Jewish world domination brought to an end. That is why there is hate, that is why there is the relentlessness of the struggle between life and death for Germany and, in the same measure as well, for the Jew.[34]

There remained for Dobers the issue of race didactics, the challenge of reaching pupils through effective teaching methods designed for the purpose of raising what he called a "racial instinct" and anti-Semitic "consciousness" among youth.[35] At this point, Dobers urged teachers to take full advantage of the anti-Semitic contents of the *Völkische Beobachter,* the major organ of the Nazi Party, and the text of speeches from Hitler, Joseph Goebbels, and Alfred Rosenberg on bolshevism and the Jews.[36] Supported by the writing of Johann von Leers from his *Fourteen Years of the Jewish Republic,* the didactics professor encouraged teachers to make their lessons as relevant as possible to the contemporary situation.[37] Dobers was especially concerned about those teachers who remained content with simply going through lessons on the Jewish question without connecting the content to the everyday lives of children. The "inner and outer dynamic" to the Jewish question could only be understood by German children if they were placed in the center of the educational process. As Deweyan as this might sound on the surface, Dobers failed to clarify just how this dynamic might come to pass.[38]

What passed for a discussion of teaching methods sometimes entered the realm of ideological justification. In one of the most unusual segments of Nazi curriculum on race education, Dobers directed readers to the problem of "respectable Jews" in the populace. Such a commentary initially appeared to contradict the anti-Semitic thinking he employed earlier, although a closer reading revealed the formation of a dualistic rationalization designed to exclude any possibility of human compassion for the beleaguered Jews. The fate of some Jewish families during these years, he noted, might be tragic and pitiable, but who among Germans could allow the existence of the "respectable Jew" to hinder or distract the Reich from the uncompromising struggle against international Jewry?[39] To even raise a question about the "respectable Jew" appeared to be out of step with Nazi ideological assumptions about the nature of being human.[40] Dobers's explanation, appearing in the first and third editions from 1936 and 1939, brings to mind an observation by Victor Klemperer. The philologist noted that philosophizing required the exercise of reason and logical thinking, both regarded by the Nazi state as deadly enemies.[41]

To Dobers and many others engaged in articulating race education, such "Nazi logic" made perfect sense since it allowed them to legitimize racial prejudices against those defined as subhuman. The power of the word, augmented by the language of propaganda, also became important in the selection of teaching materials. Coming from the pen of a didactics professor, Dobers's brief section at the end of his work on the Jewish question seems rather surprising. Furthermore, one gains the impression that Dobers was more concerned about providing a compact knowledge base for teachers from the perspectives of economic history and biology before embarking on a consideration of teaching methods. In the eyes of Dobers, there existed one teaching resource that best drew from the ideas of *Mein Kampf*. The weekly newspaper *Der Stürmer*, easily the most vociferous anti-Semitic publication in the Third Reich and edited by Julius Streicher, figured prominently in Dobers's didactical conception for educating the young about Jews. As noted in chapter 5, Streicher's office in Nuremberg became intimately involved in publishing anti-Semitic children's story books. Dobers saw in Streicher's *Der Stürmer* a practical source for the formation of racial anti-Semitic instructional themes in the classroom. From these themes, focused pupil-written essays could be created and, in some cases, serve as a focus for artwork.[42] Table 2.2 shows the broad base of anti-Semitic issues, all drawn from the publication issued in 1935. In this collection, one notes the resurrection of both ancient and contemporary anti-Semitic ideas.[43]

The closing paragraph of Dobers's work on the Jewish question, added for the third edition in 1939, revealed the perceptions of one educator concerning the solution of this issue at one point in time. About two years before the Final Solution and the formation of the death camps became a matter of policy, Dobers told teachers that the Jewish question would not necessarily be dealt with if all Jews left Germany or if all Jews in the world settled in Madagascar "or wherever [they] will be interned" (*oder wo immer interniert werden*). At this point, Dobers engaged in a kind of psychologizing with the charge that

Table 2.2

Teaching Themes for Anti-Semitic Instruction
from *Der Stürmer*
(1935)

A Poor Jew

What the Jews Would Really Like to Have

The Jewish Addiction for Racial Dominance

Communism a Jewish Creation

The Jewish Butcher, the Strangler of Farmers in Lower Saxony

The Jew in Austria

Are the Jews Germans?

The Press Writes

The Laws of the Nuremberg Reichstag

The Jew Builds a State within a State

Declining Promised Land

Frederick the Great Sees through the Jews

Jewish Vultures Sell Off German Land

So Work the Jewish Cattle Dealers

Jewish Crimes in the World War

The Manipulator

Goethe and the Jews

Give Stolen Names Back

Contemporary Teaching

What They Want

Towards Deliverance

The Hell of Soviet Russia

The Haters of the New Germany

English Newspaper Brands the Jewish Rabble Rousers

Bismarck's Struggle against the Jewish Slavery

Foreign Currency Schemes in the World War

Jewish Family Names

In America

Bolshevism and World Jewry

Teaching Themes for Anti-Semitic Instruction from *Der Stürmer* (1935).

a serious challenge awaited those bold enough to enter the teaching profession under the Third Reich. "There is," Dobers wrote, "a Jew in all of us. To fight against this and, if possible, to even destroy it is perhaps the most difficult, but therefore also the most decisively important task of education in the character of National Socialism."[44] The author of the most detailed handbook for teachers on the Jewish question engaged in the ideological *Aussrottung* (rooting out) of the Jews from the German community. In doing so, he linked traditional anti-Semitic economic stereotypes and the prejudices legitimized by the pronouncements of racial science.[45] Others contributed to this nefarious curricular development and, by doing so, pointed the way toward racial anti-Semitism as an ideological leitmotif for the schools of the burgeoning Third Reich.

EDUCATION FOR THE ANTI-SEMITE: THE PERSPECTIVE OF WERNER DITTRICH

The formation of anti-Semitic curriculum materials for the Third Reich depended heavily on contributions from people representing a variety of responsibilities within the educational establishment. Ernst Dobers advanced his work largely within the context of teacher education. Another figure, Werner Dittrich, was a teacher from Bayreuth who also acted as Reich specialist for race education in the NSLB. Dittrich was also a regular contributor to *The Biologist*, the official bulletin for race and nature studies in the NSLB. His writings for teachers cut across questions relating to the character of anti-Semitism and its place in classroom instruction and the problem of teaching genetics in the New Germany.[46] One of his best-known works, *Education for the Anti-Semite: Advice on the Treatment of the Jewish Question in Racial-Political Instruction* (1937b), represented Dittrich's most focused and succinct effort on anti-Semitism as a curricular issue. The subsequent chapter on racial hygiene will take into account his thinking on genetics instruction.

Many curriculum writings from the Nazi period, Dittrich's included, came into publication after at least one manuscript review conducted by officials usually from the NSLB, Kanzlei Rosenberg, Rust's education ministry, or Phillip Bouhler in Hitler's Chancellery. Dittrich's manuscript came under the scrutiny of Ludwig Deyerling from the NSLB's periodicals section. Since Dittrich was also on the NSLB staff in the role of race education specialist, one might question whether Deyerling was in a position to deliver a genuine critique of the piece. In any case, Deyerling's review is instructive since it revealed Nazi education values regarding the place of the Jewish question in the curriculum. Deyerling's review suggested that Dittrich enjoyed the reputation as a highly respected curriculum expert on the Jewish question in the Nazi education hierarchy.

Deyerling's *Gutachten* or report offered no substantive revisions of Dittrich's text while profusely praising the school teacher's widespread use of statistics in relation to Jewish history and current developments. Dittrich's "solid, thorough work," as the reviewer called it, rightfully proceeded from the curricular principle that the Jewish question could not be treated simply as a part of one school subject. One of the greatest contributions of *Education for the Anti-Semite* was a curriculum vision based on learning about the Jewish question "at every opportunity" in the life of the school. Moreover, through Dittrich's pedagogy, pupils could clearly see a connection between the racial soul of the Jew and Jewish history. The review also said just as much about Deyerling's ideological perspective. The teaching opportunities to which Deyerling referred advanced what he regarded as the foundation stone for Nazi schooling on race. Dittrich's book showed time and again that Jews were members of a foreign race and did not shy away from laying out the iron rule for all effective anti-Semitic teaching: "The Jew *must* be shown as the *Fremdling* or stranger in all areas of German life." (Deyerling's underlining).[47]

To Dittrich, the formation of an anti-Semitic mind-set in the schools was critical in defining the educated person in the Third Reich. In echoing both Hitler's letter from 1919 and his subsequent reflections in *Mein Kampf*, the education of anti-Semites in the schools "must be entirely clear and objective without any passionate phrases. No German youth may leave the school without having learned about this [Jewish] opponent in his entire dangerousness (*ohne diesen Gegner in seiner ganzen Gefährlichkeit kennengelernt zu haben*) ... We want therefore to educate German youth to become anti-Semites who fight out of emotion and instinct, who above all, however, also possess an unconditional, necessary, and entirely sober view of the facts."[48] This emphasis on a detached and scientific approach to teaching anti-Semitism was a hallmark of the integration of racial studies throughout the curriculum. Any kind of philosophical discourse over the issue of morality or lack thereof in treating Jews as vermine or cultural parasites was, as Victor Klemperer intimated earlier, completely outside the thinking of the National Socialist worldview. The myth of objectivity and detachment claimed by Nazi writers of anti-Semitic curriculums like Dittrich, Dobers, and their colleagues, was simply a cover for strong subjective and prejudicial condemnations of the Jews.

Even with this caveat, readers will note that anti-Semitic curriculum materials published for the schools of the Third Reich, although motivated in part by either a hatred for Jews or opportunities for career advancement or both, were not monolithic in nature. Although the ideological justification for oppressing the Jews remained basically the same, curriculum writers sometimes differed in significant ways regarding the exploitation of Volkish traditions in supporting this oppression. In contrast to Dobers, Dittrich drew heavily from the vague Volkish conception of the "Jewish soul." Not only were Jews not Germans because of physical differences, Jews were also not Germanic in character because they possessed a soul profoundly different from that of the German polity. In broad and sweeping generalizations that remained the trademark of anti-Semitic curriculum development, Dittrich hammered on the *Eitelkeit*, or vanity of the Jews, all of whom were born with the assumption that they were "chosen people." This self-appointed status explained why the Jews were so bent on world domination. The advent of the Messiah was all the more important for the Jews since it marked the eventual Jewish political takeover of the civilized world. The hatred of the Jew toward all those outside the Jewish community, so Dittrich asserted, remained connected to an unswerving Jewish lust for power and the commandment to "devour all other peoples."[49]

Dittrich apparently anticipated some reticence among educators about the challenge placed before them in addressing the Jewish question. He told teachers that they need not be shy about characterizing Jews as a race since this assumption was already part of the daily political struggles taking place across the Reich. "We are at the same time aware," he wrote, "that this racial concept does not contradict certain absolute biological principles, because even Jewry is presented as a racial mixture."[50] Emerging from this discussion was the formation of a "Jewish typology" influenced by the mystical thinking, cloaked in science, of Hans F. K. Günther on "racial soul." In a general way, Dittrich attempted a connection between biology and psychology in his perspective on the Jews. He felt that a typology of the Jew revealed itself in a psychological sense over the course of centuries through a biological selection process. The racial soul of the Jew thereby represented all of those inner qualities which remained despised by the citizens of the state.[51]

Educating the young about "a low born adversary," as Dittrich called the Jew, also required the integration of racial anthropology to emphasize physical differences between Jews and Nordics as cultural types. At this point, Dittrich encouraged teachers to draw from the vast collection of stereotypical caricatures aimed at Jews that crowded the pages of *Der Stürmer*. Understanding the inner typology of the Jew required a consideration of not only how a Jew looked but also how a Jew spoke. Unlike many other curriculum writers who took pains to publish pictorial evidence marking the physical differences between the two groups, Dittrich chose his own stereotypical rhetoric to carry the message:

> The characteristic face with the fleshy pointed nose, the almost overhanging lower lip and the eyes with the heavy lids and the lurking expression, the short back of the head, are all just as easy to encounter as their small, flat footed, bandy legged general appearance. Also, the language of this type, yiddish, is easily imitated. The Jews therefore find the German language manifoldly difficult because Near Eastern linguistic tools are apparently well suited for expressing Hebrew sounds of revenge which comes through them again and again.[52]

The formation of youth with a "sober view of the facts" concerning the Jewish question brought Dittrich to an expression of doubt about the appropriateness of integrating anthropology into the center of race instruction. Remaining vague in explaining why he assumed this position, Dittrich proposed that schools embrace the murky and mysterious *Rassenseelenkunde*, or the study of racial soul, as a more effective way to study cultures. As noted earlier, the concept of racial soul, advanced earlier by Günther and later embraced by certain Nazi figures like Dittrich and others legitimized factual knowledge purely along ideological subjective lines. There was another threat to Dittrich's worldview. How would one deal with pupil observations of Jews who looked like Aryans? Anthropology, if Dittrich had anything to say about it, did not hold the answers, especially if it contradicted Nazi doctrine. Racial soul, since it was in itself almost impossible to define, provided educators with another pedagogical weapon to fight those misguided citizens who cherished the radical thought that Jews might be human beings.

Teachers had to be perfectly clear in their understanding that since mixed bloodlines existed in every race, some Jews naturally would carry some traits of the master race. This development would not pose a serious problem for the teaching of sound racial anti-Semitic principles, Dittrich thought, if a certain propaganda strategy was followed without question. Teachers would instruct their charges that only "superficial observers" would claim that Jews are "people just like us" or share similar physical appearances. Such erroneous assumptions simply opened the door to the so-called respectable Jews who were all the more dangerous because they were especially efficient at taking over the press. Blood defined humanity and explained why Jews were Jews. Calling forth the anti-Semitic harangues from *Mein Kampf*, one of the Reich's experts on race education resurrected the claim that in the Jewish community, "one Jewish crook was valued one thousand times more than one honest non-Jew." Wasn't it true, Dittrich asked, that the Jewish press conspiracy attempted time and time again to defend Jews around the world whenever they were sentenced for crimes? Wasn't the case of Sacco and Vanzetti in the United States from 1920 proof enough of this development?[53]

The arts curriculum provided yet another way to demonstrate the racial and cultural incompatibility between Jews and citizens of the Third Reich. Calling into question the "ice cold intellect" of Jews and an associated lack of creativity among Jews in the arts, Dittrich suggested that German schools devote part of the art curriculum to expose "the facts about the "entirely different inner nature" of Jewry that differentiated itself from German culture. He urged art educators to draw from numerous examples from the arts to contrast "the production of Jewish trash art to the creations of German geniuses." As usual, Dittrich remained unclear about the criteria for making such artistic judgments. Just who from the German artistic legacy fell within his definition of genius was also left unaddressed.

Concerning artistic figures from Jewish cultural tradition to act as foils for this instruction, Dittrich was more specific. Even the more intellectually mature boys and girls could put selected Jewish works of art to the test. How they would accomplish this task revealed Dittrich's reliance on the mystical traditions that marked Volkish thinking. The pupils could draw from "techniques of expressiveness from our racial soul" to evaluate the paintings of Max Liebermann, songs from Mendelsohn-Bartholdy, or poems by Heinrich Heine including "Lorelei."[54] Dittrich's vagueness about the application of artistic standards, one can only assume, must have caused confusion for some teachers who may have wondered about not only the specific meaning of these mysterious techniques but also the means to apply them.

In contrast to Dobers's approach to the Jewish question, Dittrich singled out the intellect of the Jew as his sharpest weapon in gaining control of the professions. On the other hand, similar to Dobers, Dittrich relied on a bevy of statistical evidence to show that Berlin, that harbinger of Jewish culture, reflected Jewish influence in the professions far out of proportion to the 1 percent of Jews who made up the German population. Doctors, dentists, druggists, attorneys, and notaries came under special consideration in this discussion. Unlike many other curriculum writers working in the Nazi educational establishment on anti-Semitic affairs, Dittrich documented the sources of his statistical evidence. He closely associated himself with the Institute for the Study of the Jewish Question, the major source of his numbers. The institute, founded with the enthusiastic support of Alfred Rosenberg and Bernhard Rust, proposed a scientific study of Jewish history and culture.[55]

The credibility enjoyed by the institute under the Third Reich, supported further by the high priority placed by the regime on the persecution of the Jews, made it a perfect wellspring for writers like Dittrich bent on the formation of obedient and loyal anti-Semites among the young, the future of the Reich. Developing the illusion of objectivity to advance anti-Semitic thinking, Dittrich certainly did not forget how statistics, when linked to traditional stereotypes of the Jew, could be manipulated under the guise of "scientific fact." Behind his rhetoric was the clear implication that the "creative unproductivity and commercialism"[56] of the Jew had to be held in severe check if National Socialism was to survive. Simply setting down numbers on Jewish professions in Berlin and the percentage of Jewish faculty and students at Berlin University was not enough. Children, as Dittrich insisted, had to understand the larger picture of legitimized work and the Jewish place within and outside of it.

Raising again the specter of the *Ostjuden* migrating into Germany at the rate of thirteen per day from 1913 to 1933, Dittrich chided members of this group for how quickly they acclimated themselves to the conduct of business while embracing every opportunity to make money. Laced within these accusations was the use of name-calling of an especially incendiary nature to support anti-Semitic assertions. This same kind of economic success, Dittrich angrily declared, could not come to Germans unless they lowered themselves to become "fat eating bloodsuckers."[57] The figurative meaning of bloodsucker, in this context, connoted the vampire.

The relationship of Jews to work and the marketplace manifested itself in another way, this time by yet another exploitation of statistics. Using census data on the professions in Prussia from 1925, Dittrich implied that Jews avoided the physical labor that the Nazis continually extolled in the farmer. The economic activities of farming, forestry, gardening, and stockbreeding, taken as a whole, constituted gainful employment for just over 29 percent of the total German population, contrasted with a little less than 2 percent of Jews in the country. The powerful Volkish implication was that the Jews were not a people of the soil. Domestic service figures showed that 5.75 percent of the general population engaged in this economic activity, contrasted with 3.32 percent of the Jews. Another implication arose from the data. Jews apparently felt themselves above this kind of humble labor. Instead, the vast majority of Jews focused their energies on taking control of the institutions of law, trade, industry, transportation, and the health professions.[58]

The layers of anti-Semitic rhetoric extended to the power of family names to disguise the real Jew. In a tone of consternation, Dittrich bemoaned the fact that the baptism of Jewish converts to Christianity in German towns during the seventeenth and eighteenth centuries was often staged as a festival for the entire population. Also serious for avowed anti-Semites was the practice among some Jewish families after the Prussian emancipation of the Jews in 1812 to change their family names to Christian ones in order to disguise their essential Jewishness. In Dittrich's ordered world, Jewish names were for Jews and that was how the laws of race intended it. Of special interest to Dittrich were those names that reflected Jewish commercial activities like Kassirer, Wechselmann, Wechsler, Silbermann, and Goldstein. There was a certain stereotypical order to the tradition of family names which made the process of classifying Jews much easier. Dittrich's thinking reflected the policy of the Nazi hierarchy, initiated in 1938, requiring that all identity papers for Jews use the name "Israel" and "Sarah" to make it easier for security forces to keep track of them.

The dark threat of blood mixing through intermarriages between Jews and Germans made the issue of family names all the more important for Dittrich's approach to race education. Assuming a racial disguise through hiding behind a German name was an affront to the spirit of the Nuremberg Laws of 1935 that legally defined the Jew. Dittrich printed a long list of original Jewish family names along with their alleged German counterparts to illustrate the extent of this false attempt at assimilation. "The meaning of this Jewish experience," he noted, "is very clear for every kind of racial political schooling. We will not fail to point out to our youth again and again how perniciously only one individual Jewish family effects others and how necessary the National Socialist laws on marriage and kinship are." Pupils should come to an understanding that the marriage bond was not only important in supporting higher birthrates for the nation. The Nazi legal conception of marriage, as Dittrich dutifully pointed out, also ensured that fewer and fewer offspring would be of Jewish or mixed blood.[59]

Racial insults and character assassination, all cast under the broad sweep of the Jewish question, represented critically important elements in the expression of racial anti-Semitism in the curriculum guides written by Dittrich and other Nazi educators. Dittrich's spurious claims for objectivity in advancing a study of the Jews for the purpose of forming dedicated anti-Semites in the schools suffered under a serious contradiction. Much of his language appealed to the emotions. Since weighing evidence and reasoned debate were not perceived as part of the process of becoming an educated person in Nazi Germany, and even seen as a threat to the racial community, writers like Dobers and Dittrich could give vent to all kinds of spurious anti-Semitic claims with the blessings of the state. Dittrich, for example, unleashed an attack on Jews calling them cowards for enlisting for duty on the front during World War I in what to him were relatively low numbers. At the same time, he ignored Jews who died serving the fatherland or were decorated for bravery with the Iron Cross First Class.[60]

Of an even more vicious nature was Dittrich's use of a double meaning in reference to the term *Saujuden*, associating Jews with the pigsty and, on another level of meaning, suggesting that Jewry was a chaotic mess. The insulting expression linked with Luther's story from 1543 about Jews from Wittenberg. The reform theologian, as noted earlier in the examination of Dobers's thinking, remained a star in the firmament of dedicated Nazi anti-Semites. Heedless of the historical context defining Luther's religious anti-Semitism, Dittrich followed the path of so many other curriculum writers in exploiting the fanatical hatred imbedded in "The Jews and Their Lies" (1543). A key conclusion from Luther's polemic bears closer attention because of Dittrich's subsequent reaction. Luther wrote that he would much rather live as a sow than a human being if God had sent no messiah other than the one expected and hoped for by the Jews. To this, the enthusiastic Dittrich exclaimed that this was a sentence "that could be written in the family bible of a good many pastors!" (Dittrich's exclamation).[61]

Drawing relationships with Luther's choice anti-Semitic rantings held its own explosive potential for educating young anti-Semites in the Third Reich, but Dit-

trich was hardly at the end of his dedicated efforts to draw on other traditions
as well. Going much further than Dobers in resurrecting nefarious assertions
about criminality among Jews, Dittrich drew up an extensive statistical table
with data on sentencing trends for 1910–14 from the Institute on the Study of
the Jewish Question. The data from table 2.3 are important not only for understanding the specific nature of anti-Semitic claims about Jewish criminality.
Carried forth in these statistical relationships are stereotypes about Jews with
roots, in some instances, dating back as far back as the Middle Ages. Once again,
the Jew is presented up and against the dominant culture with the use of numbers designed to encourage pupils and their teachers to draw false generalizations
about Jewishness. Table 2.3 told a statistical story about the Jewish community,
one which suggested that Jews were part of an inferior race because they possessed a criminal nature. Comparative data showed the extent to which Jews
were more likely to be sentenced for crimes relative to the general population.[62]

Table 2.3 Sentencing Trends Comparing Jews and Non-Jews, 1910–14

Offense	Sentencing of Jews Relative to General Population, Times as Often
Embezzlement	1.1
Evading Compulsory Military Service	1.2
Misdemeanors Relating to Religion	1.2
"Other" Sentences Related to Punishable Self-Interest	1.2
Abuse of Obligatory Oath	1.3
Pimping	1.3
Slander	1.4
Blackmail	1.5
Violations/Security Devices at Factories	1.7
Crimes and Misdemeanors against Public Order	1.7
Falsifying Contents of Food Stuffs/Tobacco	1.7
Removal of Property with Threat of Execution	1.7
Treason	1.8
Spreading Obscene Literature	1.8
Fraud	2.2
Producing and Selling Health-Threatening Food	2.2
Falsification of Documents	2.3
Active Bribery	2.6
Offenses/Lottery and Games of Chance	3.1
Offenses Relating to Livestock Disease	3.1
Disloyalty	3.2
Habitual Fencing of Stolen Goods	4.5
Defying Laws on Keeping Business Hours/Sundays	5.4
Defying Laws on Employing Women, Youth, and Children	6.7
Offenses Relating to Intellectual Property	7.8
Usury	12.3
Bankruptcy	13.6

From Werner Dittrich, *Erziehung zum Judengegner: Hinweise zur Behandlung der Judenfrage
im rassenpolitischen Unterricht* (*Education for the Anti-Semite: Advice on the Treatment of the
Jewish Question in Racial-Political Instruction*). Munich: Deutscher Volksverlag, 1937b,
pp. 20–21.

The evidence, Dittrich insisted, was "indisputable" that Jews were much more likely to commit crimes than Christians.[63] As the figures showed, the Nazis once again exploited the old associations between usury and fiscal greed. The Jews were themselves portrayed in these numbers as exploiters of young children and women in the marketplace, a charge all the more sensitive because of traditional anti-Semitic charges of Jewish sexual exploitation, pimping, and spreading obscene literature.[64] Ever the opportunist, Dittrich made certain his readers knew that certain practices honored among Christians, such as observing Sunday as a day of rest, were generally ignored by Jews in order to make more money. His generalization was duplicitous at best. Hitler Youth usually included Sundays on their schedule of activities for hiking and other activities until challenged by parents who insisted on reserving Sundays for the family.

The power of these numbers might have remained somewhat muted, dealing as they did with German Jewry from the Kaissereich, were it not for Dittrich's immediate follow-up with a tightly written paragraph that crammed even more crime statistics from the late Weimar and early Nazi periods. The circle of stereotypical assumptions about Jewish criminality extended to drug trafficking, illegal gambling, and pickpocketing, the frequency of which allegedly increased among Jews from 1931 to 1933. After presenting the most densely concentrated grouping of statistics in his entire book, Dittrich reminded teachers that the data on criminality were even more amazing since Jews made up just under 1 percent of the current population. The data served a useful ideological purpose. Dittrich further extended his call to educators to join the anti-Semitic mission of the schools. The enterprise could proceed with the propaganda of distorted statistics and half-baked truths to serve racial preconceptions of the Jew.[65]

No longer, Dittrich concluded, would anyone be able to talk about "coincidence" or the "illusion of statistics" in regard to the Jews. The statistics "showed here, beyond a doubt, a specific racial predisposition of Jews." Looking to the eugenic implications of his position, Dittrich boldly asserted that "similar gruesome numerical relationships arise from observing the sum of Jewish hereditary factors, where also the share of inferior heredity is meaningfully higher when considered inside the German population."[66] Perhaps in no other segment of Dittrich's work do statistical bias, traditional anti-Semitic stereotypes, and the Nazi language of racial science intersect more clearly. As seen in a later chapter, Dittrich will also contribute to the burgeoning growth of racial hygiene in Nazi schools.

The multifaceted nature of racial anti-Semitism is further evidenced though Dittrich's interpretation of history. He delighted in citing a Jew, British Prime Minister Benjamin Disraeli, for his famous dictum that the racial question was the key to world history. While assuming that the only worthwhile interpretations of Jewish history could be authored by non-Jews, preferably disciples of Adolf Hitler and Julius Streicher, Dittrich proposed that the history of Jewry was the history of anti-Semitism. Again, Dittrich remained enthralled by racial soul. Dedicated anti-Semites had to grapple with the "inner Jew" which, at the very least, demanded an understanding of history and its eternal link to race biology. While the Nazi perspective on history curriculum relative to racial anti-Semitism will be addressed later in the book in greater detail, some broad outlines of Dittrich's thinking are necessary in order to grasp his vision of the educated anti-Semite.[67]

As before, Dittrich turned to Ludwig Clauß, a Nazi racial philosopher deeply influenced by Houston Stewart Chamberlain and Paul de Lagarde. To understand the historical dimension of Judaism and racial soul required a deeper look at the oriental racial background of the people. The inner qualities of this "desert country type," as Dittrich called Jews, deserved much closer study in order to better understand what he called "the racial unity" defining Jewish culture. The race education specialist for the NSLB proposed a curriculum reform in which the teaching of religion would be more closely tied to a study of the Old Testament. These ancient writings, Dittrich thought, held a key to understanding Jewish history and religion and, thus, racial soul.[68]

In one broad propagandistic stroke, Dittrich reduced the racial history of Jews to one central development: the racial mixture of oriental Hebrew and Near Eastern blood. For the first time, Dittrich went beyond statistics and strategically placed quotations to explain the actual elements constituting the racial soul of Jews from this racial union. His explanations offer insights into the dynamics of anti-Semitic thinking as well as the endurance of traditional stereotypes cloaked now in racial terms. Race instruction in the classrooms of the Third Reich would articulate the ancient Hebrews as either wandering shepherds or nomads in the land of Caanan. Many inner qualities of the Jew as nomad, Dittrich insisted, originated from the oriental racial soul, including "the rigid image of God, the tradition of intolerant faith, the tenacious willpower, the cowardly intellect, and wild vindictiveness."[69]

Canaanite blood from the Near East mixed yet other critical elements of racial soul. This is where Dittrich's concept of racial soul takes on a more expanded purview to included physical elements. Jews became Jews not only because of their inner qualities but also because of their dominant physical appearances. The Near Eastern race, most purely represented in contemporary times by the Armenians, explained certain racial characteristics. In deference to Hans F. K. Günther, Dittrich now linked racial anthropology with the mysticism of racial soul. The Near Eastern connection for Jews explained why they had "pronounced, protruding hooked noses, fleshy nostrils, and rather large and fleshy ears," with "dark hair, skin and eyes."[70]

Pointing teachers to anti-Semitic caricatures of Jews popularized by Nazi culture, Dittrich informed his readers that Near Eastern blood connections also explained the commercial spirit of Jews. Another equally insidious quality of Jewish racial soul entered the picture, one which remained intolerable to the deeply committed Nazi. Especially troublesome to Nazi intellectuals like Dittrich was the Jewish possession of "an extraordinary gift to empathize with foreign ways of thinking" (*eine ausgesprochene Gabe zur Einfühlung in fremdes Seelenleben*).[71] This veiled attack against the spirit of inquiry, as alluded to earlier by Victor Klemperer, helped define the culture of Nazi Germany and, more specifically, legitimized knowledge in the schools.

Digging deeper into Dittrich's worldview revealed another quality of the racial soul of Jews so controversial that certain aspects were even considered off-limits in the curriculum. The disagreeable racial characteristics of the Jews, Dittrich insisted, were without a doubt associated with their "unlimited eroticism." This aspect of Jewish sexual life was to Dittrich so offensive and disgusting that any presentation of the issue before schoolchildren was out of the question. Still, to rationalize his revulsion and advance stereotypes associated with the unlimited sexual avarice of Jews, teachers are advised to read the story of Sodom and Gomorrah from the Book of Moses. The story earned Dittrich's accolades as the best source on Jewish racial soul, its propensity for sexual excess, and "lust for the flesh." This example demonstrated for readers that "the flood of immorality from Jews in all the world always has and will flow outward!" (Dittrich's exclamation). The claim of immorality, when linked with earlier statistics on Jewish criminality, provided a strong propagandistic thrust for Dittrich's anti-Semitic teachings.[72]

A recasting of history and religion along racial anti-Semitic lines was absolutely necessary for Dittrich in order for readers to swallow without question the message underlying his propaganda. Jews at that time and throughout history remained deadly enemies of civilized peoples. There was a sense in reading Dittrich that National Socialism was a logical fulfillment of anti-Semitic developments that had transpired over the centuries. Thus the ancient Egyptians around 1600 B.C. had fomented the earliest anti-Semitic revolution in world history aimed at ridding the kingdom of Jews. In a classic instance of historical victim blaming, Dittrich insisted that the enslavement of the Jews triggered the revolution. The term *Fremdlinge,* or foreigners, is associated with Jews in this context and, as we have seen, was also connected later in history with the compound word *Fremdrasse,* or foreign race.

Dittrich's own cynicism about this chapter in Jewish history is revealed in his use of quotation marks around the word *bedrückt,* meaning oppressed, when he referred to the slavery suffered by Jews under Ramses II. Moreover, another powerful and even more contemporary historical association manifested itself through Dittrich's interpretation of the ancient Egyptian period and its place in Jewish history. The tone of his very last sentence in the paragraph invited a striking parallel to the oppression of contemporary Jewry in Nazi Germany: "Physical labor, like lugging stones, has ever since been experienced by the nomads as an especially terrible burden."[73] His remarks foreshadowed the deportation of Jews to concentration camp Mauthausen in Austria in 1941 and events that followed. The camp became notorious for its penal brigade of forced laborers who carried heavy rock on their backs up 186 steps from the quarry often under the whip and indiscriminate shootings. Both Jews and Soviet POWs were among those who suffered under this sentence.[74]

Opening a section on the decay of kingdoms, Dittrich predictably blamed Jews for everything associated with the collapse of great civilizations. The Jewish Diaspora, Dittrich insisted, did not initially take place under the ancient Romans but, instead, began in 536 B.C. under the Babylonians. In a flight of historical fancy and mythologizing, he recounted the decision of King Cyrus to allow Jews to return to their homeland after the Babylonian Captivity as "a type of Nordic tolerance." How Dittrich justified this conclusion remained wholly mysterious.

The Persians entered the picture as well, but under different circumstances. What followed was a revision of sacred history under the pen of an anti-Semitic pedagogue. The Book of Esther provided the context for examining what Dittrich regarded as the second great anti-Semitic movement in world history. Dittrich turned first to Haman, the powerful adviser to King Xerxes of Persia who plotted the mass murder of all Jews in the empire. Haman's plot is motivated by his hatred of the Jewish servant Mordecai, called a "court Jew" by Dittrich, who refused to pay him homage for religious reasons.[75] Esther, the niece and adopted daughter of Mordecai, eventually became the queen chosen by King Xerxes to replace Vashti.

The resourceful Esther then joined forces with Mordecai to avert the catastrophe through reversing Haman's decree. The plot eventually turned against Haman who was hanged by the order of the king. How Dittrich framed this victory of the Jews is instructive. Esther and Mordecai are preserved in Nazi memory as models of Jewish deceit and masterminds of subversive conspiracy. In language that became a dynamic part of the Nazi policy of mass murder, Dittrich used the biological term *Ausrottung*, or extermination, to describe the legacy of this action. Aryan blood was at stake. "Through the extermination of leading noble Aryan stratum," he wrote, "the racial strength of the Persians became weakened." A further reference is paid to the Feast of Purim honoring the Jewish triumph, seen by Dittrich as a celebration of "every gruesome bloodbath" marked with a great deal of drunkenness and alcoholic frenzy.[76]

In contrast to Dobers, Dittrich remained focused on providing a historical narrative that preserved the legacy of anti-Semitism for schools while not devoting effort to uncovering alleged "Jewish lies" about the past. He simply continued to sow historical illusions of his own. Similar to Dobers, however, Dittrich repeatedly warned readers about the growing danger of the *Ostjuden* as the penultimate threat coming from the counter race.[77] Dittrich's narrative carefully reconstructed a medieval solution to the Jewish question through religious means. Earlier, we noted what forms this religious anti-Semitism had taken under Luther. The race education specialist did not want ardent, young anti-Semites to leave the classroom with the misunderstanding that Luther alone defined this crucial period in the history of anti-Semitism.

Earlier developments, like the formation of anti-Semitic policy in the Catholic Church, provided Dittrich with opportunities to exploit parallels with the Nuremberg Laws of 1935. He delighted in pointing out that church policy during the late fourth century made illegal any marriages between Christians and Jews. Baptized Jews did not escape his attention since he had already dismissed them as essentially Jews with a false Christian exterior. Thus, committed anti-Semites would not be surprised to read that the baptized Jew Torquemada played the role of grand inquisitor of Spain in the fifteenth century. Curiously enough, in conveying a grossly inaccurate and one-sided history, Dittrich mourned the deaths of executed Aryans while completely omitting any mention of the Jews who died under the torture of the Inquisition.[78]

Dittrich did not promise a tight chronological history of anti-Semitism with a sharp eye for historical process. Thus, the reader jumps immediately from Luther and the Middle Ages to the nineteenth century. In a formula that has already become familiar to us, Dittrich grounded the discussion in statistics and selected quotes warning of the overt Jewish control of many aspects of German culture in the 1800s. The racial instinct of great Germans like Kant, Herder, Fichte, Goethe, Schiller, and Arndt, proudly declared by Dittrich as anti-Semites, had protected German culture from the worst excesses of the Jewish threat. Returning once again to the Nuremberg Laws of 1935, Dittrich interpreted the Nazi racial legislation as a necessary counterbalance to the wretched Edict of 1812 by Minister Hardenberg opening the door to Jewish emancipation.[79]

Recognizing his own ideological debt to Hans F. K. Günther and Julius Streicher, Dittrich presented educators with a surprisingly brief examination of the Jewish question as it related to the Third Reich.[80] In his most concentrated discussion about the role of schools in the process of anti-Semitic education, Dittrich told teachers that the Nuremberg Laws alone were not enough to secure an anti-Semitic mind-set in Nazi society. A systematic anti-Semitic schooling from childhood under German educators was also necessary to form "convinced" anti-Semites among the young. The foundation stone for the "correct knowledge of the Jewish question" could best be laid, he wrote, if racial science became part of all school subjects. There were age-appropriate limits to this ambitious project. Even an enthusiastic race educator like Dittrich recognized that elementary schoolchildren were not ready to grasp the more difficult processes associated with race eugenics.[81]

Returning yet again to the Nuremberg Laws that symbolized a historical turning point in German-Jewish relations, Dittrich joined Dobers in emphasizing that one of the highest duties of the school was to provide pupils advice on choosing racially healthy marriage partners. The prohibition against blood mixing, one of the greatest racial sins threatening the Nazi regime, took on a central focus in the curriculum. Behind these considerations was the question of extramarital relations with Jews. Dittrich sternly reminded teachers of a special gender-based racial responsibility. Female pupils entrusted to the care of educators must come to understand that they were not in any way to allow themselves to become economically dependent on any Jews. The implication was that such dependence would lead to sexual involvement. The omission of any reference to male pupils in this racial and sexual relationship is most instructive.[82]

The issue of didactics, in contrast to Dobers, was of relatively little importance to Dittrich in this slim volume. The Nuremberg Laws and essays from Streicher's *Der Stürmer* relating to Jewish commerce were to Dittrich among the most important teaching resources for the classroom, although he offered readers few didactical insights about instructional methods. However, his closure pointed to an instructional development in race education that gained some popularity across the Reich during the 1930s. The creation of exhibits centering around pictorial presentations contrasting Nordic and Jewish racial types held great aesthetic promise, Dittrich predicted. Images inviting comparisons between the Master Race and Jews "strengthened a strong sense of natural beauty in German youth and with this, awakened their racial feelings." Dittrich would leave the task of integrating instructional pictures into the formal race curriculum to others like Fritz Fink and Alfred Vogel. The contribution of the NSLB's race education specialist to the Jewish question was words and numbers to advance his own racial and anti-Semitic imagery of the Jews.[83]

FRITZ FINK AND THE FACE OF THE JEW

Bringing the perspective of the *Schulrat*, or school inspector, to curriculum formation, Fritz Fink published *The Jewish Question in Instruction* in 1937 to introduce into the elementary school classroom some of the most vociferous forms of anti-Semitism to be found anywhere in print. The sponsorship of Fink's work by Julius Streicher, the author of the foreword to Fink's volume, certainly explains the sharp tone of much of Fink's writing. One of the most distinctive contributions Fink made to the larger process of anti-Semitic curriculum development was the integration of pictorial evidence, some of it gathered from earlier work by Hans F. K. Günther, to emphasize physical differences between Jews and Aryans. He also brought to the curriculum guide a set of Nazi ideological interpretations of Jewish religion that made the language of Dittrich pale in comparison by both tone and substance.

The language of Fink's introduction offered teachers and school administrators a certain curricular vision about the importance of understanding just how important the Jewish question was for the entire Nazi regime. Again, as in the works of Dobers and Dittrich, one notes a sense of urgency in securing a solution to this racial problem. What Fink added was a powerful religious fervor and symbolism for the pedagogical mission at hand:

> The racial and Jewish question is the central problem of the National Socialist worldview. The solution to this problem secures the existence of National Socialism and with it the existence of our people for all time. The dreadful meaning of the race question is almost completely recognized by the German people. In order to come to this realization, our people had to bear a long way of the cross. So that coming generations remain spared of this way of the cross, we want German educators to sink into the hearts of our youth, already from childhood onwards, a knowledge of the Jews. It shall and may not grow in our people who do not know the Jews in their entire outrageousness and danger.[84]

Fink sought a certain organic integration for the anti-Semitic curriculum. He warned teachers that following the curricular tradition of creating a single-standing, independent course would simply be unnatural and ineffective. Racial science and the Jewish question must be present like "a red thread" at all age levels wound throughout the entire curriculum. Observing that current individual school subjects did not integrate the Jewish question in a fashion that did justice to the issue, Fink staked out his approach. His curriculum guide would not include "well known model teaching examples which had been corrupted by the instructional style and instinct of some teachers." Instead, Fink would show readers how his "natural" approach to teaching the Jewish question might be integrated throughout the elementary curriculum. There was no doubt that the *Stadtschulrat* wanted to break new ground in the way that schools approached the Jewish question.[85]

Among fellow authors of anti-Semitic curriculum, Fink remained exceptional for he eschewed the integration of statistical evidence and generally restricted the use of quoted language to a discussion of Jewish religion and the views of famous Germans regarding Jewish culture. For the most part, Fink's style was to provide educators with a story about Jews that could be easily translated into daily instructional practice. Departing from Dobers and Dittrich, Fink took the time to develop a more direct connection with the concerns of teachers stepping into race curriculum reform for the first time.

In his first major section on "the German child and the Jew," Fink anticipated practical pedagogical questions from teachers uncertain about how to proceed through what truly was a unique development in the history of modern education. To those worried about how to bring the Jewish problem to children or those with apprehensions about whether the young really held an interest in the subject, Fink had words of reassurance: "The conscientious pedagogue can be comforted. In the child, everything is there. Interests and links are already in existence."[86] His words were also directed to future pedagogues interested in the theory of apperception with its suggestion that children learned best when subject matter was connected to already existing interests and related to their experiences. If what Fink suggested was true, the success of an anti-Semitic curriculum would rest, at least in part, on the formation of attitudes and values about Jews in children through the family and other institutions before and after they started school.

Tapping his skill as an anti-Semitic storyteller, Fink related the tale about a farmer who was once approached in the barnyard by a Jewish cattle dealer. Immediately, the children fled to a small room and the mother hid behind a rock. This happened because their "purely racial instinct sensed a foreign race which brought danger and misfortune." Fink opined that the elderly had generally lost this healthy instinct. They had forgotten to see racially, so confronting something different meant nothing to them at all. Such a catastrophic racial situation was now changing. Unspoiled German youth developed a genuine aversion for the Jews. After all, they were bombarded with propaganda from many quarters. Anti-Semitic messages came to them daily from newspapers, speeches, and songs from the Hitler Youth, and they all bore the name of the Jew.[87]

While Fink praised the racial idealism of youth, he had special words of scorn for those teachers lacking the courage to instruct their charges about the Jewish question in a firm and forthright manner. These shy and hesitant instructors were the bane of Nazi education. There were also those educators who, falling prey to the Jewish propagation of "objectivity, decency, and humanity" drummed into their heads, still sat on their knees. Worse yet to Fink was that some teachers, at the behest of the churches, brought against the deadly enemy of the Jew both "compassion and brotherly love." Behind Fink's veiled rage is a deep mistrust for part of the teaching profession to effectively deliver racial anti-Semtic instruction. In few other Nazi sources will one find a deeper loathing expressed for those teachers held under ideological suspicion. Their greatest crime was that they stood in the way of anti-Semitic learning and thus killed the child's natural intellectual curiosity for the Jewish question.[88]

After venting his tirade against wayward teachers, Fink returned to the problem of content and method. Nature study provided an intellectual basis for young children to grasp some of the basics of anti-Semitic learning through transferring laws from the animal kingdom to the racial community. The same kinds of insects like anteaters, wasps, bees, termites, and others each built their own nests. In the fall, when the migratory birds prepared to leave for the south, the starlings flew only with starlings, the storks only with storks, the swallows only with swallows. Although they were all birds, they held a strict separation between themselves according to their genus or biological type. Teaching these facts of nature study, as Fink called them, would one day lead to the hour when the boy or girl would jump up and enthusiastically make the critical anti-Semitic connection. As it was with nature, so it must also be with the human family. Using a narrative style, Fink put into the lips of a child what he hoped might be the ultimate conclusion from this relationship: "Our German people had at one time, however, allowed themselves to be led by those of a foreign race, the Jews."[89]

Older pupils, in connecting to sex education, could study the ways of the starling. A male starling mated only with a female starling and they built a nest, incubated eggs, and cared for the brood that grew as young starlings. One type of biological life form felt attracted to the same type in nature and eventually parented a generation of similar biological types. Children would learn that a transgression of this law of nature among human beings led to disastrous racial consequences in the creation of mixed bloods and a bastardization of the race. A reinforcement of this assumption could come through posing the example of human breeding practices through sexually uniting horses with donkeys resulting in mules, a type of bastard. Though not the way nature had intended, the mule would continue to have effects on the blood of the descendants.

So it was with the racial nature of being human. Human beings alone set themselves above this will of nature. The legacy, Fink told educators, was devastating to the racial and moral fiber of the human community. To develop a critical understanding among the young for the importance of the Nuremberg Laws, Fink advanced the concept of racial consciousness, a consciousness which rejected not only Jewish blood but also the blood of Black Africans and members of the Asian community.[90] As before, Fink called upon Providence to legitimize his assumptions. Seriously misguided people

approved and even advanced the union of Black and Yellow races with Whites, of Jews with non-Jews. Every valuable member of a race is racially conscious. No racially conscious and racially proud White mates with a Negro or Jewish woman, as no racially conscious Negro joins a White. The biological type remains by its own kind. Only inferior members of a race are inclined toward other races or allow themselves to be abused by them. From different races are found only unworthiness linked to those unworthy, inferiority to those deemed inferior. So it is clear that the bastard must always follow the troubled hand. That means that only the inferior qualities are united in the paired races. An educator who confronts youth with such thinking will find it easy to introduce these young people to a sense of the Nuremberg Laws. The children will then see these Nuremberg Laws in no other way than the return to the natural, divine order.[91]

To add more weight to his argument and further justify the necessity of racial anti-Semitism in the classroom, Fink deferred to an even more drastic example from nature. He introduced a story about a termite colony through references to the work of a certain Dr. Escherich, a natural scientist and privy councillor from Munich who supposedly dedicated much of his life to studying the creatures. The termite colony, so the story goes, continued to grow as long as the established order was followed and the queen received protection, care, and nourishment. Large soldier termites armed with sharp jaws preserved this order as guardians of the colony. One day foreign insects attacked the nest. Unfortunately, some areas sensitive to attack were neglected. The invading foreign insects were able to penetrate these parts of the colony. The overwhelmed inhabitants of the colony decided to befriend the enemy. This unfortunate turn of events created an illusion among many termites that they could actually get along with their new guests. They let down their guard. To make things worse, the foreign insects arrived in larger numbers. One day, a tremendous excitement broke out in the colony. A terrible battle ensued in all corners of the structure. The foreigners murdered the termite queen. The termite state was now ruled by revolution. A gruesome murder of all the inhabitants followed, and a few days later the colony completely died out.[92]

Anticipating that some pupils might not grasp the racial moral of the story, Fink created a conversation between a star pupil and the teacher to clarify the ideological implications of the tale. Reflected in this constricted dialogue was a Nazi worldview, one which defined how a good anti-Semite was expected to think. Ideological star pupils in Fink's curricular world are always "jumping up" in the classroom supposedly moved through discovering parallels between the laws of nature and the attractive power of anti-Semitic thinking. The pupil readily noted that the Jew symbolized the foreign insects. Once again, the greater threat came from the East with Jews arriving in the fatherland in greater numbers after the war. They brought the threat of revolution and would eventually try to chase away the Führer. With order coming to an end, the land became drenched in the blood of murder. The Jews now assumed power. The curriculum guide reinforced the canned pupil response with the words of a model teacher who "expanded" on the seriousness of the Jewish threat. The fight against Jewry, the school inspector reminded educators, was not a question of mood or caprice but a matter of emergency.[93]

Who indeed was the Jew, and what did a Jew look like? These questions dogged Fink and many other curriculum writers involved in the formation of anti-Semitic elementary school curriculums. To suggest that murderous Jews ruled Germany through storylines and references to laws of nature did not take anti-Semitic education far enough. Fink insisted that young children also had to see pictures of those Jews who held power and influence in the culture. Furthermore, they should be introduced to images of schoolchildren, both Jewish and German, to grasp the major racial differences between the two groups. Seeing pictures of children chronologically close to their own generation might also augment the racial anti-Semitic implications from the nature stories. If Jews really were different from Germans, then how would one differentiate between the two on a physical basis? Questions like these suggested that some pupils were moved more by the power of image than the power of the word.

The fact that Fink's curriculum guide originated in Bavaria influenced his choice of notable Jewish politicians to target in the section he called "The True Jew." Sizable pictures of Jews involved in the German revolution of 1919, derisively called "the Soviet Republic" by the Nazis in reference to events in Munich, stressed Marxist connections to the Jewish community. Included were Erich Mühsam, Kurt Eisner, and Viktor Adler. Here again was evidence that Jews were behind yet another revolution. Missing from Fink's writing is any real context beyond the pictures and brief captions using the highly charged Soviet title of "Volkskommissar" in reference to Mühsam and Eisner. Fink encouraged teachers to post these pictures of Jews in the classroom so that pupils could see faces of the racial enemy. Immediately following the pictures of the three Jewish leaders was one large picture of a German male with obligatory blond hair.[94]

What followed was a classic piece of anti-Semitic curriculum linked with Volkish assumptions about differences in physical appearance, a crucial element in building among German youth an appreciation for the "us-them" dichotomy. Fink, following the tradition of Günther, lined up "representative" images of thirteen- and fourteen-year-old Jewish and German boys and girls. Combined with frontal views of the face were profile shots to emphasize differences in nose size and shape. After immersing themselves in the study of these images for only a few minutes, Fink chortled, pupils will see for themselves that Jews really do have noses, ears, lips, chins, and even entire faces very different from those of Germans. Racial models helped define Fink's work. Posted at the end of the collection on an entire page, the largest image from the volume showed a thirteen-year-old German girl with blond hair in pigtails. The picture symbolized a propagandized Nazi view of the racially pure young woman.[95]

Reinforcing the role of physical differences in racial anti-Semitism could start with picture study, but a subsequent assignment for pupils to observe Jews on the street could open even more conclusions. The young observers could see that Jews also walked differently and possessed fallen arches. Their posture was also different, and they had longer arms than Germans. Their manner of speaking was unusual. As important as these observations of racial differences were to forming young anti-Semites in Fink's curriculum, another even more important factor emerged. Once more, racial soul assumed its proper role in the scheme of anti-Semitic education. The exterior appearance of a person was connected to the soul of the race. Therefore, teachers held the sacred duty of pressing home to youth the cardinal principle of all sound racial anti-Semitic instruction. Not only do Jews look different from Germans. They also thought, felt, and acted differently than Germans and therefore "stood in stark opposition to our morals, to our laws."[96]

The path to this understanding of racial difference was, if Fink's assumptions were accepted without question, simple and clear. The power of the rhetorical question, evidenced throughout Fink's writing, provided a certain kind of instructional simplicity since it was the teacher who always asked the questions. To ask children what drove the Jew begged an answer similar to those already seen in other curriculum guides. What set Fink apart from other curriculum writers was his propensity to devote more attention to those occupations he felt were traditionally outside the realm of Jewish culture. Moreover, statistical evidence remained outside his purview. His conclusion for teachers was blunt. Jews are not seen in the occupations of factory worker, bricklayer, blacksmith, locksmith, miner, farmer, plasterer. In other words, the Jew avoided work with his hands and avoided heavy labor while "living off the sweat of his neighbors. He is a parasite, like the mistletoe on the tree." Fink suggested that teachers of mathematics organize lessons centered around practical examples illustrating the dominance of Jews in key professions including medicine and law as well as occupations like junk, cattle, and rag dealing along with management of apartment stores and clothes businesses.[97]

To avoid creating the impression that the Jewish question was only contemporary in nature, Fink recommended for teachers the use of the Nuremberg Chronicles, a historical resource that included references to Jewish misdeeds in the marketplace going back some 500 years. The usual anti-Semitic charges of high interest rates, dishonesty in changing money, cheating with weights and measures, poisoning wells, engaging in the ritual slaughter of children, and violating women appeared. A greater historical vision of these developments, Fink insisted, would prevent Germans from once again falling prey to the nonsensical assumption that Jews were capable of assimilation into German society. Assuming a patriarchal tone, Fink pleaded with German educators to take special care of the task at hand. This meant destroying the illusions that baptized Jews as well as Jews carrying German names could ever be Germans. The racial gulf remained purposely wide. None dare cross it.[98]

Fink saved some of his most strident anti-Semitism for a discussion of the religious and moral dimensions of Jewish culture. As was also the case with the other curriculum writers under investigation thus far, Fink was in a position to exploit the long history of anti-Semitism in Christianity. From his perspective, Jews were condemned as Old Testament people whose God, Yahweh, was not the God of the Germans. Fink's opening salvos on "the God of the Jews" revealed his thinking about the most important theological implication of Yahweh's relationship with the Jews. Yahweh's pact with the Jews as the chosen people, a status Fink insisted was merely concocted by the Jews for their own political benefit, directed them to take on "a ruthlessness against all non-Jews, against the nonbelievers, and uncircumcised heathens."[99]

Following the tradition of many other anti-Semitic writers, Fink exploited the use of both undocumented quoted language along with selected and documented expressions from the Old Testament. Both the order and the timing of this language was important to Fink's goal of deepening anti-Semitic attitudes and values among schoolchildren. In the opening paragraph of this section, Fink quoted Yahweh's commandment that those not circumcised would fall under his wrath and be exterminated: *"Alles, was nicht beschnitten ist, wird meiner Rache verfallen und ausgerottet werden."* That the actual source of these words remained undocumented was not of any importance to the writer. What was of significance was the brief conclusion which immediately followed in which Fink once again anticipated the reactions of children to anti-Semitic pedagogy. The children will feel, he wrote, that "we" can't expect mercy from Yahweh. Fear and loathing for Jews, one can safely assume, were emotions Fink hoped would grow from this kind of theological instruction.[100]

To develop additional classroom examples revealing Yahweh's command for the chosen people to "oppress and destroy" all those outside the Jewish community, Fink urged all German educators to immerse themselves in the Old Testament. A series of these Jewish commands must be recorded on the blackboard and children encouraged to offer their opinions. Fink's own biblical references are restricted to the Book of Psalms and the Book of Deuteronomy. The three documented biblical references set the tone for Fink's entire approach in exploiting religious texts in order to justify anti-Semitic thinking. Underlying these selected texts was the age-old fear of a Jewish conspiracy to rule the world:[101]

> Ask of me and I will give you the nations for the ends of the earth for your possession. You shall rule them with an iron rod; you shall shatter them like an earthen dish.
>
> Psalms 2:8–9

You shall consume all the nations which the Lord, your God, will deliver up to you. You are not to look on them with pity, lest you be ensnared into serving their gods.

Deuteronomy 7:16

You will lend to many nations, and borrow from none; you will rule over many nations, and none will rule over you, since the Lord, your God, will bless you as He promised.

Deuteronomy 15:6

Interjecting ideologically appropriate and desired pupil responses remained central to Fink's anti-Semitic methods. His narrative once gain revealed Nazi anti-Semitic ideals as well as the regime's perspectives on those elements which contributed to the formation of an educated person. Following these three references to the Old Testament, Fink again integrated the voice of that enlightened anti-Semitic pupil appropriately moved by the simplicity of Nazi teachings about Jewish culture and religion. Yahweh was unjust and cruel, the child would say. He demanded the destruction of all non-Jewish people. He sent his love to only one select people, even though they were the worst and depraved of all humankind. In what was one of the most insidious abuses of religious teaching, Fink's model pupil exploited the yawning gap between the Jewish and Christian religious communities. The attempt to falsify Jewish religious tradition was also connected with the power of old economic stereo- types of Jew from centuries past:

We heard that God (as opposed to Yahweh) is righteous, merciful, and gentle and embodied love. He loves goodness and condemns evil. We know the word of Christ which says that one can't serve God and mammon at the same time. Yahweh, however, speaks of power, rule, riches, and money![102]

A subversion of the Talmud provided another means by which Fink extended his anti-Semitic teachings, a tendency also shared by Alfred Vogel, whose work comes under investigation in chapter 3. Under the broad theme of "the criminal Jewish secret laws," Fink held up the Talmud as a means by which teachers could instruct youth about the religious origins of Jewish criminalty. The word of the Talmud was blamed as a justification for a great diversity of criminal acts from tax evasion, fraud, and manipulation of foreign currency to murder and theft. Unlike Dittrich and Dobers, Fink avoided the integration of statistical data to emphasize the level of crime in the Jewish community. Fink brought to the educator multiple layers of anti-Semitic evidence from sacred books while, at the same time, exploiting the historically estranged relationship between Christians and Jews. Words and meanings, stripped of context, were more important in advancing the anti-Semitic frame of mind than numbers.[103]

The result was a kind of incendiary Jew-baiting reminiscent of Julius Stre- icher. Jewish laws and traditions articulated in the Talmud took on a wholly new and twisted form under Fink's pen. Strongly encouraged to keep a note- book on what they learned about the Jews, pupils would read fabricated references to various books of the Talmud and thereby arrive at preconceived conclusions deemed ideologically appropriate by the regime. What was the source of Jewish wrongdoing? Quick answers could be gleaned by reading Fink's catalogue of Jewish laws applying to the non-Jew. One Talmudic source, according to Fink, stated that non-Jews really were not human and ate like dogs. Another emphasized the absence of any real connection between Jews and non-Jews. Moreover, ancient Jewish teachings advanced the notion that the flesh of non-Jews wasn't really the flesh of humans but the flesh of animals. The place of the Talmud in the constellation of Nazi curriculum resources on anti-Semitic learning will come under more specific examination in the next chapter.[104]

For those pupils who embraced Fink's call to carefully observe Jewish behavior outside of schools, pronouncements from the Nazi version of the Talmud provided a way of understanding Jewish motivations. Now pupils could see Jews with new pairs of eyes. They could understand, in a way not wholly apparent before, why Jews acted the way they did and followed certain strange and foreign cultural practices. Young Germans could now grasp why Jews in German restaurants brought their own food, plates, and silverware or why Jews had their own butchers. More important, pupils would comprehend that this behavior of the Jews had nothing to do with religion and everything to do with contempt by the Jewish community for non-Jews whom they regarded as nothing more than "unclean animals" and "swine."[105] The scope and nature of the Nazi oppression of the Jews, the people of Sinti and Roma, the mentally ill and the physically handicapped, reversed the order of Fink's language. Considered sub-human by the Nazi state, members of these groups became victims of the thinking reflected through this kind of language.

Fink was not about to overlook an aspect of theology that possessed an even greater potential explosiveness of its own. "Deep within the souls of the children," he wrote, "there must burn the realization that Jews killed Christ." The charge of deicide, long a rationalization used by Christians for the persecution of Jews over the long course of anti-Semitism in history, came to hold a special place in the pedagogy of Fritz Fink. To incite further hatred, Fink fabricated quotations from alleged Jewish sources laced with insulting language directed toward the legacy of Christ. By itself, the reality of Jesus Christ's Jewish identity held the potential of undercutting Fink's exploitation of anti-Semitic traditions in Christianity. As in all problems curricular in nature, Fink proposed an easy solution. Entering again was the mythical pupil off whom Fink bounced his anti-Semitic assumptions. The understanding will dawn on our youth, Fink explained, that any Christ who spent his life in a solitary struggle against the Jews, and earned hatred by Jews as a result, cannot himself be a Jew.[106]

Overt omissions in Fink's narrative revealed a decidedly narrow historical perspective and a severely distorted historical context. The critically important involvement of Roman authorities in the trial and crucifixion of Christ is completely overlooked. The emotionalism and the irrational tone marking certain junctures in Fink's curriculum guide do not rest on the biases of the more contemporary developments in racial science. This was an anti-Semitism connected to a history much older than this kind of science. In concluding his writing on the criminal intent of secret Jewish laws, Fink recorded an emotionally ladened interpretation of Golgotha supported by a gross distortion of history:

Before the eyes of the children emerges Golgotha. A place of triumph for Jewish hatred ... Jewish hatred which killed Christ on the cross also follows today in Christian churches. The destruction of churches and monasteries in Russia and Spain, the corpses of bestially murdered priests, monks, and nuns are the work of this irreconcilable hatred. Here the educator must touch on an important, and admittedly for many, a very painful question.[107]

What was framed as an ecclesiastical embarrassment in the deceitful language of Fritz Fink was actually another means by which anti-Semitic teaching could be broadened. The painful question to which Fink referred concerned the position of the churches regarding "the people who murdered Christ." To demonstrate the anti-Semitic elements from the Catholic Church's history, Fink selected an expression from Tertullian, a church father who condemned the synagogue as the source of Jewish persecution of Christians. Fink challenged teachers to compare the Nuremberg Laws of 1935 with directives from the Council of Toledo of 633, one of which sharply denounced Jews and, furthermore, disallowed them from employing Christian servants. Pope Innocent III's condemnation in 1215 of dangerous Jewish influence in public offices found a hearing in Fink's pages. He also cited the theologian Alfons Steiger who proudly proclaimed that while Judaism led to Christ, the church was Christ. Fink carefully built up readers to key questions of his own. In one of the best-orchestrated rationalizations for anti-Semitic actions found in Nazi literature, Fink asked his audience to think about the following issues.

If the popes and church fathers enacted such laws and one such struggle against Jewry followed, can the struggle of National Socialism against the Jews repudiate a commandment of God? How can one such struggle be unchristian, if the church itself fought it for centuries long?[108]

Underlying these queries is the assumption that the interests of National Socialism are inherently similar to the anti-Semitic interests of the Catholic Church. Fink's words suggested that the ground was already theologically and ideologically well prepared for the Nazis by the time they assumed power in 1933. He further supported this assumption by quoting the words of Christ as recorded in the New Testament Gospels of John and Matthew. Reinforcing an old medieval charge that Jews were born of the devil, Fink cited from John's Gospel the strong rejection by Christ of Jews who did not accept his teachings. The Gospel of Matthew, known for its strong tone of antipathy against the Jews, became another source for anti-Semitic teaching. In the Gospel of Matthew, Christ condemned the scribes and Pharisees as frauds willing to travel over sea and land to make a single convert who, after conversion, became "a child of hell twice as wicked as yourselves." The association of Jews with hell and the devil, part of an ancient anti-Semitic portrayal of Jews, found a home in Fink's pedagogy. Moreover, as we witnessed earlier, the charge of fraud reappeared time and time again in anti-Semitic discussions about the criminality of Jews.[109]

The placement of Christ's words was significant. In a section devoted to what Fink called the "Judgments of Great Men over the Jews," the author devoted no less than five pages to anti-Semitic pronouncements from the lips of notable Gentiles. Fink presented a line of anti-Semitic thinking from Christ to Hitler, thus reinforcing the myth of Hitler as a religious figure in his own right. This calls to mind one especially popular Nazi propaganda poster titled "Germany Awaken," which depicted the Führer as a savior of Germany with a dove shown above his head, an unmistakable symbolic reference to Christian art of the Renaissance.[110] Of course, the fire of Martin Luther's anti-Semitism certainly was not ignored. Fink wanted to ensure that young and educated anti-Semites possessed a thoroughgoing understanding of Luther's perspective on the Jews. Going beyond Luther's "The Jews and Their Lies" (1543), a primary focus for the theologian's anti-Semitism in Dobers and Dittrich, Fink integrated Luther's language from the Erlangen edition of Luther's *Tischreden* or table talk. Prominent in Fink's conception of the anti-Semitic curriculum was Luther's sharp condemnation of the Talmud and the rabbinical tradition.[111]

Bringing pupils back to their special notebooks on the Jews, Fink urged young people to always treasure in their memories the names of great heroes in the pantheon of anti-Semitism. In addition to Christ and Luther, the school inspector included the Roman historian Tacitus, Frederick the Great, Goethe, Napoleon, Fichte, Moltke, Bismarck, Hitler, Herder, Kant, Schiller, Arndt, Hebbel, Richard Wagner, Treitschke, and Mommsen. Last, but certainly not least, on the list was Henry Ford. This group of notables, when taken as a whole, provided Fink with another propaganda opportunity for his mythical pupil. Armed with the names of these immortal thinkers and anti-Semitic learning gained through history, natural science, religion, and culture studies, the young German could now confidently go forth into the world knowledgable about the Reich's most deadly enemy.[112]

The dynamic power of race in the Nazi perspective of the citizen is seen once gain in the way Fink closed his discussion about the anti-Semitic curriculum. The last section, titled "*Rassenschande,*" referred to a betrayal of Nazi laws for the preservation of Aryan bloodlines. The direct implication, already enshrined in the Nuremberg Laws, was that any sexual relations between Jews and Aryans constituted a *Schande*, or racial disgrace. Behind Fink's writing was the traditional and omnipresent stereotype of the Jewish male as sexual predator. The focus therefore remained on reaching young German girls both within and outside the school to instill a fear for any kind of sexual contact with Jews. "All of us, including parents and educators," Fink opined, "carry guilt in that countless numbers of our girls and women have perished because of the Jews." A more aggressive involvement of the families and churches with schools to impress girls about the poisonous consequences of Jewish blood was in order. The sex education Fink advocated was based on the assumption that maturing girls were better off hearing about the facts of life in school or home rather than being forced to learn one evening by "a criminal Jew under gruesome circumstances."[113] (See plate 9.)

The Nuremberg Laws of 1935 brought Fink's anti-Semitic pedagogy full circle. As shown earlier in his curriculum guide, the study of nature would impress upon the young the sexual conformity behind the mating of animals of the same kind and the unnatural outcome expected from crossbreeding and resultant bastardization. The Jews, standing outside the natural laws of breeding and racial health, revealed themselves to be members of a decidedly inferior race. Bring pupils back, Fink told teachers, to the body and the face, to appearance, as well as the thoughts, feelings, and actions of the Jew. The face of the Jew reappeared toward the end of Fink's volume. In two pictures, Fink showed the faces of *Mischlinge*, or children of mixed blood first degree, from the union of a German-blooded mother and Jewish father. Beneath these images, Fink firmly emphasized again that bastardization remained a burden to the state, sapping its strength by carrying the seeds of racial degeneration through the progeny. The Jewish question revolved around this racial issue.[114]

A close examination of Fink's curriculum resource revealed another kind of anti-Semitic image, this one created by the artistic imaginations of schoolchildren. Here, again, one notes a reflection of Nazi policy in regard to Jewish immigration. In a set of two pictures, collectively titled "How Children See Jews," the young artist portrayed a migrating Jew in 1918 walking toward Nuremberg wearing a beard and patched clothing. A signpost showed an arrow to Palestine in a direction opposite of the Jew's intended destination. The second image from 1935 depicted a Jewish couple situated near a large travel trunk labeled "to Palestine." The male brought three large money bags into the picture. The stereotypes of the Jew as stateless wanderer and as a figure consumed with amassing money survived with drawings of this nature. Some six years before the Final Solution, the message was that German Jews must leave, and indeed this was the case for 280,000 who migrated mostly to Palestine, the United States, or Latin America.[115]

How German girls should act in the presence of a Jewish man seeking her company became the theme behind a series of two drawings by a thirteen-year-old artist named Brunner. The first panel showed a street scene in which a Jewish man tipped his hat to a German woman with a caption: "A Jew wants to win over a German girl for himself . . ." But, as portrayed in the second image, he quickly experienced the scorn of the girl who greeted him with a slap to the face so hard that his hat flew to the ground. The political socialization reinforced by this student artwork, appearing at the end of Fink's volume, begs a further question about gender relationships under the Third Reich. The responsibility for maintaining a sexual distance from Jews, as Fink's work suggested, rested solely on the shoulders of girls. Where boys came into the picture regarding sexual relations with Jewish girls is left unaddressed in Fink's propaganda.[116]

There is something of what Hans-Christian Harten called "the mythical character of nordic pedagogy" in the curriculum perspectives of Dobers, Dittrich, and Fink on the Jewish question. The myth advanced the notion that the Germans, although actually a racially mixed and heterogeneous people, were a people generally defined by "Nordic blood."[117] Dobers himself noted that the presence of Jews in German culture symbolized a rejection of claims for blood purity. No other people in Europe, he wrote, possessed so much Nordic blood as the Germans and, at the same time, such a mixture of foreign racial elements.[118] Although different in their points of emphasis and in some of the methods advocated to advance the teaching of the Jewish question, the three authors, as expected, shared an ideological unity of thought on the importance of this issue for defining the educated person under the Third Reich.

They also were firm in their insistence that educating young anti-Semites required a new curricular vision in which the Jewish question must not be consigned to the narrow strictures of any single subject matter discipline. Thus, the curriculum guides, in following Rust's directive of 1933, articulated an integration of anti-Semitic learning in natural science, history, geography, cultural studies, and religion. The anti-Semitic education advocated here did not symbolize a clean break with the past. As the three writers demonstrated, the exploitation of old economic and religious anti-Semitism was just as important in the scheme to educate German youth as the racial component. The next chapter, which begins a more specific examination of race biology and its place in the anti-Semitic orientation of Nazi schools, will reveal an ever-increasing blurring of lines between the traditional school disciplines. All of this happened within a curricular process that blended old and new kinds of anti-Semitic thinking.

Chapter 3

The Jew as Racial Pariah in Race Hygiene and Biology

> National Socialism is nothing but applied biology.
> —Fritz Lenz, *Menschliche Auslese und Rassenhygiene*, 1931.

Six months after Hitler's rise to power, the race biologist and teacher Jakob Graf delivered a lecture before a convocation of science educators from Hessen. His words tapped an idealism characteristic of Nazi ideology and the significant role he felt teachers should play in the legitimation of the Third Reich and the racial state. Speaking at a conference on "The Educational Value of Teaching Heredity and Race," Graf raised a rhetorical question about what teachers could contribute to morally uplift the German people and reconstruct the nation. The ideological implications of his own response to this query foreshadowed subsequent curriculum developments in the elementary and secondary schools of Nazi Germany. The results from research in heredity and the study of race, he noted,

> formed one of the most important cornerstones of the national socialist edifice. Teachers, especially those of us in biology, are under the obligation to establish the deep associations between hereditary science, the Volkish world view and the life of our people.[1]

Under the Third Reich, biology attained a great deal of prestige in school curriculum since it most clearly reflected the central tenets of the Nazi worldview and thus possessed great propaganda value for the regime.[2] As suggested earlier, this biological conception of school knowledge would profoundly influence many other parts of the curriculum including the formation of racial anti-Semitism. The earliest Nazi curriculum policy statement to reach the Prussian school administrators, issued in August of 1933, emphasized the importance of race biology as the basis for all school studies. Drafted by Rudolf Benze from the Prussian Department of Science, Art and National Education, the measure informed school leaders that principles of race biology, taught in the spirit of national community, formed the basis for all educational endeavors under the Nazi regime. Biological knowledge and understanding were not to be restricted to the natural sciences but were to permeate all disciplines.[3]

Benze's policy statement prized curriculum integration and a "freedom of movement between individual subjects" over the traditional fragmentation of educational topics in the secondary schools. On the secondary level, two instructional hours for biology were to be offered weekly for males and females even at the expense of mathematics, foreign languages, and other natural sciences. The call for an integrated perspective on race biology brought into focus a number of topics which, when taken collectively, provided opportunities for curriculum writers to integrate multiple elements of racial anti-Semitism. The ministerial counsel stressed that "genetics, race studies, personal hygiene, public hygiene and racial hygiene as well as family studies and population studies" were to be given preference especially in the last four years of the secondary school.[4]

The actual restructuring of the schools, which did not take place until 1937, reflected these expectations. (See appendices for the order of classes and instructional hours for the elementary schools.) *Rassenkunde*, or racial science, was to be the conceptual glue holding most of the curriculum together. Rust's curriculum directive, "Genetics and Racial Science Instruction," which appeared about one month after Benze's order, told curriculum directors and teachers that the schools must preserve the "biological-racial scientific basis of experience for the national community." In classroom discussions of the races of Europe, and especially the racial science of the German people, teachers were reminded about the importance of impressing upon their young charges a principle central to biology instruction. To be stressed with the greatest emphasis was the Nordic racial composition of the present-day German people as opposed to the different bloodlines represented by foreign peoples, especially the Jews.[5]

That this held implications for the study of population politics and family life in the curriculum became evident when Rust discussed the importance of teaching young people how to wisely choose a future spouse. In what became a familiar theme in Nazi language, especially applied to education, the ministry raised the four concepts of race, people, state, and soil as the support for the development of a healthy family life. By definition, this idea of family was based on a biological abhorrence of race mixing to ensure an acceptable genetic and racial composition for future offspring. Nazi curriculum philosophy did not stop there in terms of content focus. Race biology, in conceptualizing the racially healthy family and population policy, connected with other disciplines as well including geography, history, mathematics, and foreign language.[6]

These early curriculum directives, appearing as they did during the early years of the fledgling Third Reich and inspired in part by Hitler's ideas from *Mein Kampf*, provided an ideological framework for future curriculum development in the biological sciences. During the years leading up to the outbreak of the World War II, the Jewish question remained a cogent issue for the definition of the educated person in schools under Hitler's regime. The spirit of Fritz Lenz, Hans F. K. Günther, and earlier Volkish thinkers are evident in the curriculum plans, teacher guides, and textbooks that come under investigation in association with the Jews. Nazi science in school curriculum, as we are about to see, became a handmaiden to all kinds of rationalizations for characterizing Jews as cultural parasites and racial pariahs. Just how the Nazis articulated the Jewish question in race biology is the focal point for this chapter.

The professor from Elbing, whose curriculum ideas on the Jewish question came under scrutiny in the previous chapter, would have something to say about the important place of biology in the curriculum. Like many of his colleagues, Dobers decried the underrepresentation of biology in the curriculum of Weimar Germany.[7] Another aspect of Dobers's background merited attention. Similar to the ministerial counselor Benze, Dobers developed close ties with the SS. He joined the Black Corps as an adviser for research and the teaching of heredity eventually placed under the purview of Section A attached to the office of Reichsführer Heinrich Himmler.[8] In a book edited with Kurt Higelke, a school rector in Berlin, Dobers railed against the dry formation of biology instruction centered on scientific systems and a meaningless emphasis on research procedures. All of biology instruction was to engage the young in a veritable "struggle against hereditary inferiority, a drop in the birth rate, and racial interbreeding."[9] The first four grades of the elementary school would engage children in the integrated study of nature with history and geography. Grades five through eight examined more complex biological issues including the law of species as applied to human beings and the Jewish question. Principles of heredity would be demonstrated through drawing connections between the results of Gregor Mendel's experiments with plant hybridization and the crossbreeding of humans. All of this was aimed at developing an understanding for the necessity of hereditary health laws and the importance of marriage counseling.[10] The Mendelian connection, about which more will be said later, eventually became a major feature for the entire Nazi race biology curriculum.

A curriculum reform more specifically aimed at the elementary schools expounded on the place of *Lebenskunde*, or life sciences. Unlike secondary school studies, which legitimized biology as a single standing subject, the elementary curriculum included general science, which, like history, geography, and German, integrated concepts from racial science. However, race biological thinking in all areas of school studies remained the curriculum ideal under the Third Reich for both levels. A curriculum directive handed down from the RMEWVB in late 1939 reflected the regime's desire to link the study of plant and animal organisms with *Menschenkunde*, or anthropology:

Instruction in life sciences makes known to the child the most important animals and plants and the life of people. It should awaken a joy for the beauty of nature and bring forth an awe for creation and its works. It opens the eyes to essential life events and to general as well as humanly applicable laws leading to anthropological thinking and acting. At the same time, there is to be shown the harmony between the National Socialist attitude to life and nation with the laws of nature from the organic life and the necessity to emphasize insistently and dutifully the preservation and care of the racial values of our people. Heredity brings in the most simplified form the most important teachings about Mendelian laws and germ cells. The meaning of conception, selection, counter selection, and eradication is clarified for the child. Simple observations from plant and animal breeding leads to the application of this knowledge to the heredity of humans. For an under-standing of essential differences between the races and the dangers of race mixing, the basis is to be laid in the study of animals and plants. Consequences for the lives of people and their educational evaluation in the elementary school falls primarily to the teaching of history, German, and geography.[11]

This passage remains an especially important expression of the Nazi cur-riculum vision for the new biology. For the youngest children attending schools, the value of human beings was to be expressed implicitly and explicitly through biological language applied to history and the social sciences. The directive made it abundantly clear to teachers that the kind of anthropology legitimized for Nazi schools was first and foremost rooted in race biology. This intersection of the natural and social sciences defined the nature of racial studies in the school curriculum of the Third Reich. The directive did not mention Jews or any other negative others deemed biological enemies of the state, but the implication was unambiguous. Teaching children the meaning of natural selection and erad-ication in regard to plants and animals invariably, in Nazi pedagogy, implied human volition in the biological manipulation of the races. Thus, the basis for instruction about heredity and race hygiene, initially developed in elementary schools, represented an ideological kingpin in the Nazi curriculum. How these curriculum ideals were translated into actual curriculum in race biology is an issue that demands further attention.

PAUL BROHMER AND THE NEW BIOLOGY

One of the leading figures in the formation of the new biology for Nazi schools was Paul Brohmer (1885–1965), whose professional contributions to biology instruction spanned three historical eras including the Weimar Republic, the Third Reich, and the Federal Republic. Brohmer's ideas represented a the-oretical foundation for Nazi race biology, including the formation of eugenics or racial hygiene. From 1933 to 1940, Brohmer served as a professor of genetics, racial science, biology and methods of teaching nature study at the College for Teacher Education at Kiel. He was also active as the Kiel district NSLB leader on racial political education. To this day, biology educators remember the prolific Brohmer for his pedagogical contributions to the identification of fauna.[12]

Brohmer's own intellectual journey represented a decided shift in his views on the relationship of party politics to biology education. His first notable work, *Inculcating State Consciousness by Practical Education in Biology* (1923), antic-ipated subsequent Nazi perspectives on biology instruction and the organic curriculum. Drawing a relationship between what he called "the cell-state" and the political state, Brohmer conceived the individual citizen as an organism inex-tricably tied to political culture. The pragmatism suggested by the title of Brohmer's work called forth a new way of defining biological knowledge and understanding. Teaching biology was not merely an activity defined by imparting knowledge and scientific insights to youth. Brohmer insisted that biology, by its very nature, was bound up in ethical and ideological questions.[13]

In this volume, readers found one of the most strident voices in support of teaching young people about race hygiene. Instructing pupils about the laws of biology meant very little by itself. The authentic meaning of such laws could only become evident for pupils if they were challenged to think about applying the laws to larger human issues. As friendly as this thinking later became to National Socialist assumptions about biology and the citizen, Brohmer still held a position at this time in his professional life that strongly questioned the role of the state in the schools. From the standpoint of civic education, Brohmer soundly rejected the influence of party politics in the biology classroom. To Brohmer, standing in the Weimar Republic, biology education and party politics occupied two entirely different intellectual spheres. The machinations of party politics could not be grasped with laws from the natural sciences. As we will see, the professor from Kiel eventually performed an ideological *volte-face* as one of the Third Reich's most famous pedagogues on the new biology.[14]

Brohmer was not among those who penned detailed curriculum guides on how to approach the Jewish question. One will not find in his numerous publications the vociferous kind of anti-Semitic language that marked the pedagogical writing of other noted biology educators. Hermann Holle, for example, anticipated the Nazis when he argued in 1925 that a stronger emphasis on biological thinking would serve as a cultural antidote against the mechanistic mind-set of the Jews and reconnect Germans to an inherited love of nature.[15] This does not suggest that racial anti-Semitism was not one of the logical outcomes stemming from Brohmer's articulation of science. To the contrary, Brohmer embraced the thinking of Hans F. K. Günther on the nature of racial degeneration, which, to Günther, was inconceivable without the fear of blood mixing with Jews and other racial undesirables.[16] What best characterized Brohmer's writing was an assumed objective detachment he associated with the scientific mind. Racial anti-Semitism, if it was to become a vital and organic part of the new biology, was best justified and supported with the language of science and not advanced by enflamed emotions.

The legacy of Charles Darwin's ideas on selection and survival of the fittest, later popularized by social Darwinists like Herbert Spencer, presented Brohmer and other Nazi educators with a formidable interpretive challenge. Social Darwinism provided support for Nazi propaganda campaigns warning of the threat of Jewish blood to German population policy. Maintaining the blood laws of the state meant the survival and growth of Nordic cultural heritage with the Jew serving as the eternal enemy and foil for this biological and political process.

The theory of evolution itself presented a different problem. Within the Nazi educational establishment there existed a conflict of opinion over the place of Darwin's theory in the curriculum. Brohmer would play a significant role in the discussions. The prominent Nazi educational theorist Edward Krieck, along with others, remained particularly adamant in their opposition to evolution. Evolution offered a mechanistic view of nature and, moreover, carried an implied biological insult by claiming that humans evolved from lower life forms. Krieck's position sparked a spirited debate in the pages of the professional journal *Der Biologe*. Ferdinand Rossner (1900–1987), a professor at the Female Teacher Training College in Hannover, expressed vigorous disagreement with Krieck's interpretation saying that the concept of evolution remained closely intertwined with the taxonomy of species. The taxonomy provided the basis for the study of racial science and laws on the preservation of species as well as a framework for classifying and comparing the races. Subsequently, Konrad Lorenz, a professor from Vienna and later director of the Institute of Comparative Psychology at Königsberg, took Rossner's response a step further. He observed that evolution not only supported the National Socialist worldview but also emphasized for biologists the fact that human beings were related to other living things. This supposition brought pupils in science education closer to nature. "The logical force of the simple facts of natural science," Lorenz insisted, would do more than anything to win over people to Nazi ideals.[17]

Paul Brohmer came down closest to the thinking of Lorenz on the issue of evolution in biology instruction. He saw in Darwin's work one of the greatest expressions of the human spirit. Brohmer thought it wholly inappropriate for biology teachers to treat Darwinism as a false doctrine. At the same time, the professor from Kiel criticized those who would hold the special thinking of Darwin as absolutely valid and use it as a basis for a National Socialist worldview. Many advancements in research from the natural sciences, including those related to cell biology and developmental physiology, introduced new insights about biological processes. From Brohmer's standpoint, the speculative nature of Darwin's theory of evolution had eventually given way to causal-analytical research. This kind of research method, when supported by anthropological assumptions about culture created under social Darwinism, provided a powerful legitimacy for racial science and its place in the new biology. Brohmer would wield some influence over how biology instruction translated the ideological language of the Third Reich concerning matters of race.[18]

Writing to an audience of teachers and pupils in elementary education, Brohmer tapped race biology as one of the best ways that children could join the community in fighting against a host of "racial sins." His slim volume of sixteen pages outlined the nature and scope of these transgressions against German blood. Like many of his colleagues engaged in writing curriculum, Brohmer used the Nuremberg Laws of 1935 as a justification for harsh measures taken against those who crossed the racial line. Among the items on the list of racial transgressions was miscegenation with the Jews, called "sins against the law of race." Married couples without children were guilty of "sins against the law of species preservation." Against the backdrop of offenses against the law of heredity, Brohmer defended the compulsory sterilization of criminals, alcoholics, and those suffering from hereditary illnesses. Jews, and all others deemed enemies of the state, carried the charge of criminality and thus fell under this broad category.[19]

Pupils also learned about the importance of the law to restore the professional civil service as a bulwark against Marxists and Jews. How Brohmer conceived of instructing youth on the ideal Nazi society came in closing remarks. Marxism, in contradicting the laws of nature and community life through its support of the workers' right to strike, created an economy harmful to the racial community. The model economy conceived by National Socialism was more holistic and organic in nature since the people existed as an organism. Each racially conscious citizen was responsible for carrying out a specific duty in service to the whole while acting dependently on the whole community. Each person, whether among the workers, followers, leaders, engineers, or others, remained of equal importance to the state. The organic conception of citizenship advanced by National Socialism made superfluous the misguided idea of class struggle. The crass materialism of Marxism and its Jewish cohorts became history. A new age dawned.[20]

The concept of *Lebensgemeinschaft*, so central to Brohmer's ideas about institutionalizing the new biology in the elementary school setting, meant in Nazi parlance a symbiotic community in which people from the same racial family lived together in harmony. This organic community was real since its identity was drawn from nature and defined by the laws of race as opposed to the mechanistic and illusory world represented by *Gesellschaft*, or society which reflected the empty values of commercialism and modernity. Brohmer joined other thinkers who saw in Nazism a means of restoring an authentic sense of community that had been destroyed through the horrific experience of World War I. Race ideology, supported by a curriculum integrating biological principles and the pronouncements of racial science, would offer prescribed answers to the omnipresent question about what it meant to be human. Beginning as early as the eighth and last year of the elementary school, pupils in Brohmer's curriculum vision engaged themselves in the study of racial anthropology conceived in intimate connection with biology. Leading up to this study was a science curriculum beginning in the fifth year that initiated a study of life sciences using a cluster of instructional thematics. Fifth-year pupils examined biological relationships evidenced in and around home and playground, street, factory, and park. Pupils in the sixth year studied garden, meadow, beech woods, and marshland. The focus for the seventh year shifted to field, sea, and lake.[21]

Trying to pull children and their teachers away from a traditional reliance on textbooks to legitimize school knowledge, Brohmer placed a higher value on the power of observation in forming a more racially conscious youth through biology in the elementary schools:

> We are not teaching out of a book. Therefore, do not teach lessons about heredity, race, and racial hygiene according to one of the countless themes which, during the last era, joined biology school books on the book market in great numbers. Rather, we basically build our teaching on actual observation and on the experiments of pupils. This applies not only for genetics, family science and racial science as well as racial hygiene, but also for all special areas of biology. We do not want completeness and no overview of the current situation in biology, rather we seek to lead the pupils to recording the important laws of life. With that, the purely theoretical laws are of lesser importance than those which come into question regarding attitudes toward life and life style.[22]

The important place of character education suggested by this passage for pupils in the elementary schools of the New Germany remains worthy of note. Biology and racial science, one Nazi pedagogue wrote, were also significant in forming the character and values of young Germans since they represented the keys to understanding world events.[23] The introduction of racial hygiene, perhaps more than any other element of the biology curriculum, symbolized a constellation of racial and anti-Semitic attitudes and values about Jews. Although the Nazis certainly were not the first to introduce race hygiene as a matter of public policy, they were the first to legitimize the subject as part of school curriculum using the Jews, Sinti, and Roma as well as the mentally ill and handicapped as target groups. Paul Brohmer, as previously noted, helped establish a pedagogical framework for the introduction of biological concepts in the general science curriculum of the lower grades. Racial hygiene, with all of its implications for understanding heredity and genetics as well as racial anti-Semitism, will come under more specific scrutiny later in this chapter. Brohmer will be among those contributing. The study now turns to a more micro perspective through the examination of one particular science curriculum devoted to the upper grades of the elementary school. The work of Alfred Vogel symbolized the union of history and biology in the teaching of race education.

SCHOOLING FOR A NEW MYTHOS: RACE, ANTI-SEMITISM, AND THE CURRICULUM OF ALFRED VOGEL

The recent discovery of a previously uncatalogued collection of Nazi school materials in the Special Collections at Hofstra University (Long Island) uncovered a number of books and teaching charts written for race education in the *Volksschule*. The entire Henry Kroul Collection of Nazi Writings at Hofstra, of which the school materials are but a part, numbers some 370 pieces. Henry Kroul, a U.S. Army intelligence officer with the Office of Strategic Services, assembled the materials from a number of German libraries at the close of World War II while attached to forward bases. The books eventually arrived at a bookstore in the Catskill Mountains owned by Kroul's wife where they remained until sold to Hofstra in 1969. The collection remained untouched for twenty years until catalogued by the author in the summer of 1989. About one-third of the volumes still revealed the institutional stamp from the school libraries or Nazi Party organizations where they originated. Most frequently found in these books were stamps from the academic reading room at the University of Göttingen, the Reich Institute for the History of the New Germany, and teachers' reference collections at schools in Münster, Bad Sooden Allendorf, Metz, Kassel, and Witzenhausen.

Of greatest significance for the present study were a rare series of teaching charts on anti-Semitism intended for classroom instruction from the Kroul Collection and the Library of Congress. The title page of Vogel's book *Erblehre und rassenkunde in bildlicher Darstellung* (*Teachings on Heredity and Racial Science*), which appeared in 1938, was stamped with identification from the library of the NSLB.[24] The charts authored by Alfred Vogel remained part of a collection of seventy-one teaching diagrams using visuals, text, and statistics published by National Literature in Stuttgart. Many of Vogel's anti-Semitic teaching charts were profusely illustrated using the latest technology in color printing under the hand of the artist Eberhard Brauchle. Our purpose is to examine the significance of this collection, complete with accompanying text, within the larger framework of Nazi race biology.

Schools embodied but one foundation within the larger Nazi institutional framework imbued with the task of advancing a racist and anti-Semitic ideology. This position does not minimize the function of political socialization in the elementary schools under the Third Reich but merely assumes that one school or race curriculum author cannot be held up as a conclusive or generalizable model characterizing all of race instruction in Hitlerian Germany. What is apparent in examining Vogel's curriculum in race eugenics is that his writing for teachers and pupils was wholly consistent with the official Nazi educational policy on race instruction and the emphasis placed by the regime on the predominant position of biology in the natural sciences.[25]

Vogel's teaching charts on anti-Semitism crossed history and biology instruction. These charts served as a companion to the volume *Erblehre und Rassenkunde fur die Grund- und Hauptschule* (Baden: Konkordia, 1937), a teacher's text written for instructors in the elementary schools. A close examination of his work should build a greater understanding of how one Nazi race educator articulated anti-Semitism for the classrooms of Nazi schools. Vogel published his work while maintaining his position as *Rektor*, or headmaster, of a *Volksschule* in Baden.

The work of Nazi race educators, as suggested previously, did not come to fruition in a political or social vacuum. At the same time, classroom materials in the form of textbooks and visual aids on race education did not suddenly appear in German schools immediately after Hitler's rise to power on 30 January 1933. Textbooks bearing the race ideology promoted by the Nazi Ministry of Education for elementary and secondary schools were not wholly integrated into the classroom until the last Weimar-era schoolbooks were removed in 1938. This did not pose any immediate ideological difficulties for the Nazis since many Weimar history textbooks, for example, continued on the tradition of nationalistic historical writing for school curriculum carried over from the *Kaiserreich*.[26]

Vogel's writings and teaching charts appeared some four to five years after the *Machtergreifung* at a time when Hitler was in the initial stages of restructuring the German school system. Race biology constituted the major focus in the newly revised curriculum for the natural sciences in the *Volkschule*. As school rector, Vogel published the accompanying teacher resource book in 1937. The anti-Semitic teaching charts were to be used in tandem with the book for grades four through eight. Major aspects of Vogel's pedagogical thinking in the teacher text are examined in order to provide a framework for a subsequent investigation of the anti-Semitic teaching charts.

Teachers reading Vogel's book were urged to instruct the next generation of German youth in the biological laws of nature rooted in race consciousness and a Volkish perspective on history. Hereditary biology and racial science, the author insisted, were the cornerstones in a sound National Socialist education charged with the preservation of the larger *Blutgemeinschaft*, or community of blood.[27] Pupils entering the fourth and fifth years devoted a great share of their studies to experiments in color variation and cross-pollination conducted by the nineteenth-century monk Gregor Mendel. The words *Mischlinge* (a term with negative, racist connotations meaning "half-breed" in the lexicon of National Socialism) and *bastardization* appeared frequently in the prescribed lessons. Vogel used the two terms in an attempt to draw an association between cross-breeding in plant biology and the development of race in human culture. The *Rektor* encouraged instructors to continually reinforce the notion that Mendel's experiments actually demonstrated the weakening of plant life through cross-breeding.[28]

The word of the instructor would not simply be handed down to the young charges in the traditional form of lecture. Vogel directed school officials to establish a *Rassenecke*, or race corner, in the school garden in order to conduct experiments on various plants for the direct observation of pupils. The association was also not lost on the social institution of the German family. Vogel used the familial terms "children," "parents," and "grandparents" in illustrating a three-tier generational chart on leaf development in the text. He included a brief commentary on the strengths of the *reinrassige*, or purebred plants, versus the less desirable *Mischlinge*.[29]

The race educator then extended his perspective to the "hidden tendencies" in the heredity of biological life forms. The words given here serve as a foundation for Vogel's later discussion of the handicapped and Jews in the blood community of Nazi culture:

> The *Mischlinge* deceive us through their outward appearance. Next to their visible structure, they possess hidden tendencies. These are also inherited. We differentiate between heredity and the visible characteristics of the organism. The two are not the same. One therefore can never pre-judge a living thing according to visible characteristics. The most important factor is heredity. One can not see from the outward aspects of the living thing which inherited tendencies have been hidden.[30]

A curious contradiction arose from Vogel's biological pronouncements. In one part of his text, Vogel devoted almost six pages of narrative and drawings to explaining how "the six German races" possessed certain skull shapes. This step into phrenology, with its dominant emphasis on physical shape and measurement, does not logically follow his assertion that one should not prejudge living organisms on outer, visible characteristics.[31]

The most direct pedagogical consequences of this argument can be seen in the instruction for classes seven and eight. Table 3.1 shows the table of contents from Vogel's teaching volume listing curriculum topics.[32]

Vogel's instructional text, like his teaching charts under subsequent examination, reflected a pedagogical support for the anti-Semitic policies of the Nazi state. The integration of race biology under Vogel's pen also formed a subtle rationale for the practice of euthanasia on the mentally ill, blind, and infirm. Vogel told his readers that the Prussian state paid some 125 Reichmarks per year to support one "normal" child attending the elementary school. A child born blind required funding from the state amounting to 500 Reichmarks on an annual basis. Even more serious to Vogel was the possibility that the offspring of the handicapped would continue as wards of the state and eventually drain Prussian coffers. Although Vogel did not specifically advocate outright euthanasia as an instrument of national policy, less than subtle suggestions toward that conclusion were evident. The German race, he told educators, must be kept pure from these detrimental elements.[33]

German history also became a vehicle for Vogel's race biology. A brief generational history of the Siemens family, known for its development of the electrotechnical industry, was held up as a model to emulate. The success of the Siemenses stemmed not from German business tradition but from the "inner

Table 3.1
Table of Contents
Heredity and Race Science
ALFRED VOGEL
1937

Table of Contents from Alfred Vogel, *Erblehre und Rassenkunde für die Grund-
und Hauptschule* (*Heredity and Race Science for the Elementary and Main
School*), Baden: Konkordia, 1937, pp. 33–34.

hereditary character" and pure genes of the family.[34] Deemed even more appropriate as racial models for the New Order were "great statesmen and soldiers"
like Hitler, Bismarck, and von Moltke as well as the Teutonic knights from the
Middle Ages who sought conquest and settlement of the East. The latter
theme of eastern expansion was clearly drawn from Hitler's own ideas in
Mein Kampf.[35] Adding to this pantheon of heroes were the bearers of German
cultural life in the legacies of Goethe, Schiller, Mozart, and Wagner. "The strong
and capable," Vogel reminded the next generation, "died on the battlefield
and at their work."[36]
   Vogel saved some of his most vociferous language for the creation of anti-
Semitic lessons in the eighth class. Building on previous themes, Vogel reminded
teachers that bastardization and race mixing were biological developments with
serious consequences for the survival of German culture. What held for the plant
and animal kingdoms also held true for the German body politic. The Jews, he
maintained, offered the most extreme example of any cultural group in history. Denying that the Jews were a race, Vogel went on to condemn a growing
Jewish influence in German economic life (the Rothschild family), politics
(Walther Rathenau), cultural life (80 percent of all theatre directors in Berlin

were Jewish in 1933), and the professions (Jews made up 48 percent of lawyers in the Reich). Moreover, the "Red Flood" inspired by the Russian Bear to the East linked Marxist party politics to such Jewish notables as Ferdinand Lassalle, Rosa Luxemburg, and Wilhelm Liebknecht. These are some of the dark themes developed with even greater force in the words and visuals used by Vogel in the teaching charts accompanying the text. In closing the narrative in the final section titled "Nazi Race Thinking and the Volk," the headmaster presented educators with an ominous portent for the future of Germany: "Our people will again become racially healthy."[37]

THE VOGEL TEACHING CHARTS

Alfred Vogel apparently was not satisfied with following one of the traditional German didactical paths in the education of classroom teachers. Unlike most other contemporary race educators who were content with remaining within the boundaries of a textbook, Vogel extended race theory from the confines of textbook narrative to a series of images and quotations in highlighted charts. The picture presented here centers on the latter part of Vogel's collection intended for classes seven and eight and identified under the heading of *Rassenkunde*, or racial science, the most overtly anti-Semitic part of his curriculum. In one of the popular Nazi lexicons of the period, *Rassenkunde* is defined as the "science of the races of mankind, their characteristics and their history."[38] Racial science thus brought in its train strong anthropological and historical dimensions, all of which, as we will see with even greater clarity in Vogel's teaching charts, remained important elements in framing racial anti-Semitism. As witnessed before in the curriculum guides on the Jewish question, Vogel's anti-Semitic thinking freely exploited both contemporary science and anthropology as well as traditional economic stereotypes to advance his pedagogical message.

In the foreword to the collection of teaching charts, Vogel insisted that the drawings created for the race eugenics curriculum were not only appropriate for elementary schools but perfectly suited for pupils in the secondary school classroom as well. Educators serious about advancing race eugenics in the schools of the Third Reich, Vogel remarked, would discover "a new way of teaching" departing from the old recitation methods of the past. Moreover, rejection of the Jews would remain the centerpiece of the new race eugenics curriculum. Still, Vogel made it very clear that he was not wholly at peace with the form and scope of curriculum development in racial science thus far:

> The main goal must be knowledge of the racial value of our people and the tireless struggle over the preservation of our racial character. The concise allocation of instructional time can not be overly concerned with the detailed examination of the individual races of our people and the mechanical cramming [*Einpaukung*] of countless racial characteristics thus leading to a loss of perspective for our people in its entirety. Much more important is a corresponding focus on the energetic life. It is therefore through the selected instructional materials, especially those concerning the racial character of our people and the emphasis placed on the rootedness

of German cultural achievement, that one counters opposition to foreign races, especially the Jewish people. This must be the best way to educate our young in the present and future struggle for the complete rejection [*zur völligen Ablehnung*] of the Jews.[39]

The teaching visuals for the eighth class would not represent the first overt anti-Semitic aspect of Vogel's curriculum. In a unit of study on hereditary blood diseases, members of the fifth class (age ten/eleven) were told in a series of generational diagrams that Jews were eight times more likely to contract blood diseases than the general population of the Reich. Imitating a practice assumed by Fritz Fink and taken up in later classes, Vogel subverted the meaning of the Talmud. In this same chart, Vogel pointedly ridiculed Jewish laws pertaining to circumcision.[40]

Pupils completing the sixth and seventh classes heard the prediction that without the benevolent population policies of the Third Reich and a revision of the birthrate among "racially healthy families," some 77 percent of all German racial stock would be represented primarily by racially inferior families with four or more children in the next hundred years. Included among the qualities of the inferior family structure were drunkenness, propensity toward criminal behavior, mental illness, physical handicaps and Jewish blood.[41] Omitted from discussion were details of what actually constituted Nazi population policy beyond the public campaign for a higher birthrate among Aryan women. Great German men, Vogel wrote, came from large families. He cited Albrecht Dürer (born second of eighteen children), Immanuel Kant (fourth of nine), Wolfgang Amadeus Mozart (seventh of seven), Frederick the Great (fourth of fourteen), Bismarck (fourth of six) and Werner Siemens (fourth of fourteen.) Left out of this gathering of heroes were any Nazi leaders, an omission all the more noteworthy when Vogel told readers that "out of our people blessed with children have grown men who moved the world."[42]

The succeeding chart titled, "Expenditures for Hereditary Diseases: Social Effects," showed a drawing of a school for the mentally ill at Ettlingen with the inscription that annual expenditures for the institution amounted to 104,000 Reichmarks. The adjoining drawing depicted an orderly village of some seventeen private homes owned by families of workers, presumably requiring the same total cost as the annual budget for the school. The theme of wasteful state social programs was one which Vogel stressed with additional examples in the text for teachers. The last line printed on the chart reads: "Hereditary disease is a burden to the state."[43] Closing the lesson for the seventh class, Vogel declared to teachers and pupils that Germany "must once again become a land of children" while singing the praises of rising birthrates initiated under National Socialism.[44] In the eighth class, the end of formal education for the vast majority of young Germans in the Third Reich, Vogel clarified in a most direct way whose children alone would be accepted for citizenry in the new racially conscious Nazi state.

The images and language developed by Vogel for the *Rassenkunde* curriculum and the charges populating German classrooms included almost all of the dominant anti-Semitic stereotypes that existed in European culture since the time of the Middle Ages. There is a force in Vogel's use of imagery in this stage of the curriculum that one does not find in the printed word of his accompanying teacher text. Yet, of all sections devoted to the race eugenics curriculum in this collection of teaching charts, Vogel recorded the most detailed commentaries on teaching methods for *Rassenkunde*, the last section of the curriculum encompassed by the remaining twenty visuals in the program. In the teacher notes for the section titled "The German People and the Jews," Vogel informed educators that they had a racial mission to accomplish in the classroom. His chilling words came some four years before the Wannsee Conference of 25 January 1942 that set down plans for the Final Solution:

> Just as the Führer on the Reich Party Day in 1936 exposed the Jews for all the world to see as the mortal enemy of the German people, one can not separate the race question from the Jewish question in classroom teaching. In the following pages, moreover, the conflict between the Jewish people and the Jews and the blood distinction between the two groups will be brought out. Therefore, the youth must know the danger of the Jews for our people in order that they will reject everything Jewish with complete unanimity.[45]

In two of the charts, Vogel identified what he felt were the six archetypes of German racial superiority and detailed the dominant physical characteristics of each group through the color of skin, eyes, and hair as well as facial features and body size.[46] The photographs used to demonstrate these features preceded the publication of another chart in the series that differentiated Jewish children from "German" children through a series of additional pictures. The chart, "German Youth–Jewish Youth" provided pupils in the *Volksschule* with images exemplifying acceptable and unacceptable racial qualities among children ranging in ages from seven through fourteen. This part of the collection is especially profound in that the three Jewish children shown in the photographs probably died in the concentration camps. Below the pictures of two seven-year-old boys, one exemplifying the blond Nordic race and the other the Jewish community, was written a Volkish assertion: "From the face speaks the soul of the race."[47]

As with every generation, decisions were made by the elders concerning acceptable cultural heroes for the adoration and imitation of the young. Contributions of Jews to the fields of science, art, music, and literature were ignored. Among others, Wagner, Beethoven, Luther, Goethe, Kant, Zeppelin, and Siemens served as models of resourcefulness and the fountainhead of German cultural identity. Those looking for evidence of the theory of relativity, the brainchild of Albert Einstein, were most likely disappointed. Vogel's pattern was not unique. A physics textbook intended for boys from grades six through eight completely overlooked the accomplishments of Einstein and his theory of relativity in a section on the history of research in physics.[48]

Although the mass deportation of German Jews to the concentration camps did not begin until 14 October 1941, some three years after these charts first appeared, the assumptions contained therein provided a rationalization for the mass murder to come. In the "Racial Composition of the Jews," Vogel reproduced a map of the Middle East and a series of drawings showing the faces of Jews of various mixed racial origins. Among the occupations combining to form this "strange Near Eastern, Oriental, Hamitic and Negroid race" were the traders and nomads of the world.[49]

In the subsequent chart, "German Ways–Jewish Ways," a peasant is represented in a drawing planting seed as "a secure German who loves his Fatherland." (See plate 2.) A Jewish man, dressed in a long black coat and using a cane, walks the face of the earth: "The always restless Jew wanders from one people to another." The bottom of the drawing places a well-dressed Jewish banker holding a stock certificate in one hand and a bag of money in another. He stands between a German farmer holding a scythe on his right and a foundry worker standing in front of a factory with a steel maul on his left. The description below the men reads: "The German works, the Jew rests." The image calls to mind the highly visible Nazi propaganda campaign "to put Jews back to work" by forcing them to scrub sidewalks in public view.[50]

One of the anti-Semitic ideals that Vogel took great pains to develop was the subsequent historical degeneration of German life stemming from a measure written by a Prussian minister in 1812 granting Jews citizenship. In the "Equality of the Jews in the 18th and 19th Centuries," Vogel included this measure along with the French Revolution and the presence of the "unbaptized" Jews in the National Assembly of 1848 on a timeline. Yet even here, Vogel did not strictly follow the party line. Nazi race policy remained adamant in its rejection of baptized Jews as well since citizenship was defined on the basis of bloodlines, not religious identification. A Jew remained a Jew on this basis. Nazi officials, for example, hounded diocesan and parish offices of the Catholic Church to uncover records identifying Jews who received the sacrament. Still, even with this qualification, the thrust of Vogel's message to pupils was the same. Where once monied Jews during the Middle Ages were "favorites, advisers, and dictators" in princely courts, Jews in the twentieth century virtually ruled the modern industrial state of Germany. Vogel used drawings symbolizing the world of politics, finance, and the media to relate Jewish institutional control.[51]

Using stereotypical drawings of a well-dressed Jew and a German worker, Vogel manipulated statistics on occupations to expand on the theme of "Jewish Rule over Germany, 1918–1933." In a slam against the Weimar Republic, Vogel used percentages to demonstrate a series of discrepancies in the German population as a whole and the Jewish community. Figures on employment in farming and forestry, for example, showed that 1.74 percent of Jews were engaged in these occupations contrasted with 29 to 47 percent in the total "German" population. The situation was reversed in trade and transportation where the percentage of Jews (58.80) was more than three times higher than the percentage of Germans (17.11.) If Vogel's statements were believed, Jews would have a disproportionate control over medicine, civil service, and trade, but were underrepresented in the "labor of the hands." Once again, as was standard practice for many Nazi curriculum writers, Vogel conveniently omitted any mention of the source for his statistical claims.[52]

In the map "Jews Overflow Germany—Germans Emigrate," Vogel depicted huge numbers of Jews from foreign lands, especially eastern Europe, entering the Reich while 390,000 "valuable German people," shown leaving their plows and factories behind, are lost forever to the fatherland. In an image as old as anti-Semitism itself, the Jews are shown as stateless intruders dressed in black with suitcases in hand marked with the cultural label of the *Fremdstättige*, or "foreign born" people alien to the German body politic.[53]

As a further way of supporting the teacher text, Vogel printed a copy of the painting *Kriegskrüppel* (War cripples) by the Jewish artist Otto Dix for the chart "The Jew Falsifies German Art." Like the novel *All Quiet on the Western Front* by Erich Marie Remarque and his fellow artist George Grosz, Dix called attention to the futility of the Great War. The position was antithetical to the canons of National Socialism that glorified war as a way of establishing *Lebensraum* and purifying the race.[54] In quoting from *Mein Kampf*, Vogel accused the Jews of "destroying all concepts of beauty and solemnity, of nobility and goodness."[55]

Nowhere else in this sordid gathering of images for race didactics does one find a more detailed set of written anti-Semitic pronouncements than in the "Jewish Secret Law Book." Writing in the anti-Semitic spirit of Fritz Fink and Julius Streicher, Vogel once gain exploited an old conspiracy theory through completely subverting the meaning of the Talmud. The race educator drew an open volume of the Talmud with the words "Murder, war, betrayal, revolution" on the left page. The right page reads, "Lies, deceit, defilement, profiteering." To accentuate the conspiracy theory, already heightened by the Nazi revival of the forgery the *Protocols of the Elders of Zion,* Vogel recorded what he felt were eight secrets from the Talmud to be perpetrated on the world by the Jews.[56] (See plate 3.)

The seventy-third teaching chart in Vogel's curriculum is itself a model of Nazi anti-Semitic propaganda. Accentuating the Jew once again as negative other, Vogel skillfully exploited the traditional Christian rejection of Jewish culture and theology. There was much more to this use of Nazi language. What greater insult could one perpetrate than to imply that the sacred law books of the rejected minority culture, steeped in moral theology, were themselves models of lawlessness and moral degradation? Vogel's words came into print the same year that copies of the Talmud were burned and strewn in the streets of Germany in the wake of the Night of the Broken Glass. The schoolmaster's manner of expression would offer pupils reasons why Jews were to be mistrusted and, more seriously, hated. Departing from many other Nazi curriculum writers, Vogel saw the intrinsic propaganda value of uniting the power of the word with image. Below an image of an open volume from the Talmud, Vogel recorded eight quotations from "Jewish law" that defined Jewish immorality. (See table 3.2.)

The conspiracy theme introduced in Vogel's pictorial rendition of the Talmud extended to "Jews–Free Masonry: World Politics, World Revolution." The European continent is shown with various revolutions marked by year and location followed by the words: "Free Masonry is a Jewish, international organization with the political goal of gaining control through world revolution." Moscow is termed "the Internationale of World Bolshevism." On top of the chart, a sextant is drawn with a Star of David, and they are flanked by a Jewish temple on the left and the Apron of Free Masons on the right.[57] Such teaching aids as these reinforced the traditional anti-Semitic view of the Jew as the great destabilizer while, at the same time, reviving fears of the Bolshevist threat made even more ominous by its secretive nature.

The chart titled "Mixed Marriages Between Germans and Jews" accentuated Vogel's earlier notion that the *Mischlinge* from these unions would harm the

Table 3.2

"The Jewish Secret Law Book:
Hear What the Talmud Speaks!"
Vogel, *Erblehre und Rassenkunde*, 1938

"The Jews alone were to be called human. Non-Jews were however not to be called human, but called animals instead."

"Whoever eats with a non-Jew eats with a dog."

"The most honest among the non-Jews is to be killed."

"It is a commandment for the Jews that they must make great effort to destroy everything that is associated with the Christian Church."

"What does Mount Sinai mean? It signifies a mountain from which all of the hatred of the world is spread."

"The Jew may not follow the laws of the state. He is to follow the laws of the Jews which would of course make the laws of the state rather superfluous."

"If a Jew defrauded and stole from a non-Jew and he must take an oath (in court), he may swear falsely if he is certain that the perjury will not be discovered. It therefore follows that a Jew saves himself from death through perjury. At the same time, he may swear falsely whether the perjury is discovered or not."

"The Jews teach five things: First, love one another. Second, love robbery. Third, love excess. Fourth, hate your master. Fifth, never speak the truth."

Translated text from teaching chart #73, "The Jewish Secret Law Book," Vogel, *Erblehre und Rassenkunde in bildlicher Darstellung* (*Heredity and Race Science in Pictorial Depictions*). Stuttgart: National Literatur, 1938).

German race. Using a rural/urban motif, Vogel offered statistics to show an increase in mixed German/Jewish marriages in Berlin form 553 in 1926 to 712 in 1928. The lower section included a diagram relating different degrees of racial mixing in marriages from the rural village "Dorfe L." Again, Vogel relied on *Mein Kampf* to legitimize his work. The onset of physical and intellectual regression and "progressive infirmity" from mixed racial marriages spelled the inevitable decline of German civilization.[58]

The negative legacy of the *Mischlinge* in nature, a biological development Vogel introduced as early as the first class, also held a position of some importance in the charts drawn up for pupils in the last year of the *Volksschule*. Vogel already subverted the work of Gregor Mendel when he argued that crossbreeding plants usually led to a weakening of plant life. He would consistently extend this faulty conclusion not only to the Jews but also to the human community at large. In a starkly simple set of visuals, Vogel reproduced a series of photographs showing the offspring of mixed marriages between Germans, Blacks, Chinese, and Jews with an enjoinder from *Mein Kampf* that all great cultures from the past perished because the original creative race died out from poisoning of the blood lines.[59]

In the concluding section of the curriculum, "Cultivation of Race in the Third Reich," Vogel formed a series of three charts recounting the dominant legal measures concluded by the Nazi state to subjugate the Jews. Unidentified statistical sources were tapped to graphically demonstrate to pupils the definite results of the Aryan Paragraph, the legislation written to "cleanse" the professions of the Jewish presence. Vogel could report that after 1934, 121 Jewish attorneys in Frankfurt am Main, or 44 percent of the entire legal profession in that city, were summarily dismissed from the practice of law. The Nuremberg Laws for the Protection of German Blood from 1935, which Vogel reprinted on a map of Germany, created the illusion of a benevolent Nazi state determined to preserve German blood and civilization from the threat of Judaism.[60]

The last chart in Vogel's series foreshadowed the imminent mass destruction of the Jews. Using the heading "Avoid the Jews," Vogel integrated drawings urging doctors to buy only from Aryan grocers and to "visit only German doctors." (See plate 4.) Farmers were warned that in history "wherever Jews ruled, so also died the farmer." In a last attempt to resurrect the threat of Jewish conspiracy, Vogel quoted from the *Protocols of the Elders of Zion*: "In our [the Jews'] hands one finds mountains of money. From it, we have created a sea of blood and tears." Similar to his work in subverting the Talmud earlier in the curriculum, Vogel falsified a Jewish commandment when he claimed that all Jewish doctors were duty bound not to treat a non-Jewish person suffering from a life-threatening illness or injury.[61]

The biology curriculum developed by Alfred Vogel through printed word and illustration conformed closely to the official Nazi pronouncements on the formation of studies for the racially conscious German *Volksschule*. The National Socialists, buoyed by the loyalty of such educators as Alfred Vogel, saw in the classroom another means of extending racist ideology into the political socialization of German youth. Vogel obviously was not alone in this endeavor. His contribution remained important because of his attempt to blend Nazi ideas on racial anti-Semitism with the language of propaganda through word and image. In the field of race hygiene, central to the pedagogical identity of Nazi schooling, others would vigorously advance the mission of racial anti-Semitism.

RACE HYGIENE AND THE NEW BIOLOGY

Race hygiene, as interpreted by National Socialism, directly implied that some races were superior to others. Originally defined by Alfred Ploetz in 1895 as the "science of the optimal preservation and development of the race," the idea of race hygiene took on an air of greater scientific legitimacy when it became closely associated with eugenics during the Weimar Republic.[62] This was not the conception of eugenics originated by Francis Galton in 1883. Galton conceived of eugenics as a science that studied the favorable living conditions of genetically healthy families and their care. To dedicated geneticists under the Third Reich like Fritz Lenz or Hans Günther, such a conception of eugenics, by itself, made little sense since it failed to take into account the preservation and care of certain racial elements of a people as opposed to others falling under the classification of racial undesirables.[63] Even in the late nineteenth century, fears about the influx of *Ostjuden* were already part of the German cultural landscape. Fritz Lenz, as noted earlier, played a central role in the articulation of race hygiene not only during the Weimar era but even more so under the Nazis as a member of the Kaiser Wilhelm Institute.

Used interchangeably by the Nazis, race hygiene and eugenics came to be closely associated with the dynamics of population policy through the control of human mating and racial classification.[64] Nazi language itself revealed the prominence accorded to the ideal of racial purity that defined the scope and purpose of race hygiene. The Nazi lexicon integrated at least twenty-five compound words using race as the root, many of which related directly or indirectly to the necessity of maintaining strict boundaries between Germans and racial undesirables like the Jews along with Sinti and Roma.[65] Therefore, it was not difficult to understand why the Nuremberg Laws of 1935 assumed such a preeminent position of authority in Nazi curriculum plans on race education. Race hygiene in schools, and in other institutions like medicine and law, foreshadowed horrific consequences for the Jewish community and all other peoples whose racial classification fell outside the Nazi definition of citizenship.

As reflected in the curriculum of Alfred Vogel, race hygiene was not exclusively conceived from a biological perspective. History and geography, interpreted in racial terms, were also significant since they provided a further means of legitimizing the estrangement of the races. To return to Brohmer, another qualification supported race hygiene as part of the Nazi definition of the educated person. Beneath all of the learning about eugenics was an even more important long-range goal, that of taking action in the biotic community to preserve the race. To Brohmer, the elementary school would become the first proving ground for educating racially conscious youth and eugenics would become the curricular vehicle. There was an almost desperate kind of Romantic idealism in Brohmer's words to educators, words that called forth Germans to reaffirm blood relations in the larger community. He also revealed a sharp philosophical opposition to certain pedagogical traditions in helping pupils reach this ideal:

> It is not so much a question of making a student knowledgeable on all questions of eugenics, but of creating motives for his action. If the emphasis on the ideology of the biotic community creates a sense of belonging to our people and state, then racial eugenics creates the will to struggle, body and soul, for the growth and health of this biotic community. He [the student] will see Germany as his living space and himself as a link in the German biotic community and the German destiny; and he must regard all Germans as his blood relations, his brothers. If we reach this goal, then all party and class divisions sink into nothingness and more is accomplished for education in citizenship than is done by studying governmental and administrative structures . . . Not one elementary school pupil should leave school without having internalized the iron command that he is the only link in the chain of his ancestors and descendants and the carrier of the future generation.[66]

Writing in this same spirit three years before, Brohmer traced his own ideological heritage to the geneticist Fritz Lenz and his pathbreaking text on human genetics and racial hygiene. Perhaps more than any other figure in the circle of Nazi scientists, Lenz saw in the Nazi political agenda the means and will to equate the two terms in building community. Brohmer's introductory remarks on race hygiene from a teacher text on biology instruction, published the year Hitler came to power, reflected Lenz's unmistakable influence originating in the Weimar era. At one with Lenz, Brohmer took on the mantle of science in the name of the elementary school curriculum. This was not a science, according to the professor from Kiel, steeped in details of intellectual education of little value in building a genuine sense of racial community. "Still much more important," he concluded, "is education over the individual will which places itself in the service of the biological health and the strengthening of the entire people." Moreover, race hygiene, at least in the beginning of a child's studies, had little to do with hygiene associated with one or more of the races, but rather focused on the recovery of the community's racial health.[67]

This explained why overt racial anti-Semitism in the elementary curriculum remained uneven. Brohmer rarely mentioned the Jews. Others, like Vogel, devoted themselves to integrating anti-Semitism into the seventh or eighth year of studies. Children's literature, as will be noted in the last chapter, introduced young children to anti-Semitic storylines as early as the third grade in the elementary school. In a pattern eerily similar to the timing of Nazi policy on the treatment of the mentally ill, Jews, and Sinti and Roma, Brohmer advocated the following curriculum plan for race hygiene. Drawing on his own passion for plant biology, Brohmer pushed a parallel that defined an essential organic principle of Nazi race education:

> While a merciless eradication in free nature takes place in the struggle for existence among inferior plants and animals, the culture of humans pushes a counter selection in which the weak are protected and cared for. We are far from handing down the tradition of ancient Sparta in which the weak children are set outside to die. No serious race hygenicist wants to return to such barbaric customs and it would definitely cheapen Christian compassion for the homes established for the crippled, deaf mutes, blind, the feeble minded, and mentally ill. It is another question if such unfortunates should further reproduce and through this bequeath their suffering to their offspring. In the case of war, the inferiors stayed at home, while the best members of the national community were exposed to death. Pursuant to this is the fact that the inferiors, especially the mentally ill have, on the average, reproduced at a stronger rate than those who are among the hereditary healthy.[68]

While not mentioning the Jews as a focal point for race hygiene, the implications inherent in Brohmer's question about the place of racial inferiors in Nazi society as a whole still merit special attention. At stake was the status not only of the mentally ill but anyone else defined as enemies of the state. Brohmer published these observations in 1933, the same year that the Nazis set up Hereditary Health Courts to support forced sterilization and some six years before the institution of the infamous T-4 killings legitimizing the murder of those suffering from hereditary and mental illnesses. The technology used in the creation of gas chambers in places like the mental hospitals at Hadmar and Bernberg eventually found its way to Auschwitz under the supervision of SS medical personnel.[69]

In a general sense, Brohmer's emphasis on informing pupils about the burden of racial inferiors on the state followed the initial order of Nazi policy. One of the first official acts of the Nazi government was to initiate the process leading to sterilization of racial undesirables. Brohmer kept much of his attention in race hygiene centered on the hereditary and mentally ill while mentioning Jews only infrequently. The point here was that the "unfortunates" whose further existence he called into question as unreasonable burdens for the state would shortly be joined by another group of negative others, the Jews. While he did not directly advocate a policy of state-sponsored murder of any groups, there lurked behind Brohmer's question the implication that people judged as racial outsiders had to be removed by some means.

Teachers reading Brohmer's curriculum philosophy on race hygiene discovered a heavy emphasis on birthrates and population trends, not at all unique in the constellation of curriculum writing under the Third Reich. His expressions are full of foreboding about the future. He complained about the fact that Poland's birthrate had increased during the interwar years at a rate much higher than that of Germany. Although Brohmer did not realize it, his choice of countries for comparison held great portent for subsequent developments. Poland claimed the highest number of Jews, almost three million, of any country on the continent before Hitler opened the war against his neighbor to the East. Brohmer saved some of his most barbed attacks for what he called unidentified liberal states that showed little or no interest in race hygiene. Germany under National Socialism was the only state to take aggressive action against those forces threatening its genetic inheritance, thereby "bringing about a racial recovery."[70]

Who else but Germany, Brohmer asked his readers, found an appropriate place for race hygiene and racial science in all schools? Yet, all of the teachings about race hygiene would remain unfruitful if pupils failed to develop a sense of responsibility toward the Volk as a whole. Once more, the place of character education in forming acceptable attitudes and values about race was deemed even more significant than factual knowledge. Yes, there were critically important facts that children needed to know if they were to grasp the nature of the problem. Brohmer predicted a graying of the German population, which if not addressed by an increased birthrate would result in a nation without youth by 1990. Other values were deemed essential if the race was to prosper. Schools must plant in the hearts of young girls the notion that motherhood and wife represented the highest of all callings. Freeing women to enter industrial labor was therefore out of the question according to the ideals of Nazi society. Another ideal advanced by Brohmer, with the ideological blessing of the regime, was a German conception of marriage effectively excluding the Jews along with an average of 3.4 offspring per Aryan union.[71]

Brohmer's perspective on race hygiene, although important to understanding the context within which the subject claimed its curriculum identity, was certainly not the only one to gain the attention of educators in the field. Curriculum authors on race hygiene came from public school classrooms as well as university lecture halls and the offices of school administration, a development seen earlier in the examination of selected curriculum guides on the Jewish question.

Jakob Graf, a teacher whose words established the tone for the opening of this chapter, had already contributed to the question of race hygiene in the schools during the waning days of the Weimar Republic.[72]

Graf anticipated opposition coming from those who questioned the wisdom of the Nazi experiment in education. In response to people who maintained that race education was immoral, Graf enlisted the support of Providence, a tactic witnessed before. God created the earth and all of the races within it, he observed, and did so under his "great, eternal, iron laws." The reign of God in nature did not desire a mixing, but rather the preservation of race purity. Coming from Graf's straw man was a second objection. What about the mixed bloods who were frequently the source of great cultural achievements? Although not mentioned by name, Graf at least indirectly implied the existence of Jewish cultural contributions. His response reflected a cultural ethnocentrism common to Nazi curriculum writers. Graf explained that such contributions, while often of questionable value, could never displace the cultural achievements of the racially pure, the genuine source of human creativity. Taking a page out of *Mein Kampf*, Graf warned readers about the historical consequences of civilizations that lost their racial consciousness and blood purity.[73]

As with others writing for the classrooms of Germany, Graf's thinking reflected the mythology surrounding Nordic pedagogy. The third objection to race education stressed the reality that Germans, like all other peoples, were not members of a pure race. This did not matter to Graf since Nordic bloodlines accounted for the largest percentage of blood composition in the German population. This was the blood element that held Germans together as a nation. There emerged in Graf's biological perspective the integration of mythological language with religious fervor that implied a Volkish worship of blood and soil. Biology thereby defined national identity with a sense of mission:

> Nordic blood flows in every German, in some more, in others less. The Nordic race is the common band which holds all Germans together in community. The German national tradition grows out of the Nordic racial soul and the Nordic soul is the holy fertile soil of all true German culture. So also will the racial soul of all future Germans be bound to national community. If shown through history and race research that Nordic blood is the actual creator and bearer of all high culture, there will grow in us the holy duty of the first order to rescue the Nordic blood of our people from destruction. The ongoing community of the Nordic inheritance binds all Germans to a higher living unity, the Volk. The German people is therefore more than merely the sum of 65 million individuals, rather it is a living whole sealed through the inner laws of its race, which encompasses all of the generations of the present, the past, and the future.[74]

This broad historical vision for the place of racial consciousness in the curriculum, certainly unoriginal in its conception, was not all that defined Graf's perspective on the curriculum. The Jews, in contrast to Brohmer's curriculum orientation, provided a much more prominent focus for Graf in discussing the educated person. How he rationalized the treatment of Jews as cultural outsiders became evident in his lecture before science educators in Hessen in the early days of the Third Reich. In Graf's ideological worldview, one could draw upon nature to justify anti-Semitism. He easily dismissed hatred as a logical element in anti-Semitic policy and instead drew attention to the profound cultural differences between the two groups. "We do not hate the beast of prey," Graf told his audience, "because it is equipped by nature with a ravenous appetite, a thirst for blood, and a terrible bite. We also do not hate the Jew because he is physically and intellectually entirely different from us, but we show our brothers and children the great irreconcilable and incomparable differences which exist here and through which no power of the world can set aside."[75] As seen before, part of the propaganda image of the Third Reich was built around Judenhaß, implying that Jews held a deep hatred for German culture and Nordic blood-lines, not the other way around.[76]

While Paul Brohmer became better known as a theorist in relating race hygiene to science education, Jakob Graf left his mark through setting down a much more substantial translation of Günther's racial anthropology in the curriculum. In one of his best-known works, *Vererbungslehre, Rassenkunde und Erbgesundheit-spflege* (Genetics, racial science, and care of heredity), Graf drew heavily from Günther's *Racial Science of the Jewish People* (1922) in describing the "racial composition" of the Jewish people. Familiar themes reappeared. The biological identity of Jews in more recent history revolved around the mixing of Jewish with Negroid blood. The incendiary nature of the "*schwarze Schmach*" resurrected during the French occupation of the Rhineland during the 1920s had already revealed long standing German antipathies against Blacks. Graf, in designating Jews and Blacks as racial outcasts, linked racial anti-Semitism with Black racism and thus further legitimized the traditional racist prejudices in German society against the two groups. To reinforce these assumptions, Graf published a picture of a Jew from Poland with the caption "Negroid element." Today, Graf wrote, one could still see many Jews who possessed Negroid features in the hair, lips, and mouth. Yes, there was also a weak Nordic element in the Hebrew people strengthened through mixing with the neighboring Philistines. His anthro-pological assumption led to a most unusual rewriting of biblical history. Graf stated that the manner of fighting taken up by the Philistine giant Goliath against David "corresponded to Nordic ways."[77] That David was the decisive victor in this struggle apparently eluded Graf's understanding.

The myth of Nordic pedagogy returned in a form that Graf readily deflected by his deference to Günther. The question of blond and blue-eyed individuals among the Jews persistently dogged race anthropologists like Günther and many others. Rudolf Virchow's survey research from the 1870s demonstrated that about 11 percent of Jewish schoolchildren carried these characteristics along with 31.8 percent of people from the German Reich proper.[78] Graf conveniently avoided any detailed discussion of the issue by directing readers to Günther's conclusion. The presence of the Nordic element among present-day Jews was of ancient Palestinian origin.[79] Deflecting readers away from the apparent con-tradiction posed by the legacy of Virchow's research, Graf pointed to the foreign bloodlines coursing through the veins of Jews originating from eastern and southern Europe. Like his protege Günther, Graf delighted in using reductionist labels to impose racial order upon humanity. The *Ostjuden* thus assumed a racial identity as "Near Eastern–Oriental–East Baltic–Easterly–inner Asian–Hamitic–Negroid." *Südjuden* also assumed these qualities except for being more western in orientation with a streak of Nordic blood and without the inner Asian complex.[80]

Brohmer exhorted teachers to draw on the innate powers of observation in the child to teach race hygiene. Graf went beyond exhortation to provide teachers with specific pedagogical strategies on how to integrate observation as a way to opening a deeper understanding about racial differences. The preservation of the racial community and Aryan bloodlines for future generations demanded a more direct instructional connection to the lives of students. In this context, Graf became a member of a rather exclusive circle of educators dedicated to specifically linking the content of racial anti-Semitism to methodology. Graf's curriculum represented the intersection of anthropology, aesthetics, and science. Applying Günther's emphasis on physical appearance as a window to racial soul, Graf created a number of assignments that reinforced the recognition of racial differences in the culture. The issues for study left no doubt about the importance of developing anti-Semitic attitudes and stereotypes among youth in the New Germany:

1. Present an overview of the mental characteristics of the individual races.
2. Collect from stories, essays and poems examples of ethnological illustrations. Underline those terms which describe the type and mode of the expression of soul.
3. Also ascertain which physical characteristics go hand in hand with psychologically determined traits for the individual figures.
4. Try to discover inner attitudes in stories and poems which describe the forms of actual intrinsic nature of racial soul.
5. Also transfer this way of observation to persons in your neighborhood.
6. What are the expressions, gestures and movements which allow us to make conclusions as to the attitude of racial soul?
7. Collect propaganda posters and caricatures for your race book and arrange them according to a racial scheme. What image of beauty is emphasized by the artist in posters about sports and travel? Publicity for cosmetics?
8. When viewing monuments, note the race of the person portrayed with respect to figure, bearing and physical characteristics. Try to harmonize these determinations with the features of the racial soul.
9. Observe the people whose special racial characteristics especially stand out to you, also their posture, the way they walk, speak, and further, their demeanor and gestures.
10. Observe the Jew: his way of walking, his bearing, gestures and movements when talking.
11. What strikes you about the way a Jew talks and sings?
12. What are the occupations engaged in by the Jews of your acquaintance?
13. In what occupations are Jews not found? Explain this phenomenon on the basis of the character of the Jew's racial soul.
14. In what stories, descriptions and poems do you find the psychological character of the Jews accurately portrayed?[81]

In support of this assignment in literature, Graf urged teachers to introduce the character of Shylock from Shakespeare's *Merchant of Venice* and "The Jew in the Briar" from Grimm's Fairy Tales. Also garnering attention was *Der Hungerpastor* (Pastor to the hungry) by Wilhelm Raabe from 1863. Raabe told the story of a German and a Jew who each took on very different lifestyles and values in trying to make his respective way in the world. The Jew is painted with the darkest of tones. Extremely self-centered, the Jew concerned himself with the pursuit of power and advancement through cunning and dishonesty. With religion as the leitmotif, Raabe portrayed the German as a thoroughly honest individual who, at peace with himself and the social order, remained content with his role as a pastor helping poverty-stricken members of his congregation.[82] This was the kind of literary character study from which Volkish dreams were made. Drawing from Raabe along with Graf's selections from Shakespeare and Grimm, teachers could reinforce traditional anti-Semitic stereotypes. (See student art work in figures 3.1, 4.1.)

The biological determinism undergirding these assignments grew out of the vital assumption that the racial character of human beings could be ascertained by a study of physical characteristics and observable behavior. The face, one teaching chart by Alfred Vogel explained, was the soul of the race. The concept of racial soul, which emerged long before in the minds of early Volkish thinkers like Houston Stewart Chamberlain and Julius Langbehn, found expression once again in the pedagogical writings of Jakob Graf. He offered nothing new in regard to the content for race hygiene, the queen of the curriculum in race biology. For the most part, the schoolmaster from Rüsselsheim presented to educators an abridged form of Günther's racial anthropology articulated under the guise of Nazi science. Graf's real contribution was in translating content on race hygiene through teaching methodologies.

The assignments after each section in his book on families studies and race biology reflected more directly Graf's instructional intentions in concentrated form than the steady pounding of his Günther-like narrative. The tasks set forth for pupils initiating the section on race mixing and disorder called them to use scientific knowledge from heredity and race studies in response to biological problems. Pupils considered whether two races could join to form a new race. They also pondered how beasts of burden and useful plants established new races. Under the Nazi tradition, questions like these invariably led to a more intimate connection with human beings in the racial community. While new races might be conceived in the plant and animal kingdoms, pupils were asked why this same biological process among humans remained unfeasible. In a bolded sentence appearing in the middle of his section on race mixing, Graf firmly declared that misinformed attempts to achieve some kind of biological balance through blood mixing would cause the loss of those peculiar characteristics that defined each race. An inescapable consequence was the destruction of the people's spiritual core leading to the race's decline. This was one of the strongest instructional principles Graf tried to communicate.[83]

The *Schicksalsfrage*, or question of destiny, to which Graf carefully led his readers regarded the unspoken fate of the Jews. Writing shortly before the

Figure 3.1 *"Der Jude richting gesehen"* ("The Jew Correctly Seen"), third prize in a regional art contest from a fourteen-year-old from Nuremberg. Contest sponsored by Julius Streicher, Gauleiter from Franconia and editor of *Der Stürmer*. From an article, "Die Arbeitern als Presiträger," ("The Worker as Prize Winner"), *Fränkische Tageszeitung*, 31 December 1936. From clippings collection of Wiener Library, Tel Aviv.

Nuremberg Laws, Graf emphasized the necessity for racial renewal in the Reich. Like many of his contemporaries, Graf fell back on statistics to demonstrate how powerful Jewish influence remained in the professions. These sobering statistics, Graf intimated, reflected just how far Jews had come in extending control over not only the economic life of the community but also all corners of intellectual activity. The solution to this fateful question could only be found in the wisdom of National Socialist measures to "turn back the Jews" through placing appropriate limitations on their activities. Praising the promulgation of the Aryan Paragraph limiting Jewish professional activity in law and civil service, Graff insisted that now was the time to force Jews into the realization that they were and had always been *Gastvolk*, or mere visitors in the Reich, as opposed to *Wirtsvolk* outside the host culture.[84]

MEDICAL DOCTORS ON RACE HYGIENE AND THE SCHOOLS

As members of the educational establishment, Brohmer and Graf brought two different approaches to the question of race hygiene in the curriculum. Distorting science to advance the racial agenda of the Third Reich through curriculum also reflected profound economic implications for population policy and those declared biologically unfit for citizenship. As witnessed earlier, a certain accounting mentality entered discussions among Nazi curriculum writers concerning the economic burden imposed on the state by the care of the mentally ill and handicapped. Among the voices contributing to this enterprise were medical doctors Rainer Fetscher from Dresden and Hans Krauß from Ansbach. In late 1933, Fetscher published a guide on the teaching of race hygiene for classroom teachers. Human physical and mental defectives, so the doctor claimed, represented a heavy economic cost for society. Like many prominent race eugenicists of his day, Fetscher inundated his readers with a bevy of statistics, usually without clarifying their sources. In a profound way, curriculum once again became a handmaiden to various forms of propaganda.

Educators learned that the number of children born to the mentally ill in Germany was double that of the average population in 1930. An estimated one million Germans suffering from hereditary diseases drained the government's coffers of no less than 497 million marks in health-care expenses. The *Hilfsschulen*—schools for "backward children" with a variety of physical and mental handicaps—were especially troubling for the author since they represented an annual expenditure of 40 million marks. To relativize these figures, Fetscher pointed to other categories in the Weimar budget from 1929 to 1930. He noted that 563 million marks supported art and science in Germany and 757 million marks constituted the budget for the army. The less-than-subtle suggestion was that new budgetary priorities were in order to benefit the Nordic part of the population at the expense of those people deemed by the Nazis as "life unworthy of life."[85]

Predictably, Fetscher sowed the illusion that racial identity could be scientifically identified in a kind of anthropological catalogue. The doctor listed unique qualities that defined eight races in and around Europe. The Near Eastern and Oriental races represented, for Fetscher, important foundation stones for the Jewish people. Readers were treated to a litany of details on relative skull

and nose sizes, physical height, and facial features. In addition to noting physical differences, Fetscher offered cultural observations, many drawing from
ancient anti-Semitic stereotypes. Jews from the Near East, he observed:

> possess a special capability for trade, cleverness, and a capacity for empathy. There
> is a marked talent for music, but also a calculated cruelty and revenge, slyness and
> a propensity for profit-making. We already encountered this in their role as money
> lenders in the early Middle Ages.[86]

As one might expect, Fetscher assumed a very different ideological tone when
describing the Nordic race from which the Aryans originated. If his tedious prose
is any indication, Nordic peoples brought to the world a special talent for war,
the formation of great ideas, rigorousness, objectivity, and a willingness to make
sacrifices. Of all the races, it was the Nordic race that provided the greatest
number of leaders in all areas of human life. The only real dangers posed by
that race were a tendency toward exaggerated individualism, political isolation,
and lack of empathy.[87] Fetscher could not have known in late 1933 that subsequent events related to the conduct of Nazi foreign policy and racial persecution
would resoundingly affirm the last two supposed Nordic qualities.

Enlisting the opinions of people from the medical community added an air
of scientific legitimacy to the program for race hygiene in the schools.[88] Noted
earlier was the contribution of Fritz Lenz in this endeavor. That race hygiene
was not simply an ideal consigned to the pages of curriculum directives
coming out of Berlin was manifest in the thinking of Hans Krauß, a medical
doctor from Ansbach. Taking an approach entirely different from Fetscher's,
Krauß established a kind of racial catechism that reduced race hygiene to its
barest essentials. His work *Basic Ideas on Heredity and Race Hygiene in
Question and Answer* (1935), appeared as part of a series called "The Doctor
as Educator" and placed population policy on center stage. Krauß's perspective
on curriculum remains of particular interest for this study. Unlike many other
authors espousing racial ideals for the education of the young in greater
depth, Krauß addressed educators through providing very brief responses to
very complex questions associated with race hygiene. The paternal tone of his
writing and the highly distilled format of the catechism marked this slim volume.
In the author's view, race hygiene was the most important formative element
of the curriculum.

Krauß's section of race hygiene does not mention Jews or any other specific
groupings of racial undesirables by name. Similar in some ways to the scientific and illusory objectivity of Brohmer's language, Krauß kept the faces of
the racial enemy cloaked behind generalized pronouncements on the need for
sterilization and racially healthy marriages. This was the kind of curriculum
resource that symbolized reductionism in the extreme. Veteran and inexperi-
enced teachers unprepared to instruct the young on race hygiene might see in
Krauß's writing an easy and quick way to boil down manageable "facts" for use
in the classroom. Race hygiene took on a strong international character under
Krauß's pen to demonstrate that Germany joined other civilized nations in using
eugenics as a tool of population policy. The study of foreign language held great
possibilities in this regard. Pupils could read Artur de Gobineau as part of the

French curriculum. Those studying English might read from the eugenics pioneer Francis Galton or the notable popularizers of eugenics in the United States like Lathrop Stoddard or Madison Grant.[89]

In raising an initial question about the goals of race hygiene in the opening lines of his section on the subject, Krauß offered words of reassurance. Race hygiene preserved the race from "threatening degeneration" while the race perfected itself through its own powers. Krauß then quickly brought his readers into the immediate implications of this view of biological science. The second question asked how the further spread of hereditary defects could be fought. Krauß placed a civilized face on race hygiene while, at the same time, offering citizens rationalizations about restricting certain racial undesirables from reproducing. What follows is the kind of Nazi language justifying the subsequent T-4 killings of the handicapped, mentally ill, and those suffering from hereditary diseases. The doctor from Ansbach qualified the conditions for sterilization, but veiled and distorted the true long-term intentions of Nazi policy. This kind of linguistic subterfuge, used under the banners of race hygiene and blood purity, is also important since it foreshadowed an increasingly harsh oppression of other racial undesirables like Jews and Sinti and Roma after 1935:

> The severe justice exercised during antiquity and the Middle Ages against such inferiors was almost like an extermination experience. Our age does not want to repeat such hard measures. We therefore want the mentally and physically infirm, who are reliant on our help, to be further looked after. But we may not allow such inferiors to pass on their infirmities to later generations. We do not concede to such people the right to reproduce. We certainly do not differ with them over the right to live, but over the right to give life![90]

Following this rationalization for forcibly sterilizing certain elements of the population, Krauß turned his attention to another related aspect of social policy that assured the preservation of racial health. Choosing the right marriage partner was fateful not only for the two families involved but also for the racial destiny of the Third Reich.[91] Even more serious than marrying for love was the matter of marrying someone racially compatible. Shortly after Krauß's tract appeared in print, the Nuremberg Laws legitimized a certain limitation of choice with the full weight of the state. Much of this meant little unless citizens were able to determine the composition of their own bloodlines. Families submitted to the appropriate government authorities proof of their Aryan ancestry. Defining Jewishness became important not only in the larger Nazi society but also for the curriculum of the school.

The creation of family trees became part of class activities in biology, race hygiene, and drawing. Krauß saw in the formation of the *Ahnentafel* (family tree) one of the most effective ways of advancing the ideas and demands of race hygiene. Drawing classes could make the *Ahnentafel* part of a major art project based on research relating to the hereditary history of the family. Such a generational chart drew close connections between the racial identity of the pupils and their families. Moreover, family history could be pressed into the service of promoting national and racial consciousness. Children could learn about the participation of their ancestors in the Peasant Revolt, the Thirty Years' War, and the War of Liberation against Napoleon. These kinds of learning experiences, Krauß believed, drew school and racial community closer together. The logical outcome, Krauß wanted readers to know, had everything to do with character education and the relationship of pupils to the racial state. The *Ahnentafel* would personalize for the child the history of the family and, at the same time, subordinate the youngster's own life to that of "greater points of view" instead of his or her choosing the senseless path of self-indulgence.[92]

This was a curriculum vision of race hygiene much broader than the sciences and art. Even those pupils studying the ancient languages had the opportunity to study the causes behind the racial decline of Greek blood in their reading of Plato. In Latin classes, pupils could read Tacitus and learn about the struggle of Caesar Augustus to raise the total population, his stirring speeches in the Senate, his respect for the Roman farmers, and his fruitful marriage with eight children. Important lessons in race hygiene also grew out of examining the fall of Rome as a world power, explained in part by a decline in the birthrate. Mathematical studies also held gems of racial learning. Pupils represented the Mendelian formula for the cross fertilization of plants through mathematical diagrams. Charts comparing birthrates of Germany with those of neighboring countries implied a deadly threat from the Slavs, especially Poland and Russia.[93]

The way Krauß closed his customary tight prose with nary an unanswered question revealed much about the intellectual predecessors of race hygiene. When asked which researchers stood in the first line as pioneers in establishing race hygiene as a legitimized area of inquiry, he tapped Gobineau of France, Galton of England, and Alfred Ploetz, the founder of the German Society for Race Hygiene. To this group's accomplishments he added the pathbreaking work of Wilhelm Schallmayer and Fritz Lenz. The ever-popular genetics textbook on human genetics and race hygiene written by Erwin Baur, Fischer, and Lenz (1932, 4th edition) received prominent mention among works recommended for those interested in developing a deeper scientific understanding of the subject. The circle also encompassed the writings of Rainer Fetscher, Jakob Graf, and Hans F. K. Günther. Even in the midst of this self-proclaimed heritage of scientific thinking about race hygiene, Krauß remained skeptical. These studies remained absolutely useless unless people developed the will to adapt their lives to the priorities of race hygiene.[94] One of these priorities was to follow the spirit of the Nazi legal system on the status of the Jew as noncitizen.[95]

Other medical opinions would take a much harsher view on the character of German citizens for not being anti-Semitic enough in everyday life. This was the view held by the doctors Philalethes Kuhn and Heinrich Kranz, authors of *Von Deutschen Ahnen für Deutsche Enkel* (From German ancestors to German grandchildren), a work released in 1933. As part of a larger treatise on heredity, race science, and race hygiene, the two authors integrated the Jewish question with a tone of anger and impatience not usually found in writings originating from the hands of medical doctors. Although Kuhn and Kranz wrote for a general audience, their ideas are important for *Volkserziehung*, that larger Nazi societal task of educating the people about racial matters. Furthermore, their thinking reminds readers once again that medicine was critical not only in carrying out the Nazi policy of mass murder but also in legitimizing racial anti-Semitism through education. This dimension of German culture was, of course, part of the milieu within which teachers lived and breathed.

The rebirth of the German nation, the doctors insisted, was not possible "without the elimination of Jewry and its influences" (*ohne Ausschaltung des Judentums und seines Einflusses.*) The eliminationist tone in Kuhn and Kranz remained stronger than in the writings from both medicine and curriculum formation examined thus far. Not only were German citizens not racial enough in their thinking, they remained, above all, too "neutral and tolerant" about the Jews. At this early stage in the Third Reich, there existed a deep concern on the part of the two doctors about those misguided Germans who feared making a "devastating appraisal of the Jews." Standing at the center of this cultural dilemma was the *hochanständige*, or "decent Jew." This feared character created a dangerous illusion in the minds of some Germans who made the fatal error of seeing Jews as human beings:

> And one soothes himself with the tightly held view that the Jews also are people and are not at all evil and that only virulent Volkish circles among the people are aroused against Jewry. Often one hears the assertion that Jews are more clever and efficient than Germans; therefore one can do nothing against them since they bring property and influence. We will see that this assertion is false. Finally, it is boastfully emphasized that the Jews stick together, possess a sense of family and are charitable toward the poor, especially the poor among their own people. These last qualities we must acknowledge. History affords us the observation that not only the Volkish awakened Germans today, rather peoples from all time have risen up and attempted again and again to drive the Jews out with fire and sword. The people have had full reasons for their aversion toward and their hatred against the Jews.[96]

Beyond the standard propaganda incantations about overwhelming Jewish influence in the political and economic spheres, Kuhn and Kranz recognized that pulling off a rigorous anti-Semitic agenda in schools and elsewhere would not be as easy as first imagined. They were among those medical minds, representing Nazi science, who were called upon to add legitimacy to racial anti-Semitism. What sets them apart from the other self-appointed educators from medicine is that under the banner of "objectivity," they displayed a much stronger purpose in stirring up the masses to anti-Semitic fervor. The authors concluded their book with the same issue raised in the opening paragraphs. The eliminationist tendency embraced here is the *endgültige Lösung*, or final solution, which took on a more radical meaning not long after the war opened with Russia. Kuhn and Kranz advanced the solution of resettling the Jews where they would take up their own domicile. The term *Wohnsitz* (domicile) appeared in the context of the authors' argument, not the more expansive expression of *Lebensraum* (living space) which carried a very different geopolitical meaning in the Nazi lexicon. Kuhn claimed that he had already proposed this solution in 1924. As reflected earlier in the curriculum guides and the artwork of pupils, the assumption that Jews should be moved en masse to Palestine or Madagascar as a major solution to the Jewish question remained official Nazi policy until late 1938. The vigorous anti-Semitism of doctors like Kuhn and Kranz spread through the printed word with the blessing of Nazi officialdom, echoed in the work of a dedicated Nazi pedagogue engaged in preparing young women for the teaching profession at Hanover.[97]

FERDINAND ROSSNER AND BIOLOGICAL CONCEPTIONS OF THE JEW

As noted earlier, Ferdinand Rossner was among those academics who maintained a strong defense of Darwinism in the teaching of biology and race hygiene. For him and other notables in the field like Konrad Lorenz, Darwin's conception of the survival of the fittest and the process of biological selection, both associated with social Darwinism, provided a strong theoretical basis linking racial anthropology with the natural sciences. The Jewish question and the education of anti-Semites, as seen thus far, were not the sum total of the biology curriculum and one of its branches, race hygiene. At the same time, dedicated ideologues like the science educator Rossner could not conceive of a curriculum for the racial state without the Jew as a biological focal point. Race hygiene would provide one of the most powerful curriculum doorways to approach this question.

In contrast to his colleague Paul Brohmer in Kiel, Rossner was much more adamant in attacking not only the Jews but also the *Zigeuner*, or Sinti and Roma. Brohmer placed a stronger emphasis on extending race biological principles to the economic and health problems associated with the state support of the crippled and insane. In another notable contrast examined later, Rossner was especially enthusiastic about connecting racial science with religion. The professor from Hanover is also important for this study since he, like Brohmer, cast a long shadow over the Nazi program in race biology. As a professor at the Female Teacher Training College in Hanover (1941–45), Rossner vigorously applied his convictions about the nature of race education to the task of preparing teachers in the natural sciences. In 1939, he assumed major responsibilities as head of the work group on biology and the schools for the Reich Federation of Biology. As a member of the editorial board of the journal *The Biologist*, Rossner regularly informed teachers about the latest research in race biology. He also acted as liaison between the NSLB and the Reich Federation. In addition to his professorial chair in northern Germany, Rossner directed the Main Office on Schooling in the Race Political Office of the district administrator for South Hanover–Braunschweig. His loyalty to the regime and his strong reputation as a leading race educator did not go unnoticed. In 1942, Rossner accepted an appointment as leader of the newly founded Institute for Germanic Volk and Racial Sciences in Hanover. Heading the research agenda for the short-lived institute were issues related to population development and the advancement of racial sciences in the schools and other institutions.[98]

As a strong proponent of social Darwinism, Rossner believed that the struggle for the preservation of the biological basis for National Socialist ideology had to be fought on two fronts. On one, there were the Communist ideologues and natural scientists who sided with the developmentalist thinking of J. B. Antoine de Lamarck (1744–1829) that called into serious question the fixed nature of race. Lamarckism, as it was called, came to be associated with environmental factors that could change the characteristics of species over time. The profound emphasis on materialism in Lamarck's theory and the implication that race remained flexible and open to change undercut Rossner's love for fixed racial classification. The battle, as we know from his clash with Ernst Krieck, did not end at this philosophical juncture. The second conflict extended to those of his contemporaries driven by the assumption that Darwinism carried with it the causes for a dangerous materialism. Rossner carried the fight not only to fellow pedagogues but also to the religious community.[99]

Working with Heinrich Ihde and Alfred Stockfisch, Rossner coauthored *The Care of Health and Race Hygiene* (1939) for educators. The detailed work included sections on human beings as intimate parts of nature as well as the Volk, all of which carried the strongest elements of race hygiene in the text. In addressing the "foreign races in Germany," the authors came first to the *Zigeuner*, a pejorative term roughly meaning "Gypsies." (Sinti and Roma is the term used in this discussion in place of the traditional translation of Gypsy.) They condemned as a major criminal element the 6,000 full-blooded and 12,000 mixed blooded Sinti and Roma living in Germany. The solution proposed was all too familiar. "A ruthless eradication" of this group through sterilization and the imposition of security measures would decrease the presence of this racial minority in the Reich. "German soil is too valuable," Rossner and his colleagues remarked, "to undertake experiments in settlement" with such a foreign element. Significant for the larger question of content is the fact that the three authors were among the very few who actually addressed, even on a surface level, the issue of Sinti and Roma as part of racial policy in the curriculum.[100]

Predictably, the Jews garnered the most ink as racial archenemy under the Third Reich. Anticipating questions from pupils concerning how Jews came to Germany in the first place, Rossner and his circle had an easy answer. Jews initially arrived with Roman legions as traders and quickly spread throughout southwest and eastern Europe. In a pattern designed to advance the image of the Jew as negative other, the authors emphasized the "race instinct" of Jews living together among their own in ghettos and closed settlements. To add greater legitimacy to their subjective science of race hygiene, Rossner and company delineated the oriental and Near Eastern racial composition of the Jews with interpretations from Günther and Lenz. In another example reflecting the myth of Nordic pedagogy, the authors insisted that the Jews could not qualify as a people since they failed to secure a unified living space and a common language. Apparently, Rossner and the others overlooked the historical and geopolitical realities confronting Germany before 1871, hardly an indication of secure living space. Nazi propaganda stressed that Germany's expansionist policy was justified, in part, because of a shortage of living space.[101]

The question toward which the authors led readers provided an instructional framework for the usual reductionist approach to anti-Semitic pedagogy: "How was the rise of this racial foreign element possible over the last hundred years in Germany and in the world?" The answers constituted a kind of Nazi pedagogical doctrine justifying the development of anti-Semitic attitudes among the young. More directly, these ideologically circumscribed responses, taken as a whole, offered pupils an uncomplicated and unquestioned set of assumptions about Jews. Rossner and his associates carefully preserved connections between race, religion, economics, anthropology, and history in framing the image of the Jew:

1. They found in the church a willing precursor [Jewish teachings, the baptism of the Jews] in support of the the myth of the Chosen People of God.
2. They promulgated the Lamarckian teachings about the equality of all people and emphasized that the ghetto was made for Jews and that they will transform life inside of the community of Germans.
3. They shattered [the nation] through mixed marriages and through the rule of public opinion, by the means of press, cleverly veiled their world Jewry.
4. They possess bank capital and a scarcely believable adaptability.[102]

Collectively, this brief set of answers to a preset query from the Nazi catechism demonstrated once again that race hygiene was not exclusively concerned with race as a concept from the natural sciences. The anti-Semitic core of the answers represent a skillful propaganda strategy of combining older with newer images of Jews. The Jew was a profoundly rejected outsider not only because of race but also because of religion and forces in the marketplace that Jews purportedly controlled. Linking Jews to Lamarckian thinking served a dual purpose as well since Nazi racial policy revolved around the value of inequality and race superiority, a direct antithesis of Lamarck's environmental thesis. On another level, Nazi curriculum writers like Rossner and his circle could link the Jews to the dark enemy of bolshevism through the association of Lamarckian theory with Moscow. There is another brief addendum to this curriculum on race hygiene that bears further consideration. Just before articulating the question, the authors raised the specter of the Jew as sexual threat to German womanhood, an "infection" of the people with horrific results that added up in the "account of racial shame."[103]

An attempt to globalize the threat of Jews to the peace of the world certainly was not exclusive to the curriculum proposed by Rossner. He, much more than many other writers, exploited a controversial speech by Ben Franklin of the United States as a source of anti-Semitic fear for the Jewish takeover of the young American republic. Quoting from remarks Franklin delivered in 1789 during the opening of the first Congress, Rossner wanted readers to know that the Jew was a constitutional issue. Rossner and his fellow authors went far beyond Dobers's curriculum guide to the Jewish question through integrating a much larger segment of Franklin's speech. Nonetheless, their choice of sentences revealed an editing process designed for maximum anti-Semitic effect:

The great danger, gentlemen, is the Jew! . . . If you do not exclude these people in the existing constitutional charter, then you will be flooded with such a mass in less than two hundred years that they will rule and devour the land and our form of government, for which we Americans shed our blood, will be abandoned. When you do not exclude these people, then your descendents will be forced to work in the fields in order to bring profit for others, while those who sit in the offices happily rub their hands. I warn you, gentlemen: If you do not exclude the Jews for all time, then the children of your children will wish they were in your graves![104]

To add punch to Franklin's words, Rossner and company followed the widespread Nazi curriculum practice of integrating statistics without reporting sources. New York, the capital of North American Jewry, claimed 2.5 million members from the Hebrew community. In a parallel to Berlin, the authors showered readers with false and grossly inflated percentages demonstrating an overwhelming Jewish presence in law, newspaper publishing, the telephone business, transportation, grocery, heavy industry and mass-produced articles. The Jew was not simply a German problem but a world affliction influencing not only the United States but also every part of global society. What made Germany special, Rossner and his colleagues agreed, was that Germany was the first state actually doing something about the problem. The Jews now found themselves confronted with the racial power of the Nuremberg Laws and the loss of citizenship. In a self-assured tone, the authors rejoiced in the fact that the census of all Jews, half-Jews, and mixed bloods would shortly be concluded and their kinship officially established through a card file system.[105]

The organization of the text suggested that the "struggle over race mixing" could not remain restricted to one concentrated anti-Semitic outrage. Later in the book, educators received a clarion call to overcome the myth of the Jews as a chosen people. Such a myth favored what Rossner and the others vaguely called "a psychological bastardization." Another stern judgment followed. Whoever believed in this myth of the Jewish people was nothing more than a propagandist for Jewry and an opponent of Alfred Rosenberg's *Myth of the Twentieth Century* that posited the racial worldview of National Socialism. Even stronger language was reserved for Sinti and Roma. In a condemnation eerily predictive of things to come, the authors declared that the state would "eradicate" (*ausmerzen*) the foreign-blooded Sinti and Roma, calling them "born crooks, thieves and nomads," characterizations similar to those often applied to the Jew in Nazi propaganda. These expressions appeared just before a new section on the colonial question. How Rossner and friends opened discussion at this point revealed one of the most duplicitous statements to ever appear in Nazi curriculum literature. "The German racial standpoint," they wrote, "emphasizes the diversity and not the value of differences of the races" (*betont die Verschiedenartigkeit und nicht die Verschidenwertigkeit der Rassen.*)[106]

The question of religion and its relationship to race was not one Rossner chose to explore in materials intended specifically for schools. The work of Fritz Fink, examined earlier, imbued, by contrast, anti-Semitism and the Jewish question in the schools with strong religious meaning. In the depths of the war, Rossner published *Race and Religion* (1942), a source worth considering since it represented another aspect of the pedagogue's thinking about the dynamics of anti-Semitism.[107] This obscure work reflected Rossner's conception of Volkish religion and the emergence of a *Rassegott* in the form of Adolf Hitler as the salvation for the Third Reich. Unlike Rossner's writings for schools, this volume imbued "the law of heredity" with deeply spiritual and mystical associations. His meandering critique of the Jewish religion, in following the party line, included obligatory attacks against the Talmud. Jewish kosher laws, especially those relating to the butchering of animals, came under Rossner's scrutiny. In an anti-Semitic theme reappearing later in children's literature under study in chapter 5, Rossner castigated Jews for what he considered a cruel practice of putting animals under the knife for food "without previous anaesthetization." Predictably, Rossner insisted that Aryans, "out of an inner sensitivity," refused to follow such practices.[108]

Taking a broad sweep of religious history, Rossner insisted that Jewish political behavior could be traced back to what he called *"Esther-Politik,"* named after the events recorded in the Book of Esther. Here was another example of a scheming Jewish woman entering into a strategic marriage with an influential statesman for the purpose of increasing Jewish presence in the halls of power. Queen Esther's victory over Haman was another indication that Jews would stop at nothing to secure influence. Couldn't this danger also be seen in Prussian Minister Hardenberg who took on a Jewish wife? Didn't this explain why Hardenberg ended the reforms of Freiherr von Stein and authored legislation legalizing the emancipation of Jews in 1812? The line, Rossner insisted, continued all the way to the Jewish Foreign Minister Gustav Stresemann of the Weimar Republic and even to *"Väterchen"* Joseph Stalin.[109]

One senses a certain desperation in Rossner's ravings, perhaps heightened during those days following the military defeat at Stalingrad. His editor, Walter Kopp, conveyed this feeling as well in the introduction for the book. That Jews must be behind the current state of affairs was a given. With the war conditions becoming more difficult, Rossner and Kopp held on to the illusion that the racial state might triumph in the end:

> Race thinking is the leitmotif for our world view. The race question stands today in the middle point of world discussion. The opponents of the ideas of blood and race are the opponents in this war who present the last contingent for world Jewry.[110]

The writings of Jakob Graf, and in particular Paul Brohmer and Ferdinand Rossner, provided the Nazi education establishment with something of a theoretical framework for the integration of race hygiene into science education and the curriculum at large. Rainer Fetscher and Hans Krauß were among those adding legitimacy to the enterprise from the medical community. We noted that one of the main features of this process was the articulation of a race biology that, as a fully politicized school subject, further legitimized the teaching of racial anti-Semitism through exploiting history, religion, anthropology, and geography. Race hygiene was not conceived as a mere branch of race biology, but was the ideological heart and soul of the subject. The Nazi preoccupation with maintaining blood purity, built as it was on the foundations of race mythology, found in race hygiene a strong curriculum voice. A number of practical problems emerged as the Nazis advanced this program in the life of the school. Getting ideologically appropriate curriculum materials to teachers early in the regime before new textbooks appeared was one. Another challenge was evident in efforts to link communities and schools more closely in support of the anti-Semitic agenda.

THE DEVELOPMENT OF RACE HYGIENE IN SCHOOLS
UNDER NATIONAL SOCIALISM

In Munich and Salzburg there emerged in 1932 a self-proclaimed association of teachers, parents, psychologists, doctors, authors, social workers, and representatives of cultural groups under the name of the Association of German-Aryan Educators and Parents. The size of this group's membership and the full nature of its activities remain a mystery. A special issue of the association's monthly journal, *Lenk ein!* (yield) from March of 1933 offers a glimpse into the perceptions held by the association and its fiery editor, Hermann Weiskopf, regarding the purpose of schooling under the Third Reich. Appearing less than two months after Hitler's rise to power, the third issue of the journal called upon all elementary and secondary school teachers to create a profession genuinely German in nature. Past school reforms had failed because they tried to bring in "new wine skins for old, sour wine." A change was in the air and teachers had to form a new vanguard in support of a more race-conscious curriculum. Implied in this challenge was Weiskopf's dismay over educators' traditional resistance to change.[111]

Posing a question about why the association existed, the editor immediately offered his own defensive interpretation of racial anti-Semitism. A close reading of the association's intention to exclude all that was un-German, particularly Jews, revealed a striking similarity to the exclusionary language used by the profoundly anti-Semitic Thule Society founded in late 1918 in Munich. "Are we anti-Semites?" Weiskopf asked. "This expression brings to light the charge of race hatred and race darkness. It is misleading." The association, he wrote, existed as a way to bring the community together in order to reject and decisively fight all foreign blood (*blutsfremd*) and any attempts to poison German nature. This applied especially to Jews "who, in the last centuries, crept into psychology and education on a massive scale and because of this lumped everyone together." After lauching into a tirade on the character of Jews, the association's mouthpiece concluded that "German education for German culture through German psychological formation is an eternal matter only for the German mind, never a matter of Jewish intellect." Nowhere did the journal propose specifics about curriculum reform per se. Unknown is the extent to which the association actually interacted with the schools. The anti-Semitic ideas printed by Weiskopf, also supported by membership in Austria, are significant in that they provided more of the critical social and ideological context legitimizing the emergence of race hygiene in schools.[112]

Creating curriculum materials for race hygiene true to the ideological aspirations of the racial state, as noted earlier, was a daunting task that involved the cooperation of many individuals from universities, medicine, public schools, and the education bureaucracy. The Nazis did not operate without the influence of intellectual forebears from the long history of Volkish thought. Racial anti-Semitism had assumed a prominent position in German culture long before the Nazis. Challenging any serious anti-Semitic curriculum writer of the time was the omnipresent difficulty of translating Nazi ideology into terms easily understood by children. Of course, in a dictatorship of this nature, this was a task too important to be left to the schools alone. The influence of the Association for German Girls and Hitler Youth in forming political and social attitudes was a factor of some importance. Encouraging the development of a stronger anti-Semitic mind-set was also part of the mission of the Office of Propaganda through its control of the media and the arts. What one notes in these pieces of curriculum history is evidence of the kind of anti-Semitic ideals the Nazi regime wanted to pass along to the next generation. Vogel already provided a glimpse into this process. Jews were not the only group targeted for racial condemnation in school materials, but in the vast majority of cases, Jews held the dubious distinction as racial enemy number one. The Nazi obsession for maintaining the "purity" of bloodlines and cultural practices in relation to Jews symbolized a powerful orientation for race hygiene in schools.

One of the earliest attempts to bring race hygiene into Nazi elementary schools came in 1934 on the heels of curriculum declarations issued by Interior Minister Hans Frick (9 May and 23 June 1933.) In the spirit of *Mein Kampf*, Frick handed down a sharp criticism of a previous tradition of German schooling he considered too theoretical and abstract. Rudolf Frercks, a medical doctor from the Office of Enlightenment for Population and Racial Policy in Berlin, and Arthur Hoffmann, professor from the Teachers College at Cottbus, responded accordingly. As the subtitle suggested, the two created a curriculum that integrated "image and counter image from life for practical schooling in race hygenics." The union of medicine and pedagogical expertise represented in this curriculum was not an unusual practice in the Third Reich. After all, race hygiene was steeped in the history of medicine as well as education.[113] What Frercks and Hoffmann brought to curriculum formation was one of the first efforts at simplifying race hygiene for young children. Pictures would speak louder than words in this curriculum experiment.

The introduction to *Erbnot und Volksaufartung* (Genetic emergency and race hygiene)[114] informed educators that this curriculum was not simply an addition to a collection of statistics prepared for population policy or a series of pictures to be added willy-nilly to teaching resources on the study of heredity. The writing of new textbooks and the creation of new subjects to test for teacher certification "only in the sense of a predominantly scientific kind of schooling" elicited strong reservations from Frercks and Hoffmann. In their estimation, a solid race hygiene curriculum "applied not so much to the intellect, than to a deeper psychological level of people which absolutely called for an inner adjustment and a new attitude." Above all, learning of this nature opened an "immediate inner call awakening the will to live in the people." Nazi curriculum writers like Frercks and Hoffmann believed that they had embarked on a new mission in character education. The two men also assumed that the ground was already fertile among the young for the development of prejudicial attitudes concerning Jews, Blacks, the mentally ill, and the handicapped.[115]

A so-called practical curriculum on race hygiene implied that pupils would eventually draw conclusions about racial undesirables consistent with the prejudices inherent in the prevailing ideology. Using collections of pictures in elementary school instruction could support this process in a way more directly, in some cases, than words on a printed page. This was at least part of the reasoning for the use of Alfred Vogel's teaching charts. Getting this material quickly and easily into the hands of teachers was behind the format chosen for the curriculum. Brief supportive notes for the teacher accompanied each of the thirty-eight pictures, each about the size of a postcard. Highlighted sentences from the notes emphasized especially important ideological conclusions. No other selected readings for pupils came with the program. If the two authors were believed, the series of pictures symbolized the power of Nazi education to spark a transformation in character among the youth of the New Germany.[116]

The pictures, when grouped, represented a study in contrasts. After images depicting a group of well-ordered SS men and a Hitler Youth, viewers saw a mentally ill child holding a puppet followed by a picture of a healthy and laughing blond-haired child. The mentally ill and those suffering from hereditary disease received more attention in the frequency of pictorial coverage than any other of the out groups. At least five additional images showed different kinds of handicaps, usually situated between pictures of robust Aryan children. Such images, although not anti-Semitic in nature, are important in that they represented part of an instructional whole. More important, the pictures stand as a reminder that the Nazi solution for handling both groups of racial undesirables eventually took on a brutal similarity.[117]

Blacks did not escape the exploitive eye of the race educators. Even though Blacks did not live in any significant numbers in the country, their existence and historical presence drew some of the most spiteful and insulting language to come from the pens of Nazi curriculum writers. Frercks and Hoffmann showed a playground picture of "two bastards on the Rhine," two mixed-blood children born of a Black mother from a circus troupe and a German man. Their value as human beings was in doubt because they strode the racial lines between two peoples and thus belonged to no one. Another image captured a contingent of Moroccan troops under the French Army as part of the forces occupying Germany after World War I. Accompanying teacher notes bolded "the danger that their Negro blood could seep further into the German population." Adjoining pictures of a solitary Black civil servant serving the French government and a Black jazz band playing "degenerate music" further heightened racial contrasts.[118]

In a special section titled, "The Racial Emergency of our People," which integrated images from all three out groups, Frercks and Hoffmann posed the threat of the *Ostjuden* to the bloodlines of the national community. Exploiting the same geopolitical map used by Vogel, the two authors wanted pupils to see droves of Jews from the East pouring over Germany's borders between 1910 and 1925. They added a picture of an unidentified Jewish artist to symbolize the presence of "new cultural values" in the Reich. If this wasn't disturbing enough to the dedicated anti-Semite, Frercks and Hoffmann made sure that pupils saw what a leading Jewish civil servant looked like. A Jewish man in tuxedo at a social gathering stands gazing at a fashionably dressed woman. What is he thinking? the viewer is invited to ask. The accompanying notes clarified the situation for the uninformed. Pupils might have been surprised to learn from the official source that this Jewish man was not thinking about sex. Instead, his mind was busy plotting ways to bring down the German nation and to recreate it on the basis of his own racial principles.[119]

In essence, the curriculum created by Frercks and Hoffmann represented race hygiene in its most simplified form. The nature and scope of this curriculum vision is best understood within a larger historical context. The Law for the Prevention of Hereditarily Diseased Progeny of 14 July 1933 set into force on 1 January 1934 legalized compulsory sterilization of people allegedly suffering from hereditary illnesses. *Erbnot und Volksaufartung* appeared shortly after the promulgation of this law and thereby reflected the early and vigorous Nazi campaign to bring an end to incurables or "life unworthy of life" as they were described by Nazi doctors. This does not suggest an absence of Nazi oppressive policies against Jews before 1934. The reader will recall that the Aryan Paragraph from April of 1933 had already banned Jews from civil service and Jewish businesses suffered under a nationwide boycott that same month. While the worst oppressive measures were yet to come for Jews, the content emphasis and timing of this race hygiene curriculum closely reflected a particular Nazi practice of which the infamous T-4 killings are a part. The mentally ill, crippled, and those suffering from hereditary illnesses would be the first victims chosen for mass murder.

The racism directed against Blacks under this curriculum raises further issues regarding racial separation and its implications for Jews. That racial anti-Semitism and racism directed against Blacks existed in the Third Reich was nothing new to the world community. The Berlin Olympics of 1936, with Hitler's public insults against Jesse Owens and German efforts to prevent Jewish athletes from competing, reflected the dynamics of Nazi racial politics. During that same year, Heinrich Krieger published an essay in the *International Zeitschrift für Erziehung* on the separation of the races in the school systems of the United States and Germany. Krieger's comparative study tried to convince the international academic community that racial separation was good public policy not only in the Third Reich but also in the most powerful democracy in the world. He drew parallels between school segregation in the United States and recent race legislation in Germany forbidding the attendance of Jewish children in public schools. Enlightened educational policy in the United States, especially the South, recognized that a strict separation of Blacks from Whites in schools was a cultural necessity. National Socialism, Krieger noted, had taken the lead in applying this same principle to the Jews.[120]

As Hermann Giesecke observed, the differences between education, propaganda, and indoctrination were blurred under the Third Reich. Every public institution had the similar task of *Volkserziehung*.[121] The integration of race hygiene into the curriculum of Nazi elementary schools was part of this larger project of educating the nation. During the same year that Frercks and Hoffmann released their curriculum, a certain Hans Heinze from Halle contributed his *Rasse und Erbe* (Race and Heredity). Unlike the vast majority of texts published for race hygiene that were directed to teachers, Heinze's book was written for pupils. Heinze's conception of race education for children, reflected in this piece, is important not only for what he actually wrote but also for what he left out. The table of contents reflected a broad range of issues as well as an effort to personalize the question of race for children. One of Heinze's major curriculum assumptions was that young children could not be brought to the issue of race hygiene unless they first developed an understanding of race and related this concept to themselves and their own families. As the table of contents (see table 3.3) showed, children approached race through a series of questions leading up to the important challenge of "Your Task!"[122]

Plate 1. Book cover, *Wie kam der Jude zum Geld*? (*How the Jew Came to Money*), by Johann von Leers (Berlin: Fritsch, 1936). Tel Aviv University, The Sourasky Central Library, Wiener Library, photo courtesy of Beth Hatefutsoth, Photo Archive Tel Aviv.

Plate 2. Vogel Teaching Chart #57, "*Deutsche Art–Jüdische Art: Der Deutscher schafft, der Jude rasst*" ("Germany Ways–Jewish Ways: The German works, the Jew rests") from *Erblehre und Rassenkunde in bildlicher Darstellung* (*Heredity and Race Science in Pictorial Depiction*) by Alfred Vogel (Stuttgart: Verlag für nationale Literatur, 1938).

Plate 3. Vogel Teaching Chart #63, "*Jüdisches Geheimgesetzbuch: Höre, was der Talmud spricht!*" ("Jewish Secret Lawbook: Listen What the Talmud Speaks") from Vogel, *Erblehre* (1938).

Plate 4. Vogel Teaching Chart #71, "*Meide die Juden*" ("Avoid the Jews") from Vogel, *Erblehre* (1938). Upper panels informs views to "buy only from Germans" and to "go only to German doctors." The lower panel proclaims, "Wherever the Jew rules, so dies the farmer."

„Die Judennase ist an ihrer Spitze gebogen. Sie sieht aus wie ein Sechser..."

Plate 5. Classroom scene depicting a lesson on racial anti-Semitism from *Der Giftpilz* (*The Poison Mushroom*) by Ernst Hiemer (Nuremberg: Der Stürmer, 1938), p. 7. Caption reads: "The Jewish nose is bent at its point. It looks like the number six." Tel Aviv University, The Sourasky Central Library, Wiener Library, photo courtesy of Beth Hatefutsoth, Photo Archive Tel Aviv.

Plate 6. Jewish Teacher and Jewish Pupils Expelled from School under the Jeers of Classmates from *Trau keinem Jud' auf grüner Heid'*: *Ein Bilderbuch für Gross und Klein* (*Trust No Jew on the Green Heath: A Picture Book for Big and Little*), by Elvira Bauer (Nuremberg: Der Stürmer, 1936), p. 18. Tel Aviv University, The Sourasky Central Library, Wiener Library, photo courtesy of Beth Hatefutsoth, Photo Archive Tel Aviv.

Hinter den Brillengläfern funkeln zwei Verbrecheraugen und um die wulftigen Lippen fpielt ein Grinfen.

Plate 7. Scene in a doctor's office, "What Happened to Inge with a Jewish Doctor," from Hiemer, *The Poison Mushroom* (1938), p. 33. Caption reads: "Behind the lens of the glasses gleamed two eyes of a criminal and around the thick lips played a grin." Tel Aviv University, The Sourasky Central Library, Wiener Library, photo courtesy of Beth Hatefutsoth, Photo Archive Tel Aviv.

„Der Gott des Juden ist das Geld. Und um Geld zu verdienen, begeht er die größten Verbrechen. Er ruht nicht eher, bis er auf einem großen Geldsack sitzen kann, bis er zum König des Geldes geworden ist."

Plate 8. Scene in front of a stock exchange from Hiemer, *The Poison Mushroom* (1938), p. 51. Caption reads: "The God of the Jews is money. And in order to earn money, he commits the greatest crimes. He does not rest, until he can sit on a big sack of money, until he has become the king of money." Compare this economic imagery with that shown in Vogel's *Erblehre*, teaching chart #57. Tel Aviv University, The Sourasky Central Library, Wiener Library, photo courtesy of Beth Hatefutsoth, Photo Archive Tel Aviv.

Plate 9. "The Servant Girl," from Bauer, *Trau keinem Jud'* (1936), p. 11. Note the depiction of the Jewish man with cloven hooves offering jewelry to an Aryan woman, presumably for immoral purposes. Tel Aviv University, The Sourasky Central Library, Wiener Library, photo courtesy of Beth Hatefutsoth, Photo Archive Tel Aviv.

Plate 10. Scene at the beach, "Jews Are Unwanted Here," from Bauer, *Trau keinem Jud'* (1936), p. 19. Tel Aviv University, The Sourasky Central Library, Wiener Library, photo courtesy of Beth Hatefutsoth, Photo Archive Tel Aviv.

Table 3.3

Table of Contents
Race and Heredity (1934)

HANS HEINZE

Part One: Your Race!
1. What is generally a race?
2. The most important racial characteristics
3. Negroes, Mongolians and higher races
4. Something from those races living in Europe and Germany
    a) Names
    b) Dissemination
    c) Particular characteristics
    d) The racial composition of the German people
    e) How did the races come into being?
5. Are all races of equal value?
6. May we be proud of our race?

Part Two: The Legacy of Your Father!
1. What is heredity?
2. The miracle of new life
    a) Asexual and sexual reproduction
    b) Cell division
    c) Maturation
3. Are there laws of heredity?
4. How is heredity shown in people?
5. Environment and aptitude

Part Three: Your Task!
1. How can you help as an individual?
2. Which task has the state undertaken as the community of all
   German people?

Table of Contents from Hans Heinze, *Rasse und Erbe (Race and Heredity)*. Halle: Schroedel, 1934, p. 59.

The pedagogical format of Heinze's text suggested that pupils learned racial concepts most effectively if *Merksätze*, highlighted sentences encapsulating core ideas, appeared at the end of each instructional section. Similar to Graff, Heinze organized specific tasks for pupils after the *Merksätze* to reinforce learning about the dynamics of race. Carried over from the early days of scientific racism into Heinze's work is the Nazi penchant for phrenology.[123] Children learned how skull and facial indexes reflected physical differences between and among human beings (see figure 3.2). In this part of the lesson, the author revealed to pupils a anthropological qualification that, at least on the surface, represented a gross contradiction in the kind of race education usually legitimized for the youth of the New Germany. In closing the discussion over skull and facial measurements, Heinze offered an uncharacteristic admission about the limitations of phrenology:

The researcher has the greatest difficulties in determining the psychological and intellectual characteristics of race. For these there are no measurements and calculations. Into the inner beings of others one can—if generally—only slowly penetrate. One must live together with people, must observe them, attempt to get to know them, if one is to know their inner beings. One must see how they live, how they act in everyday life and during holidays, which customs and traditions they know, which fairy tales, legends and stories circulate among them. Only if one observes everything, compares results and summarizes, will one perhaps be able to say with some certainty that these people are so and the others are entirely different.[124]

Words like these very rarely appeared in Nazi curriculum materials. The reductionism and biological determinism of Nazi science made such qualifica-

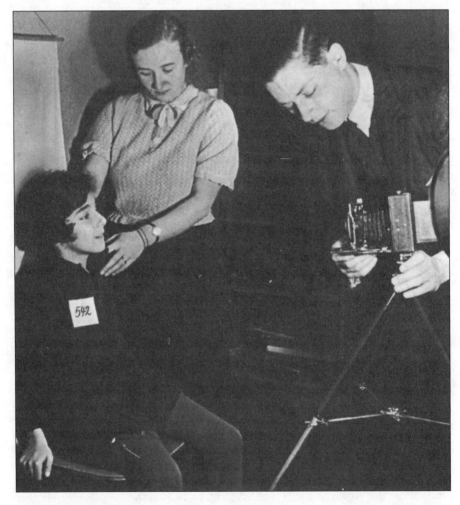

Figure 3.2 Racial examination of a Jewish child in Germany in 1936. Reprinted with permission of the Abraham Pisarek Archive in Berlin.

tions almost heretical in nature. The well-ordered universe of racial classifica-
tions and the attendant stereotypes so important to the teaching of race hygiene
still marked Heinze's writing. Over six decades later, one wonders if either
teachers or pupils noticed the inherent contradiction in this book as it circulated in the schools of the Third Reich. Only a few pages earlier, Heinze showed
pictures of a Black, a Korean, and a Nordic type from Holstein. Later, in a
section discussing "Negroes, Mongols and the Higher Races," Heinze highlighted the great differences between Germans and those of black skin and the
yellow race. He concluded that the two groups were both foreign and inferior
to the superior race of Nordics. Jews remained faceless and appeared only briefly
under the printed word on two occasions. Asked if all races were of equal value,
pupils quickly learned that only one answer would receive a hearing. Jews were
inherently unequal because their religion, customs, and traditions, as well as
their history, were so radically different from the Nordic peoples. The entire
program advanced by Heinze ended with the family tree of Adolf Hitler followed by closing words calling attention to the menacing threat of the *Ostjuden*,
especially those crossing German borders after the debacle of 1918. This was
an anti-Semitism that turned both inward and outward in focus. Apparently,
Jews and Blacks did not qualify for Heinze's anthropological call for careful
observation and indwelling while suspending judgment.[125]

Race hygiene, with its anthropological emphasis on maintaining cleanliness
and purity of blood, could not exist without the foil of others declared unclean.
The Austrian connection emerged in conveying this assumption to the schools.
One curriculum writer from Austria took special pains to translate Nazi ideology into a series of four hundred instructional drawings for use in elementary
schools and middle schools. *Erblehre, Rassenkunde und Bevölkerungspolitik*
(Heredity, race science, and population policy) appeared in Austrian schools
in 1941, some three years after the union with Germany. The etchings by Sepp
Burgstaller provide a brief glimpse into the dynamics of race curriculum as it
unfolded in the most Germanized country under Nazi occupation. Although
Austrian teachers often used curriculum materials published in Germany, this
collection is one of the few Austrian efforts to reduce the principles of race
teaching to their barest essentials. The power of image, wedded to an economy
of words, make Burgstaller's collection valuable in studying the history of
propaganda and its influence in the formation of curriculum. With his emphasis
on the use of instructional images, Burgstaller followed in the footsteps of Vogel
as well as Frercks and Hoffmann.[126]

Similar to his German counterparts, Burgstaller imposed a series of simplified categories for teaching youth about the evils of race mixing. After
bringing his young readers through pictorial renderings of cell divisions and
"cells as the building blocks of life," the author introduced a set of reductionist explanations of Gregor Mendel's findings on plant biology and the
dynamics of crossbreeding. A set of drawings under the title of "Jews Are a
Race Mixture" included a caricature of a Jew with an exaggerated hooked nose
situated at the confluence of four bloodlines. To reinforce the evils of race mixing,
Burgstaller created an image of a biological cell penetrated by the head of a
snake with a tail split into four sections. The sections delineated Near Eastern,
Hamitic, Oriental and Negroid bloodlines.[127] (See figure 3.3.)

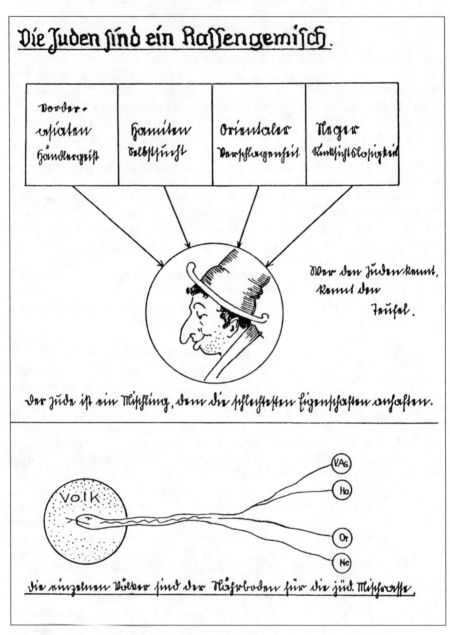

Figure 3.3 "The Jews Are a Racial Mixture," from Sepp Burgstaller, *Erblehre, Rassenkunde und Bevolkerungspolitik* (*Heredity, Race Science, and Population Policy*). Vienna: Jugend und Volk, 1941, p. 46.

Substantial sections on population policy and family drummed into the young charges the critical importance of raising the birthrate and cutting budgets for the care of the mentally ill and physically handicapped. The preservation of blood purity also meant a condemnation of "freedom, equality and brother-hood" as "slogans of world Jewry." Population figures entered the picture. Once again, as witnessed frequently in other curriculums, a geographical map of Germany, this time adorned with stick figures, informed pupils about the migration of 110,000 Jews into the Greater Reich between 1910 and 1930. A bar graph showed the increased population of Jews in Vienna: from 10,000 in 1848 to 201,000 in 1923. A table of professions pointed out that before Austria joined Germany, 52 percent of doctors in the city were Jewish.[128]

One of the most insidious uses of stereotyped images concerning those deemed racially unclean appeared late in the collection. "Bastards and Mixed Bloods under the People" portrayed images of blacks, Asians, Native Americans, and Jews. (See figure 3.4.) Beneath these drawings is the warning that race mixing between Aryans and any of these condemned races would increase the population of mixed bloods and contribute to the bastardization of the society. Burgstaller's characterization of Native Americans (identified as "Indians") and Asians is more virulent than that found in any of the race curriculums authored by Germans. There is also a subtle tendency to legitimize racial policy by appealing to religious tradition, something already well developed by Fritz Fink and Ferdinand Rossner. In a panel just below the stereotypical drawings, Burgstaller tried to convince young readers that "every race on this earth is a work of the Almighty. It contradicts the law of creation when man mixes these races." A disturbing portent for the future came with the very last drawing

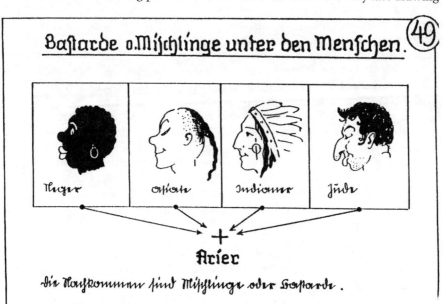

Figure 3.4 "Bastards and Mixed Bloods under the People," showing stereotyped figures representing "Negroes, Chinese, Indians, Jews," from Burgstaller, *Erblehre*, 1941, p. 49.

in the collection. Portraying a simplified map of Greater Germany crowned by a Nazi flag, youth are exhorted to greater sacrifice and obedience: "The flag of the Reich, the sign of resurrecting life, bears witness to Germany and pays heed and defends its blood, its race and its youth as its highest values."[129]

The abundance of curriculum evidence reflecting the importance of the Jewish question and the development of anti-Semitic attitudes and values among the young remains somewhat misleading. As concluded thus far, not all curriculum writers in race hygiene stressed racial anti-Semitism in the same way or with the same level of emphasis. Even in Hitler's racial state, such differences were not unusual since the Jews, although designated as the ultimate racial enemy, still remained one among other racial undesirables. Race hygiene was not only about the Jews. Werner Dittrich, whose work appeared in chapter 2 as a major contributor to the curriculum guides on the Jewish question, was another case in point. Publishing his curriculum guide in 1937, Dittrich used his post in Bayreuth in the NSLB to inform teachers about race science and hygiene. Working with Erich Meyer from Radebeul, Dittrich completed a teacher handbook, *Kleine Erb- und Rassenkunde* (Small heredity and race science) for teachers in Saxony some three years before. Nowhere in this resource are Jews mentioned. Meyer and Dittrich limit the brief discussion over foreign racial elements to the Tibetans, classified under the Mongols and African blacks. The volume was simply Nazi population policy writ large without the Jews.[130] At the other extreme, his curriculum guide from 1937 on educating the anti-Semite became one of the most concentrated curriculum resources on the subject.

What Dittrich wrote for teachers under *Vererbung und Rasse* (Heredity and race) in 1936 was a different story, one that acted as a kind of dress rehearsal for his infamous curriculum guide the following year. The section on Jews garnered significantly greater ink than that devoted to African Blacks and Mongols, this time portraying the Chinese through word and image. Dittrich's choice of picture for the discussion on Jews served a more subtle propaganda purpose. A Jew from Chicago appeared thus affirming connections between Jews and Chicago's recent history of gangsterism. Like many curriculum writers in race hygiene, Dittrich wanted readers to grasp the long historical view of his anti-Semitic ideas. He quoted Günther's racial anthropology in describing the "typical Jew," paid homage to Houston Stewart Chamberlain's thinking on the Jewish community and cited obligatory statistics from the Institute for the Jewish Question. The relatively brief, encyclopedic entry on the Jews concentrated attention on the Book of Moses, which, in keeping with Nazi doctrine, was wholly misinterpreted. Only a few months later, the fledgling contributor to race hygiene took on a much more in-depth look at the yet-unresolved problem of educating the anti-Semite across the curriculum.[131]

The place of the Jew in the curriculum, as Dittrich's case illustrated, was often not clearly articulated early in the Third Reich beyond the official curriculum directives. Some, like Frercks and Hoffmann, conceived the Jew as part of a larger constellation of racial enemies, while still devoting more attention to Blacks and hereditary illnesses. The nature and scope of anti-Semitic education were not an issue debated to any great extent among science educators as was, for example, the controversy over the legacy of Darwin and Lamarck regarding the relative importance of heredity versus environment. Albert Höft's *Arbeitsplan für erbbiologischen und rassenkundlichen Unterricht in der Schule* (Working plan for hereditary and race scientific instruction in the school), addressed to elementary educators in 1934, completely omitted discussion of any racial out group including the Jews. Höft (1901–1973) wrote in general philosophical terms about the importance of race hygiene in the curriculum but chose not to develop any content focus or offer pedagogical ideas regarding the racial enemies of the state. The native of Kiel had just completed his pedagogical exams at Göttingen before publishing this work. Unlike some of his other colleagues, Höft evidently was not moved by promises of career advancement or innate anti-Semitic passions to address the Jewish question. Following a tendency not altogether unusual in Nazi education, Höft wrote this piece for teachers and administrators without any substantive background in the natural or social sciences. His scholarly background was in German language and literature.[132]

Jakob Graf and Paul Brohmer, as well as medical people like Rainer Fetscher and Hans Krauß, demonstrated earlier that the respective beginning and ending points between biology and history often appeared indistinguishable. Technically, they wrote outside their fields when embarking on history. Yet, this was perfectly understandable from a Nazi perspective since the curriculum was best conceived as an organic whole tied together with the dynamism of race. Höft symbolized the reality that Nazi race education curriculum was not a monolithic phenomenon. When Höft communicated to teachers about "supporting and increasing the valuable nature of the German race and preventing Volkish degeneration," he said very little about those racial forces behind this degeneration. The section on race hygiene followed this same pattern. The existence of "foreign races" as a threat to the body politic only briefly crossed the pages of Höft's writing. The racial enemies of the Reich remained faceless and unidentified except for the *Ostjuden*, the negative other whose appearance in Nazi curriculum materials, as seen earlier, was almost a foregone conclusion. They remained among the most detested and feared of all the Jewish communities. Höft was not among those like Fritz Fink whose curriculum guide on the Jewish question unabashedly embraced Julius Streicher's brand of anti-Semitism. On the other hand, he chose a path similar to that of Paul Brohmer in using the language of subjective science to mask the underlying intentions of the curriculum in race hygiene. The Jewish question forever remained in the foreground in varying degrees no matter what the content focus.[133]

THE DEPTHS OF WAR AND THE ENDURANCE OF RACE HYGIENE

Even to the most casual observer, the horrendous defeat of Hitler's Seventh Army at Stalingrad during the winter of 1942–43 reflected serious weaknesses in the capability of the Third Reich to carry on a two-front war. In the face of this military debacle, and for some time afterward, anti-Semitism and the Jewish question remained of paramount importance for the further conduct of the war. Once again, the "war against the Jews," as Lucy Dawidowicz aptly described it, explained why Hitler eventually invested so much rolling stock, a tremendous number of SS personnel, and medical people as well as a burgeoning bureaucracy to conduct the Final Solution. One might call this the third front of Hitler's war. The mass murder of all Jews on the European continent was not merely an idle propaganda threat. The dictator had warned of this outcome in January of 1939 in a speech before the Reichstag should the war become a reality. A sobering affirmation of his pronouncement came with the ovens of Auschwitz that continued to burn until late 1944.

The anti-Semitic curriculum of the Third Reich closely reflected the policy orientation of the regime. The war only heightened the tone of a racial anti-Semitism that had already existed with the blessing of science decades before Hitler. The matter of educating young anti-Semites with ideologically appropriate rationalizations for treating Jews and others as subhuman was too important a value for the regime to be left to the likes of Bernhard Rust and the Ministry of Education. This was true both before and during the war. Phillip Bouhler from Hitler's Chancellery, as noted in chapter 1, became involved in a power struggle with Rust over controlling the censorship of textbooks. As the war progressed, the anti-Semitic language used by certain government offices in producing curriculum materials on the Jews became more and more vociferous in nature. Never far from the focus of these curriculum resources were the underlying ideas that had defined the character of race hygiene and the image of the Jew. Textbooks alone were not entrusted with this task.

The Main School Office of the NSDAP became involved in 1943 with the creation and dissemination of an instructional program called *Schulungs-Unterlage* (Schooling document). These relatively brief papers provided teachers with focused pedagogical themes. Their thematic paper, "3000 Years of Jewish Hatred," appeared at a time when German Jews had already either fled the country or faced deportation. The eight-page document revealed that racial anti-Semitism was still alive and well in the Nazi education establishment even though Jews ceased to exist in Germany. Jewish hatred for all things German, an old anti-Semitic theme, emerged once again. Jews are blamed for the war and become familiar scapegoats for all manner of problems in world history. This time, the invisible Jew, the one no longer seen and heard, takes on the mantle of archfiend. The fact that Jews were no longer around made them even more dangerous.

> The Jewish question is, however, in the first line not an economic, but rather a racial one. That means that the individual Cohn or Levi are not our enemies, but the race. . . . The visible opponent is never so dangerous as the invisible. Known are the most dangerous enemies of our physical existence, the bacillae, and these are invisible. We do not see them, but sense them intuitively. Therefore, the battle against them will be led. This is exactly so with the Jew: We do not see him anymore, but we *sense him intuitively (spüren ihm.)* We sensed him for years in his malicious agitation, we sense him now in the war. The war is his work.[134]

As one of the most concentrated and compact anti-Semitic writings to emerge from the war years, the treatise on 3000 years of Jewish hatred was in itself a shrill expression of German hatred for Jews. The endurance of racial anti-Semitism through the language of biology, articulated in the threat of the bacillus, found a philosophical home in this work as it had in many others. There is a certain sense of urgency in this piece. Teachers read a densely written statement on content without any discussion of teaching methodology. It was as if the authors wanted to disseminate the writing, in distilled fashion, as quickly as possible to schools across the Reich, many of which had to be relocated in the countryside in order to escape the threat of Allied bombing. Even in the darkest days of the war, racial anti-Semitism held an instructional importance for the regime.

The closing paragraphs centered on the Jew as "a blood vulture," a mass murderer, and a conspirator plotting world domination. Horst Wessl, so it was written, fell victim to Jewish hatred. Jews were behind the assassinations of Abraham Lincoln and William McKinley in the United States and the financial resources of that country. Whether his name was Moredeci or Litinov, the face of the Jew as great hater was the same. Such characterizations, although not new, came into this educational publication at a time when the machinery of death was in full swing in the East under the boot of the SS. While the death camps were not mentioned, the implied outcome for the Jews came through the last sentence of the document with great clarity: "One can not make an agreement with him [the Jew], he can only be put down" (*ihn kann man bloß niederschlagen.*)[135]

The power of race biological language in framing anti-Semitic education was even more forcefully articulated during the war by Alfred Rosenberg. His ministry, charged with oversight for "the total intellectual and worldview schooling and education for the NSDAP," handed to school officials and the SS office on race instruction one particular instructional theme for the entire 1943–44 school year. The "Jew as world parasite" was to be the formative content theme for the term. Taken as a whole, this anti-Semitic curriculum, one of the most detailed to be published that year, was an attempt to dehumanize Jews on a variety of levels. In contrast to most other anti-Semitic publications, Rosenberg's ministry was much more serious about addressing the *Protocols of the Elders of Zion*. The authors prided themselves on providing readers with extensive documentation proving the gravity of the Jewish threat to German culture. The *Protocols* was one way of demonstrating to pupils that Jews really were bent on dominating the entire world.[136]

The movement against the Jews, Rosenberg's ministry argued, was "one of the most basic and most difficult struggles of our party." Writing in the form of a tightly outlined series of arguments, Rosenberg's people wanted readers to be well informed about the multitude of ways used by Jews to destroy the host culture. The image of the Jew as a cultural parasite feeding off the blood of superior races, the centerpiece of this work, rested on both racial and religious forms of stereotyping. Pulling from an anti-Semitic strain steeped in economics, the ministry called into question the Jewish concept of work, a concept near and dear to the heart of Germans in defining the authentic citizen. Returning to the fray were anti-Semitic attitudes that earlier found expression in Vogel and Graff. Yes, they wrote, Jews devalued physical work, but how could it be otherwise? Here was a people who perceived work as just another way of making profit. The goal of the Jewish community was not to create values but to pile them up like so many commodities. This was the way of the parasite who sucked creative cultures dry.[137]

Those who worked with Rosenberg, as well as the university professors, teachers, and school administrators who advanced anti-Semitic education in the schools, did so with the assumption that Nazism would triumph in the end. Their enemy, the Jew, was demonized not only for religious reasons but also because of biology. Race hygiene, a stepchild of eugenics, appeared in the curriculum in alliance with racial anthropology as a most subjective science. Considering the dynamics of anti-Semitism in the Third Reich, it was therefore not a great mystery why the Talmud garnered so much attention. Here were the law books that set the Jews apart as the chosen people, as a mixed race whose bloodlines combined elements most abhorrent to the dedicated Nazi. The Talmud remained just as important to the curriculum of race hygiene and biology as it was for history and religion. As Vogel demonstrated through his teaching charts, learning the Nazi interpretation of the Talmud was part of the definition of the educated person.

The formative concept of racial anti-Semitism, broadly conceived as it was for almost the entire curriculum, also carried powerful historical and geographical perspectives. These elements were also part of the Nazi vision of the educated person. Like many other aspects of Nazi curriculum, they also carried the myth of Nordic pedagogy. The place of the Jews in this biological universe, as defined by history and geography, is a curricular issue which commands our attention in the next chapter.

Chapter 4

The Jew as Cultural Outsider in History and Geography

> The Jew destroys the German essence.
> —Herbert Göbel, *Deutsche Geschichte*, 1937

History as propaganda is a feature of education prevalent in both democracies and dictatorships.[1] Under the Third Reich, historical truth remained distorted by ideological bias and deceit. One particular instance in the history curriculum of Nazi Germany deserves closer attention. The threat of terror and some modicum of secrecy were important conditions in securing an efficient administration of the police state. Any discussion of concentration camps was strictly forbidden in classrooms across the Reich. Dachau, the first concentration camp created for political prisoners, opened less than two months after Hitler's assumption of power on 30 January 1933. Social Democrats and Communists, including Jews, were among the first inmates. Later, continuing violence leveled against Jews reached another brutal stage with the Night of the Broken Glass in the fall of 1938.[2]

One rare exception to the general instructional secrecy regarding the camps emerged in the publication of a National Socialist "history table for teaching aims" created by Hans Roepke for elementary pupils under the title *What Must You Know about the Third Reich?* Appearing in 1935, this history catechism of over 300 questions and answers provided a historical overview of the Nazi movement and contemporary developments. Dedicated readers soon discovered that only one answer was permissible. Alternative historical interpretations growing out of a spirit of inquiry, as Victor Klemperer observed in his reflections on the language of the Third Reich, simply remained outside the scope of Nazi mentality. In relation to one especially sensitive security issue, the legitimized answer advanced a historical lie. Question #242 asked when the concentration camps were dissolved and the prisoners released. The prescribed answer misinformed pupils into thinking that Minister President Hermann Goering had already issued the order to close the camps on the first day of September 1934.[3] Deceit intertwined with mythology became the hallmarks of the Nazi conception of history of which this example is only a small part.

Designated as special bearers of German culture, history and geography assumed an important role in the formation of the educated person in Nazi schools. Recent studies of the history curriculum in schools under the Third Reich have tended to take a macro perspective on this subject.[4] Still needed in the scholarship is a more focused examination of the place of anti-Semitism in the formation of the history and geography curriculums for the *Volksschule*. The racial orientation of these two school subjects, already articulated years before in Hitler's *Mein Kampf*, advanced anti-Semitic perspectives on Jews in a variety of ways.[5] As noted earlier, the integrated quality of the Nazi curriculum for elementary schools meant that content boundaries between school subjects often remained blurred. This was especially true for history and geography. For example, one Nazi propaganda image painted Jews as perpetual wanderers from country to country never possessing a genuine culture of their own. The Jew thereby gained the epithet as a destroyer rather than a creator of culture. The image drew from geographical concepts of place and space as well as historical perspectives on continuity and change. Geography and history, in Nazi curriculum parlance, became twin elements in the political socialization of the young of which racial anti-Semitism was a dynamic part.[6]

Hitler's own recollections of history instruction from his school days bears consideration. This was history not moved by intellectual discourse but by stirring the emotions and imaginations of youth steeped in nationalistic fervor. World history itself was to become, in the view of the future dictator, one of his great teachers. In these lines, the potential for history as propaganda became evident:

> The art of reading as of learning is this: to retain the essential, to forget the non-essential. Perhaps it affected my whole later life that good fortune sent me a history teacher who was one of the few to observe this principle in teaching and examining. Dr. Leopold Pötsch, my professor at the *Realschule* in Linz, embodied this requirement to an ideal degree. This old gentleman's manner was as kind as it was determined, his dazzling eloquence not only held us spellbound, but actually carried us away. Even today I think back with gentle emotion on this gray-haired man who, by the fire of his narratives, sometimes made us forget the present; who, as if by enchantment, carried us into past times and, out of the millenial veils of misty, molded dry historical memories into living reality. On such occasions we sat there, often aflame with enthusiasm, and sometimes even moved to tears. What made our good fortune all the greater was that this teacher knew how to illuminate the past by examples from the present, and how from the past to draw inferences for the present. As a result, he had more understanding than anyone else for all the daily problems which then held us breathless. He used our budding nationalistic fanaticism as a means of educating us, frequently appealing to our sense of national honor ... This teacher made history my favorite subject.[7]

As developments later testified, the new history for the children of the Third Reich would fire nationalistic loyalties while, at the same time, introduce the young to a strong racial sense of both past and present. As Victor Klemperer intimated earlier, German Nazism could not exist without the arch-enemy of the Jew. The German history curriculum, supported by studies in race hygiene, history and literature, and geography, reinforced this observation.

CURRICULUM DIRECTIVES

Early Nazi curriculum directives conceived of history and geography as tools of propaganda designed to recast Germany's present and past. Following a strong emphasis on warning children about the devastating consequences of race mixing with Jews, the Reich Education Ministry directed teachers to instruct young charges about the struggle of Germans to regain territory. Within this larger geographical perspective, instruction accentuated the unique and wholesome "intellectual-spiritual" and physical qualities of the "connected" Nordic race in contrast to the racially undesirable and "separated" Jews. Teaching about Europe and especially non-European countries demanded a sharp comparison of foreign races with the culture of middle Europeans.[8]

Geography educators looking for more specific content linkages to support this racial orientation would not be disappointed. Once again, as noted earlier, the immigration policies of other countries, especially the United States, France, and Australia, offered further possibilities for teachers to establish interrelationships between race, state, and culture. Without specifically naming other countries, the Education Ministry also strongly encouraged teachers to integrate historical and contemporary laws from various nations to preserve racial purity. The colonial question provided even more opportunities to stress the superiority of the Nordic race. Using what came to be known as "cultural-geographical reflections," pupils could draw racial conclusions from colonial history and offer justifications for colonial rule of subject peoples. German colonies in Africa thus provided part of the curriculum context for this aspect of race geography which, as illustrated earlier, appeared in the treatment of blacks in race hygiene.

Not overlooked was a disturbing challenge from the legacy of Lamarckian genetics and its great emphasis on the role of the environment in shaping and changing human cultures. Such thinking suggested that race was not a fixed concept and, furthermore, called into question the assumption, honored by many Nazi theorists like Ferdinand Rossner and Hans F. K. Günther, that racial classification based on innate and unchanging qualities was the defining principle of all cultures. The Education Ministry did not deny the influence of environmental factors in shaping cultural achievements. On the other hand, education officials tried to discredit Lamarckian thinking by presenting a rationalization of their own. Geography educators could show youth that the people most capable of creating culture, by racial definition excluding the Jews, usually lived under adverse environments. These conditions created a decisive source of strength in the struggle for cultural survival and growth. Race was still the overarching determinant in defining authentic culture. The cultural geography embraced by the Nazis raised historical examples from ancient Egypt, Mesopotamia, Greece, and Rome which, for primarily racial reasons, experienced both triumph and collapse.[9]

The curriculum directive from 1933 devoted more attention to history than to any other traditional school subject. A critical element of the school's ideological identity, history instruction rested on the preservation of certain myths as part of legitimized school knowledge for the young and the future vision of the Third Reich. In this sense, history joined biology, race hygiene, geography,

German literature and language, physical education, and foreign languages in the Nazi curriculum in purveying a racial mythology.[10] As with each generation, the Nazis invariably decided whose history would be legitimized as an ideologically acceptable framework for interpreting the past. The biological cast of history, rooted in a struggle to preserve racial community, supported the ideological thrust of the history curriculum:

> History has shown the meaning of the races for the development and passing of peoples while applying knowledge of our people and in translating character. A racial conception of history built on results from heredity and biology refutes views like those expressed in liberal progressive teachings. From racial thinking is furthermore the rejection of so-called democracies or other efforts derived at achieving equality and the strengthening of the sense for the leadership of the Führer. World history is presented as the history of racially determined peoples. In the place of the teaching, "Ex oriente lux," enters the knowledge that at least all of the western cultures are predominantly the work of Nordic peoples, who in the Near East, Greece, Rome and generally all other European countries—in part through conflict with other races—had asserted themselves or finally paid the price because they had unconsciously acted against the natural laws of race . . . So must youth experience German history as a continuous struggle surging back and forth over the substance and form of Germanic-German nature which protects itself against the strain of foreign influences and is encircled by living space. This violent struggle is not from the masses, but rather is carried forth by great leaders. Their lives and aspirations form therefore the firm calling for every history instruction. . . . With the biological laws of life defining this kind of historical reflection, there is also shown the tremendous, far reaching cultural meaning of the national socialist renewal of our day. The German educator and German youth must be aware that they are collectively responsible for the success of this renewal.[11]

The integration of anti-Semitic perspectives into history and geography instruction, the major thrust for this chapter, obviously did not take place within a cultural vacuum. As argued before in connection with race hygiene, anti-Semitic teachings in the Nazi curriculum drew on the thinking of Volkish forbears and more recent developments engendered by racial science. Moreover, to reinforce earlier discussions, Jews were not the only members consigned to the dubious distinction of negative others. There is a deeply imbued sense of mission and destiny in the curriculum articulated for both history and geography. Although each existed as single standing subjects in the curriculum plans of the elementary school, the curriculum directive examined above made it clear that the two stood in close relationship in defining the educated, racially conscious person. The geographical concept of *living space,* for example, was at the same time historical in nature because of the perceived threat of the *Ostjuden* to German aspirations for territory in the East. On paper, both history and geography garnered two hours of instructional time per week for grades five and six. History instruction increased to three hours for grades seven and eight, while geography remained at two. (See appendices 1 and 2.)

The Jewish Question and the New History

The place of Jews in Nazi history instruction, as in all other major courses of study, drew from both traditional and more contemporary racial forms of anti-Semitic thinking.[12] The practice of rewriting history in order to inculcate stronger anti-Semitic viewpoints was approached with great seriousness by Nazi officialdom. Researching the historical dimensions of the Jewish question took on a much greater visibility in the education community when Bernhard Rust from the Education Ministry established in Berlin the Reich Institute for the History of the New Germany in 1935. Walter Frank became president of the institute, which joined notable National Socialist historians with prominent researchers like racial anthropologists Eugen Fischer and Otmar Freiherr von Verschuer from the prestigious Kaiser Wilhelm Institute. Also part of the group was Hans F. K. Günther. Julius Streicher, Alfred Rosenberg, and Heinrich Himmler were present at the inauguration of the institute's work. The Institute for the History of the New Germany, deeply engaged as it was in the articulation of anti-Semitic historical perspectives, soon found itself in competition with other agencies like the Frankfurt Institute for the Study of the Jewish Question.[13]

The activity of the Institute for the History of the New Germany represented part of the larger bureaucratic and academic context of anti-Semitic thinking about the past. Just how much of their work influenced writers of history curriculum and textbooks for schools remains unknown. Although the institute was largely oriented toward the university research community, its efforts are worthy of note for this investigation. One of the functions of the institute was to conduct "objective" historical research on the history of the Jewish question. Such findings, so it was hoped, would find their way into university classes populated in part by future teachers of history. Another goal was to disseminate publications on the Jewish question in history to public school officials and teachers.

Wilhelm Grau, the secretary general of the institute until 1942, insisted that the Jewish question was the most important historical issue for not only the Third Reich but all of humanity. The goal of conducting historical research on Jews was to set the record straight about their real intentions over time. Grau insisted that the timing of the institute's work was most propitious. Now, for the first time, Jewish history could be taken out of the exclusive hands of theologians and placed under the auspices of historians where it belonged. Furthermore, the ideology of liberalism and "liberal science," which for so long ignored the importance of emancipation and the drive for equality in contributing to the contemporary influence of Jews, could be exposed in all of its weakness. Only a very few German scholars, Grau wrote, had taken up the subject of Jews in history as worthy of serious research. The dynamic cultural vision of the Third Reich had already changed this situation. Grau and his colleagues at the Institute for the History of the New Germany fashioned their own illusions of objectivity and scientific certainty concerning one of the central racial pariahs of Nazi culture. The institute's writing of Jewish history represented another way of extending control over historical memory. By doing so, Grau and the institute further advanced the perception of the Jew as negative other wholly separated from the German community. Most closely associated with the history and culture of the German people, he insisted, was the problem of the Jews.[14]

The work of both institutes in Berlin and Frankfurt, according to Patricia von Papen, "showed that the anti-Jewish science of propaganda was better served than the propaganda of *Stürmer* [Streicher's anti-Semitic newspaper] since it claimed a verifiable historical reality and was therefore more difficult to refute."[15] As profoundly biased and politically motivated as this "historical reality" remained under Nazi interpretations, the veneer of academic respectability afforded by institutes like these became another justification for the regime's vigorous anti-Semitic agenda. History, along with science, could be pressed into service for precise ideological reasons. The public schools, as agents of political socialization, remained important institutions in this process. The Institute for the History of the New Germany did not ignore the significant role played by history teachers in the development of anti-Semitic attitudes among young children entering Germany's classrooms.

One of the most focused pieces of writing on the implications of the Jewish question for schools came from the pen of Wilhelm Grau. His *The Jewish Question in German History*, initially published in 1936 and appearing in a fifth edition by 1943, stressed the continuity of National Socialist Jewish legislation with Germanic alien laws. Grau tried to show how Jews secured influence among Germans over time. The connection with ancient Rome was significant in Grau's historical scheme, for it was the Romans who unwittingly brought Jewish traders to the north. Here, in cities founded by the Romans, the Jews gained a foothold and survived subsequent mass migrations. On the origins of Jewish ghettos from the Middle Ages, Grau's history is veiled in a kind of victim blaming. The city of Speyer in 1084 for the first time set up a wall surrounding the Jewish quarter. Grau defended the action by saying that German citizens had no attention of turning the ghetto into a prison but rather intended the walls as protection for the Jewish community. Eventually, the ghetto had in fact took on a prisonlike environment because Jews "made the situation increasingly unpleasant for themselves" (*sich immer mehr unliebsam bermerkbar machte*). This explained why the Jews, supported by financial dealings, then turned their attention toward gaining influence among the princes and bishops.[16]

Grau's thin, thirty-two-page volume could be regarded as one of the most succinct anti-Semitic historical treatises for the school population. The secretary general of the Institute for the History of the New Germany offered nothing new to the history of Jews from Nazi and earlier Volkish perspectives. One could read much the same thing in the work of Theodor Fritsch's popular *Handbook of the Jewish Question: The Most Important Facts on the Judgment of the Jewish People*, which reached its fortieth edition by 1936.[17] What Grau's pedagogical piece contributed was the full weight of one of the most prestigious academic institutes under the Third Reich for a thoroughgoing anti-Semitic recasting of history instruction. Although he did not participate directly in the actual writing of the history curriculum, Grau nonetheless gave teachers and school administrators a useful content overview emphasizing some of the most important milestones in the history of anti-Semitism.

Grau articulated familiar anti-Semitic themes with an economy of words. Such a resource doubtlessly appealed to those educators less willing to take on tomes by Hans F. K. Günther and Theodor Fritsch, the great popularizers of anti-Semitic thinking. Readers would find in Grau's economic stereotypes and scapegoating enough prejudicial assumptions about Jews to at least form a substantive point of departure for an anti-Semitic pedagogy in the history classroom. Emerging from Grau's perspective on the Jewish experience was an implied warning. Jews made debtors out of provinces and territorial princes in the past to advance their selfish interests. Bavaria carried a debt of 5 million gilder to a coterie of rich Jewish families in 1723. If this wasn't enough, the much larger Jewish population remained in ghettos where they received deserved treatment as "foreign bodies" among the people. It was one of the darkest developments of modern history when Jews gained full emancipation in the shadow of the French Revolution with the aid of liberalism. Enjoying the rights of full citizenship, Jews ascended to even greater heights of political and economic influence under the Bismarckian era supported by a conspiratorial control of the press and public opinion.[18]

Bringing the Jews to this privileged position were key historical misjudgments that spelled disaster for Germany. The great rift between Christians and Jews was not directly exploited by Grau, in contrast to many other writers examined thus far. The big mistake committed by Christians, according to Grau, was that they simply regarded the Jew as a "missionary object" (Bekehrungsobjekt) for conversion to the Christian faith while overlooking the profound evil at the core of Jewish being. A misguided "enlightened humanism" remained bent on placing Jews on the same level as all other peoples. Grau concluded that the struggle against the cultural penetration of the Jews "would be carried forth by only a few courageous souls," thus implying the rectitude of Nazi anti-Semitic policy.[19]

HISTORY AND THE JEW: EARLY DIRECTIONS

Little time passed between the release of the Education Ministry's curriculum directive in the fall of 1933 on the teaching of genetics and racial science and the appearance of published teaching plans on the Jewish question in history. Under the broad rubric of teaching plans for "state policy" in elementary school history classes, the NSLB offered educators a means by which content on World War I and the Nazi movement could be connected to the influence of Jews. The teaching plans shown in table 4.1, presented in broad outlines, did not come in the form of a curriculum directive from either Berlin or Gau (district) education officials. The NSLB, through its various professional journals, often published curriculum ideas from teachers, professors, and school administrators in the field.[20] What follows from 1934 is a proposed set of linkages between specific historical events and their relationship to the Jew as cultural and racial outsider. The exclamation points following the expressions about Jews come from the original authorship.[21]

The appeal to emotion, a hallmark of Nazi propaganda, also became a major characteristic of this and other teaching plans on history and the Jewish question. The highly sensitive reference to Golgotha as a symbol of Germany's plight after the end of World War I drew from centuries of Christian anti-Semitism

Table 4.1
Teaching Plans on "State Policy" for Elementary Schools of the Third Reich

Week	Content Area	Relationship to Jews
1–4	Germany before the war. Class struggle, profit, strike.	The Jew plants himself!
5–8	From agrarian state to industrial state. Colonies.	The farmer in the claws of Jews!
9–12	Conspiracy against Germany, isolation, barrage around Germany.	The Jew rules! War companies.
13–16	German struggles— German distress, blockade! Death from starvation!	The Jew becomes prosperous! Exploitation of distress.
17–20	Stab in the back Collapse.	Jews as leaders of the November revolt.
21–24	Germany's Golgotha. Erzberger's crimes! Versailles.	*Ostjuden* migrate. The Jew triumphs!
25–28	Adolf Hitler. National Socialism.	The opponent of the Jews!
29–32	Bleeding boundaries. Enslavement of Germany. Free Corps.	The Jew pulls out profit from German distress. Loans (Dawes, Young).
33–36	National Socialism in a struggle with the underworld and criminality.	Jewish instigators of murder. Jewish press.
37–40	Germany's youth forward! The victory of faith.	The final struggle against the Jews.

"Teaching Plans on State Policy," from *Der Nationalsozialistische Erzieher*, Nr. 42/1934, cited in Jochen Herring et al. *Schüleralltag im Nationalsozialismus* (Dortmund: Pädagogische Arbeitsstelle, 1984), p. 269.

with a curious parallel made between the suffering and death of Christ on the cross and the tribulations of Germany in the shadow of the Great War. One will not find any anti-Semitic references of a racial nature in this piece. While the grade level recommended for the curriculum proposal remains unclear, there appears to be an underlying assumption that at least younger children investigating Jews and Germany's recent past were better informed if they maintained a focus on more traditional forms of anti-Semitism.

One notes the resurrection of old economic antipathies directed against Jews because of shady dealings with German farmers. Jews are also accused of greed and a lust for profits at a time of German national emergency. The ancient charge of conspiracy resonated in this curriculum as well. The dark specter of the *Ostjuden*, one of the most persistent themes throughout the entire anti-Semitic curriculum of Nazi schools, found another means of expression. Castigated in this curriculum was the Catholic Center Party politician Matthias Erzberger who signed the armistice for Germany and worked for the acceptance of the dreaded Versailles Treaty. He joined that condemned circle of November criminals made up mostly of Jews conspiring to bring Germany's war efforts to naught. The Jew, as scapegoat for Germany's troubles, maintained the dubious role as main actor in this sordid historical drama.

As in race hygiene and biology, there was a flurry of activity in the writing and publishing of curriculum materials on history during the early years of the Third Reich by a broad circle of people. Publishers, professors, teachers, and school administrators joined the fray. For some, publishing curriculum in this and other areas promised career advancement and possibly curried favor with the Nazi Party. One publisher especially interested in conveying a history of the Third Reich to youth was Werner May of Heinrich Handels publishing house in Breslau. He created a *German National Catechism: What a German Boy and German Girl Should Know about the Third Reich* (1934). Much more detailed in its responses to a preset collection of questions than the volume by Hans Roepke discussed earlier, this work provided pupils with an overview of major Nazi personalities, highlights from the biography of Adolf Hitler, and the political program of the Nazi Party. An equally important part of the catechism was a section on "Race and People." The pattern of questions and the ideologically correct answers developed by May left concerning little doubt the identity of the biggest racial enemy in German history. The author's purpose was to persuade young readers that the most significant history regarding German-Jewish relations was contemporary in nature encompassing their own lives:

> With which race had National Socialism to take up the struggle? Why? What created this impression? With what did the Jews subjugate the peoples? What happened to the farmers who were driven off the land? What is, furthermore, the great guilt of the Jews? What is *Rassenschande* [sexual relations with a non-Aryan]? What must the National Socialist movement do?[22]

To pound home the gross distortion that Jews were historically responsible for the nation's misfortune, May crafted answers that exploited economic stereotypes while reminding pupils that Jews really were members of a race. Emerging once again is an image of the Jew whose concept of work profoundly differed from that of the Aryan community. "The work of the Aryan people," May wrote, "is a true creation." On the other hand, Jews had always pursued the devious ways of the trader. The honorable and authentic work of the construction worker, miner, blacksmith, and sailor were not part of the Jewish view of the world. After all, May insisted, the great discoveries in technology were made by Aryans. Jewish subjugation of the entire population through the power of money was a matter of even greater seriousness for young minds to grasp. The ancient association of Jews with the lending of money and interest income brought many Germans to poverty. High interest rates charged by Jewish financial dealers forced countless peasants to sell land that had been in their families for over one hundred years. In an example of twisted logic, May accused

Jewish leaders of severely persecuting the Nazi movement through control of the press and law courts.[23]

Creating and distributing to schools ideologically sound curriculum materials for the teaching of history with a decided anti-Semitic bent tested the resources of both the Education Ministry and the NSLB. The Nazis obviously were not the first to publish Volkish curriculum ideas on history instruction. Georg Collischonn and Max Maurenbrecher, right-wing pedagogues from the Weimar era, were among the people who pioneered efforts to inculcate a stronger Volkish agenda into the teaching of history in German schools.[24] However, the Nazis were the first and only regime to fully institutionalize a racist and anti-Semitic history curriculum. At the same time, the Nazis could draw on continuities supportive of the regime including the imperialist and nationalist tendencies already prevalent in the profession of history teaching during the Wilhelmian era.[25] There emerged another development in curriculum writing already evident in the work cited earlier by Ferdinand Rossner, the Hanover pedagogue. Rossner, as a didactics professor in science, readily integrated history and religion into his perspective on race education. Karl Hahn, a teacher of science at a secondary school in Hamburg, was also a member of the faculty at the Teachers Training College there. Although Hahn was most intimately involved with physics and the natural sciences, his strongest contribution to curriculum came through a series of essays on the historical and anthropological implications of the Jewish question. Once again, people from the fields of science and history readily crossed disciplinary lines to strengthen the integration of race education.

Hahn was part of the daunting effort to bring together teaching resources on the subject of anti-Semitism not long after Hitler assumed power and several years before new and Nazified textbooks came off the press. Leading a project on *Volk und Rasse*, Hahn supervised the creation of brief, tightly written essays for teachers published in a journal format. The major purpose was to deliver content that could be used in a variety of course settings. Very possibly, these essays were among those used in teacher seminars since they were billed as working papers for curriculum and instruction in the schools. First published in 1934, a second edition appeared the following year.

Of special import for the present study are two papers out of a special collection of ten dealing with various aspects of racial science. Essays on "The Racial Science of the Jewish People" and "The Jewish Question," among the longest of the entire collection, retained a strong historical focus with support drawn from racial anthropology. The racial composition of Jews, a staple for both science and history curriculums, was always presented as a way of reinforcing the reality that Jews really were different from Germans on the basis of bloodlines, the issue that mattered the most for citizenship under the Third Reich. The myth of Nordic pedagogy, based as it was on the spurious assumption of racial purity, was not always expressed in the same way by race educators. Karl Hahn, like many other colleagues in education, admitted that Jews, "like all people," were a racial mixture. The key difference was in racial composition. Hahn, in contrast to the vast majority of curriculum writers, insisted that part of the early Hebrew community from 1400 to 1000 B.C. exhibited a "Nordic element." Ultimately, the Amorites came into the picture with the Hittites and the Philistines, all of whom followed Nordic leadership. Hahn, like Jakob Graf in chapter 3, made certain that readers understood that the Philistine giant Goliath was among these noble characters exhibiting Nordic qualities.[26]

The story of racial composition obviously does not end here. To Hahn and many others with a strong faith in racial anthropology, Jews were Jews because they also carried the bloodlines of the Near Eastern "race of the city," the Oriental desert race, the Ethiopian "ruling race" with Hamitic tongues, and the "childlike" Negroid race from Africa. As witnessed in the previous discussion of race hygiene, the Nazis readily exploited the alleged racial connection between Jews and Blacks with a propaganda purpose of bringing insult to both groups.

Since Jews were defined first and foremost as the biological offspring of racial mixing, Hahn saw fit to bring racial anthropology to bear on explaining the complex question of the Jewish "racial soul." Without really explaining to readers the meaning of this term, the teacher-educator took a page out of Hans Günther and Ludwig Clauß and proceeded to rationalize the entire issue.[27] Controlling the fate of racial undesirables under the Nazi system required a knowledge of the inner as the well as the outer qualities of the victims. In part, Hahn tried to oblige his readers through presenting a table that outlined specific differences in the inner life and behavior of Jews from the four racial groups. What follows in table 4.2 not only reflected racial and cultural stereotyping par excellence but also offered a superb example of a selective tradition supporting the myth of Nordic pedagogy. History intersected with anthropology in Hahn's curriculum perspective.

Even the most cursory reading of these cultural descriptions reveals a pronounced racial denigration not only of Jews as a whole but also Blacks. The most concentrated negative stereotypes appeared under criminal tendencies. Even the Shakespearean character of Shylock from the play *The Merchant of Venice* is pressed into service to accentuate the alleged cruelty of the Jews. What remained conveniently unaddressed was the suffering of Shylock in the face of unrelenting anti-Semitic practices common to his era. Negative qualities associated with Black Africans in this piece of Nazi curriculum are so common and explicit in nature that they almost overshadowed the original focus on the Jews. The common Nazi practice of associating Jewish with African blood was, by calculated design, an attempt to broaden as well as deepen the scope of racial anti-Semitism. The only people coming out of this curious exercise in gross anthropological simplification with at least some racial respectability are those connected to Ethiopian bloodlines. The legacy of ancient Egypt undoubtedly wielded some influence in fashioning Hahn's interpretations. The inclusion of an image of the famous sculpted head of Queen Hatshepsut, set beside less favorable artistic renderings of Near Eastern and "Oriental" people, symbolized yet another level of cultural bias.[28]

In fashioning a history of the Jewish people, Hahn followed the Nazi practice, not uncommon in other cultures, of exercising tight control over historical memory. Ideological control over historical interpretation also meant control over the historical identity of racial outcasts. As this chapter demonstrates on a variety of levels, preparing history curriculum for the young invariably involved an articulation of myths and cultural ideals held dear by the Nazi regime.

Table 4.2
The Soul of Non-European Races in the Jewish People

	Near Eastern	Oriental	Ethiopian	Negroid
Movement	Cunning, heavy stature	Supple, obliging	Adroit–Powerful Well-groomed	Somewhat lively, partly faint
Language	Caucasian [sic]	Semitic	Hamitic	Monosyllabic Sudanese
Creativity	Foreign attitude of mind	Sharp observer, linguistically	Observant eye	Uncreative, imitates, fortunes change with mood
Intellect	Adroit	Rational	Clever and bold	Narrow-minded, dull
Will	Cunning instead of self-trust	Dignified independence	Self-conscious	Instantaneous, driven by chance
Emotion	Calculating	Sudden passion, like flashing light bulb	Dreamlike, reticent	Good-natured but dull and some-times violent and unpredictable
Sense of Honor	Greed	Vindictive	Honor and loyalty	Dependent, without self-respect
Leadership	Agitator, disciplined exploiter	Belligerent wildness, without discipline	Wields power, organized	Slave instead of master
State	Hidden lust for power over the community	National delusion of the chosen people	Statecraft of Egypt, rule of nobles	Restrained striving for power but without capability, presumptuous
Economy	Smart trader, cautious	Herders, land to desert	Farming, cattle and horse breeding	Carefee existence, hoe farming
Human Qualities	Well-prepared	Without compassion, sense of family	Proud, taciturn	Vain, conceited
Sex Life	Fluctuates between strained sensual lust and full denial	Quickly ages, flourishes 16–20 years of age	Self-controlled	Quick sex, custom of female obesity
Criminality	Calculated cruelty (Shylock)	Thieves	Inclination toward cruelty	Sensitive to bloody revolts
Religion	Baal, the god of ecstasy; preaching (prophets)	Yahweh, the god of wrath; doctrinal rigidity, intolerance	Powers of nature and animal worship	Two-thirds of all Africans heathens, faith in powers of nature

Source: Karl Hahn, "Rassenkunde des jüdischen Volkes," in Hahn, hrsg. *Volk und Rasse: Das neue Reich*. Wittenberg: Hrosse's, 1935, 2.

Like his colleagues, Hahn wanted teachers and their pupils to grasp certain "facts" about the Jewish people and their historical development. At the center of this endeavor was the purpose of sharply differentiating the historical identity of Jews from Germans. Not only was the inner life or "racial soul" of Jews so different from that of Germans, as reflected in table 4.2; so also was their history.

Hahn apparently wanted to bring into the hands of teachers an easily digestible historical overview that could easily support classes in history or in strengthening the teaching of concepts relating to race hygiene. A brief section on the "Establishment of True Jewry" informed readers immediately that the Chosen People, a term usually mocked by Nazi curriculum writers, grew out of the formation of what Hahn called "the urban trader-priesthood." The expression represented a strong condemnation of Jewish religion as nothing more than a profane pursuit of crass materialism legitimized with a false and deceptive claim to the sacred. That Jews were associated with the vices of city life was nothing new. What Hahn highlighted in this narrative was the ancient Jewish practice of keeping certain blood laws pure through the observance of a strict racial separation from other peoples. The clever statesman Nehemiah, in league with the high priest Ezra, created a series of laws designed to preserve the racial heritage of Jews. To support the creation of an ongoing closed community, marriage laws restricted the choice of marriage partners to those inside the Jewish community. The two men, according to Hahn, created the legal structure for a community defined first and foremost by a union of money and trade with a priestly cast. Within this interpretation existed strains of deadly economic stereotypes that followed Jews from the Middle Ages through the twentieth century.[29]

Setting Jews apart as negative other was also possible through an anti-Semitic emphasis on Jews as intolerable "people of the law." Hahn, like many anti-Semitic writers of curriculum, stepped up attacks on the Talmud as another piece of evidence reflecting the arrogance of Jewish claims as the Chosen People. What he stressed even more was the strangeness of Jewish laws on purity as applied to diet and sacrificial offerings. Jewish religious laws and practices, described as rigid and unyielding, reflected values foreign to German culture. Even the Jewish religion came under Hahn's penchant for anthropological categorization. The inflexible nature of the "revealed" word in the scriptures of the Jewish community reflected the influence of the oriental "racial soul." According to Hahn, this aspect of Jewish racial heritage explained the Maccabean Revolt against the Seleucid kings from 168 to 163 B.C. The uprising reflected another example of Jewish religious fanaticism gone awry leading to the senseless slaughter of many of their own people. The Jewish religious conception of sin which assumed that every soul "always swayed between strained sinfulness and complete suffocation of the senses" claimed roots from the Near Eastern racial soul. These developments suggested to Hahn that the scholars of Jewish law were the ones who set an indelible character on the entire Jewish cultural and historical edifice. From a Jewish perspective, Hahn wrote, "religious piety is a spiritual skill, an art, learned didactically and masterfully prosecuted" (*Die Frommigkeit ist eine geistige Fertigkeit, eine Kunst, die Schulmäßig gelernt und meisterlich betrieben wird*).[30]

Religion and history were inseparable elements in the Nazi articulation of the history curriculum. Hahn exploited the differences between Jewish and Christian religious traditions to more fully stress the contention that Jews were cultural outsiders both racially and religiously. Other equally important layers of Hahn's curriculum papers merit attention for their revelations about the place of the Jews in the world community. In a succeeding section, Hahn dwelt on what he called "Scattering of the Jews over the World." The legacy of conquest by Alexander the Great and the spreading of Greek culture over the entire civilized world brought a greater form and shape to Jewish communities in the Near East and eastern Mediterranean. Citing Theodor Mommsen (1817–1903), the great German historian, Hahn wanted readers to know that Jews in Rome already exercised a "fateful influence" during the time of the Caesars. In a fashion typical of Nazi writers of history curriculum, Hahn failed to offer any real evidence to support the specious claim. The migrations of the Jewish people offered readers further reason for concern. The *Südjuden*, or "southern Jews," from the Mediterranean coasts of Spain and France settled in the area of Frankfurt am Main and Alsace 250 years after Christ. The more numerous and threatening *Ostjuden*, settling earlier around the Don and Volga Rivers, were depicted as an unresolved peril hanging over the entire Reich. A map showing the concentrations of Jews in middle Europe from 1881 assigned the highest numbers to Poland with 130–180 Jews per thousand population, Russia with 90–130, and the Ukraine with 40–90. The map left the impression that Jews were part of a big, advancing black blob poised to take over all of Europe.[31]

The Nazi penchant for exploiting statistics to advance anti-Semitic attitudes, already noted as a hallmark in race hygiene, emerged as well in a union of history and geography. In another curriculum paper on the Jewish question, Hahn dutifully recorded the populations of Jews from the early 1920s in twenty-eight European countries as well as Asia, Africa, Australia, and the United States. Streams of *Ostjuden* into western and central Europe as well as North America marked a decrease in the oriental branch of Jewish bloodlines and a precipitous increase in Near Eastern blood bringing in more of the feared "inner Asian elements." Jews were not only a pernicious problem for Germany and Europe but also an unresolved racial puzzle for the entire world. Revealing once again his love of maps and numbers to present an aura of objectivity, Hahn reproduced a map of Jewish population in Germany from Günther's *Race Science of the Jewish People* (1930) to focus pupil attention on their respective provinces. Berlin, as expected, retained the dubious Nazi distinction of being the capital of Germany's "city Jews." Hahn wanted readers to know that irresponsible border policies followed by previous governments left open eastern borders to an influx of *Ostjuden*. Outside Berlin, Jewish numbers were relatively high in the Rhineland and Hessen. There was a sense in Hahn's writing and through the presentation of these maps and tables that unless something was done, the Jewish presence would spread like a pestilence across the Reich.[32]

Even though Jews constituted only about 1 percent of the entire German population, their influence over German culture was unmistakable. Again and again, as noted across many of the curriculum investigations conducted in this book thus far, the racial identification of Jews with *Handelsblut* suggested that trading and bargaining was part of Jewish blood. Hahn engaged in a familiar litany of

Jewish family names associated with banking, including Warburg, Goldschmidt, Kahn, Kuhn, Loeb, Schiff, Mond, Speyer, Elissen, Bearsted, Lazard, and Rothschild. Just as Jews had taken over the economic life of ancient Alexandria, so Jews of contemporary times would dominate the banks and the money supply and hold positions on the administrative boards of heavy industry, department stores, transportation, and wholesale trade. To provide a more direct example, Hahn claimed that the executive board of the stock exchange in Frankfurt consisted in 1933 of eleven Jews and seven Christians. Quoting Goethe, Hahn described the soul of Jews as "earthly, temporal, and immediate" as a way of emphasizing the material focus of Jewish life. Not to be overlooked in Hahn's judgment was another element of economic disparity between Germans and Jews. A much lower percentage of Jews, in contrast with the general population, were engaged in manual labor.[33]

Hahn wanted teachers to share with pupils examples of how noted Jewish families had taken over control of almost every corner of German cultural life. Jews were behind the Marxist press houses, while others fell under the clutches of the Mosse, Sonnemann, and Ullstein families. Half of the medical faculty at German universities were Jewish, along with doctors and members of the bar. The supranational Expressionism in German art, preoccupied as it was with the pains and worries of the world, stemmed from the Near Eastern bloodlines of Jews. Christianity itself, in one of the rare occasions in Nazi curriculum, came under fire for allowing itself to become "Jewified." Fray Tomas de Torquemada (1420–1498), one of the head Catholic judges in the Spanish Inquisition, possessed Jewish blood, a secret that explained, at least in part, his hatred of Jews and his leadership in ordering the torture and burning of thousands of Jews for refusing to embrace the Catholic faith.[34] Hahn added another twist to the scenario. In a statement that defied imagination, Hahn insisted that several bishops appointed by the High Church of England were Jewish. The pedagogue from Hamburg also saw in the forged *Elders of the Protocols of Zion* another opportunity to impress readers with the threat of worldwide Jewish conspiracy.[35]

Hahn evidently failed to see a glaring contradiction in his approach to Jewish history. Shortly afterward, in his discussion of the Jew as "historical opponent" of all things German, he referred to Catholic Church laws from the eleventh century that had forbidden mixed marriages between Jews and Catholics as well as the employment of Catholics in Jewish households, renting homes to Jews, or permitting Jews to wear the clothes of a civil servant—legal religious restrictions that hardly suggested the church had become "Jewified." Hahn went on to justify aggressive measures against the Jewish community, arguing that those undertaken by the Catholic Church reflected a larger public outrage against the widespread abuses of Jewish moneylenders. Hahn insisted that Jews enriched themselves off the backs of honest citizens through exorbitant interest rates. In carefully baiting his readers, Hahn explained that the righteous anger of the people over these Jewish transgressions led to the persecutions of Jews in England in 1290 and in the German city of Trier in 1349, and to their expulsion by the Spanish in 1492. In the case of Germany, Hahn ignored the historical context. Trier was one of the most extreme examples of scapegoating leveled against Jews because of the Black Plague. Furthermore, the mass murder of

Jews that year in Trier came largely at the hands of the Crusades. Usury, while certainly part of the larger traditional Christian hatred of Jews, was a peripheral cause in this case. Of even greater importance than this oversimplification of history was the implication that Jews were a menace in the past and people had taken vengeance on them with the blessing of civil and religious authorities.

Hahn further insinuated that Jews continued to be a problem for the current German community and implied that just as in past regimes, the Nazi racial state could legitimately assume more extreme measures in answering the Jewish question. Indeed, this was how Hahn ended his foray into the history curriculum. The well-informed young pupil of German history would memorize all of the Nazi legal measures taken against Jews since Hitler's rise to power. This was more than a bland list of legal pronouncements. Hahn looked to a church policy once again to legitimize Nazi racial policy. He called into question the popular assumption among Catholic leaders that the Jewish question was first and foremost a matter of religious faith. In a mocking tone, Hahn pointed to the Viennese Cardinal Initzer who in 1934 founded an association for the conversion of Jews empowered by "biblical truth" (Hahn's quotation marks). The dedicated teachers and young pupils in the classrooms of the Reich, Hahn hoped, would find this situation racially unacceptable. The Nazi conception of Jewish history held to the ironclad racial assumption that "once a Jew, always a Jew." Religious conversion to Christianity could not change the underlying and irrefutable reality of racial identity and all of the associated qualities of "racial soul."[36]

The development of a racially oriented history curriculum for schools legitimized certain assumptions about Jews that drew from racial anthropology, geography, and race hygiene. The racial interpretation of just who was and was not a Jew, a matter of critical importance in defining the citizen of the Third Reich, rested on the classification of bloodlines. How schools translated Nazi racial policy regarding the Jews through curriculum, the centerpiece for this book, reveals broad outlines regarding Nazi claims about Jewish identity. The integrated nature of these racial connections throughout the curriculum showed the deadly seriousness with which the Nazis approached their vision of an educated person. Control over racial interpretations of the past resulted, in many cases, in ideologically similar approaches to the writing of curriculum. As the racial archenemy of the Third Reich, the Jew was very rarely overlooked by teaching books and curriculum guides on history. The same cannot be said for Sinti and Roma and the mentally ill and handicapped, groups more likely to be included in materials on race hygiene. Of all outcasts, it was the Jew who demanded a rewriting of history under the racial pen of Nazi ideology.

Not to be overlooked is the fact that Nazi writers of history curriculum already had a rich racial tradition to draw from, particularly from the Weimar era. One of the early Nazi contributors to this curriculum process was Richard Eichenauer, a teacher from Bochum. His *Race as Law of Life in History and Ethos: A Guide for German Youth* (1934) drew heavily from the first edition of Clauß's writings on racial soul from 1926 as well as Günther's book on racial science first published in 1922. What set Eichenauer's work apart from that of Hahn was his vigorous prosecution of four selected historical legends he used as the basis for explaining the power of Jews in the world community. In introducing these "legends" for young readers, Eichenauer triumphantly announced that the Jewish question had already been solved "for the time being" by the "radical change" in the political situation represented by the Nazi assumption of power. German youth deserved a clarification of the reasons for this solution. Eichenauer turned to debunking several historical legends he called "four rooms" from which spread the influence of Jews over world affairs. These legends were the oppression of the Jews, Jewish economic superiority, the special holiness of the Jewish religion, and the "fairy tale" surrounding the assumption that Jesus Christ was a Jew.[37]

Anti-Semitism, to Eichenauer, was an expression invented by Jews and proved false by racial science. All the peoples of the earth had due cause to hate the Jews, but not through any direct actions or provocations carried out by non-Jews themselves. Historical precedents revealed that no matter where Jews settled—whether ancient Egypt, Babylonia, Christian Spain, or Poland—they immediately set into motion an "emotional cycle" of hatred among the host peoples. Certain Jewish cultural patterns repeated themselves over time and unleashed intense emotional responses from the non-Jewish populace. After migrating to a host country, Jews took pleasure in the initial atmosphere of toleration that supported their success in securing power and riches. As time passed, Jewish arrogance and selfishness encouraged the development of hatred among the host people for the Jewish outsiders. Finally, the "curve" in this cycle ended with expulsion or oppression. Eichenauer advanced the rationalization that the "so-called oppression" of Jews was only a realistic answer by host peoples to the "pernicious effectiveness" of Jews in developing their role as a guest people.[38]

In what clearly became an extended exercise in victim blaming, Eichenauer turned to the economic power developed by Jews as a dominant cause for the hate response. Once again, Eichenauer turned to another Volkish thinker from Weimar to buttress his argument. He widely quoted Ludwig Schemann (1852–1935) and his three-volume work on *Race in the Intellectual Sciences: Studies on the History of Racial Thinking* (1928–31) in attacking the alleged economic basis for Jewish influence. The capitalist exploitation of the people practiced by the Jews made Germans feel as if "an entire pack of dogs had rushed at their throats." Everybody knew, Eichenauer claimed, how numerous Jews had become, how they "stuck together," and the way they dominated party politics. In following the example of Hahn and others, Eichenauer hit the monetary system and the press as additional examples of the "pernicious effectiveness" of Jews in the German body politic. Finally, the Third Reich "had taken up the enormous task" that seemed only like a distant hope when proposed by Schemann in 1928. Schemann suggested that Aryans could achieve economic independence from Jews only if they applied all of their energies to establish their own economic order on the basis of "an ethical conception of work." Jews, so Eichenauer implied, were part of an unethical race incapable of engaging in honest labor.[39]

To the special nature attributed to Jewish religion, Eichenauer devoted only sparse attention. Dismissing Jewish religion as nothing more than "a great deception," the teacher from Bochum followed the familiar path of other curriculum writers who used the issue as a way of hardening the lines of profound difference between Jews and Christians. A certain "rigid narrowness of mind and

Figure 4.1 "*Du hergelauf'ner Jud: Lass andere Völker in Ruh*," ("You Roaming Jew, Leave Other Peoples in Peace"), first prize in a regional art contest submitted by thirteen-year-old from Franconia. Drawing shows how the child perceived the local version of Santa Claus as Julius Streicher who dispelled the Jews. A signpost points in opposite directions to Palestine for the Jews and Germany for Aryan Germans. Contest sponsored by Julius Streicher, Gauleiter of Franconia and editor of *Der Stürmer*. From an article, "Die Arbeitern als Presiträger," (The Worker as Prize Winner"), *Fränkische Tageszeitung*, 31 December 1936. From clippings collection of Wiener library, Tel Aviv.

sense of moral inferiority" that stemmed from an Oriental concept of God applied in large measure to the Jews. How the author arrived at this broad and sweeping generalization remained unclear. Other related issues followed. The Jew persisted with an annoying toughness by attaching himself as a foreign body to the spiritual life of the West. Even more annoying to Nazi purists were questions regarding the bloodlines and racial heritage of Jesus Christ. The evasive Eichenauer, in deferring once again to Schemann, insisted that Christianity had initially reached its highest stage of spiritual development in the "Nordic-Germanic world." The nature of Christ's teachings revealed that, at the very least, he was of Nordic blood. This Nazi historical interpretation of Jesus Christ could still resonate in the West since ethnocentric artistic renderings of Christ as a white European had existed since the Middle Ages and the Renaissance.[40]

In further developing his case regarding the four legends associated with the Jews, Eichenauer sternly warned pupils to remember that "subversion,

exploitation, and subjugation" were behind the well-founded fear of good citizens for the "allegory of the eternal Jew." Throughout much of his work,
Eichenauer tried to persuade readers that there were defensible reasons why
Jews remained the target of tremendous hatred. The spirit of the Jew, if allowed
free reign, would continue to plague the racial community with "eternal unrest"
and a "knawing obsession with doubt." If Jews therefore suffered rejection and
hate, it was their own fault since they continued to pollute racial bloodlines as
they had done for centuries. They brought calamity upon themselves. In closing
his discussion of the Jewish question and legends surrounding Jewish culture,
Eichenauer intimated either a profound naiveté at best or a hardened cynicism
at worst: "The racial scientific understanding of the [Jewish] matter therefore
does not nourish hatred, rather by contrast exists as the only possibility of
attaining a lasting peace in the future." The so-called peace to which he referred
never transpired. Racial science, legitimized throughout the curriculum, provided a dark justification for the mass murder of the people Eichenauer so
despised.[41]

Besides playing the role of iconoclast, Eichenauer contributed to a view of
racial history through art. Writing about "art as a reflection of race," he associated Jewish artistic works with liberalism that encouraged a "removal of human
beings from a feeling of union with the whole of national community." More
seriously, this split resulted in a loss of feeling for the responsibility toward the
whole. Jews, as strangers to art, were incapable of discovering this essential
unity and responsibility. Unlike Hahn, Eichenauer launched a much more detailed
attack on Expressionism, calling it a carryover from the Near Eastern racial soul.
Descending into the international style of Expressionist art, he insisted, was
an "exercise in senseless pain caused by self-absorbed worries." Expressionism was yet another way of demonstrating just how far Jews deviated
from the Nazi artistic conception of the human being. Within this veritable
rogue's gallery of Nazi-appointed degenerate artists were placed Picasso from
France, Kandinsky, Chagall, Segall, and Steinhardt from Russia, and the
works of Pechstein, Meidner, and Feininger from Germany. When Expressionism
entered the world of music, Nazi artistic sensibilities suffered another blow. The
atonal compositions of Arnold Schoenberg, another Jewish artist, was an affront
to German musical tradition.[42]

One of Eichenauer's contemporaries, Reinhold Krause, urged teachers to integrate accounts of Richard Wagner's struggle against the rule of Jews in the world
of music. Krause's blacklist was longer. He attacked Cubism and futurism as
well as jazz, identified as *"Niggermusik,"* as examples of "poisonous blos-
soms from the Jewish parasitic plant on German national soil" (*die Giftblüten
der jüdischen Schmarotzerpflanze auf deutschen Volksboden*). A deeper ideological purpose emerged from Krause's curriculum ideas. Probing these examples
of Jewish cultural politics, he insisted, provided "powerful evidence for the necessity of a radical solution to the Jewish question." In few other places in the Nazi
curriculum is the ideological justification for the heavy oppression of Jews more
directly implied. In a theme repeated over and over throughout the curriculum, and exploited earlier by Alfred Vogel in racial science, the common
Nazi propaganda assumption was that Jews used art to establish supremacy
over the cultural life of the German people. Calling forth Günther once again,

Eichenauer advanced the concept of a "biological aesthetic" that assumed that bloodlines, more than any other factor, determined the level of artistic creativity in the history of a people. Biology, thus pressed into the service of history and aesthetics, represented another way of integrating the Nazi curriculum under the banner of race.[43]

DIETER KLAGGES AND RACE HISTORY

One of the most prominent of all Nazi history pedagogues and textbook writers was Dieter Klagges, a prolific author and one of the leading voices in the ideological transformation of the history curriculum. His *History Instruction and National Political Education*, first appearing in 1936 and its fifth edition by 1939, came to be known as the standard work in the field of history didactics. Klagges brought to this task experience as an elementary and middle school teacher. He then served as interior and education minister for Braunschweig beginning in 1931, followed by a term beginning in 1933 as minister president. Joining the Nazi Party in 1925, Klagges eventually became best known for his articulation of a "Nazi world view" in the teaching of history.

The scope of Klagges's writings ranged from a religious treatise on the *Early Gospel of Jesus, German Faith* (1925) to a strong advocacy, well into the 1970s, of an organic perspective on the nature of knowledge. The idea of an organic curriculum was already an idea Klagges championed with Ernst Krieck and other colleagues throughout the Third Reich. What also marked his intellectual life was a fashionable polemic against Marxist thinking and an interest in national economy.[44] In one of his more theoretical writings, Klagges set the tone for the creation of a curriculum in which the question of race, in borrowing a phrase from Benjamin Disraeli, became "the key to world history." His words placed the Jews at the center of all racial concerns for the history curriculum:

> The struggles between the heroic life and pacifist longing, between the *Führer*, despotism and democracy, between nation and world state are old and have basically never stopped moving historical consciousness. Different from this is meaning of race, the fifth principle which belongs to the foundation of the National Socialist world view. In the beginnings of history, almost all peoples actually came to know the importance of race and discovered its purity and health giving powers. Clearly emerging out of all of this is what we know about marriage laws, the laws of heredity and the racially unified appearance of our ancestors and other Nordic peoples like the Greeks and Romans, the Persians and the people of India. The castes in India, the legal hereditary rule of the pharoahs, the Incas and the Mayans in South America and many others were thinking in the same direction. With us, the racial institutions were established with roots going back into the Middle Ages. So everyone at that time who wanted to enter work as an apprentice in the manual trades had to prove his German descent in order to prevent the penetration of foreign racial elements. This same healthy instinct generally showed the citizens of the city that Jews refused to obey the laws. They permitted them to live only in a special Jewish quarter, a separation which incidentally was in no way detested by the Jews, but rather supported in the interests of their own people.[45]

Klagges resurrected a historical theme that resonated across the curriculum. Evidence of racial economic and interpretations of ghetto life emerged in earlier discussions of the race hygiene curriculum and curriculum guides. Jewish ghettos, wherever they existed, came into being because a strong Jewish desire to live as a separate community forced their creation. In a spirit of profound denial, non-Jewish responsibility for the ghettos and the economic and political conditions that brought them into being were carefully kept out of any discussion. The Jew was never very far from the racial and historical worldview that Klagges wanted to advance in the schools. The issue of the ghetto was but one doorway into the history curriculum.

The "biological legitimacy" of history and the National Socialist worldview, as Klagges called it, required pupils to think about certain laws of nature that bound them to a community of bloodlines across time. There was a certain sense of destiny that Klagges tried to communicate to educators about the spirit of Nazi thinking and the future of German youth. Elementary school children could grasp the essential biological and historical laws that summed up Nazi ideological principles for schooling. Pupils would learn the Social Darwinist principle that "life is struggle" and the Nazi dictum that "we are nothing without the *Führer*." These slogans reminded the young that "your people are the future" and "national comrades are the comrades of fate." One of the highest biological principles for developing historical consciousness was "your blood, the highest good."[46]

Politically socializing more mature pupils into the dynamics of race history moved Klagges to develop a collection of themes teachers could use as focal points for instruction. Pupils could write essays or create school exhibits expounding on key ideas. Internationalism, long associated with the culture of the Jew, remained a prominent feature among these themes along with the idea that Jews were responsible for Germany's troubles. A selection of themes from the work of Klagges also reveals Nazi concepts of citizenship and the relationship of the individual to the state:

1. The people are the body, you are only a tiny member.
2. You die, the people are eternal.
3. The state is valued in so far as the people who serve it, that carry it.
4. There is no other higher honor than death for the life and resurrection of his people.
5. Wherever work is dishonored, the national community is destroyed.
6. Between the peoples, there exists no equality, rather a hierarchy. In this, the German people stand first in line.
7. All preaching about international human development are dangerous seductions, lies and hypocrisies.
8. International teachings are rejected by the clear results of history and research from the natural sciences.
9. Internationalism will also be rejected by the healthy sentiment of all peoples.
10. Many can follow, only one can lead.
11. Race is destiny.
12. Happy are the people whose will to live is at one with the will of the *Führer*.
13. The Jews are our misfortune.

14. There is no organism named humanity. No such name can or should be given it.
15. Aryan blood alone creates high culture.[47]

All of these themes were part of what Klagges regarded as Volkish "laws of life." These ideological laws influenced how educators viewed the concept of historical time and the place of Jews within the history curriculum. On a more localized level, this curriculum practice found a voice through other kinds of essay writing among secondary pupils. In the Berlin-Neukölln district, pupils attending the Agnes Miegel *Oberschule* wrote on "the Jewish question in history. Adolf Hitler saw in the Jews all of the evil of the world. They were for him the calamity of history."[48] An examination of the history content outlines published for elementary grades five through eight from 1940 reveals the important place assumed by prehistory in defining the racial identity of Germans. Archaeology, pressed into the service of Nazi race ideology, could persuade young minds about the cultural and geographical rootedness of Nordic peoples in contrast to the wandering Jew who possessed no homeland of his own. Pupils in the sixth class studied the farming culture of Nordic families from the early Stone Age and the waves of early Nordic migrations. Later, the "Germans and Romans" came under scrutiny with a nationalistic focus on the great Germanic defeat of Roman legions at Teutoberger Wald. In the same content section, the outline directed teachers to instruct pupils on "Jewish traders in Germania."[49]

The seventh class learned that "liberalism and Jewry" existed as "foreign powers" on German soil after the war of liberation from Napoleon. The most concentrated attention devoted to the Jews came in the eighth class. Among the domestic weaknesses of the Second Reich and the Kaisers was the absence of a racial consciousness among the citizenry and the appalling fact that Jews were now accorded full citizenship. Part of Germany's difficulties as a burgeoning industrial power could be traced to the specter of Marxism, a tool of Jewish conspiracy to gain influence. The foundation of the Third Reich garnered a great deal of attention as well in the eighth class along with the Nuremberg Laws from 1935. These decisive legal measures, interpreted as the "Volkish renewal of the Nordic race," made certain that pupils understood the critical legal and racial differences between Aryans and Jews.[50] Klagges would join others in translating how these images of the Jew would emerge in history textbooks.

THE JEW IN HISTORY TEXT AND STORY

As indicated earlier, the writing, publication, and distribution of textbooks carrying the curriculum thrust of Nazi racial ideological assumptions took several years to implement. The initial reliance on dated Weimar texts eventually gave way to protests by education officials who grew impatient with the delays in adopting Nazified curriculum materials across the Reich. Fritz Wächtler, the head of the NSLB, appealed to Hitler in 1938 in the strongest terms to intervene on this matter. The result, without the consent or approval of Education Minister Bernhard Rust, was the creation of a special examining board headed by Phillip Bouhler to proof written materials intended for schools. The position, under the wing of the Nazi Party, was deemed important enough to be attached to Hitler's Chancellery.[51] By 1941, there was evidence that the problem of providing textbooks meeting ideological standards for Germany's classrooms remained unresolved. Bouhler, in a communication with Alfred Rosenberg, lamented that no less than 736,221 books published for teachers and schoolbooks for children were "unusable, outdated and hostile to the (Nazi) worldview."[52] Bouhler did not clarify whether school texts falling under his purview remained ideologically unacceptable because they, at least in part, failed to carry a stronger anti-Semitic message. Results from this study suggest that Nazi curriculum materials for elementary schools integrated anti-Semitic ideas as an important formative instructional theme before and after he filed his report. At least on this count, Bouhler need not have worried.

Of all the education branches, it was the elementary school that lagged behind the most in securing ideologically acceptable textbooks. The tight textbook situation prompted some publishers to create booklets centered on select historical themes. One foreign press report from 1934 announced the release of a brief work on Adolf Hitler for elementary pupils with a note of deep skepticism. The Dürrs publishing house in Leipzig advanced the familiar propaganda notion that Jews only wanted to see the German people in conflict and tried to fan the flames of hatred among the population through their control of the press. These conditions would pave the way for a stronger Jewish domination. What followed revealed a curious falsification of history and the multifaceted nature of anti-Semitic writing in curriculum materials. Karl Marx and Ferdinand Lassalle were named as the ideological originators of class struggle. Presumably excluded from this circle because of his Aryan identification was Friedrich Engels. Lassalle, whose role in developing the idea of class struggle was minimal at best in comparison with Engels', apparently found a falsified place in this Nazi history resource because of his Jewish background. This same misinterpretation of class struggle and the omission of Engels in the history of Marxism was true of the textbook series *Volk und Führer*, edited by Dieter Klagges.[53]

Other, much more developed texts attempted to place Jews within a larger historical context. Appearing in 1942, Hans Warneck and Willi Matschke's *History for the Elementary Schools* provided pupils with a broad sweep of Germa history from Charlemagne to the Third Reich. Few other texts devoted as much attention to medieval Jews as did these two authors. The following passage integrated some of the most deeply rooted historical anti-Semitism with themes that resonated across many other historical periods. This is the image of the Jew eternally tied to the marketplace and the pursuit of money. Pupils who studied the Jewish question in race biology and race hygiene in tandem with this perspective on history might become part of a fertile ideological ground for the suggested "radical solution" of the Jews articulated earlier by Reinhold Krause. "Life and the Hustle and Bustle in a German City from the Middle Ages" brought pupils into confrontation with values deemed un-German and therefore culturally unacceptable:

> Jews also lived in the city, but they were strictly separated from the general population and banished to the Jewish quarter. They stood under the protection of the princes to whom they paid a Jew tax. The people rejected the racial foreigners.

They had to wear gold, pointed hats and the same color of badge on their clothing. They were neither farmers or craftsmen. They lived off of lending money. That was forbidden by the Christians. The Jews charged high interest, they practiced usury. Even some merchants were dependent on them and in later centuries [Jews] lent money to princes and kings. When debtors could not pay back the money with the high interest, they were driven away from house and home by the Jews. The rage among the German people for the Jews grew and the Jews were often thrown out of the city, their synagogues burned. Free cities banned the influx of Jews. The exiles migrated to the East and, when the times became more peaceful, they came back, first individually, then in droves. Other European peoples exiled the foreign usurers including England (1290), France (1394), Spain (1412) and shortly afterward by Portugal and Italy. But later they came back again under the protection of the princes and impoverished the host peoples.[54]

The timing of this passage and the connection of the language to contemporary events in the Third Reich suggests careful ideological preparation on the part of the authors. The image of burning synagogues, powerful in its own right as a symbol of Nazi persecution, was perhaps directly witnessed by some of the teachers and pupils who used this volume. Four years earlier, in the wake of the Night of the Broken Glass, synagogues across the Reich went up in flames and Nazi authorities threw Torah scrolls into the streets. The parallel and timing between the medieval practice of wearing the yellow badge, as noted in this passage, and the Nazi requirement that Jews wear the Yellow Star in the fall of 1941 are unmistakable. Warneck and Matschke seem to have shaped this part of their narrative to advance a sense of historical continuity with regard to anti-Semitic practices. On another level, internationalizing this history by pointing to instances of anti-Semitic actions in other European countries suggested to pupils that Germany was not the only country to react to a perceived threat posed by Jews. The passage deserves another reading. During the year this book came off the press, 300,000 Jews were deported from the Warsaw ghetto and murdered at the Treblinka death camp. Unified Jewish resistance in the Warsaw and Vilna ghettos also took shape.

The legacy of Martin Luther remained omnipresent in almost all attempts to inculcate anti-Semitic attitudes and values through the curriculum. In keeping with the spirit of outrage against Jews articulated earlier in their commentary on city life in the Middle Ages, Warneck and Matschke exploited the image of an incensed Luther. The authors recounted the religious reformer's struggle against the Jews depicted as "racial foreigners, idlers, and parasites sucking dry the German people." Quoted language from Luther's "The Jews and Their Lies" (1543), an almost obligatory resource exploited by numerous and dedicated Nazi curriculum writers, remained the centerpiece. The theological context for Luther's reforms remained unaddressed. Beyond his revolutionary contributions to the German language and his spirited fight against the church as an outside force, Luther's legacy under the Nazi history curriculum would remain closely tied to the Jews. Warnecke and Matschke made no distinction between Luther's religious anti-Semitism and the racial anti-Semitism of the Third Reich.[55]

The alleged conspiracy of Free Masons and Jews in fomenting the French Revolution, an oft-cited element of Nazi race history, found a strong hearing in this text. "Liberty, equality, fraternity," call words for the revolution, collectively rejected core Nazi values. The concept of equality was especially intolerable to the authors. The Jewish assumption that "everything carrying a human face was the same" deserved a sound and final rejection. Nazi racial principles would set young readers straight. How could such a teaching like that of equality be true, indeed even be discussed as a serious idea, if races and peoples reflected such profound physical and mental differences? Warneck and Matschke told pupils that Jews were behind the proliferation of this false idea and Jews made matters worse by leaving the ghetto and going out into the larger society to secure equal rights. This was the fateful step leading to an eventual Jewish takeover of governments. Even kings and queens failed to take this threat seriously. Queen Marie Antoinette warned her brother Joseph II on the throne of Austria about the unholy alliance of Jews and Free Masons, but he ignored her pleadings. Louis XVI also remained blind to the danger and went to the scaffold with his queen wholly unaware of Jewish machinations in toppling the government. The overarching message was that Jews brought only disaster to the host cultures.[56]

Under the Nazi vision of history, Graf Carl August von Hardenberg (1750–1822) remained one of the most castigated of all political figures ever to occupy a Prussian high office. His name reappeared in various Nazi history texts as the dark figure who signed the emancipation edict for Jews in 1812. German culture would never be the same, according to the party line. In the wake of Napoleon's defeat, some Jews changed their names or accepted baptism to appear more Christian. Such a devious move could not hide the essential underlying Jewishness of those involved. Once again, the link to contemporary Nazi anti-Semitic policy could not escape the more discerning reader, although an elementary pupil might not be in a position to grasp the subtlety behind this part of the history curriculum. The Nazi assumption that "once a Jew, always a Jew" remained in force throughout much of the regime. At this point Warneck and Matschke exploited a propaganda language much more incendiary in nature. Jews like the poet Heinrich Heine and others like him had deviously changed their Jewish names and "with a biting ridicule attacked not only the reigning government, but also threw everything in the mud that Germans held holy and honorable." The blanket condemnation was not meant to merely rest in the distant past. This curriculum conceived historical anti-Semitism as a profound and logical tie to the present reality of the racial state, an essential element in the political socialization of youth.[57]

Jews obviously were not the only figures to cross the stage of German history in the pages of textbooks intended for the elementary classroom. Warneck and Matschke, like many other textbook writers under the Third Reich, wanted pupils to gain a clear understanding that Jews were the greatest of all enemies to the state. To reinforce this message, writers tried to demonstrate that the Jewish threat cut across the generations and did not reside in just one historical era. History as propaganda under Nazi Germany, not unlike other regimes, conceived of historical process as a means of legitimizing the state. The Jew provided a convenient scapegoat upon which to heap German wrath and blame. Never far from discussion was the omnipresent Jewish manipulation of public opinion. Certain icons of German nationalism suffered under the withering attacks of the Jewish press. Behind these subversive actions was a Jewry from the early nineteenth century bent on political and economic domination at any cost. The image of the vulture, long associated with the Rothschild banking house, cast a long shadow over this rhetoric:

> The daily press constantly carried a poison to the broad masses of the German people. In the newspapers, men like Arndt and Jahn and above all the Germany army were hated. Many Jews married Aryan women and strongly thrust themselves forward into the German national community. As citizens with equal rights, they also attained entry into the secret meetings of the discontented. The unsuspecting German listened to their rabble-rousing speeches in which they attacked the government leading him to believe that soon the time would come when he [the Jew] could vote as a representative in the parliament . . . The state must not attack the life of the individual and make no regulations for him. Therein lay most of the Jews and therefore they represented the foreign world view of liberalism. The Jew wanted to come to power as a profit vulture so that he could collect his great profits undisturbed. But then also as a power vulture, this despicable man out of the ghetto wanted to rule and no one was there who knew the danger.[58]

Essential to the anti-Semitic articulation of history for the young was the repetitive reinforcement of more and more contemporary examples of alleged Jewish wrongdoing in the community. The authors used the expression *Reichsfeinde*, or "enemy of the Reich," in association with Jewish influence in the economy and active Jewish leadership in liberal political parties. That Jews were members of the Reichstag under the Kaiserreich and Weimar was more than Warneck and Matschke could stomach. Economic history, as always, provided multiple layers of anti-Semitic teachings and rested on the assumption that textbook writers never had to provide reliable historical evidence to back their claims. Racial anti-Semitism, when supported by traditional economic stereotypes of Jews, became even more vitriolic. In the text, Jewish factory owners were accused of conspiring to manipulate price levels in the marketplace in order to force workers to accept lower wages. At the bottom of this conspiracy was the intention of the owners to make as much money as effortlessly and quickly as possible at the expense of the German workers. In bold print in the lines of the history book was the insinuation that "the others had to manage for him" (*Die anderen sollten für ihn schaffen*). These words called to mind the dichotomy raised by Alfred Vogel's teaching charts (1938) when he depicted the Jew as a banker holding money bags and stock certificates in sharp contrast to the scythe-wielding German farmer and the dedicated factory worker. The economic categories, advanced as simplifications for young minds, suggested in no uncertain terms that the Germans "worked" while the Jews "rested."[59]

An appeal to the economic plight of the German peasantry, as seen throughout much of the curriculum writ large, represented another propaganda opportunity to reinforce the German/Jewish dichotomy. The familiar theme of German peasants losing their homes and fertile lands to the high interest rates of unscrupulous Jewish moneylenders took on an even more insidious air in the writing of Warneck and Matschke. The Jews, so the authors assumed, did not hold the same relationship to the land as the native German peasants. Jews only con-

cerned themselves with making land deals to line their pockets. How the authors
closed this section of their text revealed the power of the word in reinforcing
preconceptions about the negative other. Because Jews could not conceive of
land as an intimate part of the Volk and national community, "the soil became
a commodity." In the language of Volkish thinking about the relationship between
soil, blood, and race, this aspect of Jewish life was tantamount to a gross cultural insult.[60]

A broader net for Germany's domestic enemies was cast by Warneck and
Matschke when they interpreted the defeat of Germany in World War I and the
harrowing days of the Weimar Republic. Kaiser Wilhelm II came under blis-
tering criticism not only for poor leadership in failing to meet declining
conditions on the home front, but also for the more serious racial offense of
taking leading Jews into his confidence. The hapless monarch was too blind
to see that Jews like Walter Rathenau, head of the electrical industry, worked
behind the scenes to ensure Jewish profits while young Germans died by the
thousands on the war front. This time, not only Jews and Marxists earned
the dishonorable distinction of being *Reichsfeinde* but also the Center Party
and its Catholic members for supporting the signing of the Versailles Treaty.
As far as Weimar was concerned, Jews remained behind the moral and economic decay of the country. In what almost became an obligatory feature of
many curriculum pieces, the authors created a series of pie graphs illustrating
the percentage of Jews in Berlin before 1933 from law, medicine, the arts, and
the teaching faculty of universities. Corruptive Jewish influences during Weimar
created a cultural decline with disastrous consequences for the nation. The
authors practiced a special kind of deceit in fabricating stories about Jewish
economic and legal practices:

> In the economy, there were greater and greater deceptions. The shareholders of a
> large brewery lost 30 million marks through a Jewish director who fled the country.
> Because Jewish lawyers protected their racial brothers, many instances of fraud
> and bribery were undiscovered. Through the Jewish and Marxist press, dependent
> on Jewish capital, the German people were misled. Everything that was holy to
> Germans was disparaged. A Jewish professor in Heidelberg called the battlefield
> where two million German soldiers gave their lives "the field of dishonor." At
> the same time, German soldiers did not die for sport in support of this "shady
> republic." Traitors and deserters were glorified, but the heroic creations of Hin-
> denburg and Ludendorff were thrown into the mud. Theatrical performances,
> concerts and art exhibits showed a deep moral decline. Germany had experi-
> enced it: *Whenever the Jew is in power, he operates without restraint.* [Last sentence
> highlighted by the two authors.][61]

When taking into account the language from previous passages originating
from this textbook, one notes the repetition of the word "holy," used in association with the highest German cultural values that Jews rejected. To "throw"
something "in the mud," an action attributed to an extreme form of denuncia-
tion, implied that Jews practiced a behavior in diametric opposition from that
legitimized by the racial state. To Nazi propaganda of the kind found in this textbook, being racially or culturally different by itself was not the major ideological

thrust behind interpreting the history of the Jew in Europe and Germany for pupils. What Jews supposedly *did*, their cultural practices as well as their racial identification, were part of the essential mythology that defined the Jew. Critically important for this Nazi educational process was that Jews were not allowed to define themselves in relationship to the past or the present. This was part of the essential ideological justification seen earlier in the formation of the Institute for the New History of Germany. The high priority placed by the Nazis on "the war against the Jews" found a powerful corollary in the text by Warneck and Matschke. In recounting the aftermath of Pearl Harbor and the union of the United States and Britain in the war effort, the authors concluded that courage and the "Nazi worldview against Jewry and its collaborators" would ensure victory in the end. Therein lay the secret to German success, they insisted.[62]

Warneck and Matschke did not have a corner on anti-Semitic historical writing for young children. The text by Johannes Mahnkopf, *From Ancient Times to the Greater German Reich* (1941), assumed that the racial consciousness of youth would be heightened by the repetition of key anti-Semitic expressions or relationships throughout the work. Predominant among these was a description of the Jews as "foreign blood" that appeared no less than thirteen times. The connection between Free Masonry and Jews as a critical destabilizing force in history met the eyes of young readers on six occasions. Race history, as noted earlier, refashioned the past through conferring on the Nordic race a holy mission. From Mahnkopf's perspective, Nordics had preserved Greek civilization and provided the only real creative cultural creativity for the West. The close link between biology and history in defining the educated person emerged once again. In this text, pupils learned that knowledge about race and heredity from the natural sciences, supported by Gregor Mendel's experiments from the nineteenth century, provided the political force behind the honored Nuremberg Laws of 1935.[63]

The Jewish question, although approached in similar fashion by many writers through the repetition of familiar historical themes, was not a monolithic presence across the history curriculum. Some editors, like Dieter Klagges, integrated a much more detailed anti-Semitic perspective on Jews in his books for secondary students than for pupils in the upper levels of the elementary school. In one textbook edited for the middle school, the authors restricted any mention of Jews to their anti-German influence over the Austrian government in opposition to the *Anschluss*.[64]

While the history curriculum examples cited thus far assumed the traditional format of broadly conceived textbooks or relatively brief thematic pieces, two other figures in the circle of anti-Semitic writers chose a somewhat different historical approach to reach elementary pupils. The Jews also figured prominently in a collection of history stories created by Wilhelm Rottenrodt, an author whose anti-Semitic storyline assumed a tone less passionate than the rantings of Johann von Leers. *German Leader and Master: Individual Historical Images from Past and Present* (1937), part of a series edited by Klagges, brought together stories about heroes as well as "enemies and betrayers." After a story castigating Mathias Erzberger for selling out the German people to the enemy after World War I, Rottenrodt centered his sights on Walter Rathenau, the Jewish business leader and later foreign minister under the Weimar Republic. This brief vignette, completely fabricating a confrontation between Rathenau and a peasant, delivered an even stronger anti-Semitic punch than what one usually found in history textbooks. Whether the story was true was not the issue for a dedicated storyteller bent on packing a strong anti-Semitic message. Of great ideological importance was the exploitation of a certain image of the Jew that young children were capable of grasping.

Rathenau made a powerful target for anti-Semitic rhetoric. He was rich and also controlled the wartime economy. His role as adviser to Kaiser Wilhelm II made him even more dangerous. In the story, Rathenau confronted an old farmer on the way to the Kaiser's castle in Freienwalde at the beginning of the war. He found the old man by himself cutting hay in the heat. All the younger men had gone off to war. Rathenau, moved by the man's plight, suggested that workers from the city should help him harvest. The farmer only shook his head saying that the wages for farm work were too low to attract employment. A lively response followed. The worker, Rathenau noted with enthusiasm, must have a high wage and the farmer a high price for his harvest. Then everyone would be satisfied and the burdens of the war easier to bear. The wisdom of the peasant prevailed. He had questions of his own to pose to the Jewish adviser who was on his way to the royal household. Did he really believe that the war could be won through money? Was it not better for everyone with meager wages to carry his own weight for the fatherland? Our sons, the peasant sternly reminded the learned Jew, fighting and dying on the front, did not sacrifice themselves for money. To do so would bring his family great shame. Rottenrodt thus posed a sharp dichotomy between two figures each representing an entirely different worldview. Not only was there an urban-rural split in this anti-Semitic portrait but also serious differences over loyalty to the state and the purpose of money.[65]

The differences sharpened even more when Rathenau met the peasant months later. The peasant confidently told Rathenau that Germany was on the verge of winning the war. After all, German armies advanced deep into France and Hindenberg emerged victorious at Tannenberg. The "fleshy lips" of Rathenau mumbled words that the peasant could not understand. The plotting Jew shortly afterward flew into a rage, furiously denouncing any possibility that the Kaiser would return victorious through the Brandenburg Gates. "I do not want it," Rathenau said. "My people do not want it. It would be a disaster for the world. Then the world would not belong to the Jews." Again, the peasant had the last word in this drama. Staring at Rathenau, he asked him why he lived in Germany if he did not want victory for the German people. Rathenau moved away and did not answer. He left angry, knowing that his true intentions had been revealed by a lowly peasant.[66] The underlying Jewish betrayal of the war effort, captured in the anti-Semitic spirit of this story, sounded a powerful propaganda theme in the curriculum. Rathenau, murdered by far-right-wing nationalists in 1922, maintained his dark legacy as archvillain and master manipulator under the pen of Nazi curriculum writers. The simplicity of a vibrant storyline could go at least as far as the lines of traditional textbooks in expressing profoundly anti-Semitic values in the history curriculum.

Johann von Leers, the prolific author of numerous anti-Semitic works on Jews and a propaganda adviser to Joseph Goebbels, assumed that young children learned history most effectively through stories. His book *For the Reich: German History in History Stories* (1940) presented forty stories on a range of themes. Three stories focused on problems relating to money and the Jews. "The Faithful Policeman" discovered, through brave and loyal service to the German community, that the "respectable Jew" existed only as fiction. This courageous man of the law, Leers wrote, discovered the level of criminality to which Jews were capable of reaching in order to satiate their lust for money. Here was an administration of law that saw Jews for who they really were without flinching.[67]

"Jews Sell the German Navy" is a carefully crafted story showing how Bank Rothschild became involved in lending money to keep the navy afloat in the wake of the war with Denmark in the late 1840s. Germany was not yet unified into a nation, so the navy found itself without the necessary funding to continue the struggle. Leers's skill at not only exploiting historical imagination but also cleverly passing off myth as fact was a critical aspect of his writing. He wanted young children to believe that the German Navy became incapable of fully engaging the enemy because their key ships were heavily financed with Jewish money out of Frankfurt. Jewish investment in the German Union had to be protected even at the cost of the navy's security. Rothschild made matters worse by demanding full payment on all of the loans heedless of how such demands would affect the already imperiled conditions faced by the navy in its fight for national honor. In the end, the "fat Jewish brokers," as Leers called them, forced an auction of the navy to secure payment on the loans. Baron Thun, representing German interests, became the target of Rothschild's harsh insults when the Jewish financier assured him that he could still retain "a tired civil servant, a hungry wretch, and a stumbling sextant."[68]

Leers layered this anti-Semitic collection with yet another example of Jewish desire to influence young minds. "So They Became Rich" recounted events leading up to the suicide of a construction tradesman in Berlin during the closing decade of the nineteenth century. Speculation in the city's housing market, manipulated by Jews, made it impossible for the man to continue in business. High interest rates made matters worse. The refusal of Jewish bankers to lend him money for the continuation of his business insulted his pride. A broken and exhausted man, he took his own life, a victim of Jewish economic conspiracy. The last paragraph of the story brought together what Leers felt was the core message of history instruction. This collection of stories was not the only piece Leers contributed to race education, but it remained one of the few he addressed specifically to the readership of children in the elementary history classes. As was his style, Leers appealed to emotion and often used potentially explosive language to advance his anti-Semitic agenda. In this closure, Leers brought pupils to one inescapable conclusion, the nature of which offered a justification for even more brutality and death for the Jewish community:

> Jewry is unabashed swindling. The Jews, in all times, beginning from the founding fathers to the present, used the deception of working people as their weapon to gain power. In economic life, the Jews have for centuries brought that serious spirit of the black marketeer which we also must repulse from his last slippery corner. Also, the years of rapid industrialization from 1872 were in reality a Jewish era.

Those people who are harmed by Jews every day have been in large measure falsely treated. In deep shame over this, ruined economically and oppressed by crooked Jewish debt structures, many of these people have given up or hidden themselves in the darkness of poverty. Correctly handling the situation at that time were those who already freely characterized Jewish crookedness. The struggle against the Jews is a struggle against ancient evil in the world. If it comes because of that, from whoever shall survive in this struggle, so will we survive and the Jew shall perish. The fewer Jews there are, the happier is the world and all working peoples! [Leers' exclamation point].[69]

This is the kind of loud and unrelenting anti-Semitic rhetoric for which Leers became well known. There are few other passages from history instruction under the Third Reich, with the possible exception of *Mein Kampf*, which brought to children such a direct and powerful suggestion about the annihilation of the Jews. One of the most utilized words in Leers's anti-Semitic lexicon is *Gauner*, which variously means "swindler" or "crook." As noted in chapter 1, Leers devoted a great deal of attention to developing notions about Jewish criminality. The story format, meant to personalize anti-Semitism and elicit an emotional commitment to the racial state, also had great appeal to pedagogues dedicated to the integration of German literature into the curriculum. Some of the results of their work appear in the next chapter.

GEOGRAPHICAL PERSPECTIVES ON THE JEW

Anti-Semitic images of Jews, already well exploited through the history curriculum and Nazi interpretations of the Jewish past, also emerged in the study of geography. Establishing linkages between race hygiene and geography as a way of developing race and population policy was already part of discussions among educators and health professionals during the Weimar Republic.[70] The emergence of geopolitics as a way of legitimizing Germany's claims for more living space, especially to the East, implied that Slavic populations in Eastern Europe stood in the way of Germany's expansionistic designs.[71] The heaviest concentrations of Jews in all of Europe, located in Poland and Russia, represented a threat to Volkish thinkers in Germany as early as the late nineteenth century. The vast and swelling numbers of *Ostjuden*, as seen earlier in the curriculums for both history and race hygiene, were the most rejected of all migrating populations. Geography, in the service of the racial state, would further legitimize a conception of the Jew as negative other.

Before examining evidence from the geography curriculum conceived for elementary pupils on this issue, the investigation turns to a consideration of cultural geography. During the Weimar Republic, Siegfried Passarge explored the Jewish question through developing an interdisciplinary set of linkages between geography, racial anthropology, and religion. Although his involvement as a geography professor in the formation of teachers remains unclear, the appearance of his ideas in 1929 is a matter of some significance. Race geography, like race history and race hygiene, was not invented by the Nazis. Passarge saw in geography a new way of understanding Jews, an understanding couched in the language of racial science so strongly embraced by other academics like the race eugenicist

Fritz Lenz and the racial anthropologist Eugen Fischer. As they did, Passarge originally addressed readers during the Weimar era, but his ideas would resonate with a frightening force after 1933.

In proposing a study of how people related to nature and the land through various cultural phenomena, Passarge immediately assured readers that he was "simply interested in the purely scientific, established opinions." Never before, he observed, had he written a scientific piece so dispassionately while keeping his emotions under complete check.[72] Not far into the book, Passarge introduced readers to the very subjective world of Eugen Fischer's race biology relating to the perils of blood mixing and bastardization. Bound with a presumptuousness often witnessed later among confident Nazi curriculum writers, Passarge immediately delved into the problem of racial soul and the Jews. Of no small import was his emphasis on the influence of Negroid bloodlines on the formation of Jewish character. With an intellectual arrogance surpassed perhaps only by Günther, Passarge passed himself off as an anthropologist and great expert on Jewish culture and religion. One lengthy section on the Jewish ghetto implied that the ghetto was part of a natural progression of events legitimizing a segregation of Jews from non-Jewish populations. Behind all of this was the assumption that Jews could not possess a genuine appreciation for the land since they were people of the city. Passarge's claim for objective judgment on matters relating to the cultural-geographical aspects of the Jewish question led to some peculiar conclusions. Jewish financiers from New York were behind Bolshevism and the Russian Revolution. Geography from Passarge's pen, deeply layered with all manner of anti-Semitic preconceptions, foreshadowed the institutionalization of Nazi science.[73]

How Volkish racism and racial science of the kind legitimized by Passarge assumed anti-Semitic proportions in *Erdkundeunterricht* (geography instruction) remains our concern. As witnessed so many times in other parts of the curriculum throughout this investigation, geography educators exploited both old and new forms of anti-Semitic thinking. The image of the wandering Jew walking the face of the earth, captured earlier in the teaching charts of Alfred Vogel, remained potent throughout the curriculums not only for geography but also for history and race hygiene. (See plate 2). How closely aligned the geography curriculum was with the overall racial and biological emphasis in school knowledge was already clear in Rust's curriculum directive on racial science and heredity from the fall of 1933. A teacher training camp on racial science and hereditary biology organized for female teachers from all grade levels the following year reflected strong geopolitical concerns. According to an address delivered by the geography educator Konrad Bahr, racial tensions with Slavic populations to the East and borderland regions like Silesia demanded more serious attention in the curriculum. The concept of living space, applied here to Silesia, is couched first and foremost in terms of race. The geographical location is of some significance. Silesia, once part of the Kaiserreich, joined Poland through the Treaty of Versailles. Although not mentioned specifically, Jews would be among those caught in the racial net of eastern Europe including the region of Silesia. Although some eight years away, the large death camp of Auschwitz eventually opened its gates on Silesian soil:

This must be made clear to our pupils. They must learn to see that nature offers many geopolitical possibilities. Then it will be made clear to them that the struggles for Silesia's future does not depend on space, but rather on race. Maintaining the purity of the race and strengthening the race are the most important tasks which Silesia, like every other borderland, must resolve itself through its own responsibility for the continued existence of the German Reich. Every blood mixing of our predominantly Nordic conditioned people with the predominantly eastern and east Baltic classified Slavs weakens the continued existence of our typically German hereditary factors. The mixing of the races plants in the life and soul of our children not only the gulf between German and Slavic national consciousness, but rather also the gulf between Nordic and foreign racial tendencies. The heroic person, the type of political leader, will favor the pushing back of the nationally unimportant, politically useless herding peoples.[74]

The biological determinism which marked Bahr's comments before an audience of teachers further legitimized the role of racial classification in the teaching of cultural and political geography. A more direct and specific discussion of the Jews in relation to geopolitical issues in the curriculum came through the writing of Walther Jantzen, one of the most best-known geography educators of the Third Reich. From his post in the Institute for Education and Instruction in Berlin, Jantzen advised teachers primarily on issues relating to geography content. Through a series of publications, some supported with well-developed collections of maps, the education official translated Nazi ideological assumptions through curriculum formation.

Jantzen's *Geographie in the Service of National Political Education* (1936) was to Nazi geography education what Dieter Klagges's tome on *History Instruction as National Political Education* was to the formation of the history curriculum. In contrast to Klagges, Jantzen took a more direct and specific approach to the Jewish question. As with many writers of geography curriculum, he was also concerned with matters relating to the declining birth rate since the World War I. Jantzen was a leading figure in the articulation of *Wehrgeographie*, a kind of "armed geography" that helped pupils understand the importance of Germany's right to living space and territorial expansion in response to the legacy of the hated Versailles Treaty. As Bahr intimated earlier, the racial implications for this kind of teaching were of central importance. The content outlines sent to elementary school teachers in 1939 stated unequivocally that "the interaction between Volk and space, between blood and soil formed central ideas of geography instruction."[75]

The "chauvinistic charge" behind the geography curriculum, as Hugo Flessau called it, manifested itself through Jantzen's treatment of the races. His work was one of the few from the Nazi curriculum establishment that specifically singled out Black Africans, Sinti and Roma (Gypsies), and Jews. The French were on the receiving end of Jantzen's sharp invective for granting Black Africans citizenship and entry into the officer corps. As usual, the "Black shame" of Black African soldiers occupying the Rhineland under the French flag was not forgotten. The United States once again provided a rationalization for maintaining racial segregation. The reality of Black lynchings and strict separation of the races in schools and public transportation suggested the importance of keeping the White race separated from foreign racial elements.[76]

Of the three racial groups, the one appearing by far the least on the pages of Nazi curriculum materials was Sinti and Roma, who remained almost faceless. Jantzen's book was more of an exception to the rule of omission. The author stressed a similarity between the Jews and Sinti and Roma as peoples without a home who wandered from one host country to another. He summed up the character of Sinti and Roma as "work shy, adventuresome, and strangely restless." The geographer saved easily his most focused attention for the Jews. The race question, Jantzen wrote, is "fired with the realization" that there was a foreign race of peoples who, even possessing relatively small numbers, empowered themselves through trade, economy, art and literature as well as the "politics of supremacy." This Jewish "nomadic people" ingratiated themselves in the money trade and remained incapable of grasping what it meant to be German. Jantzen called on teachers and pupils to "revolt against such foreign rule," meeting the enemy with the measures passed in 1933 to "eliminate this influence" (*zur Ausschaltung dieses Einflußes*) of the Jews. Similar to Johannn von Leers, Jantzen was not afraid to advocate extreme actions in addressing the Jewish question. School curriculum became one of the ideological vehicles for this expression.[77]

In departing from Hitler's original discussion of Jews as a race in *Mein Kampf*, Jantzen informed readers that the Jews were a people, not a race. His reasoning was based on the assumption that a Semitic race did not exist, only a family of Semitic languages. On the concept of anti-Semitism, Jantzen cleverly turned readers toward a somewhat meaningless reference to the word's origins. Without providing any historical context for the expression, he simply noted that the word "merely related to the Hebrew language of the Jews" and thus derived from a larger Semitic linguistic stem. Such a strategy implied that the causes of anti-Semitism were tied exclusively to Jewish culture and history. Stripped out was any recognition that European non-Jews might hold some responsibility for hateful actions taken against Jews across time.[78]

To press a further point, Jantzen presented a table on the "spread of Jews in various countries and cities" from 1933. (See figure 4.2). Using a series of stereotypical drawings to symbolize Poles, Hungarians, Romanians, Americans, Czechs, Russians, Germans, and English, he related the percentage of Jews in each population. Exacting statistical knowledge of this nature was significant, he insisted, if citizens were to "correctly assess the meaning of the Jews." The symbol of a bearded Jewish male, highlighted with a black background, revealed that Poland, of all the countries, claimed 13 percent, the highest percentage of Jews among the population. Warsaw claimed fully one-third of its citizens among the Jews. Jantzen obviously wanted pupils to see the relative strength of the population in eastern European countries as a way of underscoring the threat of the *Ostjuden*. Jews in the United States figured prominently in this table. Although they represented only 3.1 percent of the general population, Jantzen wanted readers to see that Jews were a presence in Philadelphia, Chicago, and, especially, New York City. The prominence of Jews in New York, as noted earlier with Passarge's conspiratorial charges, deeply disturbed dedicated German anti-Semites.[79]

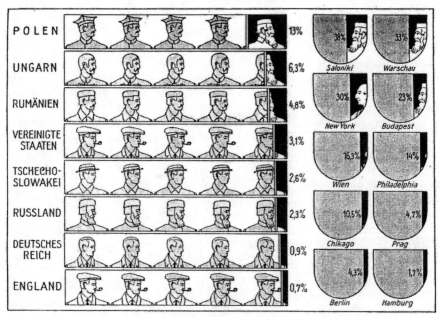

13. Verbreitung der Juden in verschiedenen Ländern und Städten (1933).

Figure 4.2 "The Spread of Jews in Various Countries and Cities," from Walther Jantzen, *Die Geographie im Dienste der nationalpolitische Erziehung* (*Geography in Service to National Political Education*). Breslau: Hirt, p. 20.

Of at least equal significance for the teaching of geopolitics and its implications for the Jewish question was Jantzen's collection of maps published as *Geopolitics in Maps: The Jews* (1941). The volume represented one of the most concentrated geographical resources on the Jewish question to exist under the regime. To Jantzen, the geographical perspectives offered by maps gave educators another pedagogical tool with which to increase an understanding of the geographical concepts of place, space, and movement. Connecting these concepts with the Jews was not an insignificant or easy matter since a historical context was demanded. Jewish migrations over time were part of the thematic glue that kept Jantzen's collection together.[80]

The first map, labeled "Restless Migration," portrayed the movement of Jews throughout Europe, northern Africa, and the Middle East during the Roman Empire. A map showing the oldest communities in Germany clearly indicated the numerous communities to which Jews belonged for centuries. The murder of Jews at Trier in 1096 during the First Crusades was not forgotten but from the Nazi perspective was seen as resulting from "Christian fanaticism against these heretics." The *Ostjuden*, "build-up and overflow," depicted the movement of Jews across Europe with broad and sweeping black-and-white arrows meant to show eastern German lands as unfortunate recipients of this change. A second map related the overseas movements of *Ostjuden* with the United States as the main destination. Jantzen exploited the theme of "Jews in America," one of the most popular in the Nazi geography curriculum. Exclaiming that over five million Jews lived in that country by 1937, he also presented circle graphs concluding that upwards of 30 percent of all practicing members of the Jewish faith resided in the United States. Not content with statistical data and maps alone, Jantzen pointed out that the movie stars Jackie Coogan and Charlie Chaplin were Jews along with Supreme Court Justice Louis Brandeis. Not to be forgotten was Mayor Fiorello La Guardia of New York who was a half-Jew. Bernard Baruch earned the epithet "Rathenau of America."[81]

The Rothschilds, the focus of more Nazi anti-Semitic rhetoric than any other single Jewish family, earned a special place in Jantzen's curriculum collection. A gigantic Rothschild family tree, spread across a map of Europe, showed the growth in power and influence of the family since the birth of Mayer Amschel in 1743. The old conspiratorial theme took on an institutional shape. His son, Nathan Rothschild, masterminded the organization of a gigantic international banking network that financed the emancipation of the Jews. The vast financial resources of the banking family supported the political ambitions of Jews in both the upper and the lower houses of the British Parliament. In one of its most "dangerous roles," the family remained behind well-funded efforts to buy influence and extend the "Jewish plutocracy" over the face of the continent. Simply providing a propagandistic description of Jewish economic and political influence through the Rothschilds was not sufficient. Jantzen called for swift action saying that "all national movements should obliterate" this international menace.[82]

As with the efforts of Nazi curriculum writers in race hygiene as well as history, Jantzen followed the general practice of exploiting the Jewish community in Berlin. The demographics of the city provided anti-Semitic propagandists with numerous opportunities to warn about the alarming growth of the Jewish community. Like Vogel, Jantzen turned to graphics as an effective way to teach anti-Semitic thinking. Coldly rational statistics, presented graphically, could be even more persuasive and, furthermore, carried an aura of scientific objectivity. Verifying the source of the data, in keeping with general Nazi curriculum practice, remained unimportant. Jantzen covered most of a page with a large line and bar graph showing the increase of Berlin's Jewish population from 1816 to 1925. A large symbol covered part of the chart. In the middle of a sizable Star of David rested a drawing of the Berlin bear, the city's symbol. There were other demographic insights Jantzen wanted readers to understand. The geographer, especially unnerved that 5,811 Jews between 1923 and 1932 had left the Jewish religious community, protested that Jews from this group remained off the city's census rolls. An action of this nature provided a stronger legitimacy for the blood laws of the racial state to maintain the iron rule of "once born a Jew, always a Jew."[83]

Jantzen's love of statistics and economic stereotypes manifested itself through a simplified rendering of the Jewish presence in the various professions. Following the practice of Alfred Vogel and others, Jantzen presented caricatures of well-dressed Jews posed against images of hardworking and industrious Germans. Under the title "1925: One Half Million Jews Enslave 62.5 million Germans," he offered drawings depicting domination by Jews among self-employed and white-collar jobs. The relative size of the drawings symbolizing Jews and Germans extended to the workers and domestic servants. Interspersed between the words of a familiar anti-Semitic pronouncement, "the Jew rules, the German must work," a much larger drawing of a big and brawny German worker standing with shovel in hand dominates a sketch of a Jewish worker who is shown seated on a rock scratching his head. The great difference between the two groups regarding employment in housework was not a small matter since the Nuremberg Laws made it illegal for Jews to employ women in the home under forty-five years of age. Jantzen's intention in this geography curriculum was somewhat different. He wanted the drawings and statistics to imply that Jews perceived themselves as above the manual labor engaged in by most Germans. Another element thus reinforced the image of the negative other.[84]

On the question of resettling the Jews, Jantzen turned to Palestine, the closing issue for his collection of maps and graphs. The timing of his remarks is significant since his publication appeared in 1941, the year of Hitler's attack on Russia. Even at this time, Jantzen's geopolitical perspective reflected an assumption that Jewish resettlement in the Middle East was still an option, although unlikely at best. Jantzen expressed serious doubts about the practicality of trying to settle sixteen million of the world's Jewish population inside the boundaries of the small land area dominated by the desert. In remarks that proved prophetic, he said that scarcity of land in Palestine was made even more problematic by the "old and established Arab population" who already expressed "violent opposition against the unwanted intruders." Remembering 1941, one might easily dismiss Jantzen's brief discussion concerning the massive resettlement of Jews in Palestine as unimportant when placed next to the policy prerogatives considered by Hitler and the SS. What remains significant about his writing are two elements. First, his curriculum reflected a certain difference in perception between educators and the SS hierarchy over the solution to the Jewish question. The SS and Hitler's inner circle had given up on the Palestinian option long before Jantzen's curriculum resource rolled off the press. Obviously, like the vast number of other educators, Jantzen was far from the center of the Nazi decision-making process. Second, the way Jantzen closed his writing reflected a basic conflict of interpretation over Hitler's "war against the Jews." The new order after the present war, he wrote, "would satisfactorily solve this question." As we have seen, Hitler eventually embraced war itself as the solution to the Jewish question. Events transpiring in 1941 and beyond made Jantzen's observations appear somewhat naive in character.[85]

Geography educators, like colleagues in most other school subjects, did not express anti-Semitic thinking in the same way. *Germany as a Whole* (1938), a popular teaching book for the geography classroom at the time, treated the Jewish question as one of several issues defining the geography curriculum for elementary and middle schools. The work, already in its ninth edition by 1938, combined physical and cultural geography. The Volkish conception of land tied to culture and race earned an honored place in this book written by a geography professor, Konrad Olbricht, and Hermann Kärgel, a school rector. The Jewish question, while not an overwhelming presence in the larger framework of this teaching resource, still assumed a form that set it apart from many other anti-Semitic curriculum writings in the field. The authors wanted teachers and their pupils to develop an understanding of the profound ideological differences between Nazism and "Jewish Bolshevism." Bolshevism certainly was not a new flashpoint for developing Nazi anti-Semitic attacks on the Jewish community. What Olbricht and Kärgel contributed was a piece of propaganda for the geography classroom differentiating the two worldviews. Few other curriculum resources for teachers set down the clash between these two ways of thinking with such propagandistic fervor. That one might find this historical, political, and economic issue addressed in a geography text was not at all unusual for the Third Reich. Geopolitics concerned itself with questions of this nature, especially in relation to the great enemy in the East that held the key to German expansion. Table 4.3 articulates how the image of both Jews and Bolsheviks became intertwined in direct opposition to the ideals of Nazism[86]:

Without labeling each column, some readers might conclude that some items recorded as characteristics of Jewish bolshevism actually came closer to describing the dynamics of the Nazi racial state. Other items carried a strong charge of wholly misrepresenting actual Nazi practice. Statement 5 on the use of forced labor to complete massive construction projects certainly was not restricted to the Russian regime. The last item on religion and the state, the only one to mention a Jewish institution, advanced a delusion. The Nazis had removed any state protection for the free exercise of the Jewish religion years before this edition of the teachers' book appeared in print. The claim that Jewish bolshevism created a police state while the Nazis developed a state characterized by "strength through joy" reinforced another deception. Such distinctions meant little when propaganda masqueraded as truth regardless of the regime. The critical element to be remembered here is that this articulation of ideological differences came with an avowed purpose of political socialization for both teachers and pupils. Sharpening the lines of difference between Jews and Germans, using bolshevism and the Russians as a foil, remained at the heart of this academic exercise while reinforcing major tenets from *Mein Kampf*. "Armed geography," with all of its geopolitical implications, could not exist without enemies.

The anti-Semitic connection with the United States and the old conspiracy charge that Jews were out to take over the world created some peculiar twists in the professional literature. That Jews might exercise some influence in the burgeoning democracy across the Atlantic drove one of the most strident of all anti-Semitic voices in the Third Reich to sensationalize the perceived threat. Johann von Leers was not a stranger to these proceedings. In an essay published in late 1938 for the NSLB journal *Deutsche Erzieher (German Educator)* the professor from the University of Berlin reprinted part of the contents of an article that appeared earlier in the pages of an anti-Semitic, Italian-American newspaper, *La Vita Italiana*. The original contributors to this essay predicted what the political leadership in the United States might look like in 1940. Their results, meant to impress readers with the depth and scope of Jewish influence, reflected the extremes of anti-Semitic conspiratorial rhetoric. All of the figures, Leers reminded readers, were Jews (See table 4.4[87]):

On only one account, in reference to the secretary of the treasury, did the predictions turn out to be accurate. Allowing for at least some element of tongue in cheek in this listing, there existed a more insidious intention behind this failed attempt at humor. Internationalizing the Jewish threat made the Jew appear even more ominous. By extending the image of the Jew beyond Germany and the

Table 4.3
National Socialism and Jewish Bolshevism Geography Instruction
Konrad Olbricht and Hermann Kärgel (1938)

National Socialism	Jewish Bolshevism
1. Leadership from the people, loyalty to the work force.	Tyranny of a foreign national authority under disguise as a democracy. Destruction of its own supporters (show trials).
2. People are the greatest wealth of Germany. A change from fragmented German classes and parties to a happy and collaborative national body.	Transformation of people into a termite-like existence in one, high capacity robot lacking its own sense of creative enthusiasm.
3. The machine becomes a valuable helper and is placed in such positions where they free human strengths for better purposes.	The machine is idolized and enslaves people (forced labor).
4. Education of a person for citizenship. Does not live in and next to the state, rather further develops a joyful sense of "his" state.	The state is only an apparatus who of the police. It shall come up later as a "world republic" and therefore has only transitory meaning.
5. The working man regards his collaboration for the expansion of German living space as an honorable duty.	Massive building construction, performed by political prisoners in the hardest slave labor, merely serves imperialistic purposes.
6. The economy serves the state and serves the people.	The economy is the state under which people are subordinated.
	The economic state devours the people.
7. A healthy peasantry and love for soil, as with the rest of the people (suburban housing), are prerequisites for healthy future. Decrease of urbanization through moving industries.	Through collectivism, the peasants are crushed. Peasant sinks to level of salaried employee without tenure. Gigantic increase of cities.
8. Foundation of a characteristic culture, which is not an "export article."	Suppression of a characteristic culture and the spread of world revolution.
9. A national army (not arming, rather "after armed") serving only defense.	A huge army, strengthened more and more at the cost of ruining the people, shall be the raiding party of world revolution.
10. Establishes a valuable heredity of past races (customs, inheritance, reviving old legal forms).	Suppression of all traditional cultural values, incapable of creating its own culture.
11. Free exercise of religion under de-politicization the same.	Godless propaganda under the protection of the synagogue.

"National Socialism and Jewish Bolshevism," from Konrad Olbricht and Hermann Kärgel, *Deutschland als Ganze. Der Erdkunde Unterricht in der Volks- und Mittelschule. (Germany as a Totality: Earth Science Instruction in the Elementary and Middle School)*. Ninth edition. Berlin: Zickfeldt, 1938, pp. 63–64.

Table 4.4
Predictions for American Political Leadership in 1940
Johann von Leers (1938)

President of the United States	Bernard Baruch
Vice President	Albert Einstein
Secretary of State	Herbert Lehmann
Secretary of Interior	Nathan Margold
Secretary of the Treasury	Henry Morgenthau
Secretary of the Army	Leon Trotsky
Secretary of the Navy	David Lilienthal
Secrtary of Agriculture	Mordechai Ezechial
Secretary of Labor	David Dubinsky
Trade Secretary	Harry Guggenheim
Postal Service	Albert Goldmann
Secretary of Education	Rabbi Stephen Wise
Attorney General	Felix Frankfurter
Press	Walter Lippmann

Ostjuden into other continents, writers like Leers could advance a stronger geographical argument. Jews had assumed control elsewhere in even a huge nation like the United States, the implication being that the same thing could happen on the German domestic front. The fact that Jews made up no more than 1 percent of the German population remained beside the point.

As a frequent contributor to professional journals for teachers, Leers exercised some influence—although how much remains unclear—in shaping ideas about what children should or should not know about Jews. He was but one voice in a vast educational enterprise that, on an ideological level, conceived geography and history as ways to advance the propaganda ideals of the Third Reich. Leers's conclusions in this essay, coming off the press only nine days after the Night of the Broken Glass, also reflected the unresolved nature, among members of the educational establishment, of Nazi policy concerning the fate of the Jews. Leers still referred to proposals to send all Jews to Palestine or Madagascar or even possibly Guyana in South America or Dutch New Guinea. As with the thinking of Jantzen, conditions surrounding the conduct of the subsequent war with Russia would nullify these considerations in short order.[88]

Chapter 5

Exemplars of Anti-Semitic Literature for Children

> Yes, my child! Like a single poisonous mushroom that can
> kill a whole family, so also a solitary Jew can destroy a
> whole village, a whole city, even an entire Volk.
>
> —Ernst Hiemer, *Der Giftpilz*, 1938

Educating young children in the *Volksschule* about the dynamics of race hygiene and anti-Semitism demanded a certain understanding of the nature of learning. There existed among Nazi curriculum writers the widespread assumption that the more complex and theoretical aspects of race education were best left to older pupils in the secondary schools. Writing in the *Handbook for Biology Instruction* (1940), Hans Keipert observed that the elementary school child was not yet able to grasp intricate "political principles and theories" relating to the Jewish question. What the child wanted, Keipert insisted, was an experiential basis for learning about the Jews. He reminded teachers that the child "still saw the matter through imagination and fairy tale" while "grasping it [the Jewish question] in his small environment as living and personified."[1]

Children's literature assumed an important role in the campaign of schools to internalize Nazi ideology and Volkish political views in the minds and hearts of the young.[2] As noted earlier, the Nazis were not the first to advance Volkish nationalism or an anti-Semitic agenda. Among earlier Volkish thinkers, the anti-Semitic writers Paul de Lagarde and Julius Langbehn strongly influenced the subsequent development of children's literature under the Nazis. Yet, even their anti-Semitism was not strong enough for the Nazis since the two men advocated the assimilation of Jews based on their degree of commitment to Nordic Germanic thinking while ignoring the issue of bloodlines. As far as establishing a racial orientation to literary policy was concerned, the Nazis drew, in part, from the example set by Adolf Bartels and Josef Nadler. Around the turn of the century, these two Volkish writers introduced the expression "decadent literature" into the cultural milieu of the Kaiserreich. In a manner prefiguring later Nazi condemnations of Jewish artists falling under Hitler's special exhibition of "decadent art" in Munich in 1938, Bartels and Nadler warned about undesirable liberal and cosmopolitan Jewish influences in literature.[3]

Jews obviously were not the only focus for children's literature under the

Third Reich. The glorification of militarism and nationalistic fervor, themes traditionally popular with history instruction from the Kaiserreich and Weimar, also marked children's readers and story collections in a powerful way.[4] German language and literature bore the special designation as one of the great bearers of German cultural values in the curriculum. Anti-Semitic learning, although certainly not an exclusive element in children's literature from the Nazi regime, still played a significant role in advancing the values of Nazi ideology. Central to the purpose of this chapter is a case study of selected anti-Semitic storybooks intended for the teaching of German literature in the *Volksschule*. It is here where one discovers Nazi anti-Semitic instruction in one of its most simplified forms through the power of the word and image. As with the race biology curriculum prepared by Alfred Vogel, publishers of anti-Semitic materials often went to great lengths to integrate artwork using the latest techniques in color printing to carry propaganda messages in the most direct way.

ERNST HIEMER AND THE DEMONIZATION OF THE JEW

Julius Streicher and the Der Stürmer publishing house in Nuremberg quickly developed a reputation as the major source for the most vociferous anti-Semitic literature written for children in Nazi Germany. As editor of a weekly of the same name since 1923, Streicher penned some of the most vile anti-Jewish passages to be recorded in modern history. The historian Gordon Craig recalled a lecture delivered by Streicher on the Jewish question in the Great Hall of the University of Munich:

> For three and a half hours, this gross bully, bulging in his brown uniform, poured forth floods of filth that I would not have thought possible in public oratory, let alone from a university lectern, and offered "scientific" evidence of the predatory nature of the Jews, at one point arguing insistently that, if one was attentive while visiting zoos, one would note that the blond-haired German children always played happily in the sandboxes while the swarthy Jewish children sat expectantly before the cages of the beasts of prey, seeking vicarious satisfaction of their blood-tainted lusts. The audience in the hall was attentive, and many took notes.[5]

One of the best-known pieces to come out of Streicher's office for a young readership was the infamous *Der Giftpilz (The Poisonous Mushroom)* from 1938. Ernst Hiemer, as one of Streicher's protégés, authored this work along with a second piece, *Der Pudelmopsdackelpinscher und andere besinnliche Erzahlungen* (The poodle-pug-dachshund-pinscher and other contemplative stories) from 1940. In Hiemer, the ex-school teacher Streicher found a most willing mouthpiece for portraying Jews as dark and devilish figures standing in diametric opposition to the aesthetically beautiful, tall blond German figures crossing his pages. The Jew became the penultimate "poison mushroom."

The Poison Mushroom is a collection of seventeen short stories with each story carrying a full-page color illustration by a draftsman who used the pseudonym "Fips." The table of contents, shown in table 5.1, makes clear the scope of anti-Semitic themes addressed in the book, many of which will sound familiar to readers of previous chapters.

Table 5.1
Table of Contents
The Poison Mushroom (1938)

1. The Poisonous Mushroom
2. How to Tell a Jew
3. How the Jews Came to Us
4. What Is the Talmud?
5. Why the Jews Let Themselves Be Baptized
6. How a German Peasant Was Driven from House and Farm
7. How Jewish Traders Cheat
8. The Experience of Hans and Else with a Strange Man
9. What Happened to Inge with a Jewish Doctor
10. How the Jew Treats His Domestic Help
11. How Two Women Were Tricked by Jewish Lawyers
12. How Jews Torment Animals
13. What Christ Said about the Jews
14. Money Is the God of the Jews
15. How Worker Hartmann Became a National Socialist
16. Are There Decent Jews?
17. Without Solving the Jewish Question, No Salvation for Mankind

Table of Contents from Ernst Hiemer, *Der Giftpilz* (*The Poison Mushroom*). Nuremberg: Der Stürmer, 1938, pp. 1–2.

This literature cleverly united traditional and more contemporary racial forms of anti-Semitic thinking. For some young readers, the illustrations undoubtedly carried an even stronger anti-Semitic punch than the words of each story. The vast majority of the pieces were limited to no more than three pages of text. A diary written by Christa Lufer, a pupil from this period, recounted the introduction of the *The Poison Mushroom* into her classroom. Writing in May of 1938, she noted the enthusiastic reception accorded the book by her teacher:

Yesterday was the first warm day this year. I played all day outside and completed none of my homework for German. I therefore was a little anxious when I went to school this morning. Herr Wenzel always shouts with the same loud voice. But I was lucky. Herr Wenzel spent the entire hour talking about a new book that absolutely should be purchased by our parents. In order not to be required to show my homework, I listened with an especially sharp ear. The book was edited by *Der Stürmer*. It is a book for children and adults with many beautiful pictures. Every good German must read the book, Herr Wenzel said. It states within the dangers threatening the German people from the Jews. Herr Wenzel read to us the first story from the book. It is called, "The Poison Mushroom." The story stated that the Jews are poison mushrooms and that we must watch out for them.[6]

With the exception of his first story, Hiemer really added little to the history of anti-Semitic thinking that had not already been expressed from Luther or Shakespeare up to the nineteenth century. The exploitation of economic stereotypes, Christian anti-Semitism, and charges of sexual perversion found a literary home in Hiemer's book along with racial diatribes using the mushroom as a potent symbol. A closer look at the language and artwork used by Hiemer in several of these scenarios revealed a carefully orchestrated effort to develop anti-Semitic attitudes among the young. When taken as a whole, his volume exemplified the great value placed by Nazi pedagogues on character education for the purpose of shaping desired political values.

In trying to establish a larger context to which readers might meaningfully associate later stories in the collection, Hiemer set the stage by telling the story of the poison mushroom. The biological implications of what it meant to be a Jew from a Nazi standpoint immediately confronted the reader in a German forest where a mother and her son are gathering mushrooms. Young Franz, after discovering some poisonous ones, heard his mother explain that just as there are good mushrooms and good people, there are also bad mushrooms and bad people. When asked what bad people represented the poisonous mushrooms, Franz triumphantly identified the Jews according to his teacher at school. The mother went on to explain the different kinds of "poisonous" Jews, including the Kosher butcher, the Jewish cattle dealer, the Jewish doctor, and the baptized Jew. "Just as a single poisonous mushroom can kill a whole family," she said, "so a solitary Jew can destroy a whole village, a whole city, even an entire Volk."[7]

The ever-inquisitive Franz wanted to know if non-Jews really understood just how dangerous Jews actually were in the community. The parallel once again was not lost. The mother told her son that German boys and girls must "learn to know the Jew." Just as poisonous mushrooms led to disastrous consequences, so too the Jew remained "the cause of misery, and distress, illness and death." The author brought the story to an end by explaining the moral:

> German youth must learn to recognize the Jewish poison mushroom. They must learn what a danger the Jew is for the German Volk and for the whole world. They must learn that the Jewish problem involves the destiny of us all. The following tales tell the truth about the Jewish poison mushroom. They show the many shapes the Jew assumes. They show the depravity and baseness of the Jewish race. They show the Jew for what he really is: The Devil in human form.[8]

The classroom itself provided the background for the next exposition of the Jews. Boys in the seventh grade were learning about how to recognize a Jew. In an exercise on racial anthropology, the teacher directed one of the pupils to come to the blackboard and interpret certain drawings. (See plate 5.) The caption to the illustration relates his explanation. "One can tell a Jew," Karl Scholz stressed, "by his nose. The Jewish nose is hooked at the tip. It looks like the figure 6." Encouraged by his teacher, the young man continued with the observation that from studying the eyes, one can safely conclude that the Jew "is a false, deceitful person." Fritz Müller, the top pupil in the class, had more to add. Jews usually possessed short arms and legs, big ears shaped like the handle of a coffee cup and walked flat-footed. Heimer made certain that his fictional pupil drew a direct relationship between the slanting forehead of Jews and their criminal behavior. All of this attention given to differences in physical qualities concluded with a recitation calling to all German youth to "get rid of the Jewish Devil." Hiemer's brief rendition of Nazi race teaching was not simply part of a fairy tale. One photograph from another source showed two Jewish pupils forced to stand in front of the class. (See figure 1.2.) Suffering from the continued derision of their non-Jewish peers, the boys stood next to a blackboard that declared the Jew the greatest enemy of the country and called on all youth to protect themselves from this great threat.[9]

As in many other parts of the curriculum, the Talmud once again provided a means by which young readers could embrace Nazi assumptions about Jewish morals and attitudes toward work. Sally, the thirteen-year-old son of a Jew, found himself attending a German school since a Jewish one did not exist in his area. Visiting the rabbi in the synagogue one day to learn Jewish religious teaching, Sally confronted once again a dual morality that tested his Jewish identity. The Talmud became the guide for his intellectual journey. The rabbi tested Sally on his understanding of the Talmud's charge that non-Jews were created for work while Jews assumed a condescending attitude toward those who worked the land. Hiemer depicted the young Jew reading aloud from the Talmud and, as was the Nazi custom, recited wholly fabricated pronouncements from Jewish law. While non-Jews said that honesty was the best policy, Jews insisted that cheating and deceiving non-Jews remained morally acceptable. To further draw the line between the two communities, Sally opened the Talmud to read the premise that non-Jews existed on earth to serve the Jews through sowing, plowing, digging, sifting and reaping. How this kind of learning played itself out in German language classes remains instructive. One historian discovered that some teachers, in order to awaken anti-Jewish emotions, developed a vivid fantasy. Pupils, under the order of their teachers, were forced to record page long excerpts from the Talmud in their notebooks until their hands and fingers hurt. The hope was that hatred for Jews could be reinforced through such an exercise.[10]

The question of religion and the Jews continued throughout several other parts of the work. The baptism of Jews, a practice common in the Catholic Church, suffered a strong rejection from Nazi racial policy. The conversion of Jews to Christianity had been a celebrated cause for Luther some four hundred years before. Predictably, Hiemer's story refuted both traditions. The illustration carried the major thrust of his anti-Semitic writing. The picture portrayed an overweight Jewish man, the owner of a local department store, accompanied by his heavily powdered wife leaving a church with large prayer books in their hands while the priest delivered a farewell blessing. The scene apparently was too much for Greta and Anne, two blond-haired German girls who witnessed this event while passing by the church. After making several remarks about the appearance of the couple, the girls agreed that baptism wouldn't make any difference. The man and wife remained Jews just the same. Hiemer, here as elsewhere in the book, often appealed to the word of authority figures in the lives of young people like teachers, parents, and Hitler Youth leaders to legitimize anti-Semitic judgments. Anne told Greta that according to her local leader in the Association for German Girls (BDM), Jews had as little a chance of being made into non-Jews through baptism as a Negro had of becoming a German. Exploiting a distortion of church history, Greta told her friend that Martin Luther and the popes had held this same conviction for baptized Jews. Once again, the term *Gauner*, meaning crook or scoundrel, appeared in this context. The scene closed with Anne angrily denouncing priests for "admitting a criminal mob into the churches."[11]

As witnessed in other parts of the curriculum, the crucifixion of Christ often loomed large in Nazi strategies to exploit religious anti-Semitism. "What Christ said about the Jews" related the story of a peasant mother returning from working in the fields with her three children. They stopped near a road-side shrine of Christ. What the mother said to her children while pointing to the cross bears closer examination. Within her exposition of Golgotha, one notes the age-old demonization of Jews carried over into the instruction of elementary school children under the Third Reich:

> Children, look here! The Man who hangs on the Cross was one of the greatest enemies of the Jews of all time. He knew the Jews in all their corruption and meanness. Once he drove the Jews out with a whip, because they were carrying on their money dealings in the Church. He called the Jews killers of men from the beginning. By that he meant that the Jews in all times have been murderers. He said further to the Jews: Your father is the Devil! Do you know, children, what that means? It means that the Jews descend from the Devil. And because they descend from the Devil, they live like devils. So they commit one crime after another. Because this man knew the Jews, because He proclaimed the truth to the world, He had to die. Hence, the Jews murdered Him. They drove nails through his hands and feet and let Him slowly bleed. In such a horrible way the Jews took their revenge. And in a similar way they have killed many others who had the courage to tell the truth about the Jews. Always remember these things, children. When you see the Cross, think of the terrible murder by the Jews on Golgotha. Remember that the Jews are children of the Devil and human murderers.[12]

The powerful religious symbolism employed by Hiemer in this passage, expressed with an incendiary appeal to the emotions, made this one of the strongest anti-Semitic statements to appear anywhere within the elementary school curriculum. The long history and traditions associated with religious anti-Semitism, deeply rooted in German society, provided the Nazi regime with a propaganda opportunity of immense proportions. Economic processes invariably remained part of the picture as witnessed by the reference to Christ and his angry reaction to the Jewish moneychangers in the temple. The association of Jews with money and the marketplace constituted an ancient link in the history of anti-Semitism. Hiemer exploited this relationship for his young readers with a ferocity unmatched by many other writers of Nazi curriculum materials.

The German peasantry once again provided the context for what became an economic disaster for people working the land. In one story, Hiemer related the misfortune of a German peasant driven from his land and farm by Rosenfeld, a Jewish financier. Breaking under the heavy weight of high interest rates for loans charged by the Jew, the ruined peasant now was forced to sell the farm. The picture accompanying the story showed a Jew in the background enforcing his claim to the land, while in the foreground a neighboring peasant and Paul, his young son, discuss what is happening. Wanting to break his water jug over the head of the Jew, Paul told his father that after growing up and working a farm of his own, he would never interact with Jews and would throw them out if they should come to his door. As with all stories in the collection, Hiemer ended it with a verse designed to capture a moral lesson—this time, from Paul's teacher. The Jew once again came to be associated with pestilence and plague, a "bloodthirsty" enemy to be shunned at all costs.[13] (See plates 6, 10.)

The layers of anti-Semitic teaching continued with Hiemer's story about a Jewish trader who tried unsuccessfully to sell bad cloth to a young German peasant girl. The girl was too smart for the peddler and refused to be taken in "by his chatter." The unmistakable moral lesson from this tale was to reject the cheating and seduction of Jewish hawkers through buying exclusively from Germans. Women were also victimized in another story when two Jewish lawyers colluded in cheating their female clients out of a sizable sum of money after losing the case in court. Congratulating themselves afterward, the lawyers lined their pockets through fraud. Readers soon learned that this was another profession where Jews could not be trusted.[14]

The practice of medicine also came under scrutiny. The young Inge, suffering from an illness, remembered the warning from her leader in the BDM about not visiting Jewish doctors. Dismissing the silly fears of her daughter, a misguided mother insisted that she pay a visit to the office of a certain Doctor Bernstein. The results were disastrous. In trying to associate Jewish males with sexual perversion, Hiemer placed Inge in the waiting room of the doctor's office waiting for an appointment. She heard the desperate screams of a girl behind closed doors demanding that the doctor leave her alone. The illustration carried an anti-Semitic power of its own. (See plate 7.) Doctor Bernstein opened the door to his office to greet Inge for her appointment. "Behind the lens of the glasses," the caption read, "gleamed the two eyes of a criminal and around the thick lips played a grin." Inge fled the office screaming after the doctor tried to "lay his fleshy fingers" on her. The mother later repented for contradicting the advice of the BDM. Playing on the theme of childhood innocence, Hiemer also integrated a story about a Jewish man who tried to entice two children into his home with candy. As in some many of the tales, fear became the handmaiden of anti-Semitic expression.[15]

Certain Jewish cultural practices, noted earlier, came under sharp criticism as well as gross distortion in considerations of the Talmud. The Jewish tradition of ritual animal slaughter did not escape Hiemer's pen or his illustrator's eye. The centerpiece of the story, Jewish cruelty to animals, took on a sharp focus after Kurt and Otto hid themselves in a Jewish slaughterhouse. In secretively witnessing the killing of a cow, the boys heard the raucous laughter of three bloodied Jewish men as the cow died a slow and painful death. "How Jews Torment Animals" carried the ancient charge of ritual murder now also applied in the story to Jewish bloodlust for young children, a myth with roots as far back as the Middle Ages. As Steven Katz observed, the charge of ritual murder, when combined with other alleged actions like the poisoning of wells during times of plague and the practice of witchcraft, bound the anti-Semitic image of the Jew even more closely to that of the Devil. Hiemer once again stepped on ancient ground.[16]

The omnipresent issues of money, work, and economic gain that dominated much of the anti-Semitic curriculum thus far examined in this study found yet another means of expression in Hiemer's tale of "Money Is the God of the Jews." The altruistic Liselotte, bemoaning the fact that her father had to work so hard, told her mother about her wish to become rich so she could help the poor. What disturbed her was the observation of a teacher who told her class that thousands of Jews in the world were millionaires and did not work. The Jew, so it seemed, only traded. The perplexed child questioned how Jews could act in such a mean way. Her mother stepped in and unleashed a torrent of anti-Semitic invective to explain the situation. The Jew as Devil "without a sense of honor dealing in only meanness and crime" stood at the center of the problem. Exploiting a misinterpretation of the Bible, the mother told her daughter that the Jewish God from the Old Testament had commanded the Jews to devour the people of the earth, bleeding and using them until they died. If these words were not enough to instill a deeper prejudice in the young charges, Hiemer's illustrator took the case a step further. In one of the most arresting images from the collection, a Jew is depicted sitting atop a huge money bag stacked in front of a stock exchange. (See plate 8). The moral of this sordid tale was that Jews committed the greatest of crimes in order to make money. "He does not rest," Hiemer wrote, "until he can sit on a big sack of money, until he has become the king of money."[17]

The tight association between Jews and communism, a staple in anti-Semitic rhetoric for many years, manifested itself through a story about the worker Hartmann. The Hitler Youth, out on a long hike, came to a stretch of autobahn construction where they met Hartmann at work. He had his own story to tell the young listeners. A former member of the Communist Party, the then unemployed Hartmann recalled the many party meetings dominated by the Jewish leadership. Enamored as the Jewish Communists were with Russia, the German workers questioned the loyalty of the Jews controlling the party apparatus. The final break occurred for Hartmann when the Jews declared that Germany meant little to them and that the only important matter was to have a good time. With words that suggested a kind of religious conversion, Hartmann described in glowing language how he saw the light and found his way to Adolf Hitler. The inspired worker concluded his conversation with the Hitler Youth with a song reminding listeners that eternal peace remained out of reach unless Germany could be freed from the clutches of the Jews. Hiemer's anti-Semitic writing for children remained at least somewhat informed by the political need to identify with key social groups like the peasants and workers. These were among the key elements of support for the regime leading to Hitler's assumption of power. Appearing late in the collection, the story implied that Jews remained incapable of understanding the value of Hartmann and other German workers since, as earlier stories intimated, they possessed little appreciation for honest labor.[18]

The Poison Mushroom raised the sensitive question about the existence of what the author called "the decent Jew." As readers will recall, Heinrich Himmler subsequently contributed his own brutal response to this issue in an address to SS Officers in Posen in 1940.[19] For Hiemer, the task demanded a direct and simplified ideological answer for young minds to grasp without confusion. A pub provided the scene in which four Germans, one a Jew named Solomon, engaged in a lively discussion. Perhaps without realizing it, Hiemer had created an exceedingly rare and ideologically unacceptable instance under the Third Reich in which a Jew was counted among Germans. Solomon broke the ice by launching into a passionate defense of the Jews as the most decent people to be found anywhere. Zimmermann simply could not abide by this assumption and rejected Solomon out of hand by offering examples of Jewish rogues who crossed his path on occasion. Seeing Zimmerman's response as an attack on his personal honor, the enraged Solomon called the three "impudent creatures" and referred to his own record as a soldier in the war to defend the fatherland. A worker from the circle called Solomon a liar and insisted that the Jew had never been to the front and, instead, stayed home to make huge profits form the war economy. If this was not bad enough, Solomon had to listen to charges that he supported the Red Revolution of 1919. The premise of the decent Jew wilted under withering attacks. Solomon grabbed his hat and fled the pub in dishonor with everyone laughing behind him. Hiemer wanted children to learn the following saying as a way of removing from their minds any possible thought that Jews were indeed human beings capable of working good in the world:

> So oft we hear the yarn
> How brave such and such a Jew was.
> How he gave his money to the poor.
> And was an angel of the world.
> A Jew, like a pure angel?
> That must be a fairy tale!
> Who invents such things?
> It is the Jew, himself, who does it! [20]

How Hiemer closed his collection of stories amounted to a form of adulation for Julius Streicher. Many children reading this volume, ranging in ages from nine through thirteen, belonged to youth organizations like the *Pimpfs*, or wolf cubs, as the boys in the *Jungvolk* were known along with the *Jungmädel* for girls. As in so many Nazi curriculum resources, authors often articulated a sense of urgency regarding a "solution to the Jewish question." The last story wanted young readers to know in no uncertain terms that Streicher remained for years one of the top campaigners in the struggle against the Jews. The *Pimpfs* shared glowing stories about Streicher's speeches. Here was a real man, they said, who was not afraid of calling the Jews to task. In typical Streicher-like rhetoric, the most notorious of Jew baiters in the Third Reich warned youth that a failure to solve the Jewish question nullified any hope of "salvation for mankind." In this way, Streicher exploited the vocabulary of religion in order to advance an anti-Semitic agenda. The volume closed with a picture of several *Pimpfs* gathered around a placard of Julius Streicher announcing his next meeting. To no one's surprise, his next speech centered on the theme of the Jew as Devil.[21]

HIEMER AND ANTI-SEMITIC FAIRYTALES

Pleased with the reception accorded Hiemer's first book, Streicher and the Der Stürmer publishing house printed Hiemer's second work two years later as *The Poodle-Pug-Dachshund-Pinscher*. The title, intended by the author to be somewhat amusing and playful for children, obscured an ideological content both deadly and serious. For young readers, the main story from this larger collection preached the profound evils of blood mixing using the animal world as an example. Very possibly, some teachers used the tale in tandem with activities associated with the *Ahnentafel*, or family tree, in which children traced their racial ancestry. Jews are not mentioned once in the featured story, but the racial target of the Jew remained unmistakable. Within this brief piece of literature, Hiemer encapsulated for young children many features of anti-Semitic teaching that cut across other areas of the curriculum witnessed in this book thus far.

As in *The Poison Mushroom*, Hiemer chose racial anti-Semitism as the leitmotif for his second work with additional support drawn from traditional economic stereotypes of Jews. *The Poodle-Pug-Dachshund-Pinscher* brought readers into an evening street scene where a "mutt" or mixed-breed dog, walked the streets. After discussing the four bloodlines emanating from the dog's lineage, the author noted how "foreign" the dog was among other dogs in the town. When one looked at this canine more closely, the racial characteristics of the grandparents became clearer. His "ruffled black hair" reminded one of a poodle, and his huge mouth called to mind the hanging lips of a pug. The bandy legs indicated the bloodlines of a dachshund, while the ears were those of a pinscher. He is a loner who, because of his unruly and cowardly nature, never fit in with the other dogs.

> The mutt is, however, still a dog whom one must hate and despise. He feels at his best in the dirt.... He especially loves to roll in the filth. His fur is caked over and over with dirt and a terrible smell comes from him. But he likes that just the same.... For years, the mutt, this racial mixture, pushed himself around in our neighborhood. We came to know him in his vileness and meanness. But we know this: One day he will fulfill his destiny. Then once again peace and order will come to the streets in our city.[22]

As was his custom in this collection of stories, Hiemer presented readers with fairy tales using animals as central characters and then made explicit the parallels between the fairy tales and Jews in adjoining essays. The carefully crafted story of the mutt immediately preceded an exploitation of both racial and religious forms of anti-Semitism. A language of dehumanization, so critically important in the Nazi rationalization of anti-Semitic attitudes, entered the picture with familiar overtones. The myth of Nordic racial purity assumed its own special place in Hiemer's purview. Without explaining the reality that the Germans themselves constituted a mixture of bloodlines, Hiemer told his audience that the Jews, like the mutts on the streets, were first and foremost biological products of race mixing. Even more insidious in nature were his observations from racial anthropology. The "creeping" manner in which Jews walked, he wrote, along with their posture, reminded one of the apes. Jews also possessed a "narrow, receding forehead and skull structure" like that of a gorilla.

Their "crinkly hair" and "overhanging lower lip" called to mind the racial qualities of the Negro. Just as important for propaganda purposes amid all of
these racial details was the rhythm of the language Hiemer employed. He used
many of the same verb forms and nouns in telling the story of the mutt and in
his exposition on the Jews. The power of repetition and association, qualities
so important in the effective development of propaganda, marked the ebb and
flow of the stories Hiemer created for his young readers.[23]

Animals in selected storylines provided the author with numerous opportunities to reaffirm the association of Jews with warmongering. In a story on "Sins
of the Blood," Hiemer portrayed hyenas as vultures who consumed the bodies
of the dead and helpless wounded soldiers on the battlefield. Wave after wave of
the animals, cowardly in nature, gathered to complete their grisly task. Consistent with conclusions from other stories in the collection, Hiemer sternly warned
readers that Jews also assumed the form of the hyena in their interactions with
other people. Just as one could readily pick out a hyena by its atrocious smell,
crooked hind feet, and thick neck, so could the sensitive and discerning eye of
the German child identify the Jew through differentiating similar characteristics
from members of the general population. Moreover, Jews and hyenas mustered
the courage to attack other people and animals through joining forces among
their own. The dark Jewish tendency for planning conspiracies, according to
Hiemer, explained why Germany fell to defeat in World War I. A fixation on the
stab-in-the-back theory was not Hiemer's intent. A vibrant anti-Semitism
demanded that he connect readers to more contemporary developments. As it
turned out, the direction and order of his charge for mass murder, published in
1940, were grossly inaccurate. He blamed Jews for a horrific act of immorality
that the Third Reich, in the end, pursued with ferocious dedication:

> In the present age, the Jews are rushing once again toward new wars. They want
> to bleed the peoples dry and through this make possible the organization of a
> new world rule. They then want again, as hyena beneficiaries, to work a gruesome
> genocide. It remains with us to spare the world of such a destiny. We must enlighten
> all people about the Jewish hyenas. The children themselves must be made knowl-
> edgeable. Then the Jewish hyenas will not be able to reach their goal and peace
> finally will be granted to the world.[24]

How this kind of anti-Semitic rhetoric from Hiemer's pen shaped or influenced the minds of readers remains undetermined. Hiemer's storehouse of
anti-Semitic teachings, broad and deep, enjoyed the enthusiastic support of
the Third Reich's loudest and most raucous voices on the Jewish question. *The
Poodle-Pug-Dachshund-Pinscher* presented a menagerie of characters, each with
an avowed purpose of reaching children with the central message that, to
paraphrase the nationalist historian Heinrich von Treitscke, the Jews were
Germany's great misfortune. One of the longest stories, set in southern Spain,
revolved around the figure of the chameleon. The ability of the chameleon to
change colors as part of a strategy to protect itself by blending into its sur-
roundings provided yet another context from nature for Hiemer to extend
anti-Semitic associations.

Repeating the mantra at least four times throughout the story, Hiemer reminded readers that "a chameleon remains a chameleon and a Jew remains a Jew." Most disturbing to the author was the assumed practice among some Jewish men to shave off their beards and ringlets. Even this could not prevent the sharp-eyed observer from picking out Jews on the street. For those who had difficulty in this process, he proclaimed, relying on one's nose was still a reliable way of discerning the Jews. Like the mutt, Jews practiced a bodily uncleanliness and gave off a terrible smell that could not be avoided. Hiemer thus connected to one of the cultural delusions that originated in medieval society. The changing of Jewish family names to downplay Jewish cultural identity and the practice of baptizing Jewish converts symbolized a changing of one's colors that, like the chameleon, could not change the person's essence. In a searing tone, Hiemer had choice words for those clergy who assumed that baptism suddenly transformed the Jewish spirit of the *Gauner*, or crook, to that of an angel. National Socialism stripped away this duplicity and broke the power of Jews once and for all. Hope for the future of the Third Reich rested in the "day to day growth in the number of anti-Semites" of which youth were the real engine.[25]

A discernible young reader would not take long to realize that the stories in Hiemer's volume rested on the brutal assumption that Jews were animals or subhuman and not people at all. Like so many other Nazi curriculum writers engaged in the ideological process of advancing anti-Semitic attitudes, Hiemer sought the simplest means of connecting prejudiced assumptions. Negative cultural associations with poison snakes were another way to communicate the idea that Jews were not only subhuman but also very dangerous. The issue of race and the question of bloodlines provided an additional biological context for the threat. A further reading also reveals the Nazi philosophical assumption that book learning and academic knowledge by themselves fell far short in creating a racially conscious society. The discipline of the will remained the critical element for realizing drastic change leading to the formation of the Nazi community:

> As the snake poisons the blood of its prey through its bite, so does the Jew poison the host peoples. People who get involved with the Jews lose the purity of their blood. In the beginning, it is scarcely noticed as the Jewish poison consumes their body and soul. Slowly they sink step by step. Their children are mixed bloods and show the physical and mental characteristics of the Jewish race. These Jewish mixed bloods further poison the people. When at once the majority of the people carry the Jewish poison, there then is no longer a chance for deliverance. The poison has done its work! The people must die ... Instruction alone, however, can not solve the Jewish question. A people which knows the Jews must also have the strength to proceed ruthlessly against the world enemy. Just as the danger of snakes is not fully removed until the poisonous snakes are completely moved out, so is the Jewish question solved when Jewry is destroyed. Mankind must know that only a hard "either-or" choice exists; namely: We do not kill the Jewish poison snake, then it kills us! (*Töten wir nicht die jüdische Giftschlange, dann tötet sie uns!*)[26]

The solution to the Jewish question, articulated here by Hiemer in even more stark and direct language than in the words and images he created for *The Poison Mushroom*, came off the press in 1940. The date holds a special significance. The following year, in the wake of the attack on Russia during the fall of 1941, Hitler set into motion the process that led to the mass murder of millions. Hiemer freely used the language of mass destruction with an elementary school readership before it became operative in the East and months before the first deportations of Jews from Germany in October of 1941. The development remained well within the spirit of anti-Semitic hatred so well developed by Streicher years before, a hatred that regularly called for the complete annihilation of the Jewish community. The author simply built on his master's tradition.

The gallery of rich biological images used to buttress this anti-Semitic hatred expanded with the usual integration of references to the practice of medicine. Hiemer enlisted tape worms, bacillae, and parasites in the service of classroom instruction. As revolting an image as tapeworms might suggest, Hiemer wanted to make sure that the negative association was not lost on his readers. Just as the tapeworm found its way unnoticed into the body of the human being, so the Jews "crept inconspicuously" into the non-Jewish people. Launching into immigration policy, the author accused Jews of keeping secret the actual numbers "of their race" who actually migrated into Germany by falsifying statistics. In this way, Hiemer lamented that good Germans had no idea about how much of the country came under the influence of the Jews. The analogy drawn between the work of the tapeworm and the activities of Jews in the German body politic took on additional features. The progressive weakening of the body through the incessant feeding tapeworm drained the host of vital juices. Likewise, the *Viehjuden*, or Jewish cattle dealers, destroyed the German peasantry, "the basis for a healthy national community," by sucking dry the economic lifeblood of those who worked the land. Devastating the vital bases for trade and economy, the Jews undermined the morality of the community. The people slowly wasted away. Calling Jews to task for creating this disaster, Hiemer resorted to using the expression *Schmarotzer*, which conveyed a dual meaning. The word, in biological usage, meant parasite. On another level, the word carried a figurative meaning of a negative nature related to social policy. The *Schmarotzer* were also those human beings condemned as spongers, scroungers, and freeloaders. Once again, like other curriculum writers, Hiemer drew a close relationship between biological processes and the social image of the Jew.[27]

The figure of the medical doctor, this time a non-Jew, entered the picture to suggest a solution. In a brief scenario, Hiemer told readers about Frau Müller who wisely took her son to the doctor's office after noticing that the boy grew steadily weak from some unknown cause. The doctor, after determining that the child suffered from a tapeworm, informed the family that only a radical cure could kill the organism. This meant mercilessly attacking the head of the tapeworm when it appeared. Destroying individual parts of its body meant little since the worm only grew back larger and stronger than before. The radical cure, a relentless attack on the organism until it finally died out, was the only answer. Closely following the formula for storytelling he embraced throughout the book, Hiemer made clear to young readers that a similar piece of medical advice had to be followed in relation to the Jews. The author appealed to history for this radical social cure. The surgical removal of the parasite from the community implied in the following passage became a justification for the mass destruction of the Jewish community:

Just as it is with the tapeworm, so also must a radical cure be undertaken with the Jews to make possible his elimination. As world history as shown, non-Jews over the centuries have risen up against the Jewish blood suckers. Millions of Jewish crooks escaped from the exploited peoples. Hundreds of thousands of these wretched criminals ended up on the gallows or were burned alive. The people hoped in this way to finally have peace from the Jewish tapeworm. But they were disappointed! The Jews propagated themselves and became numerous. Exactly then, just as the people can be saved from the plague of tapeworms only if the pest is completely destroyed, so also can the people be freed from the plague of the Jews *when they do the whole job (wenn sie ganze Arbeit machen)*. Do not do this and render only part of Jewry harmless, then the growth of the Jewish tapeworm follows again and again! Then he is more dangerous than before! Then all work was in vain! Tapeworm and Jew are parasites of the worst kind. We want their elimination, we want to became healthy and strong again. Then only one thing will help: Their extermination.[28]

The rabid anti-Semite was not finished. Closing the volume, artist Willi Hofmann sketched a stark and threatening figure of death with gaunt features wearing a cape overshadowing a community. Death crosses hovered over the town. The drawing set the tone for the story of the *Völkergift*, or "national poison." As in the preceding story about the Jew as *Schmarotzer*, Hiemer used the medical profession and the threat of illness as an essential context for his teachings. The bacillus and bacteria, Hiemer's doctor explained to a young patient, constituted a dangerous threat precisely because one could not see them with the naked eye. Therefore, people often remained unaware of which diseases attacked their bodies. Diptheria, cholera, and typhus decimated populations over the centuries as silent killers. So too would the Jew destroy the German community if not eradicated.

For all of the anti-Semitic emphases in curriculum on personal appearance as a way of differentiating the Jews from Aryans, Hiemer took a somewhat different tack. Just as it was difficult to perceive the bacillus, so it was "often impossible to recognize the Jew." Not all Jews, he admitted, possessed the same racial characteristics. Not all Jews had hooked noses, protruding ears, "typical" Jewish eyes, or walked flat-footed. His advice to young readers was to "look behind" outer appearances in order to avoid being deceived. Hiemer's advice, if taken at face value, actually required his readers to take the time and effort to get to know individual Jews. That this was not his real intention is obvious from the multitude of negative stereotypes and prejudgments he articulated throughout the book. Still, he wrote, no nation to this day "succeeded in fully removing the Jews." Even if a country became fully free of Jews, no one could say with certainty that the community would remain *Judenrein*. The "Jewish bacillus" always found a way to breed and multiply throughout other nations. As always, the "Jewish epidemic" always posed a threat by returning to infect host countries. As long as there existed the bacillus for diptheria, Hiemer concluded, so there must be diptheria. And so long as Jews lived in the world, there then would exist a Jewish danger.[29]

Hiemer's use of biological language to buttress racial anti-Semitism in children's literature connected with the vision of the Jew from the Middle Ages as "unproductive parasite" and the emergence of racial science in the nineteenth century.[30] His call for citizens to "do the whole job" of mass extermination and the powerful negative associations he so freely employed from biology and medicine to justify these actions make this volume one of the most violent pieces of school material to come off the press. In order to persuade his young readers about the righteousness of this anti-Semitic cause, Hiemer had first to succeed in persuading them that Jews simply were not human. They remained equated with revolting animals or deadly diseases. The Nazi penchant for racial purity, subsumed under Hiemer's use of the expression of *Judenrein*, implied that radical steps were necessary to rid the community of these negative elements. The rationale for the subsequent formation of the death camps in Poland shone through Hiemer's pen with a profound clarity.

THE DARK IMAGE OF THE JEW AND ELVIRA BAUER

Julius Streicher and Der Stürmer publishing house could rightfully lay claim to the distinction of printing some of the most vociferous anti-Semitic literature to enter school libraries and classrooms in the Third Reich. Hiemer was not the only author to emerge in Streicher's shadow. Elvira Bauer, an elementary school teacher, joined Der Stürmer to publish *Trust No Fox on the Green Heath and No Jew upon His Oath*! in 1936. She dealt with many of the same themes later embraced by the more prolific Hiemer. As standard fare for Streicher's circle, Bauer demonized the Jew throughout her work and provided pupils with bold illustrations to communicate anti-Semitic ideas. In contrast to Hiemer's *The Poodle-Pug-Dachshund-Pinscher*, Bauer's perspective on the Jews did not encompass biological considerations. When taken as a whole, Bauer's book came closer to reflecting the more traditional anti-Semitic themes as expressed in Hiemer's first and best-known work, *The Poison Mushroom*, which followed her book by two years. The content of Bauer's book was intended for a younger elementary school audience. Even though the format was similar, how much of Bauer's writing and approach to the problem of telling anti-Semitic stories through art and printed word influenced Hiemer, if at all, remains unclear.

Bauer's opening lines created an image of the Jew as devil by advancing her own version of the Genesis story. Her restrictive racial interpretation placed God as the creator of five major races whom she called Indians, Negroes, Chinese, Jews, and Germans. God gave to all peoples a piece of the earth to cultivate through their labor. In place of honest work, Bauer wrote, the Jews engaged themselves in all manner of deception blessed by their father, the devil. The Talmud remained as the "book of Jewish thieves" from these early times. Ancient Egypt and the Jewish experience provided a historical context, albeit a false one, for demonstrating the laziness of Jews. The pharoah forced the Jews out of their sloth by requiring them to carry loads of bricks. Bauer concluded that carrying this heavy weight under the whip explained how Jews developed bent backs and flat feet along with their hanging jaws and hooked noses.[31]

The Jew as wanderer made a special appearance in Bauer's vision of the Jews. Her writing did not always relate clearly to each anti-Semitic theme. Just as Bauer rewrote the scriptural story of Genesis, she also twisted the meaning of the New Testament to fit her ideological assumptions about the relationship of

Jews to Jesus Christ. The status of Jews as the chosen people, frequently derided and demeaned by other curriculum writers and propagandists, came under a totally different interpretation with Bauer's writing for children:

> The Jew from the beginning
> Is a murderer, says Jesus Christ.
> And since the Lord Jesus had to die,
> So did the Lord God know no people
> Which was capable of torturing him to death.
> Therefore he chose the Jews.
> That is why the Jews claim
> To be the chosen people.[32]

Bauer's anti-Semitic theology overshadowed the image of the Jew as wanderer in her verses. The image of the sly and creeping fox associated with the Jew wandering from one land without knowing a real home loomed large in her writing. For some young readers, as in most picture books, the illustrations undoubtedly carried more meaning and, perhaps for some, shaped anti-Semitic attitudes more effectively than the printed word. This indeed was the assumption behind *The Poison Mushroom*, for example. Bauer created a picture of a bearded and grizzly-looking man with two knapsacks on his back making his way with a coarse walking stick and dressed in black. Here was a person, Bauer implied, who lacked roots and did not belong in Germany.[33]

Contrasting concepts of work, witnessed earlier in the chapters on history and race biology and variously reiterated by Hiemer, entered Bauer's world of the Jews in numerous ways. In a set of verses on "the Sabbath," Bauer poked fun at Jews who dressed in their finery for the Sabbath observance. Here again was another occasion when Jews "won't stir a finger" and relied on "innocent Gentiles" to carry out their labors. Jewish laws and customs came under Bauer's biting commentary. The religious Jew, she mocked, even had to rely on Gentiles to turn off their lights during the Sabbath. The story of the servant girl drew from old anti-Semitic attitudes relating not only to work but also to sexual relations. The Jewish aversion to housework became evident when the young Teresa, a girl from a rural community, came to the city in search of gainful employment. After agreeing to work for the Jewish family Katz, Teresa engaged herself in the honest labor of cooking, cleaning, and sweeping. The wife and three daughters in the family, much to Theresa's amazement, were so lazy that they lounged around all morning and slept in the afternoon.

The ideological plot thickened. Herr Katz, the prototype of the rich Jew, exploited Teresa in more ways than one. She quickly learned about the tendency of Jewish families to overwork their servants, treat them "worse than cattle," and severely underpay those involved in common labor. The industrious Teresa from the country symbolized all of those wholesome values of the peasantry so highly praised by Nazi ideologues. Something else is awry according to Bauer's vision of a racially ordered society. In a disarming illustration, a Jewish man dressed in top hat and tuxedo has his arm around a blond-haired, blue-eyed German woman. The Jew appears to offer the woman some jewelry with the implication that he may be asking her for sexual favors. "What a poor wretch is the Jew," Bauer wrote. "He doesn't want his own women. He thinks himself awfully slick when he steals for himself a German woman ... What a dreadful spectacle he is." The stereotypes of wanton sexual exploitation and the abuse of labor in the marketplace included in this single story taught important anti-Semitic lessons to young readers. (See plate 9. Note the Jewish man depicted with cloven hooves.) Not the least of these lessons was that German and Jewish culture were universes apart.[34]

As numerous other curriculum resources embracing an anti-Semitic agenda so often demonstrated, Bauer's literature singled out law and medicine among the professions for special attention. The round and fat Jewish attorney, reflecting a stereotype of Jewish body shape that reappeared time and again across the curriculum, portrayed an image of excess and dishonesty. The formerly skinny Jewish attorney, humbled by bad times, eventually fattened himself from the lard, eggs, and flour he extracted as payment from his peasant client, a certain Mr. Michael. The innocent and unsuspecting Michael paid the scrupulous attorney much more than he deserved and found himself impoverished in the end. His goods and money now rested in the hands of the Jew paid with the high price of his livelihood and family prosperity.

Citing the Talmud, Bauer opened an attack on Jewish doctors. Fabricating a Jewish law calling all Jews to love Jews alone, the author told a story about a Doctor Hurter called to the deathbed of a fellow Jew. Not certain of a remedy for this man's serious illness, the doctor rushed to a hospital to test a medicine on several German patients who unknowingly act as guinea pigs for the doctor. After the three patients and several others in the hospital died from the medicine, the doctor conducted additional similar tests until he found a safe remedy for his Jewish patient. The deaths of Germans thus paid for the survival of a Jew. The moral of the story was for Germans never to trust a Jewish doctor. After all, Bauer argued, didn't the Talmud say that the non-Jew was nothing but a dog and therefore should be destroyed?[35]

Beyond extending her role as a self-appointed expert on Jewish law, Bauer saw fit to use school life as another way to separate Jews from the German community. She portrayed a scene in front of a school where Jewish children were being expelled amid the jeers and taunting of blond-haired, blue-eyed pupils. (See plate 6). Accompanying the group was a tense-looking adult, presumably a Jewish teacher, who had lost his position at the school. Bauer's exaggerated and stereotypical depiction of Jewish physical features commanded an important point of focus for her young viewers. All of the Jewish figures had black hair and black eyes. The ardent wish for the purging of Jews from public schools expressed in *Trust No Fox on the Green Heath* foreshadowed what eventually became Nazi policy. Two years after Bauer's work appeared in 1936, a complete purge of Jewish pupils from German public schools took place in the wake of the massive destruction unleashed on the Night of the Broken Glass. "Now it will be nice in the schools," the teacher wrote, "for all the Jews must go."[36]

Bauer's artistic style placed great value on showing young children openly ridiculing Jews as a model for civic behavior. The school scene was not the only part of her work to reflect this tendency. One picture showed a Jewish family on a path toward a public bathing area. A sign that soon became quite familiar throughout the country confronted the parents and their child: "Jews are unwanted here" (*Juden sind hier unerwunscht*). Two Aryan children ahead of the Jews responded with laughter and derision as they witnessed the shocked surprise of the family in reading the sign. Bauer once again offered a physical interpretation of Jews meant to convey the message of racial undesirability. Her gross rendition of the Jewish nose, an element with an exceedingly long history in anti-Semitic circles, remained a central feature of this drawing. A short, stocky Jewish husband accompanied an overweight wife carrying a book and a looking glass, symbols of the intellectual (see plate 10). The last image Bauer conveyed in her collection showed a mass exodus of Jews out of the community amid the cheers and ridicule of German children. Ladened with their belongings and setting out for an uncertain future, the Jews of Bauer's vision were on their way to Palestine:

> In the far South lies the land,
> Where once stood the cradle of the Jews.
> There must they go with wife and child
> As quickly as they came.
> Look at the pitiful picture!
> The nasty Jews, impudent and uncouth,
> Abraham, Solomon,
> Blumenfeld, Levinson,
> Little Rebecca with son Jonathan
> and Simon and Aaron Kahn,
> How they roll their eyes
> and waddle along.[37]

The writings of Hiemer and Bauer from the Der Stürmer publishing house represented some of the harshest anti-Semitic writings to be found anywhere in children's literature. Yet, even with the common hatred of Jews that created the central theme for these works, significant differences existed in how each author interpreted the fate of the negative other. Bauer, as the chapter on race hygiene demonstrated earlier, wrote at a time when Nazi policy remained open to possibilities for the forced mass migration of Jews to Palestine and even Madagascar. Hiemer's writing in *The Poodle-Pug-Dachshund-Pinscher* from 1940 took a much more deadly direction by openly advocating the mass destruction of Jews. Underlying these three pieces of children's literature was the instructional goal of engendering enthusiastic support for anti-Semitic policies. Riemer and Bauer were among the most successful writers for children in concentrating the power of negative associations through drawing from both racial and traditional anti-Semitic perspectives. Since these writings came with the blessing and financial support of Julius Streicher and his publishing business, their success was not a great surprise.

The two authors, although the creators of exceptional anti-Semitic storybooks, were certainly were not the only players in this endeavor. When placed within the larger context of school readers, anti-Semitism was but one theme among many others in children's literature. A closer look at the case of Phillip

Bouhler merits attention since he assumed considerable authority as a censor of schoolbooks and curriculum materials in Hitler's Chancellery. Bouhler's works, along with other sources for schools, reflected the fact that anti-Semitism was part of a multilayered process of instruction. Books like those written by Hiemer and Bauer might be seen as the most extreme examples of anti-Semitic rhetoric in children's literature. On another level, represented by Bouhler and others, anti-Semitic teachings even became obscured.

PHILLIP BOUHLER AND THE NAZI MOVEMENT

Bouhler remained unique within the Nazi hierarchy because of his dual responsibilities as schoolbook censor and, acting with Karl Brandt from medicine, administrator of the T-4 killings of the mentally ill and handicapped. His work as head of the Reich Office for Writings on School and Instruction placed him in a position of influence in the formation of curriculum materials. In the fall of 1936, according to Bouhler's account, Hitler directed him, while the two were on a walk through the forests of Obersalzburg, to write a concise school reader on the history of the Nazi movement. In the foreword to the *The Struggle for Germany: A Reader for German Youth*, Bouhler expressed the hope that the work would deepen the "fanatical faith" of youth for the Volk and Hitler. The volume traced the history of Nazism from its proclaimed origins in the Second Reich to Hitler's rise to power and the union with Austria. The last chapter, "Victory of Faith," written with a kind of religious fervor, presented Hitler as a savior figure who solved all of Germany's most pressing problems. In Bouhler's writings, one does not find the inflammatory anti-Semitic language that commonly flowed out of books released by the Der Stürmer publishing house.

For all of Hitler's expressed loathing for Jews as the Reich's archenemy in *Mein Kampf*, Bouhler devoted surprisingly little attention to the issue. In the most concentrated section regarding the Jews in his entire book, Bouhler attacked Marxism and liberalism as creations of Jewish agitators and misguided intellectuals. The deeper cause of the Jewish problem, the censor insisted, originated with Jews' winning legal equality as a legacy of the French Revolution. Bouhler observed that this unfortunate change meant that Jews were no longer confined to the ghetto and now moved about all too freely in the world. His only other mention of Jews came with brief references to Julius Streicher's "uncompromising struggle against Jewry" and the Nuremberg Laws of 1935, to which he devoted a mere three lines. Considering Bouhler's intimate experience with the T-4 killings beginning in September of 1939, his preceding commentary in the same paragraph on the necessity of Nazi policies to curb the growth of "hereditary idiots" remains worthy of note. Within one year after *The Struggle for Germany* came off the press, Bouhler was in the thick of the bureaucratic process of mass murder associated with the T-4 program, elements of which included the technology of experimental gas chambers later used in Auschwitz.[38]

Bouhler avoided using invective in explaining the place of the Jewish question in describing Hitler's biography or in any other aspect of modern German history interpreted with a Nazi bias. Remembering that Hitler's directive was to produce a concisely written history of the Nazi movement, Bouhler did just that. The legacy of Hitler's years as a young man in Vienna, in Bouhler's writing, parroted *Mein Kampf*. Paraphrasing the dictator, Bouhler informed readers that Hitler's harrowing experience in the Austrian capital greatly influenced his later thinking about the evils of Marxism and its close ties to the Jewish question. The contents of the book reflected the assumption that young children need not read the twenty-five points of the Nazi Party program that established the ideological cornerstone for the movement. Bouhler thus remained content with infrequent and extremely brief references to Jews while limiting any mention of race to the Nuremberg Laws in one scant instance. Since the book came off the presses of the central publishing house for the Nazi Party, one can safely assume that it gained broad distribution to schools across Germany and Austria. That the author was one of the most powerful censors of school materials in the entire Reich was not a matter of small concern. His growing influence over matters of curriculum did not endear him to Bernhard Rust who engaged the younger Bouhler in a protracted conflict over the preogatives of the education ministry.[39]

As noted in chapter 4, Bouhler became increasingly embittered by what he perceived as a major failure of numerous texts to present school knowledge truly supportive of a strong Nazi worldview.[40] While Bouhler does not provide more specific indications as to how schoolbooks failed to meet his version of Nazi pedagogy, there is within his April 1941 communication to Alfred Rosenberg a veiled criticism of Rosenberg and his inflated title as head of "world view education," Bernhard Rust of the Education Ministry, and the NSLB. All three parties shared with Bouhler the sometimes conflictive process of censoring manuscripts for publication. If the scope and depth of curriculum materials integrating anti-Semitic ideas were any indication, then at least on this aspect of Nazi race education Bouhler had no real cause for concern. After all, even his own biography of Adolf Hitler published in 1938 for the international market scarcely mentioned the Jews as a formative influence over the future dictator's political ideas. Marxism, with its call to left-wing politics and revolution, was the real enemy to Bouhler precisely because a Jew founded the movement and Jews carried forth Marxist ideas to the present.[41]

The scapegoating that marked so much of the curriculum in science, history, and geography simply did not find a significant hearing in Bouhler's literature for children. Bouhler's office edited another school reader in 1943, this one marked with a more general selection of literature than his earlier, more focused work on the history of the Nazi movement. Jews remained conspicuously absent by name. An introductory section on "Blood and Volk" and "Your Ancestors Are Our Volk from the Past" integrated quoted language from Hitler, Rosenberg, and Chamberlain and warned pupils about the brutal necessity of fighting for blood purity. At the same time, the blood enemies of the Reich, be they Jews, Gypsies, or the mentally ill, did not get serious consideration in this wartime writing. Other people like Werner Dittrich, Johann von Leers, Ferdinand Rossner, Fritz Fink, Ernst Hiemer, Alfred Rosenberg, and Ernst Dobers, to name but a few, would take up the banner of anti-Semitic pedagogy with a much greater seriousness and devotion than one of Hitler's grand censors.[42]

RACE HYGIENIC FABLES AND THE OBSCURE JEW

The children's literature authored by Ernst Hiemer and Elvira Bauer, as exemplars of anti-Semitic hatred and linguistic violence, represented an extreme not embraced by many other writers of curriculum resources. As the example of Phillip Bouhler illustrated, writers involved with the creation of literature in race education intended for schools did not follow a template handed down from Berlin. Anti-Semitism, as shown in the previous chapters, took on a variety of expressions. *Mein Kampf,* more than any other single resource, provided the ideological guide for curriculum writers in regard to the Jewish question. This did not mean that Jews always appeared in books or other published curriculum sources with great frequency. *Race Hygiene: Written for the Sake of German Youth,* published early in the regime, is a significant case in point. This collection of over fifty brief vignettes reflected the curricular interrelationship between the teaching of science and of literature. The slim volume, touting the necessity of racial cleanliness, focused almost exclusively on the hereditary ill of the great racial undesirables.

Jews, in contrast to their treatment in the racial science advocated by Jakob Graf and Ernst Dobers, among others, remained quite obscure throughout much of the work. In one way, such an approach exemplified the initial direction and timing of Nazi policy. Those suffering from mental illness and hereditary disease were the first victims of mass murder before the Nazi state turned its attention to administering the mass killings of Jews and Gypsies. On the other hand, a close reading of the "fables of the well born" reflected a stern rationale for a strict separation between those judged racially pure from those deemed racially unclean. This orientation, eventually supported with legislation from the Nuremberg Laws of 1935, eventually opened a path to more serious forms of oppression against the Jews.[43]

Although Jews made only one appearance in *Race Hygiene,* their relative obscurity in the writing of Emil Jörns and Julius Schwab made them even more dangerous when mentioned in the same breath with Blacks, another racial pariah in the Nazi state. The association, witnessed repeatedly across the curriculum in previous chapters, remained a hallmark of anti-Semitic and anti-Black teachings. Children learned that it was their "holy duty" to keep these foreign racial elements out of the community. After all, the authors asked, "How could a person who was a half Negro or Jew fully understand a Goethe, a Fredrick the Great, a Beethoven?"[44]

GERMAN STUDIES, THE JEW, AND CONNECTIONS WITH PHYSICAL EDUCATION

Teaching morals through telling stories, a tradition at least as ancient as Aesop's fables, assumed an important place in the teaching of German language and literature. The task of teaching race morality, so significant to German studies and the place of race hygiene in the total curriculum of Nazi elementary schools, involved physical education as well. As in all other school subjects, physical education became another means of shaping moral character among the young.

Two Nazi physical education curriculum philosophers blamed liberal education for creating a misguided tradition in which intellectual prowess attained a higher status than physical education. National Socialist pedagogy drew a close connection between "political physical education" and the principles of "blood and honor" coming from race biology.[45]

What implications this view of physical education held for Jews can be grasped through a set of writings appearing before and during the war. Bruno Malitz, a sports consultant from Berlin-Mitte, angrily denounced Jews in 1934 for "poisoning the idea of physical education" through advancing liberal teachings like class struggle, equality, and pacifism. The biggest future battle, he warned, would come against the Jews. Physical education carried the responsibility for helping youth prepare for the great racial conflict. The author compared the threat posed by leading Jewish athletes with a host of diseases like cholera, syphilis, and tuberculosis—disasters worse than "a hoard of Mongols, a conflagration, poverty, the breaking of a dike, a great draught, a plague of grasshoppers, and poison gas." His list of disasters was long. The last misfortune symbolized the yet unrealized horror awaiting millions of Jews. Two years after Malitz's essay appeared, Jewish athletes suffered exclusion from the Berlin Olympic Games in 1936 when Avery Brundage and the International Olympic Committee bowed to Hitler's pressure to prevent Jews from competing.[46]

Some teachers of physical education undoubtedly read the words of Otto Rauscher whose ideas on Jews and athletics symbolized the Nazi Party line. Writing in 1942, Rauscher called into question the athletic prowess of Jews for the purpose of drawing cultural boundaries between the races and physical education:

> Never has a Jew appeared as a fist fighter or high jumper; never has a Jew come up to the diving platform to jump into the water; never has a Jew dared the ski jump. And all of this is understandable since the Jew is a coward according to his nature . . . There were Jewish soccer players. They attracted attention through yelling and argued with the referees, but when things got tough around the ball, the Jew either got out of the way or other [Jews] became worn out and had to leave injured.[47]

Wilhelm Schneemann, a noted writer on physical education and the Jews, saw in the racial care of the body another special opportunity to teach the young about the physical attributes of racial undesirables. Using the anthropology of Hans F. K. Günther, Schneemann centered his observations on selected stereotypes marking the appearance of Jews. For the author, physical education held a great promise in contributing to the racial consciousness of youth. Proper health habits and vigorous exercise were only two, albeit important, aspects of the physical education curriculum. Developing a sharp eye for the physical movements of the Jew was an important objective in this element of race education. The skill of racial observation, Schneemann told educators, would help pupils pick out Jews on the street. In keeping with the stereotypical nature of his comments, the author informed his readers what they might expect to find differences in the way Jews walked and in a familiar litany of physical qualities. Understanding these profound differences between Jews and Germans,

Schneemann insisted, pupils would soundly reject the "fairytale" of the "respectable Jew." The racial pride of physically fit and racially conscious German youth would see and ultimately reject the "dripping Jewish poison" in German culture.[48]

The perceived racial and cultural dichotomies between Jews and Germans, the anti-Semitic grist for elementary school curriculum, became part of the Nazi conception of the educated person. The various degrees of anti-Semitic expression across children's literature and physical education, both deemed essential to the definition of Germanness, reflected a range of responses to the racial enemy. Years before death camps became a reality to the East, Hiemer's story book openly called for the extermination of Jews. Others, like Bauer, speaking from an earlier perspective, called for the removal of Jews to the Middle East while fully exploiting traditional forms of anti-Semitic rhetoric. Her words and images are no less important in this story. Indeed, Nazi curriculum writers cast a wide net. Voices from physical education exploited the myth of German physical prowess and advocated the integration of racial anthropology as powerful pedagogical means of building an anti-Semitic racial consciousness. Bouhler, the master bureaucrat, practiced a no-less-virulent form of anti-Semitic thinking in that he exhibited an illusory detachment from both the Jewish question and the T-4 killings. His unquestioning obedience and loyalty were qualities that undoubtedly gained Hitler's trust. Bouhler was the kind of young bureaucratic operative whose opportunities for career advancement reached an apogee in Hitler's Chancellery. He did not write with the same anti-Semitic virulence of others, but his loyalty to Hitler's plans to annihilate racial undesirables remained firm to the end. Bouhler committed suicide in 1945 as American troops came for his arrest.

Chapter 6

Conclusion

The Nazi experiment in race education, steeped in a strong anti-Semitic agenda, came to an end with the military victory of the Allies in May of 1945. No other society has ever devoted such a focused effort at integrating anti-Semitic thinking into curriculum intended for young children. As in all regimes, the Third Reich articulated ideals for the educated person. That this idealism was profoundly destructive in nature became evident in school subjects across the curriculum. While the Nazis were the first and only entity to institutionalize anti-Semitism in state schools, their efforts still embraced a continuity with the past. The Nazi exploitation of hatred against Jews drew from a long and brutal history of religious and economic forms of anti-Semitism, some of which resonated throughout the Middle Ages.

For many Nazi curriculum writers, Martin Luther became a kind of prophetic figure justifying contemporary government policies against the Jewish community. Even after the collapse of the Third Reich, Julius Streicher, in testifying before the Nuremberg Tribunal, told the court that Martin Luther "would be called to sit in my place in the defendant's dock if this book (Luther's *The Jews and Their Lies*) had been taken into consideration by the prosecution."[1] The language of religion expressed by various Nazi curriculum writers became another effective way in which Jews could be categorized as the negative other. The image became all the more potent through the exploitation of Golgotha. The charge of deicide against the Jews, one which survives to this day in anti-Semitic circles, carried a powerful emotional appeal for Nazi propagandists both inside and outside schools.

In a sense, the debate over Nazi Germany as a decided break in continuity with the past usually does not serve historians well in contemplating the legacy of anti-Semitism in Nazi elementary school curriculum. The either-or approach omits significant evidence reflecting the presence of both developments. The ground was well prepared before 1933 for the Nazi exploitation of older and more traditional forms of anti-Semitic thinking along with the more recent contributions from racial science. As Hitler's letter from 1919 suggested, his call for the overall removal of the Jews demanded the formation of a society in which a more rationalized and scientific approach to anti-Semitic thinking was the order of the day. The Nazis did not invent this form of anti-Semitism, but they were the first to legitimize its presence in school curriculum with the full legal weight of the racial state. Part of the genius of Nazi propaganda was its ability to fully exploit both continuity and change in addressing the question of the educated person. Obviously, anti-Semitism was not the only factor in this relationship. The glorification of militarism and the development of nationalistic fervor were also part of this educational process.

Heinrich von Treitschke, the overtly nationalistic German historian from the Kaiserreich, coined the expression "the Jews are our misfortune."[2] His words later resonated across the entire elementary school curriculum under Hitler's regime and found a strident voice in the work of numerous curriculum writers. The anti-Semitic content of the curriculum, when taken as a whole, constituted a bold Nazi attempt to rewrite Jewish history and religion. Control of the language, a power brilliantly elucidated by Victor Klemperer, was the key to legitimizing anti-Semitic school knowledge. The legal problem of defining the citizen along biological lines became a hallmark of the Third Reich and, thus, remained a question of great importance in a curriculum that glorified the Nuremberg Laws of 1935. The fact that academics from the Institute for the History of the New Germany and the Institute for the Jewish Question remained deeply involved in this issue added further legitimacy to the enterprise. Rewriting the history of Germany under the aegis of Nazism invariably meant rewriting the history of the Jews as Hans F. K. Günther, Wilhelm Grau, Johann von Leers, and others readily attested. The Nazis demonstrated all too effectively that oppression can come in the form of grossly distorting the history and culture of the victims.

There exists the temptation to treat the integration of anti-Semitic teachings into the Nazi elementary school curriculum as a monolithic process made possible by simply translating ideas from Hitler's *Mein Kampf* into the life of the school. This study reaffirmed the importance of his book as an ideological guide for education bureaucrats, teachers, and curriculum writers in shaping educational policy and in determining what children should or should not know about race and the Jews. Hitler's call for the education of a racially conscious youth ready to sacrifice for the survival and growth of Aryan bloodlines remained a staple of Nazi curriculum policy. The anti-Semitic component of Nazi race education, although offering serious deference to *Mein Kampf*, spawned a massive series of curriculum projects that allowed for differences in tone and level of attack against Jews. On one extreme, representing the most lurid anti-Semitic curriculum material for children, were writings by Ernst Hiemer, Elvira Bauer, and Johann von Leers. At the other extreme was the decidedly detached and "scientific" tone assumed by Paul Brohmer and Dieter Klagges who rarely mentioned the victims by name. This differentiation implied that anti-Semitic expression in curriculum writing was not ruled by an overarching uniformity, even though the end of such expression was the same: the isolation of the

Jews and the denial of citizenship. Hitler's tome provided the general anti-Semitic ideal while allowing curriculum writers and other authors a certain leeway in expressing their common rejection of a racial outsider and negative other.

Just how these anti-Semitic ideals would be carried out through the curriculum was another matter. One of the legacies of the Nazi state was the interdepartmental conflict stemming from a struggle over control of the curriculum. Bernhard Rust, for all of his activity in administering curriculum directives on race education, existed as only one relatively minor player within the larger process of institutionalizing anti-Semitic education. Alfred Rosenberg, the self-appointed guardian of Nazi intellectual tradition, viewed his own role as chief educator of the Nazi Party as one that also legitimized his contributions to the education of youth in the state schools. The question of teaching materials and texts was simply too important to be left in the hands of Rust. Even Rust himself recognized his limitations to some degree while agreeing to work with the NSLB in clearing manuscripts for publication. Phillip Bouhler and, eventually, even Martin Bormann from Hitler's Reich Chancellery entered the discussion over legitimized school knowledge and control over the publication of schoolbooks. Rust stood on the periphery and was never considered part of Hitler's inner circle. His influence over educational policy declined as the years passed. For all of the Nazi rhetoric in support of bureaucratic centralization, questions related to curriculum policy and the learning of children lent themselves to an increasing split over educational lines of authority. The issue of anti-Semitism did not escape this tension. Others, like Julius Streicher, wielded his own peculiar and sometimes more independent authority in these matters through his publishing activities.

While serious conflicts over the important place of anti-Semitic learning in the curriculum accorded by *Mein Kampf* and later curriculum directives did not emerge, there did exist a difference of opinion on how far educators in elementary schools should go in teaching racial anti-Semitism. As the numerous curriculum resources across the school subjects demonstrated, some authors reflected the assumption that small children would benefit most from a greater focus on the traditional religious and economic forms of anti-Semitic teaching. The ancient pedagogical practice of telling stories to young children carried more ideological potential in shaping the minds of the young in Nazi elementary schools than weighty texts of race theory. This explained why most pupils usually confronted the racial aspects of anti-Semitism in more concentrated form no earlier than sixth grade.

Not all elementary educators agreed on how early children should be exposed to the complexities of race education. In some cases, when race education initially entered materials published for elementary classrooms during the early years of the Third Reich, more attention was paid to the problems of the hereditary ill and those suffering from mental illness and to the threat of Blacks than to the Jewish question. The solution to the Jewish question ranged from proposals for forced migration to Palestine or Madagascar and general expulsion to outright annihilation. The differences among these proposals in curriculum materials is not surprising when one remembers that Nazi policy in regard to the fate of the Jews remained in flux until the war with Russia in 1941. Of particular importance among these findings is that the call for the mass murder of Jews already existed in the writing of Ernst Hiemer's *The Poison Mushroom* from 1938 and in the history stories by Johann von Leers from two years later. The common cry for "getting rid of the Jew" appeared in a variety of ways throughout the curriculum. Bringing children to this outcome, whether through racial science, medieval stereotypes, or demonization via religion, was behind much of the Nazi efforts in educating the informed anti-Semite.

One of the most disturbing aspects of Nazi education, and one that casts a long shadow over the pages of numerous curriculum materials examined in this study, is the manner in which science was transformed as myth for the presumed benefit of the young. Nazi science, influenced by the thinking of earlier Volkish forerunners and the subsequent emergence of racial anthropology, articulated concepts from race hygiene that could shape the thinking of future generations about what it meant to be a human being. Teaching the young about the necessity of state-sponsored sterilization of the hereditary ill and about choosing racially healthy marriage partners reflected Nazi thinking about the important place assumed by racial consciousness in the daily lives of citizens. Embracing the language of science, Nazi pedagogues could purposefully blur the lines between the disciplines in order to advance a more organic conception of the curriculum. They also created the powerful illusion, legitimized with the findings of racial anthropology emerging from the late nineteenth century, that the perceived outer characteristics of human beings could be linked to assumptions about behavior through racial identification.

The Nazi penchant for using unverifiable statistics along with skull and facial indexes from phrenology, pressed into the service of the racial state, contributed mightily to this illusion. Here again the Nazis did not stand on their own. Many of the practices relating to race hygiene, including racial classification and sterilization, claimed an international history. The international eugenics connection, exploited by the Nazis to add further legitimacy to their policies of racial anti-Semitism and the treatment of the hereditary ill, depended heavily on the equation of racial myth with science. The racial end of this myth never wandered far from the curricular exploitation of older kinds of anti-Semitic prejudices. Nazi science, sometimes articulated with a kind of religious fervor, could not be grasped without the power of mysticism, an element with deep roots in the Volkish thought of the nineteenth century. The assumption popularized by Fritz Lenz, Ludwig Clauß, and others laboring under the shadow of Houston Stewart Chamberlain and Paul de Lagarde was that Jews possessed a particular "racial soul." This mystical concept supposedly explained all Jewish psychological characteristics and found a hearing not only in the elementary school curriculum but also in the thinking of Heinrich Himmler and the SS. What came under the broad banner of science in the hands of the Nazis, especially when directed to the Jewish question, often took on a religious tone of its own.

Another dynamic emerged from this relationship. Understanding the nature of racial anti-Semitism within the context of Nazi curriculum demands a recognition of Nazi policies toward Blacks, for both groups were often treated as the lowest racial outcasts in Nazi society. Tensions surrounding racial segregation and the reality of Black lynchings in the United States (the latter remaining generally ignored to this day in the U.S. history curriculum), became excellent propaganda grist for the Nazis in justifying their loathing for both Blacks and Jews. To somehow suggest that Jewish and Black bloodlines were interrelated, as Günther and others repeatedly claimed during the Weimar years and later, provided another celebrated propaganda cause for the Nazis. All of this took place under a regime that ruled only a miniscule population of Blacks. The big difference with the Jews was not only their perceived influence in German society but also their alleged power in the world political and economic community. This is why the Nazi experiment in race education, especially in relation to sterilization and anti-Semitism in particular, took on a strong international flavor. The Nazis could justify their own handling of the Jewish question by exploiting the illusion, secured by the language of science and medicine, that Jews were a pressing problem for the world and not just the Third Reich.

Stepping back from this foray into curriculum as a vehicle for propaganda, one is reminded that the considerable resources the Nazis brought to bear on creating anti-Semitic school materials were largely due to the enthusiastic participation of many well-educated people. Streicher, behind some of the most lurid anti-Semitic pieces ever to appear in the classroom and even regarded by some Nazis as no more sophisticated than a street thug, was a former elementary school teacher. Alfred Vogel acted as rector of an elementary school. Johann von Leers engaged students as a professor at Berlin University. Ferdinand Rossner was a professor of science education in the teacher training program for women at the University of Hanover. Hans F. K. Günther espoused his theories on racial anthropology as a professor at the universities of Jena, Berlin, and Freiburg. Rudolf Frercks practiced medicine at the Office of Enlightenment for Population and Racial Policy (*Aufklärungsamt für Bevölkerungspolitik und Rassenpflege*) in Berlin. Fritz Lenz, one of the highest-ranked Nazi racial anthropologists, had in 1923 assumed the first chair ever created for race hygiene at the University of Munich and became a member of the prestigious Kaiser Wilhelm Institute. In what now appears to be a shocking lapse of judgment, the German postwar government brought Lenz to a new academic post at the University of Göttigen and Otmar von Verschuer to a professorial position at the University of Münster. These professionals and others too numerous in number to mention here, constituted the core of active curriculum writers on the Jewish question or became noted authorities on race education cited frequently by these writers. Like some ranking SS officers, many of these figures held doctorates.

As Klaus Fischer so wryly concluded, the growth of hatred for Jews among members of Germany's professional class reminded one of the painful reality that "education does not always equate with enlightenment or the moral improvement of its recipients."[3] Passing off prejudice as scientific fact remains a significant part of the legacy left by Nazi education. Democracies as well as dictatorships engaged in this spurious activity, including the race eugenics movement in the United States that flowered from 1910 to 1940. At the same time, Nazi education can not be held directly responsible for Auschwitz. The grave responsibility for Nazi schools lies in creating the ideological justification for what eventually became the Nazi policy of mass murder not only for Jews but also for the hereditary ill, Gypsies, Soviet POWs, and gays. Those standing at the beginning of the twenty-first century and the frontiers symbolized by the Human Genome

Project would do well to revisit the history of race eugenics. Those on this journey are likely to confront issues relating to the biological definition of the human person that so deeply engrossed the Third Reich. As with Nazi education officials and others engaged in translating race eugenics and anti-Semitic thinking through curriculum from six decades before, decisions will be made in the current age about the nature of the educated person. Race is still an important part of the social and political agenda of the United States, for example, and remains important in the process of legitimizing certain kinds of school knowledge. Bloodlines as a condition for citizenship continues to stir debate in Germany over the definition of the citizen in that country's constitution.

The Nazis thought that they had embarked on a new frontier in recasting a racial conception of the citizen with the full support of a modern state. Hitler and the Third Reich failed in their goal to completely destroy European Jewry, but not before taking millions of lives on the basis of racial assumptions. What survived the conflagration was anti-Semitism, one of the oldest forms of prejudicial hatred that continues to reveal itself in a variety of ways across the world. Looking back into the curriculum created to educate young anti-Semites in the Third Reich continues to raise questions about the nature of education under the command of the state and its potential in legitimizing prejudicial attitudes and values.

What came under scrutiny with this study represented only one part of the larger picture of anti-Semitism and education under the Third Reich. Still demanding closer attention are the important roles played by the Hitler Youth and the SS in teaching anti-Semitism. Both institutions, partly out of mistrust for the public education system, created their own education programs on the Jewish question. They also created their own elite schools to advance their respective ideals. The heavy hand of the propaganda ministry and the work of Alfred Rosenberg, to mention only two parties, reminds researchers that anti-Semitic policy remained part of a much larger bureaucratic universe going beyond the SS, Hitler Youth, and the public schools. Future inquiry might focus on the similarities and differences in the anti-Semitic curriculum created for pupils by these three groups.

A frustrating puzzle continues to trouble historians of education. Still unclear is the influence anti-Semitic education had on the development of subsequent attitudes and values among former pupils of Nazi schools. Individual oral histories and diaries offer some important evidence, but even these sources must be used with great caution because of the problem of selective memory and the distance of time from the events. Recollections of race biology instruction among former pupils, a noted researcher recently pointed out, are often characterized by an entire range of responses. Some witnesses are able to quote from memory without error content from race biology lessons sixty years ago, while others insist that this kind of instruction remained nonexistent in their schools. Still others recall isolated instances from race education that apparently failed to change the overall tone of the curriculum.[4]

Part of the reason for these apparently contradictory interpretations may be that the Nazi school system did not exist long enough for the planning, organization, and institutionalization of the curriculum to take hold. The first five years of the Third Reich witnessed a focused effort on the retraining and indoctrination of teachers loyal to the party program. At the same time, reforms relating to school structure did not come to pass until 1938–39. In many cases, new textbooks written in accordance with the new curriculum directives finally appeared in the schools between 1939 and 1942 in the midst of wartime. The conditions for a comprehensive school reform simply came too late. Added to this was the reality that not all teachers shared the same degree of commitment to the ideology of the regime.

All of these interrelated factors suggest that anti-Semitism was not taught across the curriculum in any uniform fashion. What long-term impact anti-Semitic curriculum and teaching had on the lives of former pupils is still a question that demands a systematic investigation. A series of interviews conducted by the Office of Military Government for the United States (OMGUS) during the early years of the occupation offers some insights into the matter. Conducted in April of 1946, a study of "attitudes toward the reconstruction of Germany" involving a sample of 1,192 Germans revealed the survivability of anti-Semitic and racist attitudes among some elements of the population. A minority of respondents (14 percent in the American zone and 3 percent in the American sector of Berlin) agreed with the Nazi prewar assumption that "international Jewry alone would profit from the war." The same percentage in the American zone and 12 percent in Berlin still held to a belief in Nordic racial superiority. More significant in a generational sense were results from OMGUS surveys on prejudice and anti-Semitism administered in December of 1946 and April of 1948 indicating that about two in ten Germans in the American zone were "clearly anti-Semitic." Those between the ages of fifteen and nineteen, the report concluded, reflected more anti-Semitic attitudes than any of the other age groups. Two or three years after the Nazi capitulation, members of this generation were among those pupils who once attended elementary schools under the Third Reich.[5]

The exceedingly short time frame for institutionalizing anti-Semitic learning in Nazi schools and the possible long-term influences of anti-Semitic curriculum are not the only issues. Anti-Semitic hatred already existed as a cultural tradition outside the schools for many centuries. This, after all, was the argument of Fritz Fink, who insisted that the anti-Semitism taught in the schools would be authentic and meaningful for the young because the instruction connected to preexisting anti-Semitic attitudes and values developed in the larger society. Perhaps without realizing it, Fink articulated one of the cardinal principles of the Nazi curriculum. He also brought readers back to the ancient relationship between schools and society. Progressive thinkers like John Dewey suggested years ago that schools never stood in isolation from the community. Dewey argued that schooling was not only part of the community, but part of life itself. Moreover, he reminded his contemporaries that some institutions, particularly the family, might hold a deeper influence over the formation of attitudes and values among youth than the schools.[6] The Nazis' understanding of this relationship in the starkest political terms explained why they devoted so much effort to displacing the influence of the family over the socialization of the young. Those families deeply imbued with anti-Semitic fervor, including generations shaped by traditional Catholic and Protestant hatred for Jews, represented a set of prejudicial family influences over the young that the Nazi regime wholeheartedly embraced and encouraged. This is where the influence of the family was to be exploited, not displaced. Thus, the curriculum, as noted throughout this study, placed a high value on manipulating religious anti-Semitism. The Nazis created their own theology for the young not only by rewriting and fabricating Jewish religion and moral philosophy to create the illusion that all Jews hated Germans. They also falsified the Jewish identity of Jesus Christ in the New Testament of the Christian religion. The integrative function of anti-Semitic learning became especially evident not only through racial science but also through the teaching of religion, elements of which appeared across the curriculum. The controversy over the relationship of organized religion to the Third Reich continues to spark lively debates among scholars. Questions about the moral responsibility of the churches in relationship to crimes against humanity perpetrated by the regime are likely to remain part of the dialogue for some time to come.

Another angle for future research became self-evident. A yawning gap remains in the investigation. The thrust of this study encompassed the perspectives of perpetrators as articulated in official sources and curriculum materials. The integrative function of anti-Semitic teaching and learning became a hallmark of Nazi pedagogy while providing insights into the dynamics of Nazi ideology. Investigating this curricular phenomenon provides a glimpse into Nazi ideals and the kind of future society envisioned by the Third Reich. What is still lacking is a systematic investigation of the historical meaning attributed to anti-Semitic education by both Jewish and non-Jewish pupils from both private and public school traditions during the Third Reich.

There may be some who will derive from this study a strong affirmation of the controversial thesis advanced by Daniel Goldhagen. On the contrary, the dynamics of anti-Semitism in Nazi society and the nature of the Third Reich call into question the paucity of Goldhagen's position. The professor of government and social studies at Harvard University opened a fierce debate among historians when he argued that anti-Semitic hatred, nurtured in the soil of Christianity, was *the* central cause of the Holocaust and that such hatred was imbedded in German culture. He attacked the cherished assumption that most Germans were guilty only of obedience to authority. Like many other institutions under the Nazi process of *Gleichschaltung*, Goldhagen insisted, the churches participated in an already deeply rooted German tendency toward "eliminationist anti-Semitism."[7] His exclusive emphasis on this single cause is too simplistic and virtually ignores the social and economic conditions in Germany leading up to the World War I. Moreover, he paints anti-Semitism with one broad stroke while overlooking the reality that different kinds of anti-Semitism existed in nineteenth-century Germany, not all of which called for the radical elimination of the Jews. Also disregarded by Goldhagen was the assimilation of Jews into German society through mixed marriages with Germans into the 1930s, hardly a condition reflecting a widespread eliminationist anti-Semitism.

Even with these serious qualifications, Goldhagen's scholarship deserves praise for rekindling a useful debate over the central role played by anti-Semitism in the ideology of the Third Reich. At least indirectly, his writing also continues to raise questions about the importance of education in explaining how a humane and advanced culture moved away from what Yehuda Bauer called "a traditional moral reluctance to commit mass murder or condone it—or, in other words, accepted as good what until then had been understood as evil." The attempt to build a consensus, he wrote, invariably brought together "education, preparation, and propaganda," all of which drew from "pre-existing forms of rejection," but not all of which involved eliminationist anti-Semitism. To this we add, as reflected in the curriculum itself, the subjective judgments and prejudices advanced by Nazi science.[8]

This author remains haunted by a statement delivered several years ago by the renowned historian Raul Hilberg who humbly admitted, after dedicating over forty years of his life to researching the Holocaust, that he still could not answer the question of why in relation to one of the greatest tragedies of modern history.[9] Perhaps this explains, at least in part, why countless books keep appearing every year on the Third Reich. The dark legacy of Nazi rule beckons us to contemplate the implications of racism and anti-Semitism for living in community, the relationship between schools and society, the ancient debate over the moral responsibility of citizenship, the place of science in modern society, and the prospect of closer relations between Christians and Jews. Trying to understand how the institutionalization of anti-Semitic prejudice could become reality in the schools of one of the most literate and advanced civilizations in the West poses a similar challenge of enormous proportions.

Appendix 1

Curriculum for the *Volksschule*
Weekly Class Hours for Boys,
1939

	Grade							
	1	2	3	4	5	6	7	8
Physical Education		3	3	4	5	5	5	5
German*		11	12	13	7	7	6	6
History					2	2	3	3
Geography					2	2	2	2
Science**	16				2	2	3	3
Arithmetic and Geometry		4	4	4	4	4	4	4
Music		1	2	2	2	2	2	2
Drawing and Crafts			2	2	2	3	3	3
Class Hours Weekly Total	16	19	23	25	26	27	28	28

Source: Rudolf Benze, *Erziehung im Grossdeutschen Reich* (Frankfurt am Main: Diesterweg, 1939), 18. The edition from 1943 was the third in a series from the same publisher.

Note: Religious Instruction (optional) for one to two hours weekly.

*German studies during the second, third, and fourth grades included German language, literature, and *Heimatkunde*, or local history.

**The science curriculum instituted in 1943 for boys increased the weekly hours to three hours each for grades five to six and four hours each for grades seven to eight (26). Sixteen hours represents the total weekly instructional time for *all* combined subjects for grade one.

Appendix 2

Curriculum for the *Volksschule*
Weekly Class Hours for Girls,
1939

	Grade							
	1	2	3	4	5	6	7	8
Physical Education		2	2	3	5	5	5	5
German*		11	12	13	7	7	6	6
History					2	2	3	3
Geography					2	2	2	2
Science**	16				2	2	3	5
Arithmetic and Geometry		4	4	4	4	4	4	
Music		1	2	2	2	2	2	2
Drawing		1	3	3	1	2	2	3
Hand Crafts					2	2	2	
Home Economics								4
Class Hours Weekly Total	16	19	23	25	27	28	29	30

Source: Rudolf Benze, *Erziehung im Grossdeutschen Reich*, 1939, 19.

Note: Religious Instruction (optional) for one to two hours weekly.

*German studies during the second, third, and fourth grades included German language, literature, and *Heimatkunde*, or local history.

**The science curriculum instituted in 1943 for girls changed the weekly hours to three hours each for grades five to eight (27). Sixteen hours represents the total weekly instructional time for *all* combined subjects for grade one.

Appendix 3

Male Plan of Study for the Two-Year
Teacher Training College,
1938

Subjects	Semester and Class Hours			
	I	II	III	IV
Educational Science	3	3	2	4
Character and Child Behavior	2	2	2	2
Ethnology and Racial Science	1		2	1
Popular Culture	1		2	1
General Pedagogy	2			2
Specific Pedagogy				
Visitation and Practice	4	4	4	
Lectures and Seminars	3	6	5	
Physical Education	4	4	3	3
Music Education	3	2	2	2
Speech Education	2	2		
Art Education	2	2		
Craft Education		2	2	
Elective	3	3	2	2
Weekly Hours	30	30	26	17

Source: Rudolf Benze, *Erziehung im Grossdeutschen Reich*, 1939, 91.

Appendix 4

Female Plan of Study for the Two-Year
Teacher Training College,
1938

Subjects	Semester and Class Hours			
	I	II	III	IV
Educational Science	2	2	2	4
Character and Child Behavior	2		2	2
Ethnology and Racial Science	1		2	1
Popular Culture	1		2	1
General Pedagogy	2			2
Specific Pedagogy				
Visitation and Practice	3	4	4	
Lectures and Seminars	3	6	5	
Physical Education	4	4	3	3
Music Education	2	2	2	2
Speech Education	1	2		
Art Education	2	2		
Craft Education			2	
Domestic Skills	2	2	2	
House Work	3	3		
Elective	3	3	2	2
Weekly Hours	31	30	28	17

Source: Rudolf Benze, *Erziehung im Grossdeutschen Reich*, 1939, 92.

Appendix 5

A Chronology of Persecution against German Jews

1933

January 30	President Paul von Hindenburg appoints Adolf Hitler chancellor of Germany.
February 2	General ban ordered on all demonstrations.
February 24	SA and SS become "Auxiliary Police."
February 27	Reichstag fire.
March 5	Reichstag elections, independent actions against Jews.
March 23	Dachau, the first concentration camp, is opened. Enabling Act passed by the German Reichstag surrendering its power to Hitler and his cabinet.
April 1	Nazis proclaim a general boycott of Jewish-owned businesses. Actions against Jewish doctors, lawyers, and students.
April 4	The German Boxing Association forbids the participation of Jews in boxing matches.
April 7	Jews dismissed from civil service and denied admission to the bar.
April 21	Ritual slaughter forbidden.
April 22	Exclusion of non-Aryan teachers from teaching associations. Introduction of the "Aryan Paragraph" in the German Association of Druggists.
April 25	Law Against Excessive Enrollment in German Schools and Universities limits Jewish enrollments to no more than 1.5 percent of the Jewish population. Aryan Paragraph introduced by the German Sports and Gymnastics Association.
April 26	Founding of the Gestapo (secret police).
May 2	Dissolution of free trade unions. No Jewish membership allowed. Jewish workers and salaried employees lose paid union dues.
May 10	Book burning of works by Jews and Nazi opponents.
June 16	About 500,000 Jews live in the German Reich.
July 14	German nationality stripped from Jews; action especially aimed at those originating from the East.

July 20	Conclusion of the Reich Concordat with the Vatican.
July 26	Decree from the Finance Ministry supporting the emigration of German Jews.
August	In numerous places, mayors and city offices forbid Jews from entering beaches and swimming pools.
September 13	Introduction of heredity and race as a required subject in school instruction.
October 19	Germany leaves the League of Nations.
November 12	The single-party state holds its first elections. No less than 92 percent of the votes cast for the NSDAP.

1934

March 7	Members of Jewish youth organizations not allowed to wear uniforms.
May	Publication of the ritual murder issue of Julius Streicher's *Der Stürmer*.
June 21	The Old Testament is no longer treated in classes on religious instruction in the schools of Hessen.
June 30	Opening of the Night of the Long Knives, sealing the murder of SA leader Ernst Roehm and targeted political enemies of the Reich.
July 20	The SS established as an independent organization within the NSDAP.
August 2	Death of Hindenburg. Hitler assumes power as head of state and the armed forces.

1935

May 21	Signs declaring "Jews unwanted" increase in frequency around entries to towns, restaurants, and businesses.
July 25	Armed Forces Law "releases" Jews from military service.
September 6	Sale of Jewish newspapers forbidden on the streets.
September 10	Separation of the races in elementary schools decreed.

1935

September 15	Laws for the Protection of German Blood and German Honor, known as the Nuremberg Laws, are decreed. Marriages between Jews and German nationals forbidden. Jewish households not to employ German females under forty-five years of age.

1936

August 1	Opening of the Olympic Games in Berlin. International Olympic Committee Chair Avery Brundage bows to pressure from Hitler to disallow Jews from competition.

1937

July 2   Further decreases in the number of Jewish pupils in German schools.

July 16   Buchenwald concentration camp opens.

November 16   Jews allowed to hold passes for foreign travel only in special instances

1938

April 26   Jews must turn over property to the state.

July 27   All Jewish street names removed.

August 17   The first names of all Jews must be changed to begin with "Israel" for males and "Sarah" for females beginning 1 January 1939.

October 5   All Jewish passports marked with the letter "J."

1938

November 9   Ernst vom Rath, German ambassador to Paris, dies after assassination by Herschel Grynszpan.

November 10   Night of the Broken Glass.

November 11   Jews forbidden to possess weapons.

November 12   Decree for the Exclusion of Jews from Economic Life. Jewish shops and businesses closed. Additional ban on Jews in the trades. Twenty-six thousand Jews arrested and sent to concentration camps. "Debt of atonement" set at one million marks for the entire German Jewish community. Jews not allowed to visit theaters, cinemas, concerts, and exhibitions.

November 15   All Jewish children expelled from German schools.

December 3   Jews forced to sell their businesses and stocks and hand over jewelry. Jews also lose driver's licenses and authorization papers for motor vehicles.

December 8   Jews not allowed to attend German universities.

December 13   Decree on "Aryanization" results in expropriation of Jewish industries, businesses, and shops.

1939

January 30   Speaking before the Reichstag, Hitler prophesies the "destruction of the Jewish race in Europe" if war should come.

May 17   About 215,000 Jews live in the German Reich.

1939

September 1   Germany Army invades Poland to begin the World War II. Jews may no longer leave their homes or apartments after 9 P.M. in the summer and 8 P.M. in the winter.

September 21	Reinhard Heydrich issues guidelines for the mobile killing squads in Poland.
September 23	All Jews must hand over radios to the police.
October	Hitler empowers Phillip Bouhler and Karl Brandt to organize the T-4 killings of mentally ill and handicapped. Order back-dated to September 1.
October 19	"Debt of atonement" for the Jews raised to 1.25 million Reich-marks.

1940

February 6	Jews no longer hold clothing coupons.
July 29	Jews not allowed to possess telephones.

1941

June 26	Germany attacks the Soviet Union.
September 17	Compulsory wearing of the Yellow Star by all German Jews.
September 23	First experiments with gassings at Auschwitz.
October 14	Deportation of German Jews begins.
November	Beginning of the mass murder of Jews at Minsk, Chelmo, and Riga.

1942

January 1	About 130,000 Jews live in the German Reich.
January 10	Jews must hand over all fur and woolen articles in their possession.
January 20	Wannsee Conference meets to organize an efficient and systematic process of mass murder.
May 15	Jews forbidden to own dogs, cats, and birds.
May 29	Jews forbidden to visit barber shops.
June 9	Jews must hand over all unnecessary clothing pieces.
June 11	Jews prohibited from holding smoking coupons.
June 19	Jews must hand over all electrical and optical equipment as well as bicycles and typewriters.
June 20	All Jewish schools officially closed.
July 17	Blind and deaf Jews may no longer wear armbands as a label for transportation.
September 18	Jews not allowed to have meat, eggs, or milk.
October 4	All Jews in German concentration camps transferred to Auschwitz.

1943

April 19	Jewish revolt in the Warsaw ghetto begins.
June 11	Himmler orders destruction of all Jewish ghettos in Poland.

1944

September 1   Around 15,000 Jews still live in the German Reich.
November 13   Jews forbidden to use warming rooms.

1945

January 17   Russian troops liberate Auschwitz-Birkenau.
May 8   Unconditional surrender of Germany.
Spring   Johann von Leers escapes to Argentina and subsequently settles in Buenos Aires under the Peron regime where he edits the anti-Semitic journal *Der Weg*. The Nazi propagandist meets Adolf Eichmann in the Argentinian capital that same year.

1955

August   Johann von Leers moves to Cairo where he begins service as propaganda adviser to the Egyptian strongman Gamal Abdel Nasser. He embraces the Moslem faith in 1957 and takes the name of Amin Omar.

1965

Leers dies at age sixty-three in Cairo and is buried according to Moslem tradition. Unrepentant to the end, he insisted that Hitler's greatest achievement was his policy of mass murder aimed at destroying all of European Jewry.

Sources: Hans Richter, *Damals war es Friedrich* (München: Deutsche Taschenbuch, 2000), 168–172; Günther Ginzel, *Jüdischer Alltag in Deutschland 1933–1945* (Düsseldorf: Droste, 1984), 8–12; Anti-Defamation League, *The Holocaust, 1933–1945: A Chronology of Social Education* (New York: ADL, 1978), 265. All entries reprinted with the permission of Droste, Deutsche Taschenbuch, and the Anti-Defamation League. Background on von Leers taken from clippings collection in Wiener Library, London.

Notes

Introduction

1. Eberhard Jäckel, hrsg., *Hitler: Sämtliche Aufzeichnungen, 1905–1924* (Stuttgart: Deutsche Verlags-Anstalt, 1980), 88–90.
2. Karl Rotteck and Karl Welcker, *Das Staats-Lexikon: Enzyklopädie der sämmtlichen Staatswissenschaften für alle Stände* (Altona, 1845 and 1846), cited in Cornelia Schmitz-Berning, *Vokabular des Nationalsozialismus* (Berlin: Walter de Gruyter, 2000), 344.
3. George Mosse, *Toward the Final Solution: A History of European Racism* (Madison: University of Wisconsin Press, 1985), 202–214.
4. George Mosse was one of the first historians, almost forty years ago, to argue this point in relation to Nazi culture. See his *Nazi Culture: Intellectual, Cultural, and Social Life in the Third Reich* (New York: Grosset and Dunlap, 1966), 263–318.
5. Aristotle, *Politics*, Book Eight, Part One, trans. Ernest Barker (New York: Oxford University Press, 1998), 298–299.
6. Raymond Williams, "Hegemony and Selective Tradition," in *Language, Authority, Criticism: Readings On the School Textbooks*, ed. Suzanne and Alan Luke (New York: Falmer Press, 1989), 58.
7. Lucy Dawidowicz, *The War against the Jews, 1933–1945* (New York: Free Press, 1986).
8. Victor Klemperer, *LTI: Notizbuch eines Philologen*, 18. Auflage. (Leipzig: Reklam, 1999a), 31. An English translation by Martin Brady appeared under the title *The Language of the Third Reich* (London: Athlone, 2000). Pages from the original German text are cited for this study.
9. Klemperer, 1999a, 199.
10. Klemperer, 1999a, 225–227. Also see Klemperer's diaries, one on the most important sources on everyday life in Nazi Germany, first published in German as *Ich will Zeugnis ablegen bis zum letzten: Tagebücher 1933–1945 von Victor Klemperer* (Berlin: Aufbau, 1995) and in English in two volumes as *I Will Bear Witness: A Diary of the Nazi Years, 1933–1941*, trans. Martin Chalmers (New York: Random House, 1998) and *1942–1945* (1999b).
11. The "Jewish question" initially came into public discourse as part of the ongoing discussion of the emancipation and social integration of the Jews in the 1830s. Karl Marx equated Jewish emancipation with trade, banking, capitalism, and exploitation in his *On the Jewish Question* (1844). The Zionist Theodore Herzel (1860–1904) concluded in *The Jewish State: The*

Attempt at a Modern Solution to the Jewish Question (1896) that the issue
was neither social nor religious in nature but first and foremost a national
problem. The solution, he insisted, could only come if the Jewish question
was raised to the level of international political importance. Subsequently,
National Socialism invariably cast a strong and singular anti-Semitic hue
over the expression. For a more detailed historical outlook on the origins of
this and other expressions related to Jews and exploited by the Third Reich,
see Schmitz-Berning, 2000, pp. 330–341.

12. For additional works on Nazi racial ideology and culture, see Lisa Pine,
    Nazi Family Policy, 1933–1945 (New York: Berg, 1997); Alan Steinweiss,
    Art, Ideology, and Economics in Nazi Germany (Chapel Hill: University of
    North Carolina Press, 1993); Bernard Schwartz and Fredrick DeCoste, eds.
    The Holocaust's Ghost: Writings on Art, Politics, Law, and Education
    (Edmonton: University of Alberta Press, 2000); Michael Burleigh and Wolf-
    gang Wippermann, *The Racial State: Germany, 1933–1945* (New York:
    Cambridge University Press, 1993); Gerhard Rempel, *Hitler's Children: The
    Hitler Youth and the SS* (Chapel Hill: University of North Carolina Press,
    1989); David Bankier, ed. *Probing the Depths of German Anti-Semitism:
    German Society and the Persecution of the Jews, 1933–1941*. Jerusalem:
    Yad Vashem, 2000.

13. For insightful works on Jewish schooling in Nazi Germany, see Joseph
    Walk, *Jüdische Schule und Erziehung im Dritten Reich* (Frankfurt am
    Main: Meisenheim, 1991) and Heinemann Stern, *Warum hassen sie uns
    eigentlich? Jüdisches Leben zwischen den Kriegen* (Düsseldorf: Droste,
    1970). Stern was headmaster at a Jewish middle school in the Großer Ham-
    burger Strasse in Berlin from 1931 to 1939. Walk taught in German schools
    for three years before emigrating to Palestine in 1936.

14. Heinz-Elmar Tenorth, "Deutsche Erziehungswissenschaft 1930 bis 1945,"
    Zeitschrift für Pädagogik 32 (1986): 299–321.

Chapter 1: The Emergence of Racial Anti-Semitism
and Nazi Educational Philosophy

1. George Mosse, *The Crisis of German Ideology: The Intellectual Origins of
   the Third Reich* (New York: Grosset and Dunlap, 1964), 4–5.

2. See Franz Neumann, *Behemoth: The Structure and Practice of National
   Socialism: 1933–1944* (New York: Harper, 1963), 108; Michael Burleigh
   and Wolfgang Wippermann, *The Racial State: Germany, 1933–1945* (New
   York: Cambridge University Press, 1993), 113–197.

3. Two elements of German intellectual history, although not by themselves
   anti-Semitic in nature, deserve attention because of what they revealed
   about the exploitive dynamics of Nazi ideology. The thinking of Friedrich
   Nietzsche (1844–1900), which strongly rejected anti-Semitism, subsequently influenced the language of Nazi propaganda. The Nazis exploited
   Nietzsche's ideas on the "superman" and "will to power" to advance their
   own political agenda. The philosopher's magnum opus, *Also Sprach
   Zarathustra* (1883–1885), articulated the myth of the *Übermensch* engaged
   in the heroic strivings of the superman. Nietzsche called anti-Semitism
   "the lowest level of European culture, its morass" (XVI, 391), and his ideas
   remained decidedly opposed to those of Nazism. Selectively quoting

Nietzsche out of context, the Nazis grossly twisted the writer's respect for Jewish culture into the language of racial anti-Semitism. Part of this distortion became evident after his sister Elizabeth, an avowed anti-Semite, assumed control over her brother's archives. She played a critical early role in the misinterpretation of his intellectual legacy. Nietzsche's writings later influenced Oswald Spengler (1880–1936) who credited the philosopher's "questioning faculty" in helping him form ideas for his famous work, *Decline of the West*, which first appeared in 1918. Spengler's cultural pessimism and his prophecy that Western culture would eventually go under resonated with Nazi thinkers who resoundingly agreed with his rejection of democracy, liberalism, and the Weimar Republic. Once again, the Nazis used an opportunity to selectively exploit the writings of one whom they regarded as among their ideological predecessors. This was true even though Spengler repeatedly rejected Nazi race theory and the entire Nazi movement as expressed in his political work *Preussentum und Sozialismus* (1934). After the Nazi seizure of power in 1933, Hitler quickly dismissed Spengler from the Nazi ideological pantheon, chiding him for being a prophet of doom, a quality that no longer found a home in the official optimism of the Third Reich. See Friedrich Nietzsche, *Gesammelte Werke*, Bd. XVI (Munich: Musarion, 1920–1929); Walter Kaufmann, *Nietzsche: Philosopher, Psychologist, Antichrist*, 4th ed. (Princeton, N.J.: Princeton University Press, 1974); Eric Heller, *The Disinherited Mind* (New York: Farrar, Straus and Cudahy, 1952). See the preface to Spengler's 1922 revised edition *Decline of the West* in which he acknowledges his debt to Goethe and Nietzsche (New York: Knopf, 1934), xiv, and his *Politische Schriften* (Munich: Beck, 1924). See also Henry Hughes, *Oswald Spengler: A Critical Estimate* (New York: Scribner, 1952).

4. Houston Stewart Chamberlain, *Die Grundlagen des neunzehnten Jahrhunderts* (Munich: Brückmann, 1900), 26–32.

5. Paul de Lagarde, *Deutsche Schriften* (Göttingen: Diederichs, 1878), 22–48.

6. Arthur de Gobineau, *Essai sur l'inegalite des races humaines* (Paris: Firmin-Didot, 1884), 58–62.

7. Adolf Hitler, *Mein Kampf*. trans. Ralph Manheim (New York: Houghton Mifflin, 1971), 294–300.

8. Paul de Lagarde, *Deutsche Schriften* (Göttingen: Diederichs, 1878), 216–218.

9. Lagarde, 1878, 74–79.

10. Paul de Lagarde, *Deutscher Glaube, Deutsches Vaterland, Deutsche Bildung* (Jena: Diederichs, 1914), 191–192.

11. Jules Langbehn, *Rembrandt als Erzieher* (Leipzig: Hirschfeld, 1900), 203.

12. Mosse, 1964, 44.

13. Fritz Stern, *The Politics of Cultural Despair* (New York: 1961), 291.

14. Mosse, 1964, 4.

15. Daniel Kevles, *In the Name of Eugenics: Genetics and the Use of Human Heredity* (New York: Knopf, 1985), ix.

16. Steven Selden, *Inheriting Shame: The Story of Eugenics and Racism in America* (New York: Teachers College Press, 1999); William Schneider, "Toward the Improvement of the Human Race: The History of Eugenics in France," *Journal of Modern History* 54 (1982): 268–291; Donald MacKenzie, "Eugenics in Britain," *Social Studies of Science* 6 (1976):

499–532; Mark Adams, *The Wellborn Science: Eugenics in Germany, France, Brazil, and Russia* (New York: Oxford University Press, 1990); Stephan Kühl, *The Nazi Connection: Eugenics, American Racism and German National Socialism* (New York: Oxford University Press, 1994).

17. Hans-Christian Harten, "Pädagogik und Eugenik im rassenhygienischen Diskurs vor 1933," *Pädagogica Historica* 33 (1997): 765–800.

18. Wilhelm Schallmayer, *Vererbung und Auslese im Lebenslauf der Völker* (Jena: Fischer, 1903), 25–48.

19. See Sheila Weiss, *Race Hygiene and National Efficiency: The Eugenics of Wilhelm Schallmayer* (Los Angeles: University of California Press, 1987), 156–158; Raul Hilberg, *The Destruction of the European Jews* (New York: Holmes and Meier, 1985), 221–222.

20. Wilhelm Schallmayer, *Vererbung und Auslese: Grundriss der Gesellschafts-biologie und der Lehre vom Rassedienst* 3. Auflage. (Jena: Fischer, 1918), 414.

21. Rudolf Virchow, *Archiv für Anthropologie* (1886), cited in Mosse, *Toward the Final Solution*, 1985, 91–93.

22. Alfred Ploetz (1860–1940), the founder of the Racial Hygiene Society in 1905, challenged Christian anti-Semitic traditions when he insisted that Jews had more Aryan than Semitic blood. Like Virchow, Ploetz believed that all races were of mixed blood. His admiration for Jews, however, remained restricted to those of the Old Testament. He maintained scorn for contemporary Judaism. See Alfred Ploetz, *Die Tüchtigkeit unserer Rasse und der Schutz der Schwachen: Ein Versuch über Rassenhygiene und ihr Verhältnis zu den humanen Idealen, besonders zum Sozialismus* (Berlin: Lehmanns, 1895), 137–140; Alfred Ploetz, *Archiv für Rassen- und Gesellschafts Biologie*, I (1904): 892–893.

23. Erwin Bauer, Eugen Fischer, and Fritz Lenz, *Menschliche Erblichkeitslehre und Rassenhygiene* (Munich: Lehmanns, 1927), 557–558.

24. Kristie Macrakis, *Surviving the Swastika: Scientific Research in Nazi Germany* (New York: Oxford University Press, 1943), 128–129; Benno Müller-Hill, *Murderous Science: Elimination by Scientific Selection of Jews, Gypsies, and Others in Germany, 1933–1945* trans. George Fraser (Plainview, N.Y.: Cold Spring Harbor Laboratory Press, 1998), 23–25, 35–41.

25. Fritz Lenz, *Über die biologischen Grundlagen der Erziehung* (München: Lehmans, 1925), 36. Copy from IZG, Munich, Wk150. Stamped "Deutsche Arbeitsfront/Amt für Berufserziehung und Betriebsführung."

26. Lenz, 1933, 2d ed., 30. Copy DIPF, Berlin, NS 4847. Stamped "Bücherei, Reichsführer SS."

27. Bauer, Fischer, and Lenz, 1927, 554–566.

28. Bauer, Fischer, and Lenz, 1936, 748–749. For a study of key figures in the history of race hygiene in Germany including Wilhelm Schallmayer, Alfred Ploetz, Fritz Lenz, Willibald Hentschel, Christian Freiherr von Ehrenfels, and Jörg Lanz von Liebefels, see Peter Becker, *Zur Geschichte der Rassen-hygiene: Wege ins Dritte Reich* (Stuttgart: Thieme, 1988).

29. Paul Weindling, *Health, Race and German Politics between National Unification and Nazism, 1870–1945* (New York: Cambridge University Press, 1993), 312.

30. Hans F. K. Günther, *Rassenkunde des deutschen Volkes* (Munich: Lehmanns, 1935), 7.

31. Hans F. K. Günther, *Rassenkunde des jüdischen Volkes* (Munich: Lehmanns, 1930), 17–19.

32. Günther, 1930, 226.

33. Günther, 1930, 210–239.

34. Horst Siedler and Andreas Rett, *Das Reichs- Sippenamt entscheidet: Rassenbiologie im Nationalsozialismus* (Wien: Jugend und Volk, 1982), 59.

35. Some of the most notable figures in the Nazi movement became part of the Thule society, founded in Munich just before the end of the First World War. The racist and anti-Semitic program on which the society was founded attracted such Nazi luminaries as Julius Streicher, Rudolf Hess, Hans Frank, Gottfried Fedder, Dietrich Eckert, and Alfred Rosenberg. Among the principles written for the organization were "to place special emphasis on the propaganda value of racial science" and to "fight against everything un-German." Streicher and Rosenberg would later find themselves in positions of influence in the Nazi state that provided them ample opportunity to expound racial anti-Semitism through the educational system. See Ian Kershaw, *Hitler: 1889–1936*, vol. 1 (New York: Norton, 2000), 138–139; "Principles of the Thule Society," part of an exhibit at Dachau Concentration Camp, 11 February 2001.

36. The high value placed on the development of healthy bodies under the Third Reich was evidenced by the fact that *Leibeserziehung* (physical education) claimed five hours per instructional week, the highest concentration of hours for any single school subject with the exception of German. See Paul Cretius and Martin Spielhagen, *Ziele und Wege des neuen Volksschulunterrichts* (Berlin: Zickfeldt, 1940), 161. See Hitler's commentary on the importance of physical training for the self-preservation of the Volkish community in his *Mein Kampf*, trans. Ralph Manheim (Boston: Houghton Mifflin, 1971), 408–410.

37. Hitler, *Mein Kampf*, 427. The last sentence in this passage was directly quoted as part of a detailed initial policy statement on curriculum regarding race education for Nazi schools by Bernhard Rust, minister of education, on 13 September 1933. See "Vererbungslehre und Rassenkunde im Unterricht," in *Amtsblatt des Reichsministeriums für Wissenschaft, Erziehung und Volksbildung*, 1, Jahrgang, 1935, 43–46. DIPF/Berlin 2A2547.

38. Hitler, *Mein Kampf*, 108, 300–308. The *Protocols of the Elders of Zion*, a forgery revealing the profoundly irrational nature of anti-Semitism, promulgated the myth of a Jewish world conspiracy supported by plots to take over governments of Christian countries. The crudely forged *Protocols*, written during the closing years of the nineteenth century and first appearing in Russia, articulated plans for the establishment of a Jewish world state. The work did not receive much attention until after its introduction in Germany and England in 1919, and later in the United States where Henry Ford facilitated its widest circulation through three editions. See Leo Ribuffo, "Henry Ford and the International Jew," *American Jewish History* 69 (June 1980): 437–477 and Neil Baldwin, *Henry Ford and the Jews: The Mass Production of Hate*. New York: Public Affairs, 2001, 274–275, 280.

39. Hitler, *Mein Kampf*, 306–307.

40. Georg Collischonn, *Geschichte und Volksaufgabe* (Frankfurt am Main: 1922), 22–25; Max Maurenbrecher, *Völkischer Geschichtsunterricht* (Langensalza: Beyer, 1925), 12–18.

41. Hitler, *Mein Kampf*, 422–423.
42. Arthur Suzman and Dennis Diamond, "Der mord an sechs Millionen Juden: Die Wahrheit ist unteilbar," in *Politik und Zeitgeschichte* (1978), B30-78, 4–21.
43. Reichsgesetz vom 25. April 1933, *Zentralblatt für die gesamte Unterrichtsverwaltung in Preussen*, 87.
44. Wolfgang Wippermann, "Das Berliner Schulwesen in der NS-Zeit: Fragen, Thesen und methodische Bemerkungen," in *Schule in Berlin: Gestern und Heute*, ed. Benno Schmoldt (Berlin: Colloquium, 1989), 61f. The teaching profession in Germany experienced a series of no less than three purges in fifty-seven years. The first purge came under the Nazis in 1933, the second under Allied occupation beginning in 1945, and the most recent beginning in 1990 with German reunification.
45. Joachim Remak, ed. *The Nazi Years: A Documentary History* (Englewood Cliffs, N.J.: Prentice Hall, 1969), 149.
46. Burleigh and Wippermann, 1993, 89–90.
47. Victor Klemperer, *LTI: Notizbuch eines Philologen* (Leipzig: Reklam, 1999a), 213–219.
48. For an insightful essay on Jewish schooling under the Third Reich, see Wolfgang Benz, "Jüdische Selbsthilfe bis 1938: Schulwesen," in *Die Juden in Deutschland, 1933–1945*, hrsg. Wolfgang Benz (Munich: Beck, 1988), 330–363. See also Joseph Walk, *Jüdische Schule und Erziehung im Dritten Reich* (Frankfurt am Main: Meisenheim, 1991); Ruth Röcher, *Jüdische Schule im nationalsozialistischen Deutschland, 1933–1942* (Frankfurt am Main: DIPA Verlag, 1992); Yfaat Weiss, *Schicksalsgemeinschaft im Wandel: Jüdische Erziehung im nationalsozialistischen Deutschland, 1933–1938* (Hamburg: Christians, 1991); Benjamin Ortmeyer, *Schicksale jüdischer Schülerinnen und Schüler in der NS Zeit: Leerstellen deutscher Erziehungswissenschaft und die Erforschung der nazistischen Schule* (Bonn: Weile, 1998). One of the earlier publications to appear on the issue of Jewish education under the Third Reich came from Solomon Colodner, *Jewish Education in Germany under the Nazis* (New York: Jewish Education Committee, 1964). Jewish pedagogy in Germany from the Enlightenment up to the Nazi regime is examined in Zwi Kurzweil, *Hauptströmungen jüdischer Pädagogik in Deutschland: Von der Aufklärung bis zum Nationalsozialismus* (Frankfurt am Main: Diesterweg, 1987).
49. Joseph Walk, *Das Sonderrecht für die Juden in NS-Staat*, 2. Auflage (Heidelberg: C. F. Mueller, 1996), 47, 69.
50. The author of this letter, from the Brandenburg Department of Secondary Education, told Rust that he would "enthusiastically greet" any policy to end religious instruction for Jewish children in public schools. Letter from Zander, Abteilung für höheres Schulwesen, Der Oberpräsident der Provinz Brandenberg, 12. März 1936 to RMWEVB, Brandenburgishes Landeshauptarchiv, (hereafter cited as BLHA.Potsdam), Pr. Br. Rep. 34, Provinzial-Schulkollegium Berlin, 3995-Religion, Konfirmation, Kommunion, Hebräisch (1930–1943).
51. Joseph Walk, *Das Sonderrecht für die Juden*, 47, 69, 208.
52. Erlass from RMWEVB, 15 November 1938, "Schulunterricht an Juden," BLHA.Potsdam, Pr. Br. Rep. 2A Regierung Potsdam Abteilung II: Kirchen und Schulen. II. Generalia. Das Schulwesen fur jüdische Kinder. 1260-Bd. 3 (1908–1944).

53. Joseph Walk, "Jüdische Schüler an deutschen Schulen in Nazideutschland," *Bulletin des Leo Baeck Instituts* 19 (1980): 101–109. For works on Jewish schools in Berlin, see Willi Holzer, *Jüdische Schulen in Berlin: Am Beispiel der privaten Volkschule der Gemeinde Rykestrasse* (Berlin: Edition Hentrich, 1992); Rita Meyhöfer, *Gäste in Berlin? Jüdisches Schülerleben in der Weimarer Republik und im Nationalsozialismus* (Hamburg: Kovac, 1992); Jörg Fehrs, *Von der Heidereutergasse zum Roseneck: Jüdische Schulen in Berlin, 1712–1942* (Berlin: Edition Hentrich, 1993).

54. Runderlass, RMWEVB, "Schulunterricht für Juden," 17 December 1938, cited in Walk, 1996, 268–269.

55. Letter from Schulverwaltung der Jüdische Gemeinden to RMWEVB, 16 April 1936, BLHA.Potsdam, Pr. Br. Rep. 34, Provinzial-Schulkollegium Berlin, 3995-Religion, Konfirmation, Kommunion, Hebräisch (1930–1943).

56. "Richtlinien zur Aufstellung von Lehrplänen für jüdische Volksschulen, Neue Fassung, 1937," Reichsvertretung der Juden in Deutschland, Schulabteilung, RMWEVB, 29 October 1937, BLHA, Pr. Br. Rep. 2A, Abt. II, Generalia. 1260. Bd. 3, ss. 127–128.

57. Ausschaltung des Judentums aus der Verwaltung. Niederschrift über die Besprechung betr. die Neuregelung der Erteilung des Schulunterrichts an Juden am 1. Dezember 1938. RMWEVB, R4901/11787, BArch.Berlin.

58. Runderlass von Zschintzsch, RMWEVB, 14 Februar 1939, Geheime Runderlassen der Abteilung ZII u.a. Judenangelegenheiten, R4901/R21/217, BArch.Berlin.

59. Christopher Browning, *Nazi Policy, Jewish Workers, German Killers* (New York: Cambridge University Press, 2000), 39.

60. This conclusion was similarly drawn from a study of the Institute for the Research of the Jewish Question by Dieter Schiefelbein, "Das Institut zür Erforschung der Judenfrage Frankfurt am Main: Antisemitismus als Karrieresprungbrett," in *Beseitigung des jüdischen Einflüsses: Antisemitische Forschung, Eliten, und Karrieren im Nationalsozialismus*, hrsg. Fritz Bauer Institut (New York: Campus Verlag, 1999), 43–71.

61. Walter Scharrer, *Jewish Opposition and the Secondary Schools* (London: St. Clements Press, 1936), 6–9. See also "Jewish Pupils in Secondary Schools: Why a Clean Sweep Should Be Made," *Manchester Guardian*, 3 August 1936.

62. Scharrer, 1936, 10.

63. Bernhard Rust, *Education in the Third Reich* (London: Butterworth, 1936), 4–10.

64. This journal was edited by Paul Monroe of Teachers College at Columbia University and Friedrich Schneider from the University of Cologne.

65. Ernst Krieck, "The Education of a Nation from Blood and Soil," *International Education Review* 3 (1933–1934): 309–313.

66. Ernst Krieck, "Die Judenfrage," *Volk und Werden* 1 (1933): 57–62.

67. Ernst Krieck, *Völkisch-politische Anthropologie* (Leipzig: Armanen, 1936), 70–77, 135–136.

68. Johann von Leers, *Wie kam der Jude zum Geld?* (Berlin: Theodor Fritsch, 1939), 51, 55. In 1950, Leers left Germany and settled in Argentina, where he contributed many writings to *Der Weg*, a neo-Nazi publication in Buenos Aires. In 1955, as newly appointed propaganda adviser to the Egyptian strongman Gamal Abdel Nasser, Leers moved to Cairo, where he

eventually changed his name to Omar Amin von Leers and became a
Moslem. He was buried in 1965 according to Moslem tradition. Unrepentant to the end, Leers continued to spew anti-Semitic rhetoric through his
final days. See *Die Welt*, 5 March 1965. For a detailed file of clippings, let-
ters, and periodicals on Leers, see WLLondon.

69. Johann von Leers, *Juden sehen dich an* (Berlin: NS Druck, 193?), 6–48.
70. Johann von Leers, *Judentum und Verbechen: Die Kriminalität des Juden-
    tums* (Berlin: Deutscher-Rechts Verlag, 1936), 14–42.
71. Johann von Leers, *Die Verbrechernatur der Juden* (Berlin: Hochmuth,
    1944). pp. 8–9, 113–116, 117–120, 142.
72. In a special issue on the Jewish question, see Johann von Leers, "Stein der
    Hilfe und Schild des Rechtes" and "Islam und Judentum im Laufe des
    Jahrhunderte," *Der Deutsche Erzieher* 5 (1938): 425–427. This same issue
    included a bibliography of books on Jews (442–444) presented under var-
    ious categories including "The Jew as Parasite," which cited thirty-two
    works, by far the largest number of any grouping. Additional categories
    included the History of the Jews, Freemasonry and Jews, Jews and Crimi-
    nality, Great Germans and Jews, and the Talmud. The Institute for
    Contemporary History in Munich holds the largest collection of writings by
    Johann von Leers. Among his other works, see "Der Kampf gegen die Juden
    im Altertum," *Der Deutsche Erzieher* 6 (1939): 267–269; "Der gegenwär-
    tige Stand des Judenproblems in der Welt," *Der Deutsche Erzieher* 5
    (1938): 402–406; "Das wir nicht in der Hand der Juden fallen," *Der
    Deutsche Erzieher* 10 (1943): 65–67. For other works, including those with
    an education emphasis, see Johann von Leers and Willy Becker, *National-
    sozialistische Staatskunde* (Potsdam: Hachfeld, 1942); Johann von Leers
    and Heinrich Hansen, *Der Deutsche Lehrer als Kulturschöpfer* (Frankfurt:
    Diesterweg, 1939); *Geschichte auf rassischer Grundlage* (Leipzig: Reclaim,
    1934); *Spenglers Weltpolitische System und der National Socialismus*
    (Berlin: Junker und Dünnhaupt, 1934); *Rassische Geschichtsbetrachtung:
    Was muss der Lehrer davon wissen?* (Leipzig: Beltz, 1934); *Die Grosse Auf-
    gabe!* (Berlin: Siemens, 1933); *Forderung der Stunde: Juden Raus!* (Berlin:
    NS-Druck, 1933); *Unser Glaube Deutschland! Gedanken um das Ewige
    Reich* (Erfurt: Sigrune, 1940); *Blut und Rasse in der Gesetzgebung: Ein
    Gang durch die Völkergeschichte* (Munich: Lehmanns, 1936); *14 Jahre
    Judenrepublik: Die Geschichte eines Rassenkampfes* (Berlin: Verlag
    Deutscher Kulturwacht, 1933); *Die Geschichtlichen Grundlagen des
    Nationalsozialismus* (Berlin: Deutscher Rechtsverlag, 1938); *Volkskunde im
    Deutschen Unterricht* (Darmstadt: Schlapp, 1934).
73. Alfred Rosenberg, *Der Mythus des 20. Jahrhunderts* (Munich: Hoheneichen
    Verlag, 1930), 459–466, 471, 518–523. In this same volume, Rosenberg
    also offered deference to Paul de Lagarde whom he regarded as a great
    prophet of Volkish thinking. See 457.
74. NS8/128. NS Geschichtsbild. Kanzlei Rosenberg. 1 March 1934.
    BArch.Berlin.
75. Alfred Rosenberg, *Die Entwicklung der deutschen Freiheitsbewegung*
    (Munich: Eher, 1933), 18–30.
76. Alfred Rosenberg, *Die Spur des Juden im Wandel der Zeiten* (Munich: Eher,
    1937), 117–123. For a text of Rosenberg's address to teachers marking the
    opening of a new Reich School for the NSLB at Donndorf near Bayreuth in

the fall of 1938, see "Alfred Rosenberg über Aufgaben des Lehrers und Erziehers," *Weltanschauung und Schule* 2 (1938): 512–516.

77. Ernst Klee, *Euthanasie im NS-Staat: Die Vernichtung lebensunwerten Lebens* (Frankfurt am Main, 1983), 45–79; Weindling, 1993, 543–544.

78. Phillip Bouhler, *Adolf Hitler*

79. Phillip Bouhler, *Kampf um Deutschland: Ein Lesebuch fur die deutsche Jugend* (Berlin: Zentralverlag der NSDAP, 1939). Copy found in DIPF/ Berlin NS5896. Insight into the language of censoring printed matter under the Third Reich is provided in an obscure letter to Alfred Rosenberg from Hederich, a representative of Hitler's staff on the proofing commission "for the protection of NS literature," dated 25 March 1939. Hederich censored the authors Julius Mosen, Jakob Loewenberg, and Friedrich von der Leyen "because of non-Aryan descent." Leyen was singled out as "jewish interrelated" and thus attracted the heavy hand of the censor. Other censorship categories included "questionable morals," followed by "unclear, in part negative attitude," and "one-sided confessional tendencies." See letter from Hederich, Stellvertreter des Führers Stabb, Parteiamtliche Prüfungskommission zum Schutze des NS-Schriftums to Rosenberg, 25 March 1939, BArch.Berlin, NS8/209, Kanzlei Rosenberg, 129.

80. Letter from Minister des Kultus und Unterrichts (Haanz) in Karlsruhe to RMWEVB, 16 Februar 1938 with Richtlinien für den Stoffplan und den Unterrichtsplan: Unterricht über Deutsche Sitte und Deutsche Art, R21/531 Amt E. Lebenskunde-Unterricht der Weltanschauungsgememeinschft "Deutsche Gotterkenntnis," BArch.Berlin.

81. Rudolf Benze, *Rasse und Schule* (Braunschweig: Applelhaus, 1934), 12–14.

82. Wilhelm von Humboldt (1797), "The Limits of State Action," in *The Limits of State Action*, ed. J. W. Burrow (Cambridge: Cambridge University Press, 1969), 54.

83. Walter Gross, *Rassenpolitische Erziehung* (Berlin: Junker und Dünnhaupt, 1934), 28.

84. RMWEVB, *Amtsblatt*, 1. Jahrgang, 1935, "Vererbungslehre und Rassenkunde im Unterricht," 43. The directive was actually released on 13 September 1933 but republished in the first volume of the offical newpaper of the RMWEVB in 1935.

85. Rudolf Benze, *Nationalpolitische Erziehung im Dritten Reich* (Berlin: Junker und Dünnhaupt, 1936), 20.

86. RMWEVB, *Amtsblatt*, 1935, 44.

87. RMWEVB, *Amtsblatt*, 1935, 45–46.

88. NSLB, *Lehrerfortbildung, Sommer, 1934* (Berlin: NSLB, 1934), 13–16, 18, 21, 23, 21, DIPF/Berlin, 2A 2648.

89. Horst Schallenberger, *Untersuchungen zum Geschichtsbild der Wilhelmischen Ära und der Weimarer Zeit* (Düsseldorf: Schwann, 1964), 69–79, 127–139.

90. Note the *Heimabend*, or evening instructional programs and weekend curriculums, through which Hitler Youth frequently integrated ideological teachings of an anti-Semitic nature. See Walter Gross, *Die Ehe ist die Treue zum Blute deines Volkes.* Shriftenreihe für die Wochenenschulungen der Hitler Jugend, Heft 3. (No imprint, 1943), 13–22, WLLondon, 395/B146. For two examples of ideological schooling for Hitler Youth, both edited by the Reichsjugendführung of the NSDAP, see *Sport-Tagebuch der deutschen*

Jugend (Berlin: Wirtschafts-Werbeverlag, n.d.), WLTel Aviv, B916; *Juden und Lords Hand in Hand* (Berlin: Limpert, 1940), WLTelAviv, B149. Walter Scharrer publicly chided German public schools for supporting a circle of teachers who remained ideologically unreliable and saw in Hitler Youth a way of reaching young people more effectively with strong racial and anti-Semitic instruction. See Scharrer, 1936, 13. For a detailed primer for Hitler Youth including several references to Jews, see Fritz Bennecke, *Handbuch für die Schulungsarbeit in der Hitler Jugend: Vom Deutschen Volk und seinem Lebensraum* (Berlin: Zentralverlag des NSDAP, 1937), 8–13, 56, 77–79.

Chapter 2: The Jewish Question

1. Ernst Dobers, *Die Judenfrage: Stoff und Behandlung in der Schule*, 1. Auflage (Leipzig: Klinkhardt, 1936), 3.
2. Ernst Dobers, *Die Judenfrage: Stoff und Behandlung in der Schule*, 3. Auflage (Leipzig: Klinkhardt, 1939), 6–7.
3. Dobers, 1939, 10–11. See also John Farquharson, *The Plough and the Swastika: The NSDAP and Agriculture in Germany, 1928–1945* (London, 1976).
4. Dobers, 1939, 13.
5. Dobers, 1939, 13–14.
6. Dobers, 1936, 14–15 and 1939, 15, 66. Note that an even more detailed Nazi documentation of anti-Semitic developments in the history of both Catholic and Protestant churches is recounted in "Einmal hin im Katholizismus und einmal her im Protestantismus," from a special issue of the NSLB journal, *Der Deutsche Erzieher* 5 (1938): 446–447. This special issue appeared within only a month of Dobers's publication since he wrote the foreword to the third edition during November of 1938.
7. Steven Katz, *The Holocaust in Historical Content*, vol. 1 (New York: Oxford University Press, 1994), 389.
8. Katz, 1994, 394.
9. Dobers, 1939, 66.
10. *Grosswörterbuch Klett* (London: Collins, 1983), 780.
11. Dobers, 1939, 14.
12. Also appearing in the book were spurious claims that the deaths of the Russian Czars Alexander II and III and Nicholas II came at the hands of Jewish cliques. See Dobers, 1939, 25.
13. Dobers, 1936, 27; 1939, 27–28.
14. Dobers, 1939, 28. The reference to the *Talmud* under discussion was added to the third edition and had not appeared as part of the first edition in 1936. The translation of "handeln" as "trade" must be clarified within the context of Nazi language. Nazi usage cast a negative tone over the terms connoting "wheeling and dealing," "bargaining," or "haggling."
15. Dobers, 1939, 31. The 1936 edition included a foreword written in October of that year.
16. Dobers, 1939, 33.
17. Dobers, 1939, 55.
18. Dobers, 1939, 55.

19. The story of Jud Süß transcends the history of anti-Semitism under the Third Reich. The Jewish author and playwright Lion Feuchtwanger created the drama *Jud Süß* for the stage in 1917 and later completed a novel in 1925 under the same title. The actual historical character was Joseph Süß Oppenheimer, born in Heidelberg in 1692. As financial adviser to the duke of Württemberg, Oppenheimer fell into great disfavor among Protestants opposed to his power to tax and collect tolls as well as control the finances of the Duchy. After the duke's death, Süß Oppenheimer was condemned to death by hanging in 1738 because he had "mixed carnally with Christian flesh." Feuchtwanger presented a vision of Süß that challenged the prevailing stereotypes of the conniving court Jew and figure of consummate evil. The character of Jud Süß became a literary focal point for the issue of Jewish identity. In 1940, Nazi filmmaker Veit Harlan joined forces with Joseph Goebbels in producing the film *Jud Süß* that, in the words of David Bathrick, portrayed the Jew as "perpetrator, not victim, and his brutal execution a 'horrible example' of what should and must be done to all Jews who violate the codes of biological, as well as cultural, assimilation." Harlan's film created a Jewish monster. During the same year, two other anti-Semitic films appeared under the titles of *The Rothschilds* and *The Eternal Jew*. In both films, producers tried to educate audiences about the so-called biological truth lurking behind every Jew, that a Jew was and must remain a Jew because of the reality of bloodlines. In the latter film, the figure of the sinister *Ostjude* played a major role. See David Bathrick, "1925: Jud Süß by Lion Feuchtwanger Is Published," in *Yale Companion to Jewish Writing and Thought in German Culture, 1096–1996*, ed. Sander Gilman and Jack Zipes (New Haven, Conn.: Yale University Press, 1997), 434–439.
20. Dobers, 1939, 15, 38.
21. Dobers, 1939, 38–39.
22. Dobers, 1939, 39.
23. Dobers, 1939, 42.
24. A classic example of this tendency to mislead the reader is found in Dobers's discussion of Jewish soldiers in World War I. He contrasted 1,850,000 German war dead with 12,000 Jews who had fallen at the front, concluding that Jewish casualties accounted for 65 percent less than the loss suffered by the German population. What Dobers conveniently omitted was that Jews numbered about 500,000 in Germany and made up only about 1 percent of the population. His proportional argument rested on sand. See Dobers, 1939, 24.
25. Dobers, 1939, 42–43.
26. Dobers, 1939, 44.
27. Henry Friedlander, *The Origins of Nazi Genocide: From Euthanasia to the Final Solution* (Chapel Hill: University of North Carolina Press, 1995), 288, 290; Martin Gilbert, *The Holocaust* (New York: Holt, Rinehart and Winston, 1985), 581; Peter Black, *Ernst Kaltenbrunner: Ideological Soldier of the Third Reich* (Princeton, N.J.: Princeton University Press, 1985), 26–27.
28. Dobers, 1939, 51–52, 57.
29. Dobers, 1939, 47, 57, 59.
30. Dobers, 1939, 63.
31. Dobers, 1939, 63–64. The timing of Dobers's earliest edition on the Jewish

question predated the subsequent mass arrests and deportations of Jews. Dachau, the first concentration camp, opened its gates within thirty days of the Nazi assumption of power on 30 January 1933. Jews did not enter Dachau in any significant numbers until after 1938. Deportations of German Jews did not begin until 14 October 1941.

32. Dobers, 1939, 66–73.
33. Dobers, 1939, 73.
34. Dobers, 1939, 72.
35. Dobers, 1939, 74.
36. Ernst Dobers was one of the most outspoken supporters of using newspapers to teach racial science. Among his teaching examples is one dedicated to "Jewish Destructive Rage–Nordic Will to Build," which combined excerpts from newspapers to reinforce the stereotypes of Jews as assassins, corrupt politicians, Communists, and the force behind revolutions. See Ernst Dobers, *Die Zeitung im Dienste der Rassenkunde* (Leipzig: Klinkhardt, 1936), 46–48.
37. Johann von Leers, *14 Jahre Judenrepublik: Die Geschichte des Rassenkampfes* (Berlin: Deutsche Kulturwacht, 19?), 107–108, cited in Dobers, 1939, 74. Dobers also relied on the work of Fritz Lenz in his discussion of the Jewish question. See Dobers, 1939, 11.
38. Dobers, 1939, 74.
39. Dobers, 1939, 75.
40. That there existed a kind of "Nazi logic" may seem debatable to some, but to Heinrich Himmler there was a perfectly sound logic to the Final Solution and the reasons why SS officers could ill afford to maintain the illusion of the good Jew in their midst. See Himmler's speech at Posen before a meeting of SS major-generals at Posen, 4 October 1943, quoted in Henry Gwiazda, "World War Two and Nazi Racism," *Prologue* 25 (1994): 156–159.
41. Victor Klemperer, *LTI: Notizbuch einer Philologen* (Leipzig: Reclam, 1999), 186.
42. Julius Streicher, as gauleiter of Franconia, sponsored an art contest in the schools of that province at the end of 1936. The first-prize drawing from a thirteen-year-old Franconian depicted Father Christmas chasing a group of Jews from the outskirts of a German community with the outcasts running toward Palestine. The title of the drawing was "You Roaming Jew, Leave Other People in Peace." The artwork for third place, created by a student from a *Realgymnasium* in Nuremberg, advanced a stereotypical conception of two cigar-smoking Jewish men haggling in the street. See "Die Arbeitern der Preisträger," *Fränkische Tageszeitung*, 31 December 1936 from the Clippings Collection of the Wiener Library at Tel Aviv University. (Note figure 4.1.)
43. Dobers, 1939, 77.
44. Dobers, 1939, 79.
45. For other related works by Ernst Dobers, some of which come under further scrutiny in later chapters, see Ernst Dobers and Kurt Higelke, hrsg., *Rassenpolitische Unterrichtspraxis: Der Rassengedanke in der Unterrichtsgestaltung der Volksschulfächer* (Leipzig: Klinkhardt, 1938); Ernst Dobers, *Rassenkunde: Forderung und Dienst* (Leipzig: Klinkhardt, 1939); and "Zur weltanschaulichen Begründung von Rassenkunde und Rassenpflege,"

Deutsche Volkserziehung 1 (1934): 34–39.

46. Werner Dittrich, *Vererbung und Rasse: Hand und Hilfsbuch für den Lehrer* (Stuttgart: Fränckh'sche Verlagshandlung, 1936); Werner Dittrich, "Rassenkunde und Biologieunterricht," *Nationalsozialistisches Bildungswesen* 4 (January 1937a): 18–22.

47. Gutachten über Werner Dittrich, Bayreuth: *Erziehung zum Judengegner: Hinweise zur Behandlung der Judenfrage im Unterricht* by Ludwig Deyerling, NSLB Abteilung Zeitschriften (undated). See BArch Berlin, NS12/554, Angelegenheiten betr. Juden 1935–1938.

48. Werner Dittrich, *Erziehung zum Judengegner: Hinweise zur Behandlung der Judenfrage im rassenpolitischen Unterricht* (Munich: Deutscher Volksverlag, 1937b), 4. Original in WLTAV, B2a/DIT.

49. Dittrich, 1937b, 7.

50. Dittrich, 1937b, 3.

51. Dittrich, 1937b, 3; Günther, *Der nordische Gedanke unter den Deutschen* (Munich: Lehmanns, 1925), 18. More contemporary Nazi ideological influence concerning the idea of racial soul was represented in the thinking of Ludwig Clauß, *Rasse und Seele*, 6. Auflage (Munich: Lehmanns, 1936). Alfred Rosenberg elevated "racial soul" to a new level under National Socialism. Speaking before the NS Union of University Students, he noted that "the discovery of racial soul constituted a revolution just as the discovery by Copernicus had four centuries before." See Alfred Rosenberg, *Deutsches Philologen Blatt* 42 (14 November 1934): 502. Wilhelm Schallmayer, the geneticist, had observed some thirty years before that the idea of racial soul was so complex that it could scarcely be conceptualized. Capriciousness and fantasy, he observed, often had more to do with the formation of a concept like racial soul than did scientific research. See Wilhelm Schallmeyer, "Vererbung und Auslese im Lebenslauf der Völker," *Natur und Staat*, 3. Teil (1903), 80.

52. Dittrich, 1937b, 6.

53. Dittrich, 1937b, 6, 21. Nicola Sacco and Bartolomeo Vanzetti were two Italian-born immigrants who were convicted and sentenced to death for allegedly killing a paymaster and guard at a Massachusetts shoe factory in 1920. Their conviction, under the most questionable conditions and without solid evidence, raised a furor among those who thought that justice had been denied and the men executed because of prejudice against foreigners. That Jewish newspapers in the United States raised objections to this outcome was evidence enough for Werner Dittrich to connect the Jewish press to a sense of lawlessness. See Daniel Boorstin and Brooks Kelley, *A History of the United States* (Upper Saddle River, N.J.: Prentice Hall, 1999), 580–581.

54. Dittrich, 1937b, 9.

55. Dittrich, 1937b, 9; see Dieter Schiefelbein, "Das Institut zur Erforschung der Judenfrage Frankfurt am Main," in *'Beseitigung des jüdischen Einflüsses:' Antisemitische Forschung, Eliten und Karrieren im Nationalsozialismus*, hrsg. Fritz Bauer Institut (New York: Campus, 1999), 43–71; Institut zum Studium der Judenfrage, hrsg., *Die Juden in Deutschland* (Munich: Eher, 1939).

56. Dittrich, 1937b, 9–10.

57. Dittrich, 1937b, 11.

58. Dittrich, 1937b, 11–12.
59. Dittrich, 1937b, 16.
60. Dittrich, 1937b, 17–18.
61. Luther's strange essay described Jews sucking the teats of a sow carved out of stone. See Michael Behal and Wolfgang Pasche, *Juden in Deutschland* (Stuttgart: Klett, 1995), 25. See also Dittrich, 1937b, 18, 37.
62. Dittrich, 1937b, 20–21. These statistics were gleaned by Dittrich from the Institute for the Study of the Jewish Question, *Die Juden in Deutschland* (Munich: Eher, 1939), 380–404. Copy found in the collection of the former Teacher Training College for Women at Hanover opened under the Third Reich. See the Niedersächsische Landesbibliothek, Fachbereichsbibliothek, Erziehungswissenschaften und Allgemeine Lehrbücherei, University of Hanover, NS 34.
63. Dittrich, 1937b, 20.
64. Children's literature exploited this stereotype in a number of ways, as noted in chapter 5. See the story about the visit of a young girl from the Bund Deutsche Mädel to the offices of a Jewish doctor in "Wie es Inge bei einem Judenartzt erging," from Ernst Hiemer, *Der Giftpilz* (Nuremberg: Der Stürmer, 1938), 31–34. Original at WLTAV, B4a, HIE. Also see references to Jews and alleged tendencies toward the exploitation of women through prostitution in Argentina and the Weimar Republic in Dobers, 1939, 61.
65. Dittrich, 1937b, 21.
66. Dittrich, 1937b, 21.
67. Dittrich, 1937b, 22–23. A more detailed history of the Jews from the perspective of Werner Dittrich is found in an essay written for one of the NSLB journals. See his "Der Endkampf gegen das Judentum," *Der Deutsche Erzieher* 6 (1939): 403–409.
68. Dittrich, 1937b, 23.
69. Dittrich, 1937b, 25.
70. Dittrich, 1937b, 25–26.
71. Dittrich, 1937b, 24, 26.
72. To add more propagandistic support to his argument, Dittrich insisted that Soviet dictator Joseph Stalin had married a Jewish woman with Near Eastern blood. See Dittrich, 1937b, 26.
73. Dittrich, 1937b, 27.
74. Michael Berenbaum, *The World Must Know* (New York: Little, Brown, 1993), p.132. For a survivor's account of Mathhausen, see Anton Gill, *The Journey from Hell* (New York: Morrow, 1988), 335. Also see Martin Gilbert, *The Holocaust* (New York: Holt Rinehart, and Winston, 1985), 143–144.
75. The author called the character of Mordecai in the Book of Esther "the first bringer of misfortune to hold this name in world history." See Dittrich, 1937b, 31.
76. Dittrich, 1937b, 30–31.
77. Dittrich, 1937b, 35.
78. Dittrich, 1937b, 35–36.
79. Dittrich, 1937b, pp 38–39.
80. Dittrich included in his closing section a list of ten top curriculum resources for teachers and school principals. Ernst Dobers's work on the Jewish ques-

tion is recommended, especially his writing on the contemporary Nazi campaign against the Jews. Among other sources are Theodore Fritsch, *Handbuch der Judenfrage* (Leipzig: Hammerverlag, 1933); Walter Linden, *Luthers Kampfschriften gegen das Judentum* (Berlin: Klinkhardt and Biermann, 1936); Hans F. K. Günther, *Rassenkunde des jüdischen Volkes* (Munich: Lehmann, 1930); Institut zum Studium der Judenfrage, *Die Juden in Deutschland*, 2. Auflage. Munich: Eher, 1936); Wilhelm Grau, *Antisemitismus im späteren Mittelalter* (Munich: Duncker und Humblot, 1934).

81. Dittrich, 1937b, 42.
82. Dittrich, 1937b, 43.
83. Dittrich, 1937b, 44. Also published by Werner Dittrich was a handbook for teachers called *Vererbung und Rasse* (Stuttgart: Franckh'sche Verlag, 1936) for instruction in race hygiene. The work included a very brief section on the Jews, the details of which reappeared in his later curriculum guide on the Jewish question. Reflecting the influence of Hans F. K. Günther, the centerpiece of his essay recounted the racial anthropologist's stereotypical descriptions of Jews including the standard references to the hooked nose, weakness of muscles due to the avoidance of physical labor, and thick lips revealing the influence of Negroid bloodlines. See Dittrich, 1936, 75.
84. Fritz Fink, *Die Judenfrage* im *Unterricht* (Nuremberg: Willmy, 1937), 5. The back cover of Fink's book depicted a stereotyped face of a brooding Jew behind the Star of David. The caption read: "Without a solution to the Jewish question, there will be no solution to human kind." Original in WLTAV, B56.
85. Fink, 1937, 5–6.
86. Fink, 1937, 6.
87. Fink, 1937, 6.
88. Fink, 1937, 8.
89. Fink, 1937, 8.
90. The Nazi antipathy against Blacks was also evident in other curriculum resources. See Rudolf Frercks and Arthur Hoffmann, *Erbnot und Volksaufartung* (Erfurt: Stenger, 1934), 18–19 and pictures 25, 25a, and 26. Hans F. K. Günther's racial anthropology tried to convince readers that the blood mixing of Jews and Blacks resulted in the appearance of a "light negroid element" in Jews that then was passed on through the intermarriage of Jews with Germans. Günther also exploited the *Schwarze Schmach*, or "Black Disgrace," referring to the occupation of Germany's Ruhr region after World War I by Black troops from the French colonial empire, including Dahomey. Günther's reference was potentially explosive because of memories still lingering from German anti-Black propaganda coming from the interwar period that advanced gross exaggerations of Black occupation troops raping German women. See Hans F. K. Günther, *Rassenkunde des Deutschen Volkes*, 16. Auflage (Munich: Lehmanns, 1935), 170–172. German girls were strongly advised by a medical doctor from the Youth Welfare Office not to play with puppets depicting Negroes. See Emil Joerns and Julius Schwab, *Rassenhygiene Fibel: Der Deutschen Jugend Zuliebe Geschrieben* (Berlin: Metzner, 1935), 101. Johann von Leers and Willy Becker contrasted Aryan women with women from Sudan on the bases of physical beauty and intellectual capabilities. See their *Nationalsozialistische Staatskunde* (Potsdam: Bonness und Hachfeld, 1942), 24–25.
91. Fink, 1937, 8.

92. Fink, 1937, 10–11.
93. Fink, 1937, 11–12.
94. Fink, 1937, 12–14.
95. Fink, 1937, 16–19.
96. Fink, 1937, 18. For accounts of Jewish pupils who endured insulting behavior from teachers and classmates in this anti-Semitic instructional environment, see Jochen Hering et al., *Schüleralltag im Nationalsozialismus* (Dortmund: Pädagogische Arbeitsstelle, 1984), 272–275; Margaret Limberg and Hubert Rübsaat, *Sie dürfen nicht mehr Deutsche sein: Jüdische Alltag in Selbstzeugnissen, 1933–1938* (New York: Campus, 1990); Joseph Walk, "Jüdische Schüler an Deutschen Schulen in Nazideutschland," *Bulletin des Leo Baeck Instituts* 19 (1980): 101–109.
97. Fink, 1937, 19–20.
98. Fink, 1937, 20–21.
99. Fink, 1937, 22. The term *auserwählte,* meaning "chosen," always appeared with quotation marks when associated with the expression "chosen people."
100. Fink, 1937, 22.
101. Fink, 1937, 23. A Catholic version and English translation of the Old Testament texts selected by Fritz Fink can be found in *The New American Bible* (New York: Kenedy, 1974), 222, 231, 733.
102. Fink, 1937, 23.
103. Fink, 1937, 24.
104. Fink, 1937, 25. The school inspector from Bavaria acknowledged a debt to Theodore Fritsch, the author of *Handbuch der Judenfrage: Die wichtigsten Tatsachen zur Beurteilung des Jüdischen Volkes* (Leipzig: Hammer Verlag), which appeared in its forty-ninth printing in 1944. The edition from 1944 included a section on the Talmud from which Fink drew some of his material that also appeared in earlier editions. See Fritsch, 130–135. Along with the book by Fritsch, Fink recommended that the work of F. Roderich-Stoltheim, *Das Rätsel des jüdischen Erfolges* (Leipzig: Hammer, 1928) be included on every teacher's bookshelf. See Fritsch, 130–135.
105. Fink, 1937, 25.
106. Fink, 1937, 26.
107. Fink, 1937, 26.
108. Fink, 1937, 27–29. Fink cited Alfons Steiger, *Der neudeutsche Heide im Kampfe gegen Christen und Juden* (Berlin: Germania, 1924), 24–25.
109. Fink cited John 8:44–45 and Matthew 23:15. Still unclear is the source of the biblical translations that appeared in Fink's writing. See Fink, 1937, 34. For a profound historical study of anti-Semitism in the Catholic Church, see James Carroll, *Constantine's Sword: The Church and the Jews* (Boston: Houghton Mifflin, 2001).
110. See Anthony Rhodes, *Propaganda: The Art of Persuasion* (London: Chelsea House, 1976), 44.
111. Fink, 1937, 34–41. A curious and self-serving justification for the persecution and eventual removal of Jews from Danzig after the brutal pogrom of November 1938 appears in the memoirs of an SS family. SS Brigadeführer Johannes Schäfer, who participated in this action, later recalled that the guilt for this development rested with the Lutheran Church and, more specifically, with Martin Luther. After all, he observed, the Lutheran

Church even caused and helped carry out the persecutions. Conspicuous in its absence was any discussion of SS responsibility for the fate of the Danzig Jews. See Ingeburg Schäfer and Susanne Klockmann, *Mutter mochte Himmler nie: Die Geschichte einer SS-Familie* (Reinbeck bei Hamburg: Rowohlt, 1999), 56.

112. Fink, 1937, 40–41.
113. Fink, 1937, 41–42.
114. Fink, 1937, 42–43. Earlier instructional resources on the Jewish question can be found in K. Hahn, hrsg., "Die Judenfrage," *Das Neue Reich: Arbeits-Schulungs-und Unterrichtsblätter*, Blatt Nr. 9 (Wittenberg: Herrose's Verlag, 1935), 1–4. Hahn also included an essay for teachers on the "Rassenkunde des jüdischen Volkes," in the same collection, presented as Blatt Nr. 8. These two pieces were published under the auspices of the journal *Volk und Rasse*. Original in WLTAV under Ald/HAH. See also Erich Malitius, *Wir und die Jude: Was die Jugend über den Juden wissen muß* (Berlin: Jugendzeitschriften Verlag, 1935). Original in Yad Vashem Archives under 64–0159.
115. Fink, 1937, 7; Donald Niewyk, "Jews, 1933–1990," in *Modern Germany*, ed. Dieter Buse and Jürgen Doerr (New York: Garland, 1998), 527–528.
116. Fink, 1937, 45.
117. Hans-Christian Harten, "Rasse und Erziehung: Zur pädagogischen Psychologie und Soziologie des Nationalsozialismus," *Zeitschrift für Pädagogik* 39 (1993): 128.
118. Ernst Dobers, *Rassenkunde: Forderung und Dienst* (Leipzig: Klinkhardt, 1936), 79–80.

Chapter 3: The Jew as Racial Pariah in Race Hygiene and Biology

1. Jakob Graf, *Die Bildungs-und Erziehungswerte der Erblehre, Erbpflege und Rassenkunde: Nach einem Vortrag gehalten vor den Naturkundlehren Hessens am 30. Bachmonds 1933* (Munich: Lehmanns, 1934), 3. This chapter draws, in part, from two essays previously published by the author. The work of Alfred Vogel was treated in "Schooling for a New Mythos: Race, Anti-Semitism and the Curriculum Materials of a Nazi Race Educator," *Paedagogica Historica* 27 (June 1991) and is reprinted here with full permission. The discussion of the contributions to Nazi race education made by Jakob Graff, Sepp Burgstaller, Paul Brohmer, and Ranier Fetscher grew out of an earlier essay, "Legitimizing the Final Selection: Race in the School Curriculum of the Third Reich," in *The Holocaust's Ghost: Writings on Art, Politics, Law and Education*, ed. F. C. DeCoste and Bernard Schwartz (Edmonton: University of Alberta Press, 2000), 362–375.
2. Änne Bäumer-Schleinkofer, *Nazi Biology and Schools* (New York: Peter Lang, 1995), 3. See also Gertrud Scherf, "Vom deutschen Wald zum deutschen Volk: Biologieunterricht im Dienste nationalsozialistischer Weltanschauung," in *Schule und Unterricht im Dritten Reich*, hrsg. Reinhard Dithmar (Neuwied: Luchterhand, 1979), 217–234.
3. Cited in Harold Scholz, "Schule unterm Hakenkreuz," in *Schule und Unterricht im Dritten Reich*, ed. Reinhard Dithmar (Neuwied: Luchterhand, 1989), 15–18.
4. Scholz in Dithmar, 1989, 18–20.

5. RMWEVB, "Vererbungslehre und Rassenkunde im Unterricht," Erlaß vom 13, September 1933, *Amtsblatt des RMWEVB und der Unterrichtsverwaltungen der Länder*, 1. Jahrgang, 1935, 44.

6. RMWEVB, 44–46. The teaching of English language provided a context for "racial political" instruction about Jewish influence in England and the prevalence of the Jewish question in the literature of Shakespeare's *Merchant of Venice* and the writings of Somerset Maugham and John Galsworthy. See K. H. Kröger, "Der Rassengedanke im englischen Unterricht," *Die Deutsche Höhere Schule* 5 (1938): 3–10.

7. Ernst Dobers, "Biologie und neue Volksschullehrerbildung," *Der Biologe* 1 (1931–1932): 65–69.

8. Alexander Hesse, *Die Professoren und Dozenten der preußischen Pädagogischen Akademien (1926–1933) und Hochschulen für Lehrerbildung (1933–1941)* (Weinheim: Deutscher Studien Verlag, 1995), 239. The SS connection with secondary schools was significant for a number of reasons, one of the most important of which centered on vigorous SS recruitment of future members from the student body. See Gerhard Rempel, *Hitler's Children: The Hitler Youth and the SS* (Chapel Hill: University of North Carolina Press, 1989).

9. Ernst Dobers and Kurt Higelke, hrsg., *Rassenpolitische Unterrichtspraxis: Der Rassengedanke in der Unterrichtsgestaltung der Volksschulfächer* (Leipzig: Klinkhardt, 1938), 206.

10. Dobers and Higelke, 1938, 220–238.

11. "Lebenskunde," RMWEVB, Erlaß, EII a 3500/39KVa vom 15.12.1939, reprinted in Paul Brohmer, *Der Unterricht in der Lebenskunde* (Berlin: Zickfeldt, 1943), 201.

12. Paul Brohmer, *Fauna von Deutschland*, 16th ed. (Heidelberg: Quelle und Meyer, 1984). Brohmer initially lost his professorship after the war under order of the British occupation authorities and was declared a *Mitläufer* (fellow traveler) with the Nazi regime by a denazification tribunal in 1947. Eventually returning to Kiel, he continued to publish numerous editions of study and teaching books until his death in 1965.

13. Paul Brohmer, *Erziehung zur Staatsgesinnung durch arbeitskundlichen Biologieunterricht* (Berlin: Osterwieck, 1923), 3, 8–11.

14. Brohmer, 1923, 22, 50.

15. Hermann Holle, *Allgemeine Biologie als Grundlage für Weltanschauung, Lebensführung und Politik* (Leipzig, 1925), 10–11.

16. Paul Brohmer, *Biologieunterricht und völkische Erziehung* (Frankfurt am Main: Moritz, 1936a), 47–50; Hans F. K. Günther, *Rassenkunde des jüdischen Volkes* (Munich: Lehmanns, 1930), 20–115.

17. Ferdinand Rossner, "Die Taxonomie und der Begriff der Evolution im Unterricht," *Der Biologe* 8 (1939): 366–372; Konrad Lorenz, "Nochmals: Systematik und Entwicklungsgedanke im Unterricht," *Der Biologe* 9 (1940): 20–36. Lorenz was the recipient of the Nobel Prize for Medicine in 1973. Known also as a researcher of animal behavior, Lorenz advocated the elimination of *Gemeinschaftsfremden*, or "social misfits," in an essay published in 1940. People placed under this category were to be sterilized by doctors and then sent to internment camps or possibly a death sentence determined by police officials. See Konrad Lorenz, "Durch Domestikation verursachte Störungen arteigenen Verhalten," *Zeitschrift für angewandte*

Psychologie und Charakterkunde 59 (1940): 2, cited in Benno Müller-Hill, *Murderous Science.* Trans. George Fraser (Plainview, N.Y.: Cold Spring Harbor Laboratory Press, 1998), 222f.

18. Brohmer, 1936a, 3–9.
19. Paul Brohmer, *Bekämpfung der Rassensünden durch den nationalosozialistischen Staat*, 2. Auflage (Berlin: Osterwieck, circa 1936b), 8–10.
20. Brohmer, 1936b, 14–16.
21. Brohmer, 1933, 15.
22. Brohmer, 1943, 78.
23. Albert Fischer, "Die Charaktererziehung in der Schule," *Die Deutsche Höhere Schule* 4 (1937): 342–345.
24. The entire bound collection of Alfred Vogel's teaching charts is included in the collection of the Library of Congress under GN280.V63 1938. The complete, bound pedagogical volume from the Library of Congress will take readers through the entire Vogel race curriculum. The Kroul Collection from Hofstra University includes the Vogel teaching charts numbered 54–58, 60, 62–64, and 66 and a host of additional school materials from the Nazi era too numerous to mention here.
25. Bernhard Rust, *Education in the Third Reich* (London: Butterworth, 1938), 4–8; Hans Schemm, *Deutsche Schule und Deutsche Erziehung in Vergangenheit, Gegenwart, und Zukunft* (Stuttgart: Pädagogische Verlagsanstalt, 1934), 5; A. Kluger, *Die deutsche Volksschule im Grossdeutschen Reich* (Breslau: Hirt, 1940), 220–226.
26. Horst Schallenberger, *Untersuchungen zum Geschichtsbild der Wilhelmischen Ära und der Weimarer Zeit* (Düsseldorf: Schwann, 1964), 69–79, 127–139; Akademie der *Künste*, ed., *Berliner Schulalltag* (Berlin: Akademie, 1983), 13, 17.
27. Alfred Vogel, *Erblehre und Rassenkunde für die Grund- und Hauptschule* (Baden: Konkordia, 1937), 5. Hereafter cited as *Vogel Teacher Text.*
28. *Vogel Teacher Text*, 13.
29. *Vogel Teacher Text*, 19, 23.
30. *Vogel Teacher Text*, 23.
31. *Vogel Teacher Text*, 68–73.
32. *Vogel Teacher Text*, 3–4.
33. *Vogel Teacher Text*, 60, 63. For a study of euthanasia under the Third Reich, see Michael Burleigh, *Death and Deliverance: Euthanasia in Germany, 1900–1945* (New York: Cambridge University Press, 1995).
34. *Vogel Teacher Text*, 58.
35. Hitler, *Mein Kampf*, 158–159.
36. *Vogel Teacher Text*, 74–75, 85.
37. *Vogel Teacher Text*, 100–104. Vogel Chart #61 is a visual teaching aid illustrating statistics relating alleged Jewish influence among Berlin's lawyers, theatre directors, druggists, medical doctors, and dentists.
38. Volks-Brockhaus, 1940, cited in Cornelia Schmitz-Berning, *Vokabular des Nationalsozialismus* (Berlin: Walter de Gruyter, 2000), 512.
39. Alfred Vogel, *Erblehre und Rassenkunde in bildlicher Darstellung* (Stuttgart: National Literatur, 1938), 2.
40. Vogel Chart #28.
41. Vogel Chart #39.

42. Vogel Chart #47.
43. *Vogel Teacher Text*, 60, 63, Vogel Chart #40.
44. Vogel Chart #48.
45. Vogel Chart #49.
46. Vogel Charts #52 and 53.
47. Vogel Chart #54.
48. Vogel Chart #54. See P. Schauff, "Die Geschichte der physikalische Forschung," *Grimsehl's Lehrbuch der Physik* (Leipzig: Teubner, 1940), 281–284.
49. Vogel Chart #55. Each chart measures 39 cm x 29.5 cm.
50. Vogel Chart #57.
51. Vogel Chart #58; Günther Ginzel, *Jüdischer Alltag in Deutschland 1933–1945* (Düsseldorf: Droste, 1993), 108.
52. Vogel Chart #60.
53. Vogel Chart #59.
54. International Military Tribunal, Document 1919-PS, vol. XXIX, 112.
55. Vogel Chart #62; Hitler, *Mein Kampf*, 326.
56. Vogel Chart #63. (See print.)
57. Vogel Chart #64.
58. Vogel Chart #66; Hitler, *Mein Kampf*, 286.
59. Vogel Chart #67; Hitler, *Mein Kampf*, 289.
60. Vogel Charts #69 and 70.
61. Vogel Chart #71. (See print.) George Mosse observed that Wilhelm von Polenz's book *The Peasant from Büttner* (1895) held some influence over Hitler. Polenz developed a story in which a peasant lost his land to foreclosure through his indebtedness to a Jew. The same Jewish landlord who reclaimed the property built a factory on the parcel. The peasant, out of great despair in seeing his life's work come to naught, hanged himself. The Jew is thus portrayed as a dominant and hated force in modern industrial society as well as a foreigner out to destroy the peasant, seen by the Nazis as critical to the identity of the Volk. The rural association of Jews as cattle dealers and moneylenders, seen before in the curriculum guides examined in chapter 2, will appear again in the children's literature examined in chapter 5. See George Mosse, *The Crisis of German Ideology* (New York: Grosset and Dunlap, 1964), 27.
62. Alfred Ploetz, "Zur Abgrenzung und Einteilung des Begriffs Rassenhygiene," *Archiv* 3 (1906): 864. For an insightful discussion of the relationship between race hygiene and eugenics after World War I, see Peter Weingart, Jürgen Kroll, and Kurt Bayertz, *Rasse, Blut und Gene: Geschichte der Eugenik und Rassenhygiene in Deutschland* (Frankfurt am Main: Suhrkamp, 1988), 239–245.
63. *Meyers Lexikon*, 3. Band. (Leipzig: Bibliographisches Institut, 1937), 119; see also the writing of Günther Just, a professor from Griefswald who became the head of the Genetics Research Institute of the Reich Office of Health in Berlin-Dahlem. See his essay "Eugenik und Weltanschauung," in *Eugenik und Weltanschauung*, hrsg. Günther Just (Berlin: Metzner, 1932), 7–38, and also his "Eugenik und Schule," in *Erblehre-Erbpflege*, hrsg.-Zentralinstitut für Erziehung (Berlin: Mittler, 1933), 40–65; Fritz Lenz, *Die Rasse als Wertprinzip: Zur Erneuerung der Ethik* (Munich: Lehmanns, 1933).

64. Otto Helmut, hrsg., *Volk im Gefahr: Der Gebürtenrückgang und seine Folgen für Deutschlands Zukunft* (Munich: Lehmanns, 1939); Friedrich Burgdorfer, *Deutsches Volk im Not* (Leipzig: Velhagen und Klosing, 1933).

65. Among the compound expressions that became part of Nazi language are *Rassenbewußtsein* (race consciousness), *Rassencharakter* (race character), *Rassenseele* (race soul), *Rassengedanke* (race thinking), *Rassenkampf* (race struggle), *Rassenfeind* (race enemy), *Rassenschande* (part of the Nazi criminal code regarding sexual relations with a non-Aryan), *Rassenfremd* (not amicable with one's own race, especially in reference to the Jews), *Rassengefühl* (feeling for the value of one's race), *Rassegenosse* (member of the same race), *Rasseninstinkt* (instinctive feeling for the uniqueness of one's own race), *Rassenmischung* (race mixing), *Rassenkern* (the pure racial element in a racially mixed people), *rassenlos* (not racially pure, without racial consciousness), *Rassenchaos* (race mixing), *Rassenhaß* (race hatred), *Rassenfrage* (racial question), *Rassenbiologie* (race biology), *Rassenpflege* (a German translation of race hygiene), *Rassenpolitik* (race politics), *Rassenrein* (without adding foreign blood), *Rassenreinheit* (the original condition of the races, the goal of race hygiene), *Rassenverrat* (sexual intercourse with foreign races, similar to *Rassenschande*), *Rassentrennung* (racial segration), *Rassentum* (a sense for the essence of race). Many of these expressions came into use before National Socialism. See Cornelia Schmitz-Berning's *Vokabular des Nationalsozialismus* (New York: Walter de Gruyter, 2000), 481–530. The relative importance of race in defining the ideology and the educated person in the Third Reich is also evidenced in *Meyers Lexikon* (9. Band, 1942) which devoted no less than fifty-eight columns of print on race and racially related concepts along with profusely illustrated racial models àla Günther (columns 21–78).

66. Brohmer, *Biologische Unterricht und völkische Erziehung*, 1936, 68–69, 71.

67. Brohmer, *Biologieunterricht*, 1933, 51.

68. Brohmer, *Biologieunterricht*, 1933, 52.

69. Robert Lifton, *Nazi Doctors: Medical Killing and the Psychology of Genocide* (New York: Basic Books, 1986), 78–79; Ärztekammer Berlin, *The Value of the Human Being: Medicine in Germany, 1918–1945* (Berlin: Edition Hentrich, 1991), 30–36.

70. Brohmer, *Biologieunterricht*, 1933, 54–55, 58.

71. Brohmer, *Biologieunterricht*, 1933, 52, 58–59.

72. Jakob Graf, *Vererbungslehre, Rassenkunde und Erbgesundheitspflege*. 5. Auflage (Munich: Lehmanns, 1938).

73. Graf, 1934, 30–31. See the similarity between Graf's writing and language used by Hitler in describing the "culture-founding Aryan," in *Mein Kampf*, 296. Graf's practice of condemning detractors of Nazi race education as immoral also appeared in his *Vererbungslehre, Rassenkunde und Erbgesundheitspflege*, 5. Auflage (Munich: Lehmanns, 1938), 262.

74. Graf, 1934, 31.

75. Graf, 1934, 30.

76. For a well-annotated bibliography of numerous sources on racial science, see Institut für Leser- und Schriftumskunde, *Rassenkunde: Eine Auswahl des wichtigsten Schriftums aus dem Gebiet der Rassenkunde, Vererbungslehre, Rassenpflege und Bevölkerungspolitik* (Leipzig: Institut, 1936).

77. Graf, 1938, 262–263.

78. Rudolf Virchow, *Archiv für Anthropologie* 16 (January, 1886): 285–337.
79. Graf, 1938, 263. Günther wrote about a certain *Helligkeit* or fair skin among some Jews coming from western and southern Europe as well as parts of North Africa. For a more detailed discussion of this anthropological issue and Günther's racial spin on Virchow's findings, see his *Rassenkunde des jüdischen Volkes* (1930), 225–239.
80. Graf, 1938, 263–264.
81. Jakob Graf, *Familienkunde und Rassenkunde für Schüler* (Munich: Lehmanns, 1935), 114–115.
82. George Mosse, "Culture, Civilization, and German Anti-Semitism," *Judaism* 7 (summer 1958): 257–258; Graf, 1935, 115.
83. Graf, 1935, 123.
84. Graf, 1935, 142–143.
85. Rainer Fetscher, *Rassenhygiene: Ein erste Einführung für Lehrer* (Leipzig: Verlag der Dürr'schen Buchhandlung, 1933), 35.
86. Fetscher, 1933, 25–26.
87. Fetscher, 1933, 22.
88. Peter Weingart, Jürgen Kroll, and Kurt Bayertz, *Rasse, Blut und Gene: Geschichte der Eugenik und Rassenhygiene in Deutschland* (Frankfurt am Main: Suhrkamp, 1988), 400, 527–531.
89. Hans Krauß, *Die Grundgedanken der Erbkunde und Rassenhygiene in Frage und Antwort*. Der Arzt als Erzieher. Heft 71 (Munich: Verlag der Ärztlichen Rundschau Otto Gmelin, 1935), 62. Original copy in WLTLV, A434. For a more specific consideration of Grant and Stoddard in connecting racism with eugenics in public policy and education in the United States, see Steven Selden, *Inheriting Shame: The Story of Eugenics and Racism in America* (New York: Teachers College Press, 1999), 15–20, 121–122.
90. Krauß, 1935, 54.
91. The Nazi perspectives on family and community are examined by Lisa Pine in "The Dissemination of Nazi Ideology and Family Values through School Textbooks," in *History of Education* 25 (1996): 91–109.
92. Krauß, 1935, 60. For a more specific pedagogical explanation on the integration of the *Ahnentafel* into racial studies under the Third Reich, see Hermann und Stridde, *Untergang und Aufstieg: ABC der Vererbungslehre und Erbgesunheitspflege, der Familen- und Rassenkunde*, 2. Auflage (Frankfurt am Main: Diesterweg, 1934), 6–9, and Jakob Graff, *Arbeitsheft zu Graf, Familienkunde und Rassenbiologie für Schüler* (Munich: Lehmanns, 1935), 2–15.
93. Krauß, 1935, 61–62. See also "Ostisch, Fälisch, Nordisch: Rassenkunde in der Schule," *Die Woche Berlin* (Oktober 1935) in *Heil Hitler, Herr Lehrer*, hrsg. Arbeitsgruppe Pädagogisches Museum (Hamburg: Rowohlt, 1983), 104–106.
94. For a book on race hygiene from medicine intended for a general audience, see Franz Schütz, *Rassenhygiene des deutschen Volkes* (Erfurt: Stenger, 1934). The author was professor and head of the Institute of Hygiene at the University of Berlin.
95. Krauß, 1935, 62–63. One of the most intensely anti-Semitic pieces to come out of the medical community in Germany was authored by Julius Schwab, a medical adviser in Paderborn. He collected numerous proverbs related to

race hygiene. In a section on racial contrasts, Schwab recorded over thirty-five proverbs about Jews. Among them: "Where there are many Jews, there are many thieves," followed by "Baptized Jew, circumcised Christian" and "The baptized Jew seldom does good." The connection with Christianity is further exploited with: "Who ever betrays a Jew will receive a first place in heaven." See Julius Schwab, *Rassenpflege im Sprichwort: Eine volkstümliche Sammlung* (Leipzig: Fröhlich, 1937), 19–22. Original copy found in the collection of the former Hochschule für Lehrerinnenbildung Hannover at Uni Hannover ERWS, NS 743. Schwab's work is also recommended for teachers of German language and literature by Max Schwarz in his entry "Rassenkunde und Deutschunterricht," in *Handbuch für den Biologieunterricht*, Lieferung 3, hrsg Ferdinand Rossner (Leipzig: Beltz, 1939), 101.

96. Philalethes Kuhn and Heinrich Kranz, *Von Deutschen Ahnen für Deutsche Enkel: Allgemeinverständliche Darstellung der Erblichkeitslehre, der Rassenkunde und der Rassenhygiene* (Munich: Lehmanns, 1933), 62. Heinrich Himmler also spoke to the problem of the "decent Jew" within the context of the Final Solution in his speech to SS officers at Posen (Poland) on 4 October 1943. See Himmler, "Speech of the Reichsfüher SS at the Meeting of SS Major-Generals at Posen," Partial Translation of Document 1919-PS, National Archives and Records Administration, quoted in *Prologue: 25th Anniversary Issue.* (1994): 156–158.

97. Kuhn and Kranz, 1933, 70–76.

98. Ferdinand Rossner, was placed in an internment camp by British occupation authorities in 1945 and released in late 1947. Not allowed to resume professional activities as a university professor, Rossner took up work as a Gymnasium teacher in Hildesheim during the 1950s. He retired in 1963 and died in 1987 in Hanover. See Hesse, 1995, 626–627.

99. Joachim Knoll, *Zur Geschichte des naturkundlichen Unterrichts in Hannover* (Hannover: Universität Hannover, 1995), 162–163.

100. Heinrich Ihde, Ferdinand Rossner and Alfred Stockfisch, *Gesundheitspflege und Rassenhygiene*, 3. Auflage (Langensalza: Beltz, 1939), 210. For one of the most succinct explanations of the Nazi concept of race to be found in the curriculum of the period, see Heinrich Ihde and Alfred Stockfish, *Vom Natur hab' ich die Statur: Erbgesundheitspflege für Schule und Volk*, 2. Auflage (Leipzig: Beltz, n.d.), 35–36.

101. Ihde, Rossner, and Stockfisch, 1939, 210–211.

102. Ihde, Rossner, and Stockfisch, 1939, 212.

103. Ibid.

104. Ihde, Rossner, and Stockfisch, 1939, 213. For a shorter consideration of Ben Franklin's anti-Semitic remarks before Congress, see Ernst Dobers, *Die Judenfrage: Stoff und Behandlung in der Schule*, 3. Auflage (Leipzig: Klinkhardt, 1939), 14.

105. Ihde, Rossner, and Stockfisch, 1939, 213.

106. Ihde, Rossner, and Stockfisch, 1939, 310–312.

107. The proposed link between race biology and Jewish religion, cloaked in the language of science, was the central theme in a lecture by Gerhard Kittel, a professor at the University of Tübingen. Spoken at that university's "Day of Science" in June of 1937, Kittel's remarks later appeared under his authorship in the essay "Das Urteil über die Rassenmischung im Judentum und in der biblischen Religion," *Der Biologe* 6 (1937): 342–352. Kittel actively

published on the Jewish question for the research department attached to the Institute for the History of the New Germany.

108. Ferdinand Rossner, *Rase und Religion* (Hannover: Schaper, 1942), 40–41; Fritz Fink, *Die Judenfrage* Im *Unterricht* (Nuremberg: Willmy, 1937), 21–24. Original in the collection of the former Hochschule für Lehrerinnen-bildung Hannover, Uni Hannover ERWS NS 662.

109. Rossner, 1942, 39.

110. Rossner, 1942, 7.

111. Hermann Weiskopf, "Anfang aller Schulreform," in *Lenk ein* 2 (20 March 1933), 33. Original in IZG/WK933.

112. Weiskopf, 42–44.

113. Weingart, Knoll, and Bayertz, *Rasse, Blut und Gene*, 1988, 307–395.

114. *Volksaufartung*, under National Socialism, was used in place of eugenics or race hygiene. *Aufartung*, according to Duden, 11. Auflage, 1934, meant "an improvement of the species through measures of race hygiene." Race hygiene is thus used in the translation of *Volksaufartung* as part of the book title. Duden reference cited in Cornelia Schmitz-Berning, *Vokabular des Nationalsozialismus* (New York: de Gruyter, 2000), 73–74.

115. Rudolf Frercks and Arthur Hoffmann, *Erbnot und Volksaufartung: Bild und Gegenbild aus dem Leben zur praktischen rassenhygienischen Schulung* (Erfurt: Stenger, 1934), 1. Original in WLTAV.

116. Frercks and Hoffmann, 1934, 3.

117. Frercks and Hoffmann, 1934, 5–20; pictures 3, 5, 7, 9, 11, 17, 18.

118. Frercks and Hoffmann, 1934, 17–18, pictures 24, 25, 25a, 26. The anti-Black nature of Nazi race rhetoric is also found in Karl Bareth and Alfred Vogel, *Erblehre und Rassenkunde für die Grund- und Hauptschule* (Baden: Konkordia, 1937), 98–99.

119. Frercks and Hoffmann, 1934, 18–19, pictures 27, 28, 29. An essay by Frercks from 1938 argued that choosing between environment and heredity as the most important influence in human development offered a false dichotomy. "Blood is blood," he wrote, and the environment did not change this eternal verity. See Rudolf Frercks, "Der Rassengedanke: Ein Wendepunkt der Erziehungslehre," *Weltanschauung und Schule* 2 (1938): 545–549.

120. Heinrich Krieger, "Die Trennung der Rassen im Schulwesen der Vereinigten Staaten und des Dritten Reiches," *Internationale Zeitschrift für Erziehung* 5 (1936): 344–356. A condensed version of Krieger's essay is found in *Völkische Beobachter*, 22 September 1936.

121. Hermann Giesecke, *Hitler's Pädagogen: Theorie und Praxis nationalsozial-istischer Erziehung* (Weinheim: Juventa, 1993), 21–22.

122. Hans Heinze, *Rasse und Erbe* (Halle: Schroedel, 1934), 59. Original in WLTAV, A1b/HEI/W.5636.

123. Exercises on skull and facial measurement, supported by detailed diagrams and charts, are found in the writing of Alfred Weis, headmaster of Helmholtzschule in Leipzig. See his *Einfache Versuche zur Vererbugslehre und Rassenkunde* (Leipzig: Quelle und Meyer, 1934). Original at IZG/WK451.

124. Heinze, 1934, 9.

125. Heinze, 1934, 5, 10, 12, 23–25, 58.

126. Sepp Burgstaller, *Erblehre, Rassenkunde und Bevölkerungspolitik* (Vienna:

Jugend und Volk, 1941). Original at University of Wisconsin-Madison Memorial Library, Cutter Section, QH/+431/+B97.

127. Burgstaller, 1941, 46.

128. Burgstaller, 1941, 37, 43, 46–48.

129. Burgstaller, 1941, 49, 52.

130. Erich Meyer and Werner Dittrich, *Kleine Erb- und Rassenkunde*. Ausgabe für Sachsen (Leipzig: Hirt und Sohn, 1934), 32–37, 50–62. Original in DIPF/Berlin under NS 5251.

131. Werner Dittrich, *Vererbung und Rasse: Hand und Hilfsbuch für den Lehrer* (Stuttgart: Franckh'sche Verlagshandlung, 1936), 73–76. Original in WLTAV/A1b/DIT. The anti-Black propaganda, perhaps engendered from Germany's colonial experience and the occupation of Black troops in the Rhineland after World War I, was often not very different from the pages of anti-Semitic teachings in curriculum materials. Dittrich, for example, urged school children never to play with a *"Negerbastard"* since mixed bloods, from their earliest childhood on, were incapable of grasping the culture and religion of pure-blooded peoples. The myth of Nordic pedagogy presented itself once again. See Dittrich, 1936, 76.

132. After brief stints in school administrative posts in Berlin-Mitte and Lyck (East Prussia), Albert Höft started work as a lecturer in German language and methods at the College for Teacher Education at Elbing in 1939. He began army service later that year that lasted almost two years. Subsequent responsibilities in teacher education institutions in Elbing and Graudenz in the Danzig district brought him to the end of the war. He continued work as an English translator and *Studienrat* at the Ratsgymnasium in Osnabrück until his retirement in 1965. Höft died in 1973. See Hesse, 1995, 360–361.

133. Albert Höft, *Arbeitsplan für erbbiologischen und rassenkundlichen Unterricht in der Schule unter Berücksichtigung der Rassenpflege, Familienkunde und Bevölkerungspolitik* (Osterwieck: Zickfeldt, 1934), 1–3, 8, 36–42. Original in Uni Hannover ERWS, NS 77.

134. Hauptschulungsamt der NSDAP, hrsg., *Schulungs-Unterlage: 3000 Jahre jüdischer Haß* (Berlin: NSDAP, 1943), 2. Original in archives of IZG/Db08.10.

135. Hauptschulamt, des NSDAP, 1943, 6–8.

136. Der Beauftragte des Führers für die Überwachung der gesamten geistigen und weltanschaulichen Schulung und Erziehung der NSDAP, hrsg., *Der Jude als Weltparasit* (Munich: Zentralverlag der NSDAP, 1943), 41. Original in archives of IZG/Db04.12(a).

137. Der Beauftragte des Führers, 1943, 10–11.

Chapter 4: The Jew as Cultural Outsider in History and Geography

1. Laura Hein and Mark Selden, eds. *Censoring History: Citizenship and Memory in Japan, Germany, and the United States* (Armonk, N.Y.: Sharpe, 2000); James Loewen, *Lies My Teacher Told Me: Everything Your American History Textbook Got Wrong* (New York: New Press, 1995).

2. For a variety of perspectives from those who witnessed the Night of the Broken Glass, see Jörg Wollenberg, ed. *The German Public and the Perse-*

cution of the Jews, 1933–1945 (Atlantic Highlands, N.J.: Humanities Press, 1996).

3. Hans Roepke, *Was muß Du wissen vom Dritten Reich? Nationalsozialistische Geschichtstabelle für Lehrzwecke in Frage und Antwort* (Berlin: Heinz Denckler 1935), 24–25. Original in WLTAV, B4d/B228.

4. Horst Gies, *Geschichtsunterricht unter der Diktatur Hitlers* (Weimar: Böhlau, 1992); Gilmer Blackburn, *Education in the Third Reich: Race and History in Nazi Textbooks* (Albany: SUNY Press, 1985); Helmut Genschel, "Geschichtsdidaktik und Geschichtsunterricht im Nationalsozialistischen Deutschland," in *Gesellschaft, Staat, Geschichtsunterricht,* hrsg. Klaus Bergmann and Gerhard Schneider (Düsseldorf: Schwann, 1982), 261–294; Karl Werner, *Das NS-Geschichtsbild und die deutsche Geschichtswissenschaft* (Stuttgart: Kohlhammer, 1976).

5. Adolf Hitler, *Mein Kampf* (Boston: Houghton Mifflin, 1971), 407–433.

6. RMWEVB, "Richtlinien für die einzelnen Unterrichtsfächer, in *Die Deutsche Volksschule im Dritten Reich,* hrsg. A. Klug (Breslau: Hirt, 1940), 126–130.

7. Hitler, *Mein Kampf,* 1971, 14–15.

8. RMWEVB, "Vererbungslehre und Rassenkunde im Unterricht," Erlaß vom 13. September 1933, *Amtsblatt des RMWEVB und der Unterrichtsverwaltungen der Länder,* 1, Jahrgang, 1935, 45.

9. RMWEVB, 1933, 45.

10. Kurt-Ingo Flessau, *Schule der Diktatur: Lehrpläne und Schulbücher des Nationalsozialismus* (Frankfurt am Main: Fischer, 1979), 69–132.

11. RMWEVB, 1933, 45.

12. For one of the earliest publications interpreting German history from the National Socialist Library, see Konrad Maß, *Deutsche Geschichte,* Heft 24 (Munich: Eher, 1931).

13. Patricia von Papen, "Schützenhilfe nationalsozialistischer Judenpolitik: Die Judenforschung des Reichsinstituts für Geschichte des neuen Deutschland, 1935–1945," in *Beseitigung des jüdischen Einflusses: Antisemitische Forschung, Eliten und Karrieren im Nationalsozialismus,* hrsg. Fritz Bauer Institut (Frankfurt: Campus, 1999), 17–42. SS doctor Joseph Mengele was a visiting scientist in the anthropology program at Kaiser Wilhelm Institute (KWI) under Verschuer from 1943 to 1945. During that same time, Mengele acted as Auschwitz camp doctor with the rank of SS captain and conducted research for Verschuer in the camp, see Benno Müller-Hill, *Murderous Science* (Plainview, N.Y.: Cold Spring Harbor Laboratory Press, 1998).

14. Wilhelm Grau, *Die Judenfrage als Aufgabe der neuen Geschichtsforschung* (Hamburg: Hanseatische Verlag, 1935), 9–12; Wilhelm Grau, *Die Judenfrage in der deutschen Geschichte* (Berlin: Teubner, 1937), 2–6.

15. Papen, 1999, 18.

16. Wilhelm Grau, *Die Judenfrage in der deutschen Geschichte* (Berlin: Teubner, 1937). The essay appeared a year before under the same title in *Vergangenheit und Gegenwart* 26 (1936): 193–209.

17. Theodor Fritsch, *Handbuch der Judenfrage: Die Wichtigsten Tatsachen zur Beurteilung des Jüdischen Volkes,* 49. Auflage (Leipzig: Hammer, 1944), 40–113. The Nazis honored Fritsch as "master teacher," or *Altmeister,* after his death in 1933. For a closer examination of Fritsch's contribution

to anti-Semitism in Germany, see George Mosse, *The Crisis of German Ideology: Intellectual Origins of the Third Reich* (New York: Grosset and Dunlap, 1964), 112–113, 141–142.

18. Grau, 1937, 3–15.

19. Grau, 1937, 18–32.

20. For an especially useful Nazi bibliographical resource on the Jewish question, see E. Wiegand, "Zur Geschichte des Judentums: Neueres Schrifttum zur Judenfrage," *Volk und Rasse* 13 (1938): 153–155.

21. *Der Nationalsozialistische Erzieher*, Nr. 42/1934, cited in Jochen Herring et al., *Schüleralltag im Nationalsozialismus* (Dortmund: Pädagogische Arbeitsstelle, 1984), 269.

22. Werner May, *Deutscher Nationalkatechismus: Was ein deutscher Junge und ein deutsches Mädel vom Dritten Reich wissen soll* (Breslau: Heinrich Handels, 1934), 24–26.

23. May, 1934, 24–25.

24. Georg Collischonn, *Geschichte und Volksaufgabe* (Frankfurt am Main: Winter, 1922); Max Maurenbrecher, *Völkischer Geschichtsunterricht* (Langensalza: Beltz, 1925). Maurenbrecher was a Lutheran minister and a leading member of the far-right German National People's Party after World War I. His teaching plans for history were both irrational and anti-Semitic in nature. Collischonn advocated dropping the history of ancient oriental cultures while reorienting pupils to a more focused study of history through German mythology. See Gies, 1992, 51–52.

25. Klaus Bergmann, "Imperialistische Tendenzen in Geschichstsdidaktik und Geschichtsunterricht ab 1890," in *Gesellschaft, Staat, Geschichtsunterricht*, hrsg. Klaus Bergmann and Gerhard Schneider (Düsseldorf: Schwann, 1982), 190–217.

26. Karl Hahn, "Rassenkunde des jüdischen Volkes," 8. Gang, 2. Auflage, in *Volk und Rasse: Das Neue Reich*, hrsg. Hahn (Wittenberg: Herrose's, 1935), 1. Original in WLTAV, Ald/HAH.

27. Ludwig Clauß, *Rasse und Seele: Eine Einführung in den Sinn der leiblichen Gestalt*, 8. Auflage (Munich: Lehmanns, 1937); Hans Günther, *Rassenkunde des jüdischen Volkes*, 2. Auflage (Munich: Lehmanns, 1930).

28. Hahn, 1935, "Rassenkunde des jüdischen Volkes," 1935, 1–2.

29. Hahn, 1935, "Rassenkunde des jüdischen Volkes," 1935, 3.

30. Hahn, 1935, "Rassenkunde des jüdischen Volkes," 3–4. The author qualified the use of the Nazi expression *Volksgenossen*, loosely translated in a racial and political sense as "national comrade." Hahn used the word to describe the Jews who, out of a strong rejection of pagan worship and a defense of Jewish law and religious practices, willingly died under the sword of attacking enemy forces representing King Antiochus during the early phase of the Maccabean revolt. The use of quotation marks around *"Volks"genossen* informed readers that Jewish fanatics who died under the sword out of religious conviction were certainly dedicated followers of Jewish tradition, but they were categorically rejected as part of the Nazi racial community. For a greater elucidation of this term so important to the daily lexicon of Nazi language, see Cornelia Schmitz-Berning, *Vokabular des Nationalsozialismus* (New York: de Gruyter, 1999), 660–664.

31. Hahn, "Rassenkunde des jüdischen Volkes," 1935, 3–5.

32. Karl Hahn, "Die Judenfrage," in *Volk und Rasse: Das Neue Reich* 2. Auflage, hrsg. Hahn (Wittenberg: Herrose's, 1935), 1.

33. Hahn, "Die Judenfrage," 1935, 2.

34. The recent book by James Carroll examined the legacy of Torquemada's involvement in the Spanish Inquisition. Carroll observed that Hitler "was less the beneficiary than the product of religious and racial assumptions that had their origins, perhaps, in the Jew-hating sermons of Saint John Chrysostom or Saint Ambrose, and certainly in the blood purity of Torquemada." See Carroll's *Constantine's Sword* (Boston: Houghton Mifflin, 2000), 477.

35. Hahn, "Die Judenfrage," 1935, 3.

36. Hahn, "Die Judenfrage," 1935, 4. See also a textbook written by Hans Warneck for the secondary school, third class. In this work, he attributed some satirical words to Luther, without citing any further source: "The Jews have a reason to stand up for themselves and greatly defy the masses. That is, they are born as the highest people on earth, from Abraham, Sarah, Isaac, Rebecca, Jacob and so on. We goyem (heathens) are against them and, before their eyes, are not humans, rather of scarce value since we poor worms were created from nothing." See Hans Warneck, *Geschichte des Deutschen Volkes von der Grundung des Ersten Reiches bis 1648* (Berlin: Oldenbourg, 1939), 97.

37. Richard Eichenauer, *Die Rasse als Lebensgesetz in Geschichte und Gesittung: Ein Wegweiser für die deutsche Jugend* (Berlin: Teubner, 1934), 81–82.

38. Eichenauer, 1934, 82. The author relied on the work of the geography professor Siegfried Passarge from the University of Hamburg in developing his argument about historical precedents of Jewish migration and settlement as a context for hatred against Jews. See Passarge's *Das Judentum als landschaftlich-ethnologisches Problem* (Munich: Lehmanns, 1929), 23–24. Original in Uni Hannover ERWS/NS1303. Passarge's thinking about geography and the Jewish question comes under closer scrutiny later in this chapter.

39. Ludwig Schemann, *Die Rasse in Geisteswissenschaft: Studien zur Geschichte des Rassengedankes*, vol. 1 (Munich: Lehmanns, 1928–1931), 131; Eichenauer, 1934, 82–83.

40. Eichenauer, 1934, 84.

41. Eichenauer, 1934, 85–86.

42. Eichenauer, 1934, 123–124. See also Guid Waldmann, hrsg. *Rasse und Musik* (Berlin: Vieweg, 1939); Paul Schultze-Naumburg, *Kunst und Rasse* (Munich: Lehmanns, 1928).

43. Reinhold Krause, "Die Judenfrage im Unterricht," in *Rassische Erziehung als Unterrichtsgrundsatz der Fachgebiete*, hrsg. Rudolf Benze and Alfred Pudelsko (Frankfurt am Main: Diesterweg, 1937), 199; Eichenauer, 1934, 125; Alan Steinweis, *Art, Ideology and Economics in Nazi Germany* (Chapel Hill: University of North Carolina Press, 1993), 104–126; Harald Welzer, hrsg. *Das Gedächtnis der Bilder: Ästhetik und National Sozialismus* (Tübingen: Diskord, 1995).

44. Dieter Klagges articulated one of the strongest Volkish interpretations of the Gospels to be found anywhere in Weimar Germany. See his *Das Urevangelium Jesu, der deutsche Glaube* (Leipzig: Armanen, 1925). Also, see

his *Reichtum und soziale Gerechtigkeit: Grundfragen einer nationalsozialistischen Volkswirtschaftslehre*, 2. Auflage (Leipzig: Armanen, 1933); *Heldischer Glaube* (Leipzig: Armanen, 1934); *Kampf um Marxismus*, 5. Auflage (Munich: Eher, 1932); *Geschichte als nationalpolitische Erziehung* (Frankfurt am Main: Diesterweg, 1936); *Idee und System: Vorträge an der deutschen Hochschule für Politik über Grundfragen des nationalsozialistischen Weltanschauung* (Leipzig: Armanen, 1934); *An aller Völker der Erde* (Kreuzau-Stockhein: Alma Druck, 1972–1973); *Eine Tugend gegen* alle *Todsünden: Das organisches Weltbild* (Bassum-Dimhausen: Alma Druck, 1974).

45. Klagges, *Geschichte als nationalpolitische Erziehung*, 1936, 87–88.

46. Klagges, 1936, 141.

47. Klagges, 1936, 142–143.

48. *Gedankensplitter und Auskünfte zur Namensänderung einer Neuköllner Schule: 1907–1982* (Berlin: Albert Schweitzer Oberschule, 1982), 54.

49. *Kamps Stoffverteilungen für alle Jahrgänge der Volksschule*. Bearbeitet von H. Hermeler. 2. Teil. Nach dem Richtlinien vom 15. Dezember 1939. Bochum, 1940, 2–7.

50. *Kamps Stoffverteilungen*, 1939, 7–8. The Nazi intent of providing a strong place for prehistory in the curriculum is evidenced in Fritz Schwendt, *Handbuch für den Unterricht der deutschen Vorgeschichte in Ostdeutschland* (Breslau: Hirt, 1934); Hans Philipp, "Wege und Irrwege im Unterricht der Ur- und Frühgeschichte," *Die Deutsche Höhere Schule* 4 (1937): 574–584; Paul Vogel, "Vorgeschichte," in *Rassische Erziehung als Unterrichtsgrundsatz der Fachgebiete*, hrsg. Rudolf Benze and Alfred Pudelko (Frankfurt am Main: Diesterweg, 1937), 81–89.

51. See Hermann Eilers, *Die nationalpolitische Schulpolitik: Eine Studie zur Funktion der Erziehung im totalitären Staat* (Opladen: Westdeutschen Verlag, 1963), 28–33.

52. Bouhler to Rosenberg, "An die Mitlgieder des Reichsausschusses für das Schul- und Unterrichtsschriftum," April 1941, 65, BArchBerlin, NS8/209 Schul-und Unterrichtsschriftum. Kanzlei Rosenberg.

53. *Parisier Tageblatt*, 24 May 1934, the clippings collection of WLTAV; Dieter Klagges, hrsg. *Volk und Führer*, 2. Auflage (Frankfurt am Main: Diesterweg, 1941, 19.

54. Hans Warneck and Willi Matschke, *Geschichte für Volksschulen* (Leipzig: Velhagen und Klasing, 1942), 49.

55. Warneck and Matschke, 1942, 59. For an engaging discussion of distinctions between the anti-Semitic legacies of Luther and the Third Reich, see Steven Katz, *The Holocaust in Historical Context*, vol. 1 (New York: Oxford University Press, 1994), 393–394.

56. Warneck and Matschke, 1942, 96–97.

57. Warneck and Matschke, 1942, 122.

58. Warneck and Matschke, 1942, 123.

59. Alfred Vogel, *Erblehre und Rassenkunde in bildlicher Darstellung* (Stuttgart: Nationale Literatur, 1938), teaching chart #57; Warneck and Matschke, 1942, 144.

60. Warneck and Matschke, 1942, 145.

61. Warneck and Matschke, 1942, 186.

62. Warneck and Matschke, 1942, 242.

63. Johannes Mahnkopf, *Von der Uhrzeit zum Grossdeutschen Reich* (Leipzig: Teubner, 1941), 1, 61, 115–116, 123, 126, 132–134, 137–138, 140–142, 151, 173. Walter Gehl's *Geschichte für Mittelschulen* (Breslau: Hirt, 1940–1941), developed by Otto Losch, Heinrich Pahlte, and Eric Weschollet, remained one of the most popular series for middle school pupils. Substantive references to Jews are included in the volumes published for classes three (60–61), four (97–99), five (101–102, 147), and six (110–111).

64. Dieter Klagges, hrsg., *Volk und Fuhrer: Deutsche Geschichte für Schulen.* Ausgabe für Mittelschulen. Bearbeitet von Karl Grunwald (Frankfurt am Main: Diesterweg, 1943), 204. Dieter Klagges centered most of his activities as history textbook editor on volumes intended for the secondary school population, although his treatise on *History and Instruction as National Political Education* (1936) remained highly recommended by education authorities for both elementary and secondary teachers. For his textbook articulation of the Jewish question in modern German history published for the *Oberschule*, see the following references to the *Volk und Führer* series: *Preußen gestaltet das Reich* (Klasse 4), bearbeitet von Gerhard Staat und Walter Franke (1941), 191–195; *Nun wieder Volk* (Klasse 5), bearbeitet von Walter Franke (1941), 14–19, 127–129, 168–169, 270–271; *Deutsches Ringen um Lebensraum, Freiheit und Einheit* (Klasse 7), bearbeitet von Eugen Huth et al (1943), 31–32, 214–215, 268–270.

65. Wilhelm Rottenrodt, *Deutsche Führer und Meister: Geschichtliche Einzelbilder aus Gegenwart und Vergangenheit* (Frankfurt am Main: Diesterweg, 1937), 131–132.

66. Rottenrodt, 1937, 132–133. The inside cover of this collection included a famous press photo by Heinrich Hoffmann, Hitler's court photographer, showing Hitler surrounded by young admirers. The book appeared as part of the series edited by Klagges under *Volk und Führer*. The integration of anti-Semitic themes and messages was rather uneven in Nazi collections of history stories intended for young children. See, for example, Hermann Funke's *Geschichtserzählungen* (Leipzig: Teubner, 1940). His stories, thirty-two in number, emphasized the role of Great Men in History with nationalistic narratives about Frederick the Great, Otto von Bismarck, Horst Wessel, Adolf Hitler, Otto the Great, and others. Maria Theresa of Austria was the only female political figure addressed. Only one piece, a story about Martin Luther, assumed an anti-Semitic tone (84–87).

67. Johann von Leers, *Für das Reich: Deutsche Geschichte in Geschichtserzählungen* (Leipzig: Beltz, 1940), 305–312.

68. Leers, 1940, 313–321. Veiled insults were part of the anti-Semitic language used by Leers in this story. Putting words into the mouth of Rothschild, Leers used the compound expression, *Schlattenschammes*. *Schammes* is actually a Yiddish word meaning "sextant." Many thanks to Yeshaya Metal from the Library of the Yivo Institute in New York City.

69. Leers, 1940, 322–330. Leers wrote an essay for teachers on "The Question of Jewry from the Viewpoint of the Nordic Race" in his *Rassische Geschichtsbetrachtung: Was muß der Lehrer davon wissen?* (Leipzig: Beltz, 1934), 40–50.

70. Emil Jörns, *Erziehung zu Eugenischer Lebensführung als Aufgabe der*

Volksschule (Berlin: Metzner, 1933), 7, 59–66; Peter Weingart, Jürgen Kroll, and Kurt Bayertz, *Rasse, Blut und Gene: Geschichte der Eugenik und Rassenhygiene in Deutschland* (Frankfurt am Main: Suhrkamp, 1992), 367–389; Paul Weindling, *Health, Race and German Politics Between National Unifikcation and Nazism, 1870–1945* (New York: Cambridge University Press, 1993), 474–484.

71. See Karl Haushofer, *Geographie und Weltmacht* (Berlin: Vowinckel, 1925).

72. Compare Passarge's claim for a more scientific and dispassionate approach to anti-Semitic thinking with Hitler's letter to Gemlich in 1919 on the need for a "rational anti-Semitism" cited in the introduction.

73. Siegfried Passarge, *Das Judentum als landschaftlich-ethnologisches Problem* (Munich: Lehmanns, 1929), 5–6, 45–46, 49–54, 324–397.

74. Konrad Bahr, "Die Rassenfrage im Unterricht," *Deutsche Höhere Schule* 1 (1934): 109–115.

75. Walther Jantzen, *Die Geographie im Dienste der nationalpolitischen Erziehung: Ein Ergänzungsheft zu den Lehrbüchern der Erdkunde*, 2. Auflage (Breslau: Hirt, 1936), 37–41; *Erziehung und Unterricht in der Volksschule* (Berlin: 1940), 18, cited in Flessau, *Schule der Diktatur*, 1979, 87. For the most detailed *Richtlinien*, or content outlines, for the teaching of geography and other subjects in the elementary school from 1939, see A. Kluger, *Die Deutsche Volksschule Im Dritten Reich* (Breslau: Hirt, 1940), 129–130.

76. Jantzen, 1936, 18–19, Flessau, 1979, 86.

77. Jantzen, 1936, 19–20. For an engaging history of German hatred and fear of the Jews, what Klaus Fischer called "Hitler's obsession," see his *History of an Obsession: German Judeophobia and the Holocaust* (New York: Continuum, 1998).

78. Jantzen, 1936, 19–20.

79. Jantzen, 1936, 20.

80. Walther Jantzen, *Geopolitik Im Kartenbild* (Berlin: Vowinckel, 1941).

81. Jantzen, 1941, maps 1, 2, 4, 5, pp. 1–5.

82. Jantzen, 1941, map 8, "Die Verbreitung des Stammes Rothschild in Europa," p. 7. Johann von Leers delighted in smearing the Rothschild family with an inflammatory caricature of Nathan Rothschild holding the reins of a vulture symbolizing bankruptcies. See his *Wie kam der Jude zum Geld?* (Berlin: Fritsch, 1939), 51. The Hitler Youth published a special volume in 1940 on Jewish influence in England under *Juden und Lords: Hand in Hand*. Folge 6., edited by the Reich Youth Leadership of the NSDAP.

83. Jantzen, 1941, chart 12, "Der Zustrom der Juden nach Berlin," p. 10.

84. Jantzen, 1941, chart 16, "Anteile der Juden an einzelnen Berufen," p. 12.

85. Jantzen, 1941, chart 23, "Die Lage Palästinas im Verkehrsnetz des nahen Osten," p. 16.

86. Konrad Olbricht and Hermann Kärgel, *Deutschland als Ganze*. Der Erdkunde Unterricht in der Volks- und Mittelschule, 9. Auflage (Berlin: Zickfeldt, 1938), 63–64.

87. Johann von Leers, "Der gegenwartige Stand des Judenproblems in der Welt," *Der Deutsche Erzieher* 5 (18 November 1938): 405.

88. Leers, 1938, 404–405.

Chapter 5: Exemplars of Anti-Semitic Literature
for Children

1. Hans Keipert, "Die Judenfrage im Unterricht," in *Handbuch für den Biologieunterricht*, Lieferung 3, hrsg. Ferdinand Rossner (Langensalza: Beltz, 1940), 244–248.
2. Christa Kamenetsky, *Children's Literature in Hitler's Germany: The Cultural Policy of National Socialism* (London: Ohio University Press, 1984); Peter Aly, *Jugendliteratur im Dritten Reich: Dokumente und Kommentare* (Hamburg: Verlag für Buchmarktforschung, 1965).
3. Fritz Hippler, *Staat und Gesellschaft bei Mill, Marx, Lagarde: Ein Beitrag zum soziologischen Denken der Gegenwart* (Berlin: Junker und Dünnhaupt, 1941), 161, 230; Josef Nadler, *Literaturgeschichte des deutschen Volkes: Dichtung der deutschen Stämme und Landschaften* (Berlin: Junker und Dünnhaupt, 1941), both cited in Kamenetsky, 1984, 9, 27.
4. See Elke Peters, *Nationalistisch-völkische Bildungspolitik in der Weimarer Republik* (Weinheim: Beltz, 1972); Ernst Schwarzinger, "Deutsch," in *Mitteilungsblatt des NSLB* (February, 1940), 10.
5. Joshua Trachtenberg, *The Devil and the Jews: The Medieval Conception of the Jew and Its Relation to Modern Antisemitism* (New Haven, Conn.: Yale University Press, 1993), 47.
6. Aus dem Tagebuch der Christa Laufer, 7 May 1938, in Jochen Hering et al., *Schülertag im Nationalsozialismus* (Dortmund: Pädagogische Arbeitsstelle, 1984), 263.
7. Ernst Hiemer, *Der Giftpilz* (Nuremberg: Der Stürmer, 1938), 2, 4. Hiemer also wrote *Der Jude im Sprichwort des Völker* (Nuremberg: Der Stürmer, 1942).
8. Hiemer, *Der Giftpilz*, 1938, 5.
9. Hiemer, *Der Giftpilz*, 1938, 6–9; Günther Ginzel, *Jüdischer Alltag in Deutschland, 1933–1945* (Düsseldorf: Droste, 1993), 83.
10. Hiemer, *Der Giftpilz*, 1938, 13–17; Dieter Rossmeissl, *"Ganz Deutschland wird zum Führer halten": Zur politischen Erziehung in den Schulen des Dritten Reiches* (Jena: Fischer, 1985), 117.
11. Hiemer, *Der Giftpilz*, 1938, 18–20.
12. Hiemer, *Der Giftpilz*, 1938, 46–48. Translation from the Friends of Europe, *The Poisonous Mushroom* (1938) with a foreword by the bishop of Durham, 17. Copy in WLTelAviv.
13. Hiemer, *Der Giftpilz*, 1938, 21–23.
14. Hiemer, *Der Giftpilz*, 1938, 24–26, 39–42.
15. Hiemer, *Der Giftpilz*, 1938, 27–34.
16. Hiemer, *Der Giftpilz*, 1938, 43–45; see also Steven Katz, *The Holocaust in Historical Context*, vol. 1 (New York: Oxford University Press, 1994), 271–273; Leon Poliakov, *The History of Anti-Semitism*, vol. 1, trans. Richard Howard (London: Elek, 1965), 56–64. "Ritual Murder: The Great Secret of World Jewry" was the lead story in an edition of Julius Streicher's *Der Stürmer* from May of 1939.
17. Hiemer, *Der Giftpilz*, 1938, 49–52.
18. Hiemer, *Der Giftpilz*, 1938, 53–56.
19. Speech of the Reichsführer-SS Heinrich Himmler at Meeting of SS Major

Generals at Posen, 4 October 1943. Partial Translation of Document 1919-PS in National Archives and Records Administration printed in *Prologue* 25 (1994): 156–158.

20. Hiemer, *Der Giftpilz*, 1938, 57–59.
21. Hiemer, *Der Giftpilz*, 1938, 60–62.
22. Ernst Hiemer, *Der Pudelmopsdackelpinscher und andere besinnliche Erzahlungen* (Nuremberg: Der Stürmer, 1940), 58–61.
23. Hiemer, 1940, 61–64.
24. Hiemer, 1940, 23–25. The author's writing reaffirmed a famous speech delivered by Hitler before the Reichstag in January of 1939 in which he warned that dire consequences would follow for the Jews if they drew Germany into another world war.
25. Hiemer, 1940, 31–34. The association of Jews with a foul body odor had been a delusion of medieval society. For an enlightening discussion of medieval delusions about Jews, see Klaus Fischer, *The History of an Obsession: German Judeophobia and the Holocaust* (New York: Continuum, 1998), 30–37.
26. Hiemer, 1940, 72–73. The symbol of the poisonous snake also appeared among the 140 instructional drawings for Sepp Burgstaller's *Erblehre, Rassenkunde und Bevölkerungspolitik*, (Vienna: Jugend und Volk, 1941).
27. Hiemer, 1940, 81.
28. Hiemer, 1940, 82–83.
29. Hiemer, 1940, 88–91. One of the most intolerable principles of Jewish intellectual life, according to Hiemer, was the assumption that "all people are the same," a call for equality he described as "a despicable lie." See 90.
30. See Klaus Fischer, *History of an Obsession* (New York: Continuum, 1998), 35.
31. Elvira Bauer, *Trau keinem Jud' auf grüner Heid: Ein Bilderbuch für Gross und Klein* (Nuremberg: Der Stürmer, 1936), 1.
32. Bauer, 1936, 3.
33. Bauer, 1936, 3.
34. Bauer, 1936, 11–12.
35. Bauer, 1936, 10, 14. The obligatory deference to their patron, Julius Streicher, was evident in the writing of authors working for the Der Stürmer publishing house. Similar to Ernst Hiemer's, Bauer's contribution praised Streicher as a civic model for young anti-Semites since he was the biggest target for Jewish hatred. See 15–16.
36. Bauer, 1936, 18.
37. Bauer, 1936, 19, 21. Two brief writings on the Jewish question intended for a young readership appeared in Kurt Shrey, *Du und Dein Volk* (Köln: NSDAP, Gau Köln-Achen. Amt für Erzieher, n.d.), 28–29 and Franz Lüke, *Rassen-ABC* (Bochum: Kamp, 1934), 66–70.
38. Phillip Bouhler, *Kampf um Deutschland: Ein Lesebuch für deutsche Jugend* (Berlin: Zentralverlag des NSDAP, 1938), 14–16, 56, 98. Copy stamped from the Library of the Reichsinstitut für Geschichte des neuen Deutschland.
39. Bouhler, 1938, 27–28. A review of Bouhler's volume appeared in the essay "History of Nazi Movement: A School Reading-Book Prepared," in *Manchester Guardian*, 10 June 1938.

40. Bouhler to Rosenberg, "An die Mitlgieder des Reichsausschusses für das Schul-und Unterrichtsschriftum," April 1941, 65, BArchBerlin, NS8/209 Schul-und Unterrichtsschriftum. Kanzlei Rosenberg.

41. Phillip Bouhler, *Adolf Hitler: A Short Sketch of His Life* (Berlin: Terramare, 1938), 6, 13.

42. Reichsstelle für das Schul-und Unterrichtsschriftum, hrsg., *Deutsches Lesebuch für Volksschulen* (Berlin: Deutscher Schulverlag, 1943), 4–5. Contrast this volume of readings with the publication of two overtly anti-Semitic thematic curriculum booklets for teachers, examined in chapter 3, which also appeared in 1943. For a piece coming out of the office of Alfred Rosenberg, see Der Beauftragte des Führers für die Überwachung der gesamten geistigen und weltanschaulichen Schulung und Erziehung der NSDAP, hrsg., *Der Jude als Weltparasit* (Munich: Zentralverlag der NSDAP, 1943), 41 and also an instructional pamphlet published by the Main School Office of the Nazi Party under Reichsorganisationsleiter der NSDAP, Hauptschulungsamt, hrsg., *Schulung-Unterlage: 3000 Jahre jüdischer Haß* (Berlin: NSDAP, 1943).

43. Emil Jörns and Julius Schwab, *Rassenhygienische Fibel: Der Deutschen Jugend Zuliebe Geschrieben* (Berlin: Metzner, 1935), 38–48. Schwab, the reader will recall from chapter 3, also authored anti-Semitic proverbs in *Rassenpflege im Sprichwort: Eine volkstümliche Sammlung* (Leipzig: Fröhlich, 1937).

44. Jörns and Schwab, *Rassenhygienische Fibel*, 1935, 100–101. For a story-line intended for middle and secondary school audiences, see Ernst Streit, *Wissenwertiges für die deutschblütige Jugend* (Lorch: Rohm, 193?). Streit told the story of Anna Weise, a young women who drowned herself out of shame for having sexual relations with a Jewish man. Not unusual was the author's portrayal of a young German man, known here as Erich Burkhardt, as the protagonist and authority figure instructing several other women about the threat of "racial disgrace" that came at the hands of the Jews as sexual predators.

45. Johannes Dannheufer and Arno Kreher, *Zur Methodik einer politischen Leibeserziehung* (Berlin: Limpert, 1937), 8, 17–18.

46. Bruno Malitz, *Die Leibesübungen in der nationalsozialistischen Idee* (Munich: Eher, 1934), 42–45.

47. Otto Rauscher, *Volk und Leibeserziehung*, 1942, 114f., quoted in Hajo Bernett, *Nationalsozialistische Leibeserziehung: Eine Dokumentation ihrer Theorie und Organisation* (Schorndorf: Hofmann, 1966), 40. See also Bernett's *Der jüdische Sport in nationalsozialistischen Deutschland, 1933–1938* (Schorndorf: Hofmann, 1978). A guide for German studies and political education for groups in the Association of German Gymnastics included a section offering advice to gymnasts in "the struggle against Jewry" along with notes explaining the "secret of Jewish power." See Friedrich Zenker, *Deutschkunde: Hilfsbuch für die politische Erziehung in den Vereinen der Deutschen Turnerschaft*, 4. Auflage (Berlin: Limpert, 1934), 271–274.

48. Wilhelm Schneemann, *Der Dietwart* (1938), 442, cited in Bernett, 1966, 39–40.

Chapter 6: Conclusion

1. *Nuremberg Trial Proceedings*, vol. 12, 29 April 1946, Streicher Testimony. Retrieved 22 August 2001, from the Avalon Law Project at Yale University website: http://www.yale.edu/lawweb/avalon/imt

2. Quoted in Hans Keipert, "Die Judenfrage im Unterricht," in *Handbuch für den Biologieunterricht*, hrsg. Ferdinand Rossner (Langensalza: Beltz, 1940), 247.

3. Klaus Fischer, *The History of an Obsession: German Judeophobia and the Holocaust* (New York: Continuum, 1998), 138.

4. Änne Bäumer-Schleinkofer, *Nazi Biology and Schools* (New York: Peter Lang, 1995), xiii.

5. Anna Merritt and Richard Merritt, eds. *Public Opinion in Occupied Germany: The OMGUS Surveys, 1945–1949* (Chicago: University of Illinois Press, 1970), 105–106, 146–148, 239–240. Results from OMGUS surveys and interviews drawing from the postwar German populace, like any sources of a similar nature, must take into account the limited scope of the sample and the context. The repeat surveys on prejudice and anti-Semitism from December of 1946 and April of 1948 drew from a sample of 3,006 persons in the American zone and 409 in the American sector of Berlin. Report 122, released in May of 1948, noted that 503,000 Jews populated Germany in 1933. In 1948, this figure had dropped to less than 20,000 (239–240).

6. John Dewey, "My Pedagogic Creed," in *John Dewey on Education*, ed. Reginald Archambault (Chicago: University of Chicago Press, 1964), 427–439.

7. Daniel Goldhagen, *Hitler's Willing Executioners: Ordinary Germans and the Holocaust* (New York: Knopf, 1996), 383, 484–488. See also his *A Moral Reasoning: The Catholic Church during the Holocaust and Today* (New York: Knopf, 2000).

8. Yehuda Bauer, *Rethinking the Holocaust* (New Haven, Conn.: Yale University Press, 2001), 96–97.

9. See a summary of Raul Hilberg's keynote address before an international conference, "The Holocaust: Art/Politics/Law," at the University of Alberta, *Edmonton Journal* (30 October 1997). The proceedings from this remarkable interdisciplinary conference are published by Frederick Decoste and Bernard Schwartz, eds., *The Holocaust's Ghost: Writings on Art, Politics, Law, and Education* (Edmonton: University of Alberta Press, 2000).

Glossary

Anschluss Union of Austria with Germany in 1938.

Anti-Semitism Prejudice against and fear of Jews, either religiously or racially, or both. The term was first applied to a movement of opposition to Jews in the second half of the nineteenth century. [*Reprinted with permission of Simon Wiesenthal Center.*]

Arierparagraph Passed in April of 1933, the Aryan Paragraph, as part of the "the Law for the Restoration of the Professional Civil Service," called for the removal of Jews and Jewish influence from positions in the government bureaucracy.

Aryan race "Aryan" was originally applied to people who spoke any of the Indo-European languages—which had nothing to do with race. The Nazis, however, applied the term to people of "proven," non-Jewish, purely Teutonic "racial" background. Their aim was to avoid the bastardization of the German race, and they considered the main task of the state to preserve the ancient racial elements. [*Reprinted with permission of Simon Wiesenthal Center.*]

Entjudung The gradual and eventually complete suppression of Jews from the professions and the economic life of the Reich. The term eventually took on a more sinister meaning with the forced collection and sale of Jewish businesses and property followed by the subsequent deportation and mass murder of the Jews.

Erbgesundheitspflege Care of hereditary health

Familienkunde The study of families in relation to racial health and marriage policies.

Fremdblütig Foreign blooded, in contrast to German blooded as defined by the *Nuremberg Laws*.

Fremdrassig Foreign racial features or qualities.

Gleichschaltung The process of placing all institutions under the full control of the Nazi dictatorship, a kind of "meshing of the gears."

Judenfrage The Jewish question.

Judenfrei "Free of Jews," also used interchangeably with *Judenrein*, meaning cleansed of Jews." Both expressions reflected an escalation of persecution of the Jews under the Third Reich in the economy, geographical location, the professions, and government administration.

Judengegner In some cases, curriculum writers like Erich Malitius (1935, 3) used this word in the place of "anti-Semite" since the latter expression suggested a hatred for both Jews and Arabs. Arabs were also considered Semites and, according to the German Foreign Ministry, potential allies for the Third Reich.

Jud Süß German anti-Semitic movie directed by Viet Harlan in 1940. First shown in Venice, the movie was rated by the Propaganda Ministry as "especially valuable politically and artistically—worthwhile for young people." It portrayed a scheming and mentally depraved Jewish financier, Joseph Süß Openheimer (1648–1738), adviser to the Duke Karl Alexander of Württemberg. Citing these qualities as typical for the Jews, Harlan's screenplay suggested that anti-Semitism was a logical defense against Jewish immorality. The film incited attacks on Jewish individuals and businesses. [Christian Zentner and Friedemann Bedürftig, eds., *The Encyclopedia of the Third Reich*, vol. 1 (1991), 447–448.

Kristallnacht Night of Broken Glass, a violent pogrom leveled against the German Jewish community by the SA on 9–10 November 1938. Using the pretext of Ambassador Ernst vom Rath's assassination in Paris by the young Herschel Grynszpan, stormtroopers burned 191 synagogues across Germany. Almost 100 Jews lost their lives and more than 30,000 faced internment in concentration camps.

Machtergreifung The Nazi seizure of power on 30 January 1933 marking Hitler's appointment as German chancellor.

Mischlinge Mixed bloods.

Nuremberg Laws Promulgated on 15 September 1935, these laws came to symbolize the anti-Semitic mind-set of the Nazi racial state and the racial definition of citizenship under the Third Reich. Germans were forbidden to marry or have sexual relations with Jews or to hire female domestic servants under the age of forty-five, thus resurrecting the old anti-Semitic stereotype of Jewish sexual perversity. Jews could not be citizens of Germany and were forbidden to fly the colors of the Reich. Jewish civil servants faced forced retirement at the end of 1935. Defined as *Volljudisch* or fully Jewish by race were those descended from at least three full-blooded Jewish grandparents. A grandparent was considered Jewish if he or she belonged to a Jewish religious community. This critical definition of who constituted a Jew by bloodlines also extended to those partly Jewish nationals who claimed two fully Jewish grandparents and who married a Jewish person or joined Jewish congregations after the adoption of the Nuremberg Laws.

Rasse Race, the "cornerstone of the National Socialist world view" [*Volks-Brockhaus*, 1940, 555].

Rassenfeinde Race enemy.

Rassenfrage Race question. Julius Streicher, the vociferous anti-Semitic mouthpiece of *Der Stürmer*, told teachers that "the National Socialist state demanded *from* its teachers the education of German children on the question of *race*. The race question, however, is the Jewish question *for* the German people" [(Julius Streicher, foreword to *Die Judenfrage im Unterricht*, by Fritz Fink (1937)].

Rassenhass Race hatred.

Rassenhygiene Race hygiene. The Nazi regime expressed a preference for the *more "Germanized"* expression of eugenics (*Eugenik*) through *Rassenhygiene*, a term originally introduced by Alfred Ploetz in 1895.

Rassenkunde A curriculum term referring to racial science.

Rassenmischung Race mixing, seen as a defilement of Aryan blood through mixing with racial undesirables.

Rassenseele Race soul, a mystical reflection of the *Völkisch* tradition.

Rassenschande Race defilement, deemed a serious offense under Nazi law and institutionalized under the *Nuremberg Laws* of 1935 in regard to Jews as well as Germans who married Jews.

Rassenreinheit Race purity, the goal of race hygiene.

Staatsangehörigkcit Subjects belonging to the state, the legal status for the Jews legitimized by the *Nuremberg Laws* of 1935.

Der Stürmer Weekly anti-Semitic newspaper edited by Julius Streicher, Gauleiter of Franconia.

Schwarze Schmach "The black shame." Propaganda expression originating in the Weimar Republic and later exploited by the Nazis that referred to the French occupation of the Rhineland by Black African troops from French colonies after the German defeat in World War I. The incendiary nature of this language was further exploited by the reference to the "Rhineland bastards," the alleged offspring of Black occupation troops and German women.

Völkisch Anglicized as "Volkish" in the text. Almost impossible to wholly and accurately translate into English because of the historical context and strong cultural rootedness of the term, *Völkisch* refers to a mystical union of blood and soil as central to the cultural identity of the German people. Hitler, in particular, imbued the expression with both racial and anti-Semitic overtones.

Volks-Brockhaus (1940, 728) defined *Völkisch* as a sense of the "national with an emphasis on the foundational values of race and characteristic values of a people."

Volksgemeinschaft National community, conceived primarily in a racial sense.

Vererbungslehre Genetics.

Weltanschauung. Called a "linguistic mainstay of the Third Reich" by Victor Klemperer (1999, 185), this expression connotes a worldview both racial and anti-Semitic in nature. Hitler frequently used the word in *Mein Kampf*, calling his own racial anti-Semitism a "fanatical world view" more important than a political party in mobilizing the masses to victory over the competing Marxist worldview.

Bibliography

PUBLISHED WORKS FROM THE NAZI PERIOD (1933–1945)

"Alfred Rosenberg über Aufgaben des Lehrers und Erziehers." *Weltanschauung und Schule* 2 (1938): 512–516.

Bahr, Konrad. "Die Rassenfrage im Unterricht." *Deutsche Höhere Schule* 1 (1934): 109–115.

Bareth, Karl, and Alfred Vogel. *Erblehre und Rassenkunde für die Grund- und Hauptschule*. Baden: Konkordia, 1937.

Bauer, Elvira. *Trau keinem Jud' auf grüner Heid: Ein Bilderbuch für Gross und Klein*. Nuremberg: Der Stürmer, 1936.

Bennecke, Fritz. *Handbuch für die Schulungsarbeit in der Hitler Jugend: Vom Deutschen Volk und seinem Lebensraum*. Berlin: Zentralverlag des NSDAP, 1937.

Benze, Rudolf. *Rasse und Schule*. Braunschweig: Applelhaus, 1934.

———. *Nationalpolitische Erziehung im Dritten Reich*. Berlin: Junker und Dünnhaupt, 1936.

Bouhler, Phillip. *Kampf um Deutschland: Ein Lesebuch fur die deutsche Jugend*. Munich: Zentralverlag des NSDAP, 1938.

———. *Adolf Hitler: Das Werden einer Volksbewegung*. Lübeck: Coleman, 1943.

Brohmer, Paul. *Biologieunterricht und völkische Erziehung*. Frankfurt-am-Main: Moritz, 1933 and 1936a.

———. *Bekämpfung der Rassensünden durch den Nationalosozialistischen Staat*. 2. Auflage. Berlin: Osterwieck, circa 1936b.

———. *Der Unterricht in der Lebenskunde*. Berlin: Zickfeldt, 1943.

———. *Fauna von Deutschland*. 16. Auflage. Heidelberg: Quelle und Meyer, 1984.

Burgdorfer, Friedrich. *Deutsches Volk im Not*. Leipzig: Velhagen und Klosing, 1933.

Burgstaller, Sepp. *Erblehre, Rassenkunde und Bevölkerungspolitik*. Vienna: Jugend und Volk, 1941.

Clauß, Ludwig. *Rasse und Seele*. 6. Auflage. Munich: Lehmanns, 1936.

Cretius, Paul, and Martin Spielhagen. *Ziele und Wege des neuen Volksschulunterrichts*. Berlin: Zickfeldt, 1940.

Dannheufer, Johannes, and Arno Kreher. *Zur Methodik einer politischen Leibeserziehung*. Berlin: Limpert, 1937.

Der Beauftragte des Führers für die Überwachung der gesamten geistigen und weltanschaulichen Schulung und Erziehung der NSDAP, hrsg. *Der Jude als Weltparasit*. Munich: Zentralverlag der NSDAP, 1943.

Der Stürmer. May 1939.

"Die Arbeitern als Preisträger." *Fränkische Tageszeitung.* 31 December 1936. Clippings Collection WLTAV.

Dittrich, Werner. *Vererbung und Rasse: Hand und Hilfsbuch für den Lehrer.* Stuttgart: Fränckh'sche Verlagshandlung, 1936.

———. "Rassenkunde und Biologieunterricht." *Nationalsozialistisches Bildungswesen* 4 (January 1937a): 18–22.

———. *Erziehung zum Judengegner: Hinweise zur Behandlung der Judenfrage im rassenpolitischen Unterricht* Munich: Deutscher Volksverlag, 1937b.

———. "Der Endkampf gegen das Judentum." *Der Deutsche Erzieher* 6 (1939): 403–409.

Dobers, Ernst. "Zur weltanschaulichen Begründung von Rassenkunde und Rassenpflege." *Deutsche Volkserziehung* 1 (1934): 34–39.

———. *Rassenkunde: Forderung und Dienst.* Leipzig: Klinkhardt, 1936a and 1939.

———. *Die Zeitung im Dienste der Rassenkunde.* Leipzig: Klinkhardt, 1936b.

———. *Die Judenfrage: Stoff und Behandlung in der Schule.* 3. Auflage. Leipzig: Klinkhardt, 1939.

Dobers, Ernst, and Kurt Higelke, hrsg. *Rassenpolitische Unterrichtspraxis: Der Rassengedanke in der Unterrichtsgestaltung der Volksschulfächer.* Leipzig: Klinkhardt, 1938.

Eichenauer, Richard. *Die Rasse als Lebensgesetz in Geschichte und Gesittung: Ein Wegweiser für die deutsche Jugend.* Berlin: Teubner, 1934.

"Einmal hin im Katholizismus und einmal her im Protestantismus." *Der Deutsche Erzieher* 5 (1938): 446–447.

Fetscher, Rainer. *Rassenhygiene: Ein erste Einführung für Lehrer.* Leipzig: Verlag der Dürr'schen Buchhandlung, 1933.

Fink, Fritz. *Die Judenfrage im Unterricht.* Nuremberg: Willmy, 1937.

Fischer, Albert. "Die Charaktererziehung in der Schule." *Die Deutsche Höhere Schule* 4 (1937): 342–345.

Frercks, Rudolf. "Der Rassengedanke: Ein Wendepunkt der Erziehungslehre." *Weltanschauung und Schule* 2 (1938): 545–549.

Frercks, Rudolf, and Arthur Hoffmann. *Erbnot und Volksaufartung. Bild und Gegenbild aus dem Leben zur praktischen rassenhygienischen Schulung.* Erfurt: Stenger, 1934.

Fritsch, Theodore. *Handbuch der Judenfrage: Die wichtigsten Tatsachen zur Beurteilung des Jüdischen Volkes.* Leipzig: Hammerverlag, 1933.

Funke, Hermann. *Geschichtserzählungen.* Leipzig: Teubner, 1940.

Gehl, Walter. *Geschichte für Mittelschulen.* Breslau: Hirt, 1940–1941.

Graf, Jakob. *Die Bildungs- und Erziehungswerte der Erblehre, Erbpflege und Rassenkunde: Nach einem Vortrag gehalten vor den Naturkundlehren Hessens am 30. Bachmonds 1933.* Munich: Lehmanns, 1934.

———. *Familienkunde und Rassenkunde für Schüler.* Munich: Lehmanns, 1935.

———. *Arbeitsheft zu Graf, Familienkunde und Rassenbiologie für Schüler.* Munich: Lehmanns, 1935.

———. *Vererbungslehre, Rassenkunde und Erbgesundheitspflege.* 5. Auflage. Munich: Lehmanns, 1938.

Grau, Wilhelm. *Antisemitismus im späteren Mittelalter.* Munich: Duncker und Humblot, 1934.

————. *Die Judenfrage als Aufgabe der neuen Geschichtsforschung*. Hamburg: Hanseatische Verlag, 1935.

————. *Die Judenfrage in der deutschen Geschichte*. Berlin: Teubner, 1937.

Gross, Walter. *Rassenpolitische Erziehung*. Berlin: Junker und Dünnhaupt, 1934.

————. *Die Ehe ist die Treue zum Blute deines Volkes*. Shriftenreihe für die Wochenenschulungen der Hitler Jugend, Heft 3. (No imprint, 1943.) WLLondon, 395/B146.

Hahn, Karl. "Die Judenfrage." Blatt Nr. 9 und "Rassenkunde des jüdischen Volkes." Blatt Nr. 8. *Das Neue Reich: Arbeits-Schulungs-und Unterrichtsblätter*. Wittenberg: Herrose's Verlag, 1935.

Hauptschulungsamt der NSDAP, hrsg. *Schulungs-Unterlage: 3000 Jahre jüdischer Haß*. Berlin: NSDAP, 1943.

Heinze, Hans. *Rasse und Erbe*. Halle: Schroedel, 1934.

Helmut, Otto, hrsg. *Volk im Gefahr: Der Gebürtenrückgang und seine Folgen für Deutschlands Zukunft*. Munich: Lehmanns, 1939.

Hermann, Fritz, and Heinrich Stridde. *Untergang und Aufstieg: ABC der Vererbungslehre und Erbgesunheitspflege, der Familen- und Rassenkunde*. 2. Auflage. Frankfurt am Main: Diesterweg, 1934.

Hiemer, Ernst. *Der Giftpilz*. Nuremberg: Der Stürmer, 1938.

————. *Der Pudelmopsdackelpinscher und andere besinnliche Erzahlungen*. Der Stürmer, 1940.

————. *Der Jude im Sprichwort des Völker*. Nuremberg: Der Stürmer, 1942.

Hitler, Adolf. *Mein Kampf*. Trans. Ralph Manheim. New York: Houghton Mifflin, 1971.

Höft, Albert. *Arbeitsplan für erbbiologischen und rassenkundlichen Unterricht in der Schule unter Berücksichtigung der Rassenpflege, Familienkunde, und Bevölkerungspolitik*. Osterwieck: Zickfeldt, 1934.

Ihde, Heinrich, Ferdinand Rossner, and Alfred Stockfisch. *Gesundheitspflege und Rassenhygiene*. 3. Auflage. Langensalza: Beltz, 1939.

Ihde, Heinrich, and Alfred Stockfish. *Vom Natur hab' ich die Statur: Erbgesundheitspflege für Schule und Volk*. 2. Auflage. Leipzig: Beltz, n.d.

Institut für Leser- und Schriftumskunde. *Rassenkunde: Eine Auswahl des wichtigsten Schriftums aus dem Gebiet der Rassenkunde, Vererbungslehre, Rassenpflege und Bevölkerungspolitik*. Leipzig: Institut, 1936.

Institut zum Studium der Judenfrage. *Die Juden in Deutschland*. 2. Auflage. Munich: Eher, 1936.

Jantzen, Walther. *Die Geographie im Dienste der nationalpolitischen Erziehung: Ein Ergänzungsheft zu den Lehrbüchern der Erdkunde*. 2. Auflage. Breslau: Hirt, 1936.

————. *Geopolitik Im Kartenbild*. Berlin: Vowinckel, 1941.

Jörns, Emil. *Erziehung zu Eugenischer Lebensführung als Aufgabe der Volksschule*. Berlin: Metzner, 1933.

Jörns, Emil, and Julius Schwab. *Rassenhygiene Fibel: Der Deutschen Jugend Zuliebe Geschrieben*. Berlin: Metzner, 1935.

Just, Günther. "Eugenik und Schule." In *Erblehre-Erbpflege*, hrsg. Zentralinstitut für Erziehung. Berlin: Mittler, 1933, 40–65.

Kamps Stoffverteilungen für alle Jahrgänge der Volksschule. Bearbeitet von H. Hermeler. 2. Teil. Nach dem Richtlinien vom 15. Dezember 1939. Bochum, 1940.

Keipert, Hans. *Die Behandlung der Judenfrage im Unterricht.* Leipzig: Beltz, 1937.

———. "Die Judenfrage im Unterricht." In *Handbuch für den Biologieunterricht.* Lieferung 3, hrsg. Ferdinand Rossner. Langensalza: Beltz, 1940, 244–248.

Kitte, Gerhard. "Das Urteil über die Rassenmisching im Judentum und in der biblischen Religion." *Der Biologe* 6 (1937): 342–352.

Klagges, Dieter. *Reichtum und soziale Gerechtigkeit: Grundfragen einer nationalsozialistischen Volkswirtschaftslehre.* 2. Auflage. Leipzig: Armanen, 1933.

———. *Heldischer Glaube.* Leipzig: Armanen, 1934.

———. *Idee und System: Vorträge an der deutschen Hochschule für Politik über Grundfragen des nationalsozialistischen Weltanschauung.* Leipzig: Armanen, 1934.

———. *Geschichte als nationalpolitische Erziehung.* Frankfurt am Main: Diesterweg, 1936.

———, hrsg. *Volk und Fuhrer: Deutsche Geschichte für Schulen.* Ausgabe für Mittelschulen. Bearbeitet von Karl Grunwald. Frankfurt am Main: Diesterweg, 1943.

Kluger A. *Die deutsche Volksschule im Grossdeutschen Reich.* Breslau: Hirt, 1940.

Krauß, Hans. *Die Grundgedanken der Erbkunde und Rassenhygiene in Frage und Antwort.* Der Arzt als Erzieher. Heft 71. Munich: Verlag der Ärztlichen Rundschau Otto Gmelin, 1935.

Krause, Reinhold. "Die Judenfrage im Unterricht." In *Rassische Erziehung als Unterrichtsgrundsatz der Fachgebiete,* hrsg. Rudolf Benze and Alfred Pudelsko, 190–199. Frankfurt-am-Main: Diesterweg, 1937.

Krieck, Ernst. "Die Judenfrage." *Volk und Werden* 1 (1933): 57–62.

———. "The Education of a Nation from Blood and Soil." *International Education Review* 3 (1933–1934): 309–313.

———. *Völkisch-politische Anthropologie.* Leipzig: Armanen, 1936.

Krieger, Heinrich. "Die Trennung der Rassen im Schulwesen der Vereinigten Staaten und des Dritten Reiches." *Internationale Zeitschrift für Erziehung* 5 (1936): 344–356.

Kröger, K. H. "Der Rassengedanke im englischen Unterricht." *Die Deutsche Höhere Schule* 5 (1938): 3–10.

Kuhn, Philalethes, and Heinrich Kranz. *Von Deutschen Ahnen für Deutsche Enkel: Allgemeinverständliche Darstellung der Erblichkeitslehre, der Rassenkunde und der Rassenhygiene.* Munich: Lehmanns, 1933.

Leers, Johann von. *Juden sehen dich an.* Berlin: NS Druck, 193?).

———. *Die Grosse Aufgabe!* Berlin: Siemens, 1933.

———. *Forderung der Stunde: Juden Raus!* Berlin: NS-Druck, 1933.

———. *14 Jahre Judenrepublik: Die Geschichte eines Rassenkampfes.* Berlin: Verlag Deutscher Kulturwacht, 1933.

———. *Geschichte auf rassischer Grundlage.* Leipzig: Reclaim, 1934.

———. *Spenglers Weltpolitische System und der National Socialismus.* Berlin: Junker und Dünnhaupt, 1934.

———. *Rassische Geschichtsbetrachtung: Was muss der Lehrer davon wissen?* Leipzig: Beltz, 1934.

———. *Volkskunde im Deutschen Unterricht.* Darmstadt: Schlapp, 1934.

————. *Judentum und Verbechen: Die Kriminalität des Judentums.* Berlin: Deutscher-Rechts Verlag, 1936.

————. *Blut und Rasse in der Gesetzgebung: Ein Gang durch die Völkergeschichte.* Munich: Lehmanns, 1936.

————. "Stein der Hilfe und Schild des Rechtes." *Der Deutsche Erzieher* 5 (1938): 425–427.

————. "Islam und Judentum im Laufe des Jahrhunderte." *Der Deutsche Erzieher* 5 (1938): 425–427. Leers, Johann von.

————. "Der gegenwärtige Stand des Judenproblems in der Welt." *Der Deutsche Erzieher* 5 (1938): 402–406;

————. *Die Geschichtlichen Grundlagen des Nationalsozialismus.* Berlin: Deutscher Rechtsverlag, 1938.

————. *Wie kam der Jude zum Geld?* Berlin: Theodor Fritsch, 1939.

————. "Der Kampf gegen die Juden im Altertum." *Der Deutsche Erzieher* 6 (1939): 267–269.

————. *Für das Reich: Deutsche Geschichte in Geschichtserzählungen.* Leipzig: Beltz, 1940.

————. *Unser Glaube Deutschland! Gedanken um das Ewige Reich.* Erfurt: Sigrune, 1940.

————. "Das wir nicht in der Hand der Juden fallen." *Der Deutsche Erzieher* 10 (1943): 65–67.

————. *Die Verbrechernatur der Juden.* Berlin: Hochmuth, 1944.

Leers Johann von and Willy Becker. *Nationalsozialistische Staatskunde.* Potsdam: Hachfeld, 1942.

Leers, Johann von and Heinrich Hansen. *Der Deutsche Lehrer als Kulturschöpfer.* Frankfurt: Diesterweg, 1939.

Lenz, Fritz. *Die Rasse als Wertprinzip: Zur Erneuerung der Ethik.* Munich: Lehmanns, 1933.

Linden, Walter. *Luthers Kampfschriften gegen das Judentum.* Berlin: Klinkhardt and Biermann, 1936.

Lorenz, Konrad. "Nochmals: Systematik und Entwicklungsgedanke im Unterricht." *Der Biologe* 9 (1940): 20–36.

Lüke, Franz. *Rassen-ABC.* Bochum: Kamp, 1934.

Mahnkopf, Johannes. *Von der Uhrzeit zum Grossdeutschen Reich.* Leipzig: Teubner, 1941.

Malitius, Erich. *Wir und die Jude: Was die Jugend über den Juden wissen muß.* Berlin: Jugendzeitschriften Verlag, 1935.

Malitz, Bruno. *Die Leibesübungen in der nationalsozialistischen Idee.* Munich: Eher, 1934.

May, Werner. *Deutscher Nationalkatechismus: Was ein deutscher Junge und ein deutsches Mädel vom Dritten Reich wissen soll* Breslau: Heinrich Handels, 1934.

Meyer, Erich, and Werner Dittrich. *Kleine Erb- und Rassenkunde.* Ausgabe für Sachsen. Leipzig: Hirt und Sohn, 1934.

Olbricht, Konrad, and Hermann Kärgel. *Deutschland als Ganze.* Der Erdkunde Unterricht in der Volks- und Mittelschule. 9. Auflage. Berlin: Zickfeldt, 1938.

Philipp, Hans. "Wege und Irrwege im Unterricht der Ur- und Frühgeschichte." *Die Deutsche Höhere Schule* 4 (1937): 574–584.

Reichsjugendführung des NSDAP, hrsg. *Sport-Tagebuch der deutschen Jugend*. Berlin: Wirtschafts-Werbeverlag, n.d.

———, hrsg. *Juden und Lords Hand in Hand*. Berlin: Limpert, 1940.

Reichsstelle für das Schul-und Unterrichtsschriftum, hrsg. *Deutsches Lesebuch für Volksschulen*. Berlin: Deutscher Schulverlag, 1943.

RMWEVB, "Vererbungslehre und Rassenkunde im Unterricht." Erlaß vom 13. September 1933. *Amtsblatt des RMWEVB und der Unterrichtsverwaltungen der Länder*. 1. Jahrgang, 1935.

Roepke, Hans. *Was muß Du wissen vom Dritten Reich? Nationalsozialistische Geschichtstabelle für Lehrzwecke in Frage und Antwort*. Berlin: Heinz Denckler, 1935.

Rosenberg, Alfred. *Der Mythus des 20. Jahrhunderts*. Munich: Hoheneichen Verlag, 1930.

———. *Die Entwicklung der deutschen Freiheitsbewegung*. Munich: Eher, 1933.

———. *Deutsches Philologen Blatt*. 42 (14 November 1934): 502.

———. *Die Spur des Juden im Wandel der Zeiten*. Munich: Eher, 1937).

Rossner, Ferdinand. "Die Taxonomie und der Begriff der Evolution im Unterricht." *Der Biologe* 8 (1939): 366–372.

———. *Rase und Religion*. Hannover: Schaper, 1942.

Rottenrodt, Wilhelm. *Deutsche Führer und Meister: Geschichtliche Einzelbilder aus Gegenwart und Vergangenheit*. Frankfurt am Main: Diesterweg, 1937.

Rust, Bernhard. *Education in the Third Reich*. London: Butterworth, 1936.

Scharrer, Walter. *Jewish Opposition and the Secondary Schools*. London: St. Clements Press, 1936.

Schauff, P. "Die Geschichte der physikalische Forschung." *Grimsehl's Lehrbuch der Physik*. Leipzig: Teubner, 1940.

Schemann, Ludwig. *Die Rasse in Geisteswissenschaft: Studien zur Geschichte des Rassengedankes*. Vol. 1. Munich: Lehmanns, 1928–1931.

Schemm, Hans. *Deutsche Schule und Deutsche Erziehung in Vergangenheit, Gegenwart, und Zukunft*. Stuttgart: Pädagogische Verlagsanstalt, 1934.

Schütz, Franz. *Rassenhygiene des deutschen Volkes*. Erfurt: Stenger, 1934.

Schwab, Julius. *Rassenpflege im Sprichwort: Eine volkstümliche Sammlung*. Leipzig: Fröhlich, 1937.

Schwarz, Max. "Rassenkunde und Deutschunterricht." In *Handbuch für den Biologieunterricht*, hrsg. Ferdinand Rossner, 101. Lieferung 3. Leipzig: Beltz, 1939.

Schwarzinger, Ernst. "Deutsch." *Mitteilungsblatt des NSLB* 6 (February 1940): 10.

Schwendt, Fritz. *Handbuch für den Unterricht der deutschen Vorgeschichte in Ostdeutschland*. Breslau: Hirt, 1934.

Shrey, Kurt. *Du und Dein Volk*. Köln: NSDAP, Gau Köln-Achen. Amt für Erzieher, n.d.

Streit, Ernst. *Wissenwertiges für die deutschblütige Jugend*. Lorch: Rohm, 193?.

Völkische Beobachter, 22 September 1936.

Vogel, Alfred. *Erblehre und Rassenkunde* in bildlicher *Darstellung*. Stuttgart: National Literatur, 1938.

Vogel, Paul. "Vorgeschichte," in hrsg. *Rassische Erziehung als Unterrichtsgrundsatz der Fachgebiete*. Rudolf Benze and Alfred Pudelko. Frankfurt am Main: Diesterweg, 1937, 81–89.

Waldmann, Guid, hrsg. *Rasse und Musik*. Berlin: Vieweg, 1939.

Warneck, Hans. *Geschichte des Deutschen Volkes von der Grundung des Ersten Reiches bis 1648*. Berlin: Oldenbourg, 1939.

Warneck, Hans, and Willi Matschke. *Geschichte für Volksschulen*. Leipzig: Velhagen und Klasing, 1942.

Weis, Alfred. *Einfache Versuche zur Vererbugslehre und Rassenkunde*. Leipzig: Quelle und Meyer, 1934.

Weiskopf, Hermann. "Anfang aller Schulreform." *Lenk ein* 2 (20 March 1933): 33.

Wiegand, E. "Zur Geschichte des Judentums: Neueres Schriftum zur Judenfrage." *Volk und Rasse* 13 (1938): 153–155.

Zenker, Friedrich. *Deutschkunde: Hilfsbuch für die politische Erziehung in den Vereinen der Deutschen Turnerschaft*. 4. Auflage. Berlin: Limpert, 1934.

ARCHIVAL SOURCES

BArchBerlin—Bundes Archiv Berlin

BLHAPotsdam—Brandenburgishes Landeshauptarchiv Potsdam

DIPF/Berlin—Deutsches Institut für Pädagogische Forschung

RMWEVB—Reich Ministerium für Wissenschaft, Erziehung und Volksbildung

Ausschaltung des Judentums aus der Verwaltung. Niederschrift über die Besprechung betr. die Neuregelung der Erteilung des Schulunterrichts an Juden am 1. Dezember 1938. RMWEVB, R4901/11787, BArchBerlin.

Bouhler to Rosenberg, "An die Mitlgieder des Reichsausschusses für das Schul- und Unterrichtsschriftum," April 1941, 65, BArchBerlin, NS8/209 Schul-und Unterrichtsschriftum. Kanzlei Rosenberg.

Erlass, RMWEVB, 15 November 1938, "Schulunterricht an Juden," BLHAPotsdam, Pr. Br. Rep. 2A Regierung Potsdam Abteilung II: Kirchen und Schulen. II. Generalia. Das Schulwesen fur jüdische Kinder. 1260-Bd. 3 (1908–1944).

Gutachten über Werner Dittrich, Bayreuth: *Erziehung zum Judengegner: Hinweise zur Behandlung der Judenfrage im Unterricht* by Ludwig Deyerling, NSLB Abteilung Zeitschriften (undated). BArch Berlin, NS12/554, Angelegenheiten betr. Juden 1935–1938.

Hederich, Stellvertreter des Führers Stabb, Parteiamtliche Prüfungskommission zum Schutze des NS-Schriftums to Rosenberg, 25 March 1939, BArchBerlin, NS8/209, Kanzlei Rosenberg, 129.

Minister des Kultus und Unterrichts (Haanz) in Karlsruhe to RMWEVB, 16 Februar 1938 with Richtlinien für den Stoffplan und den Unterrichtsplan: Unterricht über Deutsche Sitte und Deutsche Art, R21/531 Amt E. Lebenskunde-Unterricht der Weltanschauungsgememeinschft "Deutsche Gotterkenntnis," BArchBerlin.

NS Geschichtsbild. Kanzlei Rosenberg. 1 March 1934. BArchBerlin.NS8/128.

NSLB, *Lehrerfortbildung, Sommer, 1934*. Berlin: NSLB, 1934. DIPF/Berlin, 2A 2648.

Reichsgesetz vom 25. April 1933, *Zentralblatt für die gesamte Unterrichtsverwaltung in Preussen*.

"Richtlinien zur Aufstellung von Lehrplänen für jüdische Volksschulen, Neue Fassung, 1937," Reichsvertretung der Juden in Deutschland, Schulabteilung,

RMWEVB, 29 October 1937, BLHAPotsdam. Pr. Br. Rep. 2A, Abt. II, Generalia. 1260. Bd. 3, ss. 127–128.

Runderlass von Zschintzsch, RMWEVB, 14 Februar 1939, Geheime Runderlassen der Abteilung ZII u.a. Judenangelegenheiten, R4901/R21/217, BArch.Berlin.

Rust, Bernhard, "Vererbungslehre und Rassenkunde im Unterricht," 13 September 1933, in *Amtsblatt des Reichsministeriums für Wissenschaft, Erziehung und Volksbildung*, 1. Jahrgang 1935, 43–46. DIPF/Berlin 2A2547.

Schulverwaltung der Jüdische Gemeinden to RMWEVB, 16 April 1936, BLHAPotsdam, Pr. Br. Rep. 34, Provinzial-Schulkollegium Berlin, 3995-Religion, Konfirmation, Kommunion, Hebräisch (1930–1943).

Zander, Abteilung für höheres Schulwesen, Der Oberpräsident der Provinz Brandenberg, 12. März 1936 to RMWEVB, BLHAPotsdam. Pr. Br. Rep. 34, Provinzial-Schulkollegium Berlin, 3995-Religion, Konfirmation, Kommunion, Hebräisch (1930–1943).

OTHER PRIMARY SOURCES

Archambault, Reginald, ed. *John Dewey on Education*. Chicago: University of Chicago Press, 1964.

Aristotle, *Politics*. Book Eight, Part One. Trans. Ernest Barker. New York: Oxford University Press, 1998.

Baur, Erwin, Eugen Fischer, and Fritz Lenz. *Menschliche Erblichkeitslehre und Rassenhygiene*. Munich: Lehmanns, 1927 and 1936.

Brohmer, Paul. *Erziehung zur Staatsgesinnung durch arbeitskundlichen Biologieunterricht*. Osterwieck: Zickfeldt, 1923.

Chamberlain, Houston Stuart. *Die Grundlagen des neunzehnten Jahrhunderts*. Munich: Brückmann, 1900.

Collischonn, Georg. *Geschichte und Volksaufgabe*. Frankfurt am Main: Winter, 1922.

Dobers, Ernst. "Biologie und neue Volksschullehrerbildung." *Der Biologe* 1 (1931–1932): 65–69.

Gobineau, Comte Arthur de. *Essai sur l'inegalite des races humaines*. Paris: Firmin-Didot, 1884.

Günther, Hans F. K. *Der nordische Gedanke unter den Deutschen*. Munich: Lehmanns, 1925.

———. *Rassenkunde des jüdischen Volkes*. Munich: Lehmanns, 1930.

———. *Rassenkunde des deutschen Volkes*. Munich: Lehmanns, 1935.

Haushofer, Karl. *Geographie und Weltmacht*. Berlin: Vowinckel, 1925.

"History of Nazi Movement: A School Reading-Book Prepared." *Manchester Guardian*, 10 June 1938.

Holle, Hermann. *Allgemeine Biologie als Grundlage für Weltanschauung, Lebensführung und Politik*. Leipzig: 1925.

International Military Tribunal, Document 1919-PS. Vol. XXIX, 112.

Jäckel, Eberhard, hrsg. *Hitler: Sämtliche Aufzeichnungen, 1905–1924*. Stuttgart: Deutsche Verlags-Anstalt, 1980.

"Jewish Pupils in Secondary Schools: Why a Clean Sweep Should Be Made." *Manchester Guardian*, August 3, 1936.

Just, Günther. "Eugenik und Weltanschauung." In Günther Just, hrsg. *Eugenik und Weltanschauung*. Berlin: Metzner, 1932, 7–38.

Klagges, Dieter. *Das Urevangelium Jesu, der deutsche Glaube*. Leipzig: Armen, 1925.

———. *Kampf um Marxismus*. 5. Auflage. Munich: Eher, 1932.

———. *An aller Völker der Erde*. Kreuzau-Stockhein: Alma Druck, 1972–1973.

———. *Eine Tugend gegen* alle *Todsünden: Das organisches Weltbild*. Bassum-Dimhausen: Alma Druck, 1974.

Klemperer, Victor. *I Will Bear Witness: A Diary of the Nazi Years, 1933–1941 and 1942–1945*. 2 vols. Trans. Martin Chalmers. New York: Random House, 1998 and 1999b.

———. *LTI: Notizbuch eines Philologen*. 18. Auflage. Leipzig: Reklam, 1999a.

Lagarde, Paul de. *Deutsche Schriften*. Göttingen: Diederichs, 1878.

———. *Deutscher Glaube, Deutsches Vaterland, Deutsche Bildung*. Jena: Diederichs, 1914.

Langbehn, Jules. *Rembrandt als Erzieher*. Leipzig: Hirschfeld, 1900.

Lenz, Fritz. *Über die biologischen Grundlagen der Erziehung*. München: Lehmans, 1925 and 1933.

Maß, Konrad. *Deutsche Geschichte*. Heft 24. Munich: Eher, 1931.

Maurenbrecher, Max. *Völkischer Geschichtsunterricht*. Langensalza: Beyer, 1925.

Nietzsche, Friedrich. *Gesammelte Werke*. Bd. XVI. Munich: Musarion, 1920–1929.

Parisier Tageblatt, 24 May 1934.

Passarge, Siegfried. *Das Judentum als landschaftlich-ethnologisches Problem*. Munich: Lehmanns, 1929.

Ploetz, Alfred. *Die Tüchtigkeit unserer Rasse und der Schutz der Schwachen: Ein Versuch über Rassenhygiene und ihr Verhältnis zu den humanen Idealen, besonders zum Sozialismus*. Berlin: Lehmanns, 1895.

———. *Archiv für Rassen- und Gesellschafts Biologie*, 1 (1904): 892–893.

———. "Zur Abgrenzung und Einteilung des Begriffs Rassenhygiene." *Archiv* 3 (1906): 864.

Roderich-Stoltheim, Ferdinand. *Das Rätsel des jüdischen Erfolges*. Leipzig: Hammer, 1928.

Schäfer, Ingeburg, and Susanne Klockmann. *Mutter mochte Himmler nie: Die Geschichte einer SS-Familie*. Reinbeck bei Hamburg: Rowohlt, 1999.

Schallmayer, Wilhelm. *Vererbung und Auslese im Lebenslauf der Völker*. Jena: Fischer, 1903.

———. "Vererbung und Auslese im Lebenslauf der Völker." *Natur und Staat*. 3. Teil (1903).

———. *Vererbung und Auslese: Grundriss der Gesellschaftsbiologie und der Lehre vom Rassedienst*. 3. Auflage. Jena: Fischer, 1918.

Schultze-Naumburg, Paul. *Kunst und Rasse*. Munich: Lehmanns, 1928.

Spengler, Oswald. *Politische Schriften*. Munich: Beck, 1924.

———. *Decline of the West*. New York: Knopf, 1934.

———. *Preussentum und Sozialismus*. Munich: Beck, 1934.

Stern, Heinemann. *Warum hassen sie uns eigentlich? Jüdisches Leben zwischen den Kriegen*. Düsseldorf: Droste, 1970.

Virchow, Rudolf. *Archiv für Anthropologie* 16 (January 1886): 285–337.

SECONDARY SOURCES

Adams, Mark. *The Wellborn Science: Eugenics in Germany, France, Brazil, and Russia*. New York: Oxford University Press, 1990.

Akademie der Künste, hrsg. *Berliner Schulalltag*. Berlin: Akademie, 1983.

Aly, Peter. *Jugendliteratur im Dritten Reich: Dokumente und Kommentare*. Hamburg: Verlag für Buchmarktforschung, 1965.

Anti-Defamation League of B'nai B'rith. *The Holocaust, 1933–1945: A Chronology of Social Education*. New York: Anti-Defamation League, 1978.

Arbeitsgruppe Pädagogisches Museum, hrsg. *Heil Hitler, Herr Lehrer*. Hamburg: Rowohlt, 1983.

Ärztekammer Berlin. *The Value of the Human Being: Medicine in Germany, 1918–1945*. Berlin: Edition Hentrich, 1991.

Baldwin, Neil. *Henry Ford and the Jews: The Mass Production of Hate*. New York: Public Affairs, 2001.

Bankier, David, ed. *Probing the Depths of German Antisemitism: German Society and the Persecution of the Jews, 1933–1941*. Jerusalem: Yad Yashem, 2000.

Bathrick, David. "1925: Jud Süß by Lion Feuchtwanger." In *Yale Companion to Jewish Writing and Thought in German Culture, 1096–1996*, ed. Sander Gilman and Jack Zipes, 434–439. New Haven, Conn.: Yale University Press, 1997.

Bauer, Yehuda. *Rethinking the Holocaust*. New Haven, Conn.: Yale University Press, 2001.

Bäumer-Schleinkofer, Änne. *Nazi Biology and Schools*. New York: Peter Lang, 1995.

Becker, Peter. *Zur Geschichte der Rassenhygiene: Wege ins Dritte Reich*. Stuttgart: Thieme, 1988.

Behal, Michael, and Wolfgang Pasche. *Juden in Deutschland*. Stuttgart: Klett, 1995.

Benz, Wolfgang. "Jüdische Selbsthilfe bis 1938: Schulwesen." In *Die Juden in Deutschland, 1933–1945*, hrsg. Wolfgang Benz. Munich: Beck, 1988, 330–363.

Berenbaum, Michael. *The World Must Know*. New York: Little, Brown, 1993.

Bergmann, Klaus. "Imperialistische Tendenzen in Geschichstsdidaktik und Geschichtsunterricht ab 1890." In *Gesellschaft, Staat, Geschichtsunterricht*, hrsg. Klaus Bergmann and Gerhard Schneider. Düsseldorf: Schwann, 1982, 190–217.

Bernett, Hajo. *Nationalsozialistische Leibeserziehung: Eine Dokumentation ihrer Theorie und Organisation*. Schorndorf: Hofmann, 1966.

———. *Der jüdische Sport in nationalsozialistischen Deutschland, 1933–1938*. Schorndorf: Hofmann, 1978.

Black, Peter. *Ernst Kaltenbrunner: Ideological Soldier of the Third Reich*. Princeton, N.J.: Princeton University Press, 1985.

Blackburn, Gilmer. *Education in the Third Reich: Race and History in Nazi Textbooks*. Albany, N.Y.: SUN.Y. Press, 1985.

Boorstin, Daniel, and Brooks Kelley. *A History of the United States*. Upper Saddle River, N.J.: Prentice Hall, 1999.

Browning, Christopher. *Nazi Policy, Jewish Workers, German Killers*. New York: Cambridge University Press, 2000.

Burleigh, Michael. *Death and Deliverance*: *Euthanasia in Germany, 1900–1945*. New York: Cambridge University Press, 1995.

Burleigh, Michael, and Wolfgang Wippermann. *The Racial State*: *Germany, 1933–1945*. New York: Cambridge University Press, 1993.

Burrow, J. W., ed. *The Limits of State Action*. Cambridge: Cambridge University Press, 1969.

Carroll, James. *Constantine's Sword*: *The Church and the Jews*. Boston: Houghton Mifflin, 2001.

Colodner, Solomon. *Jewish Education in Germany under the Nazis*. New York: Jewish Education Committee, 1964.

Dawidowicz, Lucy. *The War against the Jews, 1933–1945*. New York: Free Press, 1986.

Edmonton Journal, 30 October 1997.

Eilers, Hermann. *Die nationalpolitische Schulpolitik*: *Eine Studie zur Funktion der Erziehung im totalitären Staat*. Opladen: Westdeutschen Verlag, 1963.

Farquharson, John. *The Plough and the Swastika*: *The NSDAP and Agriculture in Germany, 1928–1945*. London: 1976.

Fehrs, Jörg. *Von der Heidereutergasse zum Roseneck*: *Jüdische Schulen in Berlin, 1712–1942*. Berlin: Edition Hentrich, 1993.

Fischer, Klaus. *History of an Obsession*: *German Judeophobia and the Holocaust*. New York: Continuum, 1998.

Flessau, Kurt-Ingo. *Schule der Diktatur*: *Lehrpläne und Schulbücher des Nationalsozialismus*. Frankfurt-am-Main: Fischer, 1979.

Friedlander, Henry. *The Origins of Nazi Genocide*: *From Euthanasia to the Final Solution*. Chapel Hill: University of North Carolina Press, 1995.

Gedankensplitter und Auskünfte zur Namensänderung einer Neuköllner Schule: *1907–1982*. Berlin: Albert Schweitzer Oberschule, 1982.

Genschel, Helmut. "Geschichtsdidaktik und Geschichtsunterricht im Nationalsozialistischen Deutschland." In *Gesellschaft, Staat, Geschichtsunterricht*, hrsg. Klaus Bergmann and Gerhard Schneider, 261–294. Düsseldorf: Schwaann, 1982.

Gies, Horst. *Geschichtsunterricht unter der Diktatur Hitlers*. Weimar: Böhlau, 1992.

Giesecke, Hermann. *Hitler's Pädagogen*: *Theorie und Praxis nationalsozialisticher Erziehung*. Weinheim: Juventa, 1993.

Gilbert, Martin. *The Holocaust*. New York: Holt, Rinehart, and Winston, 1985.

Gill, Anton. *The Journey from Hell*. New York: Morrow, 1988.

Ginzel, Günther. *Jüdischer Alltag in Deutschland 1933–1945*. Düsseldorf: Droste, 1993.

Goldhagen, Daniel. *Hitler's Willing Executioners*: *Ordinary Germans and the Holocaust*. New York: Knopf, 1996.

———. *A Moral Reckoning*: *The Catholic Church during the Holocaust and Today*. New York: Knopf, 2002.

Gwiazda, Henry. "World War Two and Nazi Racism." *Prologue* 25 (1994): 156–159.

Harten, Hans-Christian. "Rasse und Erziehung: Zur pädagogischen Psychologie und Soziologie des Nationalsozialismus." *Zeitschrift für Pädagogik* 39 (1993): 111–134.

————. "Pädagogik und Eugenik im rassenhygienischen Diskurs vor 1933." *Pädagogica Historica* 33 (1997): 765–800.

Hein, Laura, and Mark Selden, eds. *Censoring History: Citizenship and Memory in Japan, Germany, and the United States.* Armonk, N.Y.: Sharpe, 2000.

Heller, Eric. *The Disinherited Mind.* New York: Farrar, Straus and Cudahy, 1952.

Herring, Jochen, et al. *Schüleralltag im Nationalsozialismus.* Dortmund: Pädagogische Arbeitsstelle, 1984.

Hesse, Alexander. *Die Professoren und Dozenten der preußischen Pädagogischen Akademien (1926–1933) und Hochschulen für Lehrerbildung (1933–1941).* Weinheim: Deutscher Studien Verlag, 1995.

Hilberg, Raul. *The Destruction of the European Jews.* New York: Holmes and Meier, 1985.

Holzer, Willi. *Jüdische Schulen in Berlin: Am Beispiel der privaten Volkschule der Gemeinde Rykestrasse.* Berlin: Edition Hentrich, 1992.

Hughes, Henry. *Oswald Spengler: A Critical Estimate.* New York: Scribner, 1952.

Kamenetsky, Christa. *Children's Literature in Hitler's Germany: The Cultural Policy of National Socialism.* London: Ohio University Press, 1984.

Katz, Steven. *The Holocaust in Historical Content.* Vol. 1. New York: Oxford University Press, 1994.

Kaufmann, Walter. *Nietzsche: Philosopher, Psychologist, Antichrist.* 4th ed. Princeton, N.J.: Princeton University Press, 1974.

Kershaw, Ian. *Hitler: 1889–1936.* Vol. 1. New York: Norton, 2000.

Kevles, Daniel. *In the Name of Eugenics: Genetics and the Use of Human Heredity.* New York: Knopf, 1985.

Klee, Ernst. *Euthanasie im NS-Staat: Die Vernichtung lebensunwerten Lebens.* Frankfurt am Main: 1983.

Knoll, Joachim. *Zur Geschichte des naturkundlichen Unterrichts in Hannover.* Hannover: Universität Hannover, 1995.

Kühl, Stephan. *The Nazi Connection: Eugenics, American Racism and German National Socialism.* New York: Oxford University Press, 1994.

Lifton, Robert. *Nazi Doctors: Medical Killing and the Psychology of Genocide.* New York: Basic Books, 1986.

Limberg, Margaret, and Hubert Rübsaat. *Sie dürfen nicht mehr Deutsche sein: Jüdische Alltag in Selbstzeugnissen, 1933–1938.* New York: Campus, 1990.

Loewen, James. *Lies My Teacher Told Me: Everything Your American History Textbook Got Wrong.* New York: New Press, 1995.

MacKenzie, Donald. "Eugenics in Britain." *Social Studies of Science* 6 (1976): 499–532.

Macrakis, Kristie. *Surviving the Swastika: Scientific Research in Nazi Germany.* New York: Oxford University Press, 1993.

Merritt Anna, and Richard Merritt, eds. *Public Opinion in Occupied Germany: The OMGUS Surveys, 1945–1949.* Chicago: University of Illinois Press, 1970.

Meyhöfer, Rita. *Gäste in Berlin? Jüdisches Schülerleben in der Weimarer Republik und im Nationalsozialismus.* Hamburg: Kovac, 1992.

Mosse, George. "Culture, Civilization, and German Anti-Semitism." *Judaism* 7 (summer 1958): 257–258.

———. *The Crisis of German Ideology: The Intellectual Origins of the Third Reich.* New York: Grosset and Dunlap, 1964.

———. *Toward the Final Solution: A History of European Racism.* Madison: University of Wisconsin Press, 1985.

———. *Nazi Culture: Intellectual, Cultural, and Social Life in the Third Reich.* New York: Grosset and Dunlap, 1966.

Müller-Hill, Benno. *Murderous Science: Elimination by Scientific Selection of Jews, Gypsies, and Others in Germany, 1933–1945.* Trans. George Fraser. Plainview, N.Y.: Cold Spring Harbor Laboratory Press, 1998.

Neumann, Franz. *Behemoth: The Structure and Practice of National Socialism: 1933–1944.* New York: Harper, 1963.

Niewyk, Donald. "Jews, 1933–1990." In *Modern Germany.* Vol. 1, ed. Dieter Buse and Jürgen Doerr, 527–528. New York: Garland, 1998.

Nuremberg Trial Proceedings. Vol. 12, 29 April 1946. Streicher Testimony. Retrieved 22 August 2001 from the Avalon Law Project at Yale University (http: //www.yale.edu/lawweb/avalon/imt)

Ortmeyer, Benjamin. *Schicksale jüdischer Schülerinnen und Schüler in der NS Zeit: Leerstellen deutscher Erziehungswissenschaft und die Erforschung der nazistischen Schule.* Bonn: Weile, 1998.

Papen, Patricia von. "Schützenhilfe nationalsozialistischer Judenpolitik: Die Judenforschung des Reichsinstituts für Geschichte des neuen Deutschland, 1935–1945." In *Beseitigung des jüdischen Einflusses: Antisemitische Forschung, Eliten und Karrieren im Nationalsozialismus,* hrsg. Fritz Bauer Institut. Frankfurt: Campus, 1999.

Peters, Elke. *Nationalistisch-völkische Bildungspolitik in der Weimarer Republik.* Weinheim: Beltz, 1972.

Pine, Lisa. "The Dissemination of Nazi Ideology and Family Values through School Textbooks." *History of Education* 25 (1996): 91–109.

———. *Nazi Family Policy, 1933–1945.* New York: Berg, 1997.

Poliakov, Leon. *The History of Anti-Semitism.* Trans. Richard Howard. London: Elek, 1965.

Remak, Joachim, ed. *The Nazi Years: A Documentary History.* Englewood Cliffs, N.J.: Prentice Hall, 1969.

Rempel, Gerhard. *Hitler's Children: The Hitler Youth and the SS.* Chapel Hill: University of North Carolina Press, 1989.

Rhodes, Anthony. *Propaganda: The Art of Persuasion.* London: Chelsea House, 1976.

Ribuffo, Leo. "Henry Ford and the International Jew." *American Jewish History* 69 (June 1980): 437–477.

Richter, Hans. *Damals war es Friedrich.* München: Deutsche Taschenbuch, 2000.

Richter, Ingrid. *Katholizmus und Eugenik in der Weimarer Republik und im Dritten Reich: Zwischen Sittlichkeitsreform und Rassenhygiene.* Paderborn: Schönigh, 2001.

Röcher, Ruth. *Jüdische Schule im nationalsozialistischen Deutschland, 1933–1942.* Frankfurt am Main: DIPA Verlag, 1992.

Rossmeissel, Dieter. *"Ganz Deutschland wird zum Führer halten": Zur politischen Erziehung in den Schulen des Dritten Reiches.* Jena: Fischer, 1985.

Schallenberger, Horst. *Untersuchungen zum Geschichtsbild der Wilhelmischen Ära und der Weimarer Zeit.* Düsseldorf: Schwann, 1964.

Scherf, Gertrud. "Vom deutschen Wald zum deutschen Volk: Biologieunterricht im Dienste nationalsozialistischer Weltanschauung." In *Schule und Unterricht im Dritten Reich*, hrsg. Reinhard Dithmar, 217–234. Neuwied: Luchterhand, 1979.

Schiefelbein, Dieter. "Das Institut zür Erforschung der Judenfrage Frankfurt am Main: Antisemitismus als Karrieresprungbrett." In *Beseitigung des jüdischen Einflüsses: Antisemitische Forschung, Eliten, und Karrieren im Nationalsozialismus*, hrsg. Fritz Bauer Institut, 43–71. New York: Campus Verlag, 1999.

Schmitz-Berning, Cornelia. *Vokabular des Nationalsozialismus*. Berlin: Walter de Gruyter, 2000.

Schneider, William. "Toward the Improvement of the Human Race: The History of Eugenics in France." *Journal of Modern History* 54 (1982): 268–291.

Scholz, Harold. "Schule unterm Hakenkreuz." In *Schule und Unterricht im Dritten Reich*, hrsg. Reinhard Dithmar, 15–18. Neuwied: Luchterhand, 1989.

Schwartz, Bernard, and Fredrick DeCoste, eds. *The Holocaust's Ghost: Writings on Art, Politics, Law, and Education*. Edmonton: University of Alberta Press, 2000.

Selden, Steven. *Inheriting Shame: The Story of Eugenics and Racism in America*. New York: Teachers College Press, 1999.

Siedler, Horst, and Andreas Rett. *Das Reichs- Sippenamt entscheidet: Rassenbiologie im Nationalsozialismus*. Wien: Jugend und Volk, 1982.

Steiger, Alfons. *Der neudeutsche Heide im Kampf gegen Christen und Juden*. Berlin: Germania, 1924.

Steinweiss, Alan. *Art, Ideology, and Economics in Nazi Germany*. Chapel Hill: University of North Carolina Press, 1993.

Stern, Fritz. *The Politics of Cultural Despair*. New York: 1961.

Suzman, Arthur, and Dennis Diamond. "Der mord an sechs Millionen Juden: Die Wahrheit ist unteilbar." *Politik und Zeitgeschichte* (1978) B30–78: 4–21.

Tenorth, Heinz-Elmar. "Deutsche Erziehungswissenschaft 1930 bis 1945." *Zeitschrift für Pädagogik* 32 (1986): 299–321.

Trachtenberg, Joshua. *The Devil and the Jews: The Medieval Conception of the Jew and Its Relation to Modern Anti-Semitism*. Philadelphia: Jewish Publication Society, 1993.

Walk, Joseph. "Jüdische Schüler an deutschen Schulen in Nazideutschland." *Bulletin des Leo Baeck Instituts* 19 (1980): 101–109.

———. *Jüdische Schule und Erziehung im Dritten Reich*. Frankfurt am Main: Meisenheim, 1991.

———. *Das Sonderrecht für die Juden in NS-Staat*. 2. Auflage. Heidelberg: C. F. Mueller, 1996.

Wegner, Gregory. "Schooling for a New Mythos: Race, Anti-Semitism and the Curriculum Materials of a Nazi Race Educator." *Paedagogica Historica* 27 (June 1991): 189–213.

———. "Legitimizing the Final Selection: Race in the School Curriculum of the Third Reich." In *The Holocaust's Ghost: Writings on Art, Politics, Law and Education*, eds. F. C. DeCoste and Bernard Schwartz, 362–375. Edmonton: University of Alberta Press, 2000.

Weindling, Paul. *Health, Race and German Politics between National Unification and Nazism, 1870–1945*. New York: Cambridge University Press, 1993.

Weingart, Peter, Jürgen Kroll, and Kurt Bayertz. *Rasse, Blut und Gene: Geschichte der Eugenik und Rassenhygiene in Deutschland.* Frankfurt am Main: Suhrkamp, 1988.

Weiss, Sheila. *Race Hygiene and National Efficiency: The Eugenics of Wilhelm Schallmayer.* Los Angeles: University of California Press, 1987.

Weiss, Yfaat. *Schicksalsgemeinschaft im Wandel: Jüdische Erziehung im national-sozialistischen Deutschland, 1933–1938.* Hamburg: Christians, 1991.

Welzer, Harald, hrsg. *Das Gedächtnis der Bilder: Ästhetik und National Sozial-ismus.* Tübingen: Diskord, 1995.

Werner, Karl. *Das NS-Geschichtsbild und die deutsche Geschichtswissenschaft.* Stuttgart: Kohlhammer, 1976.

Williams, Raymond. "Hegemony and Selective Tradition." In *Language, Authority, Criticism: Readings On the School Textbooks,* ed. Suzanne and Alan Luke, 56–68. New York: Falmer Press, 1989.

Wippermann, Wolfgang. "Das Berliner Schulwesen in der NS-Zeit: Fragen, Thesen und methodische Bemerkungen." In *Schule in Berlin: Gestern und Heute,* hrsg. Benno Schmoldt, 57–74. Berlin: Colloquium, 1989.

Wollenberg, Jörg, ed. *The German Public and the Persecution of the Jews, 1933–1945.* Atlantic Highlands, N.J.: Humanities Press, 1996.

REFERENCE WORKS

Duden. 11. Auflage, 1934.

Meyers Lexikon. 3. Band. Leipzig: Bibliographisches Institut, 1937 and 9. Band, 1942.

Volks-Brockhaus. 1940.

Zentner, Christian, and Friedemann Bedürftig, eds. *The Encyclopedia of the Third Reich.* Vol. 1. New York: Macmillan, 1991.

Index